Federalism and Fiscal Transfers in India

Federalism and Fiscal Transfers in India

Second Edition

C. RANGARAJAN
D.K. SRIVASTAVA

OXFORD
UNIVERSITY PRESS

OXFORD
UNIVERSITY PRESS

Great Clarendon Street, Oxford, OX2 6DP,
United Kingdom

Oxford University Press is a department of the University of Oxford.
It furthers the University's objective of excellence in research, scholarship,
and education by publishing worldwide. Oxford is a registered trade mark of
Oxford University Press in the UK and in certain other countries

First Edition published in 2011
Second Edition published in 2024

Published in the United States of America by Oxford University Press
198 Madison Avenue, New York, NY 10016, United States of America

British Library Cataloguing in Publication Data

Data available

Library of Congress Control Number: 2024947069

ISBN 9780198930396

DOI: 10.1093/9780198930426.001.0001

Printed and bound in India by
Replika Press Pvt. Ltd.

Contents

List of Tables, Figures, and Appendices   vii
Preface to the First Edition   xiii
Preface to the Second Edition   xxv
Acknowledgements for the First Edition   xxvii
Acknowledgements for the Second Edition   xxix

1. Fiscal Federalism: Basic Tenets   1

2. Evolution of Fiscal Federalism in India   29

3. Fiscal Federalism in Practice: *Canada and India*   63

4. Fiscal Federalism in Practice: *Australia and India*   115

5. Resolving Vertical and Horizontal Imbalances in India   175

6. Dynamics of Debt Accumulation in India: *Impact of Primary Deficit, Growth, and Interest Rate*   223

7. Fiscal Deficits and Government Debt in India: *Implications for Growth and Stabilization*   241

8. Thirteenth, Fourteenth, and Fifteenth Finance Commissions   285

9. Future of Fiscal Federalism in India   313

References   341
Index   355

Tables, Figures, and Appendices

Tables

2.1 Years Covered under Different Finance Commission Recommendations   30

2.2 Inter-se Sharing of Income Tax: Phase I   32

2.3 Inter-se Sharing of Union Excise Duties: Phase I   32

2.4 Inter-se Sharing of Income Tax and Union Excise Duties: Phase II: Eighth, Ninth, and Tenth Finance Commissions   34

2.5 Criteria and Relative Weights for Determining Inter-se Shares of States: Phase III: Tenth (Alternative Scheme), Eleventh, and Twelfth Finance Commissions   37

2.6 Modified Representative Tax System Approach   58

3.1 Share in Population and All-Province GDP in Canada   67

3.2 Measuring Vertical Imbalance in Canada   72

3.3 Vertical Imbalance in India   73

3.4 Major Transfers to Other Levels of Governments: Canada   75

3.5 Central Transfers in India Relative to Centre's Gross Revenue Receipts and GDP   76

3.6 Canada: Composition of Transfers   77

3.7 Share of Equalization Payments in Total Transfers   81

3.8 Horizontal Fiscal Imbalance: Revenue Before and After Transfers: Canada   90

3.9 Per Capita Revenues Relative to 15-State Average Before and After Transfers   92

3.10 Horizontal Fiscal Imbalance in Expenditure: Canada   94

3.11 Horizontal Imbalance: India   95

4.1 Own Source Revenues by Governments, 2000–1   119

4.2 Australia: Inter-jurisdictional Shares in Expenditures, 2000–1   120

4.3 Relative Share of Centre and States in India: Selected Heads   121

4.4   Australia: Mean Resident Population: 1997–8 to 2002–3   127

4.5   Australia: Gross State Product at Current Prices   128

4.6   Vertical Fiscal Imbalance in Australia: Selected Years   132

4.7   Vertical Fiscal Imbalance in India: Selected Years   133

4.8   Main Factors Affecting Revenue and Cost Disabilities   136

4.9   Australian States: Population, Income, and 2004 Relativities   140

4.10   Australia: Per Capita Relativities: 1999–2004 Review   141

4.11   Australia: Horizontal Fiscal Imbalance Per Capita Expenditure Relative to All-State Average   148

4.12   Total Pool over the Years and Extent of Redistribution (1981–2005)   149

4.13   Relative Contribution of Revenue, Expenditure, and SPP Disabilities in the 2004 Review   150

5.1   Fiscal and Revenue Deficits of Centre and States   178

5.2   Share of States in Combined Revenues   183

5.3   Twelfth Finance Commission Recommended Transfers: Vertical and Horizontal Components   195

5.4   Illustrative Derivation of Weight for Equalization   200

6.1   Decade-Wise Decomposition of Debt Accumulation Relative to GDP   229

7.1   Fiscal Deficits and the Economy: Salient Features of Alternative Paradigms   246

7.2   Gross Domestic Savings and Capital Formation of the Public Sector Relative to GDP   267

7.3   Dependent Variable: SPVR   271

7.4   Dependent Variable: RCMCE   272

7.5   Decade-Wise Decomposition of Debt Accumulation Relative to GDP   275

7.6   Combined Central and State Finances: Structural and Cyclical Deficits Relative to GDP   279

8.1   Recommended and Effective Share of States in Sharable Central Revenues (%): FC12 to FC15 (2)   291

8.2   Relative Weights for Different Tax Devolution Criteria: Thirteenth Finance Commission to Fifteenth Finance Commission   292

8.3   Relative Importance of Tax Devolution and Grants   293

8.4   Actual Transfers Received by States (magnitude and shares)   294

8.5   State-Wise Recommended Revenue Gap Grants Per Year (INR crore)   296

8.6 Weights Allotted to Criteria for Grants to Local Bodies by the Thirteenth Finance Commission 298

8.7 Grants to Local Bodies as Recommended by the Fifteenth Finance Commission 301

8.8 Fiscal Deficit to GDP Ratio for the Central Government (%): Fifteenth Finance Commission Forecasts 308

8.9 Fiscal Deficit to GDP Ratio for States: Fifteenth Finance Commission Forecasts 309

9.1 Share of Centre and States in Combined Revenue Receipts (percent): Recent Commission Periods 322

9.2 Per Capita GSDP (INR) 325

9.3 State-Wise Per Capita Education Expenditures (INR) 327

9.4 State-Wise Per Capita Health Expenditures (INR) 328

9.5 State-Wise Per Capita Expenditures on Water Supply and Sanitation (INR) 329

Addendum 3.1 Federal Support to Provinces and Territories 101

Addendum 3.2 Distribution of Per Capita Equalization Transfers (in dollars): Canadian Provinces and Territories 105

Addendum 3.3 Distribution of Per Capita Health Transfers (in dollars): Canadian Provinces and Territories 107

Addendum 3.4 Distribution of Per Capita Social Transfers (in dollars): Canadian Provinces and Territories 108

Addendum 4.1 Summary of the Transition by Year 158

Addendum 4.2 State's Share in Nominal GDP (%) 159

Addendum 4.3 State-wise Per Capita GDP (in Australian dollars) 161

Addendum 4.4 Relativities, Shares, and Illustrative GST Distribution, 2022–3 and 2023–4 161

Addendum 4.5 Per Capita General Revenue Assistance (Australian dollars, millions) 162

Addendum 4.6 General Revenue Assistance Payments to the States, 2021–2 (Australian dollars, millions) 163

Figures

3.1 Provinces in Canada Arranged in Ascending Order of Per Capita GDP (in Canadian $) 66

5.1 Comparing Equalizing Benchmark Transfers with Twelfth Finance Commission Recommended Transfers: General States   195

6.1 Growth of Central Debt Relative to GDP: Relative Roles of Cumulated Primary Deficit and Excess of Growth over Interest Rates   230

6.2 Time Profile of Nominal Growth and Interest Rates   232

6.3 Real Growth and Interest Rates   233

6.4 Primary Deficit to GDP Ratio and Excess of Growth over Interest Rates   236

7.1 Stable Combinations of Debt and Fiscal Deficit to GDP Ratios for Different Growth Rates   258

7.2 Aspects of Fiscal and Debt Sustainability   261

7.3 Savings Relative to GDP: Household, Private Corporate, and Public Sector   265

7.4 Investment Relative to GDP: Private and Public Sector 266

7.5 Growth of State Debt Relative to GDP: Relative Roles of Cumulated Primary Deficits and Excess of Growth over Interest Rates   274

7.6 Comparison of Structural and Debt-Stabilizing Primary Deficit   280

9.1 Tax-GDP Ratio: Centre, States, and Combined   321

9.2 Weighted Average (Effective) GST Rate   333

Addendum Chart 3.1 Share in Nominal GDP (%, 2021)   103

Addendum Chart 3.2 Share in Population (%, 2021)   104

Addendum Chart 3.3 Growth in Per-Capita Health Transfer (%) 109

Addendum Chart 3.4 Growth in Per-Capita Social Transfer (%) 109

Addendum Chart 4.1 State-Wise Population of Australia (2022) 160

Appendices

3A.1 Revenue Sources   110

4A.1 Difference between GST and FAG Relativities   164

4A.2 State Taxes in Australia   164

4A.3 Australia: Main State Expenditure Categories   166

4A.4 Inpatient Services: Example of Expenditure Assessment Techniques 167

Tables

4A.1 Comparison of GST and FAG Relativities   165

4A.2 Hospital Services Assessment Structure: 2004 Review   168

4A.3 Inpatient Service Costs Derivation of the Service Factor   172

5A.1 Comparison of Equalization Transfers Based on Available Data
      with TFC Recommended Transfers   216

5A.2 Decomposition of Recommended Per Capita Transfers   218

5A.3 Decomposition of Per Capita Grants and Devolution into Vertical,
      Equalizing Horizontal, and Residual Components   219

Preface to the First Edition

This volume brings together eight chapters written by us on the subject of fiscal federalism in India since 2003. The key institutional arrangement that has guided the working of fiscal federalism in India has been the Finance Commission. The centrepiece of the recommendations of the Finance Commission in India is the scheme of fiscal transfers consisting of sharing central taxes and grants. The chapters included in this volume are interconnected with the underlying theme of the evolution of fiscal federalism in India, focusing both on its theoretical underpinnings and application to India's complex empirical setting. In particular, we look at the principles that have guided the determination of fiscal transfers from the centre to the states and the distribution of these transfers amongst the states, given the large differences in fiscal capacities and service standards across states in India.

Chapter 1 on 'Fiscal Federalism: Basic Tenets' highlights the basic tenets of fiscal federalism making a distinction between the traditional focus on the link between decentralization and welfare to its more modern day extensions. The idea of fiscal federalism is couched in the belief that multi- level governments can augment the pursuit of efficiency and equity in the provision of public and merit goods through cooperation, competition, and coordination among central and sub-national governments where these interactions take place within the framework of a set of well-defined rules, preferably through a constitutional arrangement. The working of these rules in practice can be guided by an independent body like the Finance Commission in India. The constitutional arrangements generally result in an asymmetry in the assignment of resources and responsibilities between the central and the sub-national governments. This asymmetry is such that the centre has a larger share of resources and the state governments have larger responsibilities. The system is then brought in balance by a suitable scheme of transfers from the centre to the states. The challenge is to design a scheme of fiscal transfers that provide the right incentives, and facilitates comparable standards of public and merit services throughout the country.

Chapter 1 then moves on to the modern extensions of the idea of fiscal federalism. These deal mainly with five aspects, namely, fiscal competition amongst jurisdictions, political economy aspects of fiscal federalism, market-preserving fiscal federalism, environmental federalism, and fiscal decentralization and growth. These are all aspects of federalism that have a bearing on the evolution of fiscal federalism in India and are often reflected in the changing terms of reference of the Finance Commissions.

The next chapter on 'Evolution of Fiscal Federalism in India' highlights the evolution of fiscal transfer arrangements in India over the period covered by the First to the Twelfth Finance Commissions. This chapter traces the evolution of the criteria for sharing of tax revenue in India, showing how the system moved from a tax-by-tax approach to a more global sharing of central taxes and how the criteria for horizontal distribution of sharing also converged. This chapter also examines the basic considerations in the determination of grants by the Finance Commission and the main patterns in the overall transfer of resources from the centre to the states since the First Finance Commission. The move towards sharing of all central taxes and the determination of inter se shares of states on the basis of a common set of criteria has prepared the ground for easier application of the equalization principle in India towards which we have progressively moved.

The guiding principle of fiscal transfers in theory as well as in practice in some of the well-established systems of fiscal transfers internationally has been the principle of equalization. The next two chapters on 'Fiscal Federalism in Practice: Canada and India' and 'Fiscal Federalism in Practice: Australia and India' focus on the design of fiscal transfers in two of the oldest federations, namely Australia and Canada, and compare them with the system of transfers in India. In theory, as well as in practice, a system of equalization transfers is considered desirable as it is consistent with the objectives of both equity and efficiency. The efficiency implications follow from two considerations:

1. Locational inefficiencies that can result from inefficient migration induced by fiscal surpluses are neutralized by equalization transfers; and

2. The redistribution implied by equalization transfers from the richer to the poorer states also gives a return to the richer states by avoiding congestion resulting from excessive migration in the context of services provided by these states that are in the nature of 'congestible' goods.

The Canadian system of transfers is a suitable example of application of the principle of fiscal capacity equalization. In applying this, they follow a tax-by-tax approach, which has been referred to in the literature as the 'representative tax system' approach. An alternative to this approach is to follow a more macro approach in equalizing fiscal capacities. We argue that there may be certain advantages in following a macro approach in India, both for practical reasons and for the principles involved, particularly in the light of the difficulties raised in the Canadian literature itself concerning the deficiencies of the representative tax system approach. However, the Canadian system brings home the point that a good indicator of fiscal capacity will have to go beyond using the per capita gross state domestic product (GSDP). Account has to be taken not just of production in a state but rather of the incomes that accrue to its citizens.

While comparing the Canadian system of inter-governmental transfers with the system of fiscal transfers in India, we note that while the heart of the Canadian transfer system is fiscal capacity equalization, this is supplemented by the Canadian health and social service transfers. This also serves the objective of equalization but permits inclusion of cost considerations so that each province is able to spend equal per capita amount for two major merit services, namely health and education. Thus, in Canada, fiscal capacity equalization is supplemented by cost considerations at least for select services. We argue that the need for ensuring that resources are available for maintaining per capita expenditures of select basic services at comparable levels among states, as attempted in Canada, is worth pursuing in the case of India.

We also note that incomes as well as population are concentrated in just a few provinces in Canada namely Ontario, British Columbia, Alberta, and Quebec. This facilitates a transfer system aimed at equalization since the richer provinces also have the larger populations and equalization transfers are relatively small in per capita terms and made to provinces with relatively smaller populations so that the total volume of transfers is also limited. On the contrary, redistribution in India is far more difficult because the required per capita equalization transfers are large and the poorer states have relatively larger populations.

Chapter 4 makes a similar comparison between the fiscal transfer system in Australia and India. Australia is well known for following a more comprehensive approach to equalization where fiscal capacity equalization is supplemented by a detailed analysis of cost differentials across provinces in providing public services. As compared to Australia, India has not only a larger number of states and a greater concentration of population in low fiscal capacity states but also many factors responsible for differences in per capita costs of public services. The differences in size, heterogeneity, and the scale of problems notwithstanding, the conceptual basis of the transfer system in Australia has much relevance for India. At the same time, serious difficulties have also been noted with the Australian system.

Australia has one of the most elaborate systems of determining equalization transfers. The Australian equalization payments are based on explicit principles that aim at enabling states to provide services to its citizens at comparable standards if they are willing to make comparable revenue efforts and are able to operate at comparable levels of efficiency. The overall approach to equalization is with reference to the entire transfers as most special purpose payments are integrated into the equalization calculations. The Australian system is sound in principle but the methodology adopted, particularly with respect to equalizing expenditure disabilities, has made the system unduly complex. The system is still grappling with issues of efficiency. From the Indian perspective, the major lesson to be drawn from the Australian experience is the need for a clearer enunciation of the equalization objective and its translation in practice. We argue that it may be practical in the Indian context to consider a macro base for revenue side equalization and focus expenditure equalization in only select services where mobility is limited.

In Australia, the determination of the vertical share of resources to be transferred to the states is not in the hands of the Commonwealth Grants Commission. It gets determined automatically by the amount of revenues collected under the goods and services tax (GST) supplemented by the special purpose grants that are also in the hands of the Commonwealth Government. In India, the Finance Commission determines a large part of the transfers in the form of tax devolution under global sharing and grants, requiring it to determine a significant part of the volume of the vertical transfers. The Finance Commission transfers are supplemented by the Planning Commission grants and other discretionary grants determined by the central government. Global tax sharing may have some merits over the sharing of a single tax as in Australia where the collecting agency, namely the Commonwealth Government has no revenue interest. Deciding about vertical transfer facilitates horizontal equalization and to that extent India has an institutional advantage.

The chapter on 'Resolving Vertical and Horizontal Imbalances in India' brings together the ideas developed, based on theoretical considerations, and the Canadian and Australian examples to comprehensively examine the design of fiscal transfers in India in resolving the vertical and horizontal imbalances. As far as the vertical dimension is concerned, we note that in India, there has been long-term stability in the share of the centre and the states in the combined tax revenues of the system after tax devolution. It may be considered desirable to continue to maintain this stability as long as there are no basic changes in the division of responsibilities between the centre and the states. It is further shown that maintaining such stability requires an upward adjustment in the share of states in the divisible pool of taxes in periods where the expected buoyancy of central taxes is higher than that of the states.

This chapter also shows that subject to certain assumptions, tax revenue sharing under an axiomatic framework will result in transfers that will be consistent with the concept of revenue side equalization as used in Canada. The difference is that in the Indian case, a macro base rather than a tax-by-tax approach is followed on the revenue side. While using a macro approach, there is a need to obtain a better measure of fiscal capacity as GSDP at factor cost is an incomplete indicator for this purpose. The Central Statistical Organization, which prepares comparable estimates of GSDP for the Finance Commission should be asked to prepare a more comprehensive indicator of fiscal capacity taking GSDP at market prices, and providing supplementary information on remittances and other influences that add to the spending capacity in different states. For delineating the equalizing component of transfers, we have suggested a scheme whereby the transfers recommended by the Finance Commission are decomposed into (i) the vertical component of transfers indicating per capita transfers to all states including the highest income state, (ii) equalizing transfers indicating the component of transfers only to the states with a fiscal capacity less than the defined benchmark capacity, and (iii) a residual reflecting special needs and ad hoc components. We also develop a suitable methodology to objectively determine the relevant weights that should be applied to different criteria in the tax-devolution formulae to ensure that the desired degree of equalization is achieved in the scheme of transfers.

Using the available information, it is also shown that contrary to the contention made by several economists, transfers by the Finance Commissions in India, particularly in respect of some of the more recent Commissions, are not necessarily 'gap-filling' in nature, at least for the general category states subject to the exception of one or two states for some years. Taking the transfers recommended by the Twelfth Finance Commission, it is shown, for example, that under specific assumptions and with respect to data used by the Twelfth Finance Commission, systematic elements of transfers constitute a high proportion of transfers—50 per cent of transfers were used as the vertical component of transfers and nearly 40 per cent was equalizing in nature, consistent with the revenue-side equalization approach. The degree of equalization achieved was nearly 88 per cent using the revenue-side approach to equalization. We also argue that full equalization should be attempted at least in respect of merit services like health and education. These also provide cases where revenue-side equalization should be supplemented by expenditure-side equalization where cost and use disabilities should be fully neutralized.

The volume of fiscal transfers cannot be determined independent of the profile of resources and expenditure commitments of the participating governments in the federal system. In India, both the central and the state governments are entitled to borrow to partially finance expenditures. Over time as borrowing increased and debt accumulated, interest payments relative to total revenue receipts have also increased both for the central and the state governments. Since the revenue receipts cannot indefinitely increase relative to GDP, increased interest payments imply a fall in primary expenditures. This affects both the central and the state governments. If higher and higher transfers are made to the state governments to cover their rising interest payments, the central government will be required to cut its primary expenditures or borrow more progressively. A healthy and stable system of fiscal transfers requires that borrowing by the central and state governments is kept at sustainable levels. This can be done by prescribing rules and/or targets under fiscal responsibility legislations. In addition, an autonomous supervisory body like a loan Council can be helpful in maintaining fiscal discipline consistent with requirements of macroeconomic stability. In this context the working of the Australian Loan Council has relevance for India.

Historically, in India, states used to borrow from the centre. Since the Finance Commissions often followed a gap-filling approach, there was a significant link between debt, interest payments, and fiscal transfers in India. First, with the states historically owing considerable amounts of debt to the centre, Finance Commissions were periodically asked as part of their term of reference to consider additional transfers in the form of debt relief. This gave rise to a significant adverse incentive in the sense that the states started borrowing amounts larger than what would be warranted by their borrowing capacity and created a history of expenditures based on borrowing to justify claims for higher transfers in future. These expenditures became committed expenditures in the form of salary or interest payments. The states then asked the Finance Commission to take account of these additional committed expenditures and fill the gap in the next cycle of transfers knowing that the Finance Commissions often followed a 'gap-filling' methodology. Secondly, interest payment commitments of the central government constitute a critical determinant of the available resources with the centre from which transfers could be made to the state governments.

In the following chapter 'Dynamics of Debt Accumulation in India: Impact of Primary Deficit, Growth and Interest Rate', we have examined the dynamics of debt accumulation in India for the central government bringing out the role of primary deficit, growth rate, and interest rate in the evolution of the centre's debt relative to the GDP. We note that the concerns have become quite serious in recent years when there has been an explosive rise in the debt-GDP ratio. The growth in the debt-GDP ratio has been very large in the years when the nominal growth rate was less than the nominal interest rate. One such phase was during 2000–3, when the growth rate was less than the effective interest rate and the debt–GDP ratio increased both because of cumulated primary deficits and excess of interest rate over growth rate during 2000–1 to 2002–3. High levels of debt and interest payment liabilities put a limit on the volume of transfers that could be taken up for the states.

The next chapter on 'Fiscal Deficits and Government Debt in India: Implications for Growth and Stabilization' expands this analysis in theoretical terms as also in terms of application to the combined debt and deficit concerns of both the central and the state governments. We argue that there is need for an institutional arrangement for keeping the growth of central and state debt within prudent limits and consistent with the requirements of macroeconomic stability. In fact, as in Australia, states should be allowed to raise loans in the market subject to agreed limits and there is no need for the central government to intermediate. Over time, market-based discipline would become more and more effective.

Chapter 7 also looks at the impact of fiscal deficits on saving, investment, and growth in the light of the theoretical literature on the subject in the context of the fiscal deficit and debt on the combined accounts of the central and state governments. Fiscal deficits, when these have accumulated into higher debt, lead to higher revenue deficits through higher interest payments. Revenue deficits amount to reduction in government savings, which may not be fully offset by a corresponding rise in private savings, leading to a fall in the overall saving rate. The impact of fiscal deficit on investment arises both from its impact on private investment and government investment. The adverse effects on private investment occur if fiscal deficits put pressure on interest rates, and if private investment is sensitive to the interest rate. The effect on government capital expenditure is through committed interest payments, which rise if the debt-GDP ratio rises and/or interest rate rises.

When fiscal deficits are high in magnitude relative to the GDP and largely structural in nature, the ability of the government to mount countercyclical interventions is also compromised, particularly when growth is below the trend levels. This was clearly experienced in the late 1990s and the early part of the new decade. In India, the household sector saves more than it invests, and the excess becomes available in the form of financial savings of this sector to the private corporate sector, and the government sector for their investment requirements that are not financed by their own savings. although government dis-savings increased since the late 1990s, the pressure on interest rates was not witnessed because of a fall in investment demand by the private sector.

The overall growth rate depends on the overall savings rate and the rate of investment. There is reason to believe that when government saving falls, private saving rate increases as wealth held in the private sector in the form of government bond increases. This compensatory rise in the private sector saving rate has been partial. On the investment side, government's own investment demand also fell as its debt-GDP ratio and the ratio of interest payments to revenue receipts rose. empirical tests indicate that government capital expenditures respond negatively to the interest payments and positively to revenue receipts. If interest payments rise faster than revenue receipts, government capital expenditure falls. Private investment responds negatively to a rise in expected interest rates. In the 1990s and beyond, government capital expenditures relative to GDP fell not only because interest payments relative to GDP increased but also because the revenue receipts to GDP fell. To achieve and sustain growth at high levels, it is required that the overall savings ratio is increased leading to a rise in the investment ratio, and fiscal deficit should be managed so as to serve this purpose.

Partly as a result of these considerations, the Twelfth Finance Commission (TFC) had recommended that the centre's intermediation for state borrowing, except for external loans and small saving loans, may be discontinued. further, the TFC considered it important that the centre's Fiscal Responsibility and Budget Management Act (FRBMA) should be supplemented by the state level fiscal responsibility legislations because, taken together, the states' borrowing and debt, contribute significantly to the overall fiscal deficit and the debt relative to GDP. They have significant macro implications. The analysis of the chapter on 'Fiscal Deficits and Government Debt in India' provides a framework using which the sustainable levels of debt and deficit can be fixed for medium and long runs. These considerations did inform the Twelfth Finance Commission to suggest long term debt–GDP targets for the central and state governments at 28 per cent of GDP each and fiscal deficit targets at 3 per cent of GDP each for the central government and aggregate borrowing of the state governments.

Issues of macroeconomic stability following the global economic slowdown became one of the key features of the context at the time the Thirteenth Finance Commission deliberated on its terms of reference. This chapter, which is the concluding chapter, draws attention to contemporary challenges in the working of fiscal federalism in India particularly in relation to the work of the Thirteenth Finance Commission in the background of the recent slowdown in the economy and re- emergence of high levels of fiscal imbalance. We also observe that since the time of the Fifth Finance Commission, the main gainers in fiscal transfers recommended by the Finance Commission have been the low income states and the special category states. This reflects the growing importance of the equalization objective as well as cost differentials in fiscal transfers. In the context of the proposal for implementing a comprehensive goods and services tax, we have observed that achieving equalization would require somewhat lower volume of equalizing transfers since there will be some redistribution of tax revenue in favour of the consuming states and the degree of disparity in tax bases would be less. The challenge is to capture this as GSDP would not suitably reflect the tax bases being focused only on production in the states.

It may be noted that these chapters were written prior to the submission of the report of the Thirteenth Finance Commission. It is not possible to do justice to the highly detailed recommendations of the Thirteenth Finance Commission, which would require a lengthy and separate treatment. Also, more time needs to elapse before we begin to see the impact of the recommendations of the Thirteenth Finance Commission before a critical examination is taken up. However, there are clear links on some aspects of the recommendations of the Thirteenth Finance Commission, and the issues and approach discussed in this volume, which we note below.

First, the Thirteenth Finance Commission has used and acknowledged (paragraphs 3.37 and 8.7 of the Report of the Thirteenth Finance Commission) that if the stability in post-transfer shares of revenue expenditures of the centre and the states is to be maintained, as has been noted in Chapter 5 in this volume, then in periods of reference where the central taxes have experienced a relatively higher buoyancy compared to the states, there will be a need to increase the share of the states in the central taxes. Using this argument, the Commission recommended an increase in the share of states from 30.5 per cent to 32 per cent and the notional benchmark in the overall transfers from 38 per cent to 39.5 per cent.

Second, the Thirteenth Finance Commission had agreed to the logic of the link between the saving rate and borrowing limits for the central and state governments, and has continued with the target for 3 per cent of GDP for the central government in the medium term and 3 per cent of GSDP for individual state governments to be achieved by 2014–15 or earlier as also the need for maintaining balance on the revenue account, although it has defined state-specific paths of adjustment.

We consider that the principles of fiscal transfers and the analysis of their application over a long period of time in India as examined in this volume will be of relevance to the study of fiscal federalism in India and for designing a suitable scheme of fiscal transfers in the foreseeable future.

Preface to the Second Edition

Since the publication of the first edition of *Federalism and Fiscal Transfers in India*, three more Finance Commissions have been constituted and have given their recommendations. The periods covered by the recommendations of the Thirteenth, Fourteenth and the Fifteenth Finance Commissions are 2010–11 to 2014–15, 2015–16 to 2019–20, 2020–21 to 2025–26 respectively. During this period, some salient changes happened in the organization of states. In particular, the erstwhile state of Andhra Pradesh was divided between Andhra Pradesh and Telangana in 2014, increasing the number of states from 28 to 29. Subsequently, the state of Jammu and Kashmir was reorganized in August 2019, which reduced the total number of states in India from 29 to 28 and increased the number of union territories with legislatures from 2 to 3. In the field of taxation, the Goods and Services tax was implemented in 2017 replacing a number of central and state indirect taxes. Also, major reforms were undertaken with respect to the CIT in 2019. Further, the plan non plan distinction in government expenditures was abolished in 2015-16 and subsequently, the mechanism of plan grants was also discontinued. In the context of managing fiscal deficit and government debt, Centre's FRBM was substantially amended in 2018. These changes affected the working of India's fiscal federal system in a number of ways.

In terms of events having significant economic and fiscal implications during the period under review, mention needs to be made of the impact of COVID-19 on the formulation of fiscal and monetary policy. The Indian economy suffered a major setback in terms of the contraction in growth with a negative GDP growth rate of (-)5.8% in 2020–21. The fiscal deficit of the central government and on the combined account of central and state governments had to be stretched to 9.2% of GDP and 13.1% respectively. The term of the Fifteenth Finance Commission was extended by one year as it became difficult to make projections using 2020–21 as a base year. The Commission also provided a new glide path for bringing down the fiscal deficits of the central and state governments relative to GDP. It also suggested the setting up of a High-Powered Inter-governmental Group to re-examine Centre's FRBM. Soon after the advent of the pandemic, the global and the Indian economies have had to face severe supply side disruptions. These changes and economic events have a bearing on the future of India's fiscal federalism. In the context of these developments, we have made following changes to the earlier edition.

In the first edition, Chapter 8 was entitled 'Contemporary Challenges and Issues before the Thirteenth Finance Commission'. This Chapter has now been dropped. Two additional chapters have now been added. Chapter 8 is titled 'Thirteenth, Fourteenth and the Fifteenth Finance Commissions' and Chapter 9 is titled 'Future of Fiscal Federalism in India'. In Chapter 8, the discussion of the issues contained in Chapters 2, 5, and 6 where the first twelve Finance Commissions were considered, are continued so as to bring these up to date. Aspects of fiscal deficit and debt in India which were earlier covered in Chapters 6 and 7 are also now covered in both Chapters 8 and 9. Two small appendices to Chapters 3 and 4 bring the discussion on the practice of fiscal federalism in Canada and Australia also up to date.

Acknowledgements for the First Edition

In preparing the chapter on Canada, we had the benefit of discussions with several scholars during our visit to Canada to study the operation of the system of fiscal transfers. We wish to thank the Indian High Commission in Canada, the Forum of Federations, C.D. Howe Institute, Federal Ministry of Finance in Ottawa, Provincial Ministries of Finance and Municipal Affairs in Ontario, Quebec, and Alberta. We would also like to thank Almos Tassonyi who helped us with additional material on the macro approach to equalization.

While preparing the chapter on Australia, we had the benefit of discussions with several scholars on our visit to the country to study the system of fiscal transfers. We wish to thank the Indian High Commission in Australia, the Consulate General offices in Sydney and Melbourne, and the Chancery at Canberra. We would also like to thank officials of the Commonwealth Treasury in Canberra, and State Treasuries and Finance Departments at Sydney and Melbourne. We wish to extend our appreciation to A. G. Morris and M.A. Nicholas, Chairman and acting Secretary of the Commonwealth Grants Commission respectively. We would like to acknowledge John Wallace of Ernst and Young, D. J. Collins of Macquarie University, and Raghabendra Jha of the Australian National University who in the course of our discussions highlighted some of the current concerns with the Australian transfer system.

We would like to thank Bhujanga C. Rao, who provided important inputs for some of the chapters. The final manuscript was prepared by Sudha and Jothi and we take this opportunity to thank them for their efficient work.

The following articles jointly written by us and published in the *Economic and Political Weekly* have been used for the relevant chapters, sometimes with some modifications.

- 'Dynamics of Debt Accumulation in India: Impact of Primary Deficit, Growth and Interest Rate', *Economic and Political Weekly*, 38(46), 15 November 2003, pp. 4851–8.
- 'Fiscal Transfers in Canada: Drawing Comparisons and Lessons', *Economic and Political Weekly*, 39(19), 8 May 2004, pp. 1897–1909.
- 'Fiscal Transfers in Australia: Review and Relevance to India', *Economic and Political Weekly*, 39(33), 14 August 2004, pp. 3709–22.
- 'Fiscal Deficits and Government Debt: Implications for Growth and Stabilisation', *Economic and Political Weekly*, 40(27), 2 July 2005, pp. 2919–33.
- 'Reforming India's Fiscal Transfer System: Resolving Vertical and Horizontal Imbalances', *Economic and Political Weekly*, 43(23), 7 June 2008, pp. 47–60.

C. Rangarajan
D.K. Srivastava

Acknowledgements for the Second Edition

In addition to the Acknowledgements given in the first edition, we have benefited from the papers and deliberations of the Conference on Fiscal Federalism in India: Contemporary Perspectives conducted jointly by Madras School of Economics (MSE) and EY India during 22-23 February 2019 and the Conference on India's Contemporary Macroeconomic Themes: Challenges and Prospects conducted by MSE in honour of Dr. C. Rangarajan on the occasion of his 90th birth anniversary during 6–7 January 2023. We would further like to acknowledge the help provided by Muralikrishna Bharadwaj, Tarrung Kapur and Ragini Trehan in the completion of this revised and updated Volume. As before, Sudha and Jothi were quite helpful in preparing the final version of this edition and some of the publications related to this theme.

The following articles published individually or jointly by us have also been useful in the completion of this edition.

- Rangarajan C. and Srivastava D.K. (2023). Growth, Fiscal Policy and Monetary Policy of India: Why and how to overcome economic shocks, Consumer Unity & Trust Society (CUTS International)
- Srivastava, D. K. (2023). Balancing Growth with Fiscal Consolidation, Economic and Political Weekly, Issue No. 12, Volume 58 (March 2023) - https://www.epw.in/journal/2022/13/budget-2022/future-fiscal-consolidation-india.html.
- Rangarajan, C. and Srivastava, D.K. (2023). Charting the path for the Sixteenth Finance Commission. The Hindu. 29 July 2023. doi: https://www.thehindu.com/opinion/lead/charting-the-path-for-the-sixteenth-finance-commission/article67132693.ece
- Rangarajan, C. and Srivastava, D.K. (2020). Slower growth and a tighter fiscal. The Hindu. 9 May. Doi: https://www.thehindu.com/opinion/lead/slower-growth-and-a-tighter-fiscal/article31538125.ece

- Rangarajan, C. and Srivastava, D.K. (2020). Growth Compulsions, Fiscal Arithmetic. The Hindu. 28 September. doi: https://www.thehi ndu.com/opinion/lead/growth-compulsions-fiscal-arithmetic/arti cle32709726.ece
- Rangarajan, C. and Srivastava, D.K. (2023). Balance Fiscal Consolidation with Growth. The Hindu. 17 January 2023. doi: https:// www.thehindu.com/opinion/op-ed/balance-fiscal-consolidation- with-growth/article66382844.ece
- Rangarajan, C. and Srivastava, D.K. (2021). How far can the fiscal deficit be stretched?. The Hindu. 23 February. doi: https://www. thehindubusinessline.com/opinion/how-far-can-the-fiscal-deficit- be-stretched/article33915755.ece
- Rangarajan, C. and Srivastava, D.K. (2022). The Fiscal Rethink. The Indian Express. 23 February. doi: https://www.magzter.com/stor ies/Newspaper/The-Indian-Express-Delhi/The-fiscal-rethink
- Rangarajan, C. (2022). Good and Bad Freebies. The Indian Express. 16 June. doi: https://indianexpress.com/article/opinion/columns/ punjab-govt-free-electricity-low-income-households-support-pol icy-7972197/
- Rangarajan, C. and Srivastava, D.K. (2023). Fiscal Consolidation in India: Charting a Credible Glide Path. EY Tax Insights. Issue 25. 25 March.
- Rangarajan, C. and Srivastava, D.K. (2018). Balancing Conflicting Claims. The Hindu. 19 May 2018. doi: https://www.thehindu.com/ opinion/lead/balancing-conflicting-claims/article62111589.ece
- Srivastava, D.K. (2015). Recommendations of the 14th Finance Commission will change basic architecture of Centre-state fiscal ties. The Economic Times. 25 February. doi: https://economictimes. indiatimes.com/news/economy/policy/recommendations-of-the- 14th-finance-commission-will-change-basic-architecture-of-cen tre-state-fiscal-ties/articleshow/46363348.cms?from=mdr
- Srivastava, D. K. (2021). Fiscal consolidation and FRBM in the COVID-19 context: Fifteenth finance commission and be- yond. Economic and Political Weekly, 48–55.
- Srivastava, D.K. (2023). Evolving Contours of Centre-State Fiscal Relations: Inconsistencies, Ad-Hocism and Centralization. MSE Working paper 239. July 2023.

- Srivastava, D. K. (2022). Intergovernmental fiscal relations in India: time for the next generation of reforms. MSE Working Paper 222.
- Srivastava, D.K. (2023). The Future of Fiscal Consolidation. Economic and Political Weekly. LVII(13), 29–35.
- Srivastava, D.K. et al. (2021). Covid's Economic Impact: Should India Recast its Fiscal and Monetary Policy Frameworks?: Journal of International Economics and Finance. 1(1), 63–81.

C. Rangarajan
D.K. Srivastava

1

Fiscal Federalism

Basic Tenets

> The federal system was created with the intention of combining the different advantages which result from the magnitude and the littleness of nations.
>
> —*Alexis de Tocqueville*

Fiscal federalism is the most popular form of organization of governments for the provision of public goods. The Forum of Federations (Canada) mentions twenty-five federal countries in the world today, which together represent 40 per cent of the world's population (Grifiths and Neren Berg 2002). These include some of the largest and most complex democracies like India, the US, Russia, Brazil, Canada, Australia, Germany, and Mexico. Other important federal countries include Argentina, Belgium, Malaysia, and Nigeria. The system of government in many of the federations has made some of these federal countries quite prosperous with high standards of government services. The ideas of 'fiscal' federalism have, however, a broader scope and are relevant for all kinds of governments, viz., unitary, federal, and confederal. Fiscal federalism refers to the idea that decentralization in governance leads to welfare gains. It entails the provision of public goods by sub-national governments so that public consumption levels are tailored to suit the preferences of a heterogeneous population. Fiscal federal arrangements promote both efficiency as well as equity.

A distinction is now being made (Oates 2002) between the traditional theory of fiscal federalism and its modern extensions. The three main areas considered in the traditional theory are: (a) welfare gains from decentralization, (b) assignment of resources and responsibilities between different tiers of government, and (c) fiscal instruments for the

Federalism and Fiscal Transfers in India, Second Edition. C. Rangarajan and D.K. Srivastava, Oxford University Press.

resolution of vertical and horizontal imbalances. The modern extensions deal with areas such as fiscal competition among jurisdictions, political economy aspects of fiscal federalism, market-preserving fiscal federalism, environmental federalism, and fiscal decentralization and growth.

Welfare Gains from Decentralization

The potential welfare gains from decentralization are best stated in the so-called 'decentralization theorem (Oates 1972 and Bird 1993)'. The decentralization theorem is a normative proposition. Oates (1972) has defined this as stating that 'in the absence of cost-savings from the centralized provision of a [local public] good and of inter-jurisdictional externalities, the level of welfare will always be at least as high (and typically higher) if Pareto-efficient levels of consumption are provided in each jurisdiction than if any single, uniform level of consumption is maintained across all jurisdictions' (p. 54). The theorem of decentralized provision increases economic welfare above the level that results from the more uniform levels of such services that are likely under national provision. This is so because the efficient level of output of a 'local' public good for which the sum of residents' marginal benefits equals marginal cost is likely to vary across jurisdictions due to differences in preferences as well as cost differentials. Maximization of overall social welfare requires differentiation of local outputs.

In this argument it is assumed that centralized provision implies a uniform level of output across all jurisdictions. If perfect information is available to the central planner, it should be possible to provide locally differentiated outputs which maximize overall social welfare. The magnitude of these gains, however, depends both on the extent of the heterogeneity in demands across jurisdictions and any inter-jurisdictional differences in costs of service provision and information costs in ascertaining local preferences. In practice, it has been suggested that potential welfare gains from decentralized finance may well be quite large as the demand for local public goods is typically highly price-inelastic.

Another key argument, often cited in the literature, about the gains from decentralization emanates from Tiebout's (1956, 1961) model where highly mobile households 'vote with their feet', selecting a jurisdiction that provides their preferred fiscal combination of local public goods and taxes. Welfare may be enhanced by such mobility.

There is now a widespread acceptance of the view that decentralization of expenditure responsibilities to lower-tier governments is efficiency-augmenting as they are better informed and can more readily respond to the needs and preferences of the citizens living within their jurisdictions. This 'better information' argument can be traced back to Hayek (1945). Taxation powers, on the other hand, generally tend to be more centralized. In principle, whether or not taxation responsibilities should also be decentralized remains a debatable issue (see Ter-Minassian 1997 for a discussion). A centralized tax system ensures a country-wide market with uniform tax laws and rates, which is seen to be efficiency-enhancing.

Assignment of Resources and Responsibilities

The organization of a multi-tier governmental structure requires assignments of resources and responsibilities to each tier. The theoretical framework of fiscal federalism provides the first principles for addressing this assignment issue. Musgrave (1959) and Oates (1972), among others, provide the relevant basic considerations in this context. The theory of assignment argues that the central government should have the basic responsibility for macroeconomic stabilization function and income redistribution. This is so because the monetary and external sectors are best handled by central governments which, in turn, provide the basic instruments for handling the macro-stabilization issues. Similarly, it is the mobility of households that constrains attempts to redistribute income by the sub-national governments since a more effective or generous poverty alleviation programme by a local government will simply attract migration of the poor from the neighbouring jurisdictions. This might also lead to outmigration of the richer persons if the local-level programme is financed by higher local taxation. The central government is also in the ideal position to provide public goods with an economy-wide reach.

These public goods are called 'national' public goods like defence or issuance of currency.

There is a corresponding problem of assignment of revenue sources. The determination of the vertical structure of taxes is known in the literature as the 'tax-assignment problem' (McLure 1983). The basic issue here is to determine taxes that are best suited for use at the different levels of government. Taxes can be a source of distortion in resource allocation, as buyers shift their purchases away from taxed goods. In a spatial setting, such distortions take the form of locational inefficiencies, as taxed units (or owners of taxed items) seek out jurisdictions where they can obtain relatively favourable tax treatment. High excise taxes in one jurisdiction would lead purchasers to bear unproductive travel costs in order to purchase the taxed items in jurisdictions with lower tax rates. The key implication is that decentralized levels of government should avoid non-benefit taxes on mobile units. Analysis shows that on efficiency grounds, decentralized governments should tax mobile economic units with benefit levies (Oates and Schwab 1991; Oates 1996). Such economic units should pay for the benefits received from the public service provided by the local governments.

Thus, decentralized jurisdictions should refrain from non-benefit taxation of mobile economic units, but should actively engage in benefit taxation. Gordon (1983) finds several forms of potential distortions that result from an individual jurisdiction's ignoring the effects of its fiscal decisions elsewhere in the system. These include inefficiencies involving 'exporting' of tax burdens, external congestion effects, and impacts on levels of revenues in other jurisdictions. This analysis suggests some guidelines for the use of such taxes. A reliance on resident-based taxes rather than source-based taxes, for example, can lessen tax-induced distortions by reducing the scope for tax exporting (Inman and Rubinfeld 1996; McKinnon and Nechyba 1997).

Resolving Fiscal Imbalances:
Role of Fiscal Instruments

As long as taxes are less decentralized than expenditures, there will be an imbalance between the resources and needs of different tiers of governments, with the central government having more resources than it needs and the sub-national governments having less than they need. The system is then brought into balance by fiscal transfers from the central to the sub-national governments in the form of revenue sharing and/or grants. The inter-se distribution of fiscal transfers has to take into account both equity and efficiency issues.

Intergovernmental transfers constitute an important policy instrument in fiscal federalism that can serve a number of different functions. The literature emphasizes three potential roles for such transfers: the internalization of spillover benefits to other jurisdictions, fiscal equalization across jurisdictions, and an improved overall tax system. The theory prescribes that conditional grants in the form of matching grants (under which the grantor finances a specified share of the recipient's expenditure) should be employed where the provision of local services generates benefits for residents of other jurisdictions. This induces individuals (in this case policymakers or the electorate) to incorporate spillover benefits into their decision-making framework. The magnitude of the matching shares, in such instances, should reflect the extent of the spillovers. In contrast, unconditional grants are typically the appropriate vehicle for purposes of fiscal equalization.

The purpose of these grants is to channel funds from relatively richer jurisdictions to poorer ones. Such transfers are often based on an equalization formula that measures the 'fiscal need' and 'fiscal capacity' of each sub-national government. Some observers see equalization grants as playing an important role in allowing poorer jurisdictions to compete effectively with fiscally stronger ones. In the absence of such grants, richer jurisdictions can exploit their position to promote continued economic growth, often at the expense of poorer ones. Fiscal equalization, from this perspective, helps to create a more level playing field for inter-jurisdictional competition. On the other hand, it is argued that fiscal equalization can stand in the way of needed regional adjustments that promote development in poorer regions. McKinnon (1997), for example, contends that in the US, the economic resurgence of the South following World War II resulted from relatively low levels of wages and other costs. From this perspective, fiscal equalization may hold back the development of poorer areas by impeding the needed inter-regional flow of resources (both emigration and immigration) in response to cost differentials.

The primary justification for fiscal equalization is on equity grounds. It is the redistributive issue that continues to occupy a central place on the political stage. It has also been observed that central taxes can be more progressive, without establishing fiscal incentives for relocation. There is evidence to indicate that state and local systems of taxes are typically more regressive than central taxation (e.g., Chernick 1992). There is thus some force in the argument for 'revenue sharing' under which the central government effectively serves as a tax-collecting agent for decentralized levels of government. The central government then transfers funds in an unconditional form to the states. An important consideration is that such transfers must not be too large to undermine fiscal discipline at lower levels of government.

As part of a positive theory of intergovernmental grants, Bradford and Oates (1971a and 1971b) show that a lump-sum grant to a group of people is fully equivalent in all its effects, both allocative and distributive, to a set of grants directly to the individuals in the group. These theorems are known as the 'veil hypothesis', which implies that a grant to a community is fully equivalent to a central tax rebate to the individuals in the community. Intergovernmental grants, according to this view, are simply a 'veil' for a federal tax cut. It implies that the budgetary response to an intergovernmental transfer should be nearly the same as the response to an equal increase in private income in the community. However, empirical support for this hypothesis is weak. Several studies find that state and local government spending is much more responsive to increases in intergovernmental receipts than it is to increases in the community's private income ('Flypaper Effect').

An efficient fiscal transfer system is also likely to be characterized by predictability and stability. Predictability of resource flows enables the sub-national governments to plan ahead, and stability ensures that there will not be sudden shocks in the transfer arrangements. In the consideration of the issue of equity, reference is often made to its vertical and horizontal dimensions. The main conceptual issues relate to the interdependence of the vertical and horizontal dimensions of equity and trade-off, if any, between equity and efficiency. The analysis has also to take into account the implications of vertical and horizontal fiscal externalities. These issues are discussed further in the following sections.

Fiscal Imbalances and the Role of Fiscal Transfers

Fiscal transfers play a role in resolving both vertical and horizontal imbalances in a fiscal federal system. Vertical fiscal imbalance refers to the simultaneous imbalance between means and responsibilities in two different tiers of government (Madden 1993; Walsh 1993). The vertical gap arises from the assignment of revenue sources and expenditure responsibilities. However, individual policy choices and the handling of these assignments by the governments in different tiers play a significant role in determining the actual gap that ultimately emerges. The imbalances may be mutually balancing in the sense that while in one tier, the means exceed the needs, in the other, the needs exceed the means. The system is brought into balance by the transfer of resources from the surplus tier (usually the central government) to the deficit tier (usually, the sub-national governments).

Horizontal fiscal imbalance pertains to the same level of government where the concerned tier comprises more than one government. It, therefore, necessarily refers to the lower, sub-national, tiers of government. In particular, it refers to the differences in the fiscal capacity of the states to provide services at comparable levels to the citizens residing within its boundaries, even while these governments make the same revenue effort to exploit their respective fiscal capacities. A process of redistribution can ameliorate horizontal imbalance. When explicit redistribution is not possible from one state to another due to legal or other constraints, both vertical and horizontal imbalances need to be attended to simultaneously in the process of resource transfers from the centre to the states.

There may also be an aggregate fiscal imbalance if the surplus of one tier cannot wipe out the deficit of the other. It may arise because of an overall shortage of fiscal resources compared to fiscal needs, especially if fiscal needs are judged according to some exogenous targets, for example, the universalization of elementary education. The task of designing a system of fiscal transfers becomes more difficult when the situation is that of aggregate fiscal imbalance where unless government resources are augmented, some of the governments/functions would face a shortage of resources even after transfers. Augmentation of resources may require reassignment of revenue sources between the central and state governments and/or greater revenue effort in respect of the already assigned resources. Since this may take time to translate into revenues, fiscal transfers under an overall resource shortage require greater care, as the post-transfer residual imbalances can be a cause of considerable vertical and horizontal tensions. Equalization arrangements can be severely constrained by extreme vertical and/or horizontal imbalances in the pre-transfer stage. Full equalization may require large centre-state transfers or redistribution across states, which may be resisted by the richer states. Since vertical and horizontal fiscal balances are interdependent, failure to address the problem of vertical fiscal imbalance is likely to threaten the efficacy of the horizontal fiscal equalization system as well.

Fiscal Equalization: Conceptual Issues

A fiscal transfer system may be constructed to ensure that through inter-governmental transfers all states can provide comparable levels of services if they also undertake comparable efforts to raise revenues. Fiscal capacity equalization and allocative efficiency may turn out to be mutually compatible and mutually supportive. Much depends on how the system of transfers is designed and implemented. A badly designed system may have distorting effects if it is not neutral with respect to state policies, especially if it permits states to influence the size of their grants through their own policies.

The philosophical foundation of fiscal equalization relates to the concept of equal rights and equal treatment of all citizens in all the states of a federation. This is to be complemented with greater responsiveness to the needs and preferences of citizens than would be possible in a unitary system of government.

Fiscal Residuum

One of the earliest analyses advocating the case of equalization was put forward by Buchanan (1950 and 1952). Buchanan sought an ethical justification for fiscal equalization not in terms of equality between states but as fiscal justice between individuals. Horizontal equity calls for equal treatment of equals. Using the concept of fiscal residuum, defined as the difference between taxes paid by an individual and benefits received by that individual from public spending, Buchanan showed that differences in fiscal capacity between states necessarily result, in the absence of corrective action, in unequal fiscal treatment of equals; citizens in states with high fiscal capacity have higher fiscal residuums than comparable citizens (that is, citizens with the same incomes) in states with low fiscal capacity. An important means of bringing about fiscal equalization, that is, equalization of the fiscal residuum, could be transfers between governments. Buchanan's linking of the case for fiscal equalization with the existence of economic union in a federation contained both efficiency and equity implications.

Scott (1950 and 1952) provided a counter view. Scott showed concern with a different kind of efficiency, namely the effects of fiscal equalization on the distribution of population among the states of a federation. Scott endeavoured to show that equalization transfers, by providing resources to poor people in resource-poor states, would be *inefficient* because 'the maximum income for the whole country, and so the highest average personal income, is to be achieved only by maximising national production' (p. 203). This requires labour to move from places where its marginal product is low to places where it is high. By discouraging labour mobility, fiscal equalization grants would result in allocative inefficiency. Scott recognized that equalization grants in a federation would merely treat individuals in low-capacity areas in the same way as if they were in a unitary country. However, he argued that federalism without equalization provides, through enhanced labour mobility, the opportunity to achieve greater efficiency than is possible under a unitary system.

Congestible Public Goods and Efficiency

In 1971, Buchanan, with Richard E. Wagner as co-author, renewed the debate with a paper justifying fiscal equalization grants purely on efficiency grounds. Their analysis drew on the concept of public goods and fiscal surplus. Public goods like defence are publicly provided goods and services that are supplied jointly in equal amounts to all citizens and are indivisible. Fiscal surpluses are the value citizens place on public goods over and above the taxes they are required to pay to obtain the benefits of the public goods. These benefits arise because citizens value public goods at their average and not at their marginal values, and thus exist even when the conditions for public goods efficiency have been met (that is, when marginal tax prices are equal to the marginal evaluations by citizens of the public goods provided).

The rationale that Buchanan and Wagner provided rested on a distinction between pure public goods and *congestible* public goods. They showed that because rich states can provide higher fiscal surpluses than poor states—taxes paid are lower for given benefits—there is an incentive for migration to occur from the latter to the former. In the case of *congestible* public goods, like roads and other facilities that are fixed in size, the addition of each person who shares in the public goods will partly reduce the amounts available for those in the existing population. This does not happen in the case of pure public goods, where the amounts available to individual citizens are not affected by the size of the population. As the population of the receiving state increases, congestion in the use of publicly provided goods eventually occurs, and fiscal surpluses fall.

In making their decisions to migrate, citizens are not likely to take into account the effects of their decisions on others. As such, too many people will migrate to states costing less for the same level of public goods. This will result in a loss of efficiency for the economy as a whole. Since the rich states cannot exclude migrants, another mechanism is needed to eliminate the fiscal surplus differentials. Buchanan and Wagner suggested that equalization grants from rich states to poor states could be used for this purpose. This serves as a mechanism of compensating citizens in poor states for not migrating and thereby equalizing fiscal surpluses between states.

By contrast with Buchanan's 1950 paper, the emphasis now was that even conceptually equalization transfers must be between governments and not between individuals because the source of the excessive migration lies in the provision of public goods. The corrective measures must work through the goods and services that are commonly shared.

Property Rights: Implications for Equity and Efficiency

In a later contribution, Boadway and Flatters (1982) made a distinction between two concepts of horizontal fiscal equity among individuals, which they suggested required alternative approaches to fiscal equalization. The first or broad concept postulated the equal treatment of equals in the federation, as a whole, while the second or narrow concept calls for equal treatment of equals only within each state. The reason why this distinction is important lies in the recognition of property rights and hence in the issue of what state revenues should be brought into the equalization process.

Under the broad view of equity, the goal would be to equalize the net fiscal benefits (Buchanan's net fiscal residuums) of persons with equal incomes in all states. The application of the narrow concept would allow differences in net fiscal benefits to remain to the extent that they reflected the property rights of states or citizens, revenues from which would not be subject to equalization. To help decide on the appropriate concept, Boadway and Flatters made a further distinction between two kinds of state taxes: those imposed on residents, such as personal income and consumption taxes, and those imposed on the sources of income and wealth, such as company income taxes, land taxes, and mining revenues or other taxes on resource rents.

Boadway and Flatters conclude that the application of the narrow concept would neither be equitable in the broad sense nor efficient. If resources were distributed only to the residents of a state, the allocation of labour and other factors would be inefficient across states because the movement of factors would take place to equalize their average products (including their differential fiscal benefits) whereas efficiency would require the equalization of their marginal products (in the case of labour and wage rates). Wages would thus be lower in states with high resource rents. They arrived at three main conclusions:

1. In the absence of equalization, migration decisions by individuals are unlikely to lead to an efficient allocation of labour across states;
2. state governments, acting on behalf of their citizens, are likely to take budgetary actions that lead to inefficiencies and inequities in the federation as a whole; and
3. faced with the inefficiencies and inequities resulting from individual and state behaviour, the central government is justified in using fiscal equalization to achieve nationwide equity and efficiency.

Alternative Approaches to Equalization: Musgrave

Musgrave (1961) undertook the pioneering work on theoretical models of fiscal equalization as an approach to a more general theory of political federalism. Musgrave was concerned with the distributional and state revenue effects of different kinds of equalization grants from federal to state governments. He distinguished between three approaches to fiscal equalization, described as (i) equalization of outlays or performance, (ii) equalization of differentials in need and capacity, and (iii) equalization of potentials for state finance.

Musgrave contended that intervention of the centre in the finances of the states, through fiscal transfers or otherwise, can relate to two distinguishable sets of objectives: (i) addressed to states, that is, groups of individuals comprising the states, and (ii) individual citizens of the federations, whatever state they may be residing in.

According to Musgrave (1961), the former approach is more federalist, and the latter is more centrist. In the former case, the individual citizen is subject to the policies of the state in which they are living, but the central government through its intervention may influence the terms on which public services are provided at the state level. In the second case, the central fisc may try to 'equalize differentials in the position of federal citizens which arise from their respective citizenships in particular states. Thereby, the central fisc attempts to isolate federal citizens from the fiscal consequences of their respective state citizenships' (Musgrave 1961, p. 98).

Musgrave outlined several equalization plans with alternative objectives in the context of the first alternative, that is, taking the states (groups of individuals) as a whole, rather than its citizens as individuals. In particular, he sets out alternative 'equalization plans' aimed respectively at (i) equalization of actual outlay (or performance) (two variants), (ii) equalization of differentials in need and capacity, and (iii) equalization of potentials for state finance. As against pure equalization plans, he also considers 'pure incentive plans'. In all, he puts forward seven plans. Additional plans can be generated as composite plans targeted both at equalization and incentives. In developing these plans, various assumptions have been made. For example, possibilities of tax exporting, and spillover effects of expenditures have been ruled out. Borrowing, as well as non-tax revenues through user charges for publicly provided services, have also been assumed out. Relaxing these assumptions gives rise to additional equalization plans.

Fiscal Transfers in the Presence of Externalities

Externalities could be of two types: vertical fiscal externalities and horizontal fiscal externalities. They may arise from the side of taxation as well as expenditures. Horizontal externalities refer to jurisdictions at the same level of government. Here, the tax or expenditure decisions of one state government will affect the citizens of other states. In the case of vertical fiscal externality, it is the policy of the centre which will influence the states, or that of the states which will influence the centre. Externalities are direct when either tax bases overlap (fully or partially) and/or expenditure responsibilities are shared for the same function either fully or partially.

In several recent contributions, the implications of externalities in a federal system have been examined extensively. For example, Boadway and Flatters (1982) show that the existence of fiscal externality associated with the free mobility of individuals leads to an inefficient allocation of population among regions. They further show that equalization grants can be used to internalize this fiscal externality. Myers (1990) has argued that migration efficiency can be achieved through voluntary inter-regional transfers when local authorities can use such an instrument. In such a case, federal grants are not necessary.

In a simple, partial equilibrium framework, as also in a general equilibrium framework, it has been shown that if a local government does not take into account the effect of its tax policy on the central government's tax revenue, the Marginal Cost of Public Fund (MCPF) is underestimated, which may lead to an excessive supply of local public goods (see, for e.g., in Dahlby and Wilson 1994). They have established that under conditions of the second-best optimum, it is required that social MCPFs be equalized not only among tax bases in each local jurisdiction but also among regions. The explicit form of equalization grants for achieving this objective has also been specified. The consequence of the underestimation of MCPF by the local authorities is that they may raise local tax rates beyond the second-best levels. In Dahlby (1996), it is recommended that matching grants could be used to internalize this tax externality.

Boadway and Keen (1996) raise the question as to what is the optimum level of fiscal gap between local and central governments. The kind of economy that they examined consists of homogenous regions in which a labour income tax is co-occupied by local and central governments and households are mobile. They conclude that the existence of the tax externality may make the optimal fiscal gap negative. In Sato (2000), some of these assumptions have been relaxed. Sato examines the second-best policy at the federal level in the presence of both heterogeneous regions and imperfect individual mobility. He argues that in the presence either of perfect or imperfect mobility of households, the heterogeneity of the regions gives rise to different characteristics of the second-best outcome. In partial modification to Dahlby and Wilson (1994), the second best does not generally require the equalization of the MCPFs between regions. He argues that a matching grant scheme as the function of the local tax rate or tax revenue needs to be employed to internalize the tax externalities which arise due to the misperception of the social MCPFs by the sub-national governments. The second-best provision of the national public good and allocation of the population also requires a lump-sum transfer to equate the shadow prices of raising public funds among the governments. It is also shown that the optimal fiscal gap is indeterminate. This arises from the contention that federal tax policy is redundant as an instrument to achieve the second best.

While several contributions have referred to tax and expenditure externalities, not many of them have treated them together. In Wrede (2000), an attempt is made to consider tax and expenditure externalities together under certain assumptions. On the tax side, a perfect tax base overlap is assumed. On the expenditure side, the case of shared expenditure is taken where the public goods provided by the two levels of government are perfect substitutes. It has been shown that the equilibrium is characterized by over-taxation and either under-provision or overprovision of public goods, depending on the degree of complementarity between public goods and the tax base. He has argued that the recommendation by Brennan and Buchanan (1977) that public goods should be bound to tax bases which are highly complementary with them, might be misleading in a federal nation with tax base overlaps and shared expenditures. Some of the policy implications of Wrede's analysis are that the overlapping of tax sources and expenditures needs to be restricted by constitutional provisions and that vertical cooperation between governments might be beneficial under certain circumstances.

Instruments of Equalization

The instruments of equalization available in a system comprise all instruments whereby redistribution can be affected between states. These means can be both explicit instruments and implicit mechanisms. The main explicit instruments for redistribution are revenue sharing, general purpose grants, specific purpose grants, conditional grants, and matching grants. The implicit means of redistribution may relate to central policies/rules, and centrally administered prices which may differentially affect tax rates/bases in the states. The local incidence of central expenditures, especially central investment, would also be a means by which redistribution can be affected.

Revenue Sharing
The sharing of central tax revenues, individually or globally, can be a potent means of redistribution among states. The extent of redistribution that can be affected through this means depends on the vertical shares of the centre and the states, and the horizontal shares pertaining to individual states. The horizontal shares will bring about redistribution depending on the weights attached to such criteria as can give higher shares to low revenue capacity states, and the total amount (vertical share) that is redistributed among states.

Grants
Grants, as an instrument of fiscal transfers, provide a range of options. Grants may be conditional or unconditional. The justification of conditional grants is premised on the judgement that local decision-making will fail to produce the socially optimum outcome, especially in the presence of inter-jurisdictional spillovers or externalities. Within the category of conditional grants, we may have matching grants where the sub-national government may be required to contribute matching funds.

The matching grants can be open-ended or subject to caps. An open-ended matching grant will encourage the local governments to internalize identified spillovers and provide the required level of services.

Unconditional grants are general purpose grants meant to augment the revenues of the low revenue capacity states without attaching any strings that may affect the preference pattern of spending in the concerned state. General purpose grants serve the same purpose as revenue sharing except that general purpose grants are specified in nominal terms, while in the case of revenue sharing, the amounts that actually flow to the states automatically respond to changes in the actual realizations of the central taxes.

Inter-jurisdictional Competition

One strand of literature argues that inter-jurisdictional competition among decentralized levels of government introduces serious allocative distortions. In their eagerness to promote economic development with the creation of new jobs, state and local officials tend to keep tax rates at low levels and consequently outputs of public services, to reduce the costs for existing and prospective business enterprises resulting in a 'race to the bottom' with suboptimal outputs of public services. Competition may also take place between different levels of government (Breton 1998).

There are some strong assumptions in these models. First, jurisdictions behave as price-takers in national or international capital markets; secondly, public officials seek to maximize the welfare of their constituencies with access to the needed fiscal and regulatory policy instruments to carry out their programmes efficiently. Violations of any of these conditions can lead to distorted outcomes.

Fiscal decentralization can play a most important role in constraining public sector growth. Competition among decentralized governments for mobile economic units greatly limits the capacity of Leviathan to channel resources into the public sector. As Brennan and Buchanan (1980) put it, competition among governments in the context of the 'inter-jurisdictional mobility of persons in pursuit of "fiscal gains" can offer partial or possibly complete substitutes for explicit fiscal constraints on the taxing power' (p. 184). The Brennan–Buchanan view suggests the hypothesis that the overall size of the public sector 'should be smaller, ceteris paribus, the greater the extent to which taxes and expenditures are decentralized'.

The welfare implications of inter-jurisdictional competition remain the subject of an ongoing debate. Oates (1999) argues that the existing work is not sufficient to make a compelling case for the modification of the principle of fiscal decentralization. In his view, the case remains strong for leaving 'local matters in local hands'.

Political Economy Aspects of Fiscal Federalism

Inman and Rubinfeld (1997a and 1997b) bring into the analytical framework, a set of political goals, and examine the trade-offs between such goals as economic efficiency and political participation. In one such illustration, they present a *federalism frontier* in which (over the relevant range) increased political participation comes at the expense of economic efficiency. The basic presumption here is that more decentralized political systems are conducive to increased citizen impact on political outcomes and political participation. The basic political objectives strengthen the case for increased decentralization. They point to a system that is more decentralized than the one chosen simply on the grounds of an exercise in economic optimization. The political objectives seem, on the whole, to strengthen the case for fiscal decentralization (Pommerehne 1997).

Rather than viewing politicians as either revenue or social welfare maximizing entities and focusing on the size of fiscal externalities and the relative elasticities of tax bases, these models treat government decisions as bargains struck among self-interested politicians attempting to form winning coalitions. Gramlich (1989), Inman and Rubinfeld (1996 and 1997c), Persson et al. (1996), Lockwood (2002, 2005), and Besley and Coate (2003) argue that the case for decentralization depends critically upon the nature of legislative bargaining over distribution.

Political economy in the analytical and policy literature on fiscal federalism has developed along several interconnected strands. Four important strands relate to (i) the benefits of competition, (ii) principal-agent problems, (iii) common pool problems, and (iv) the role of the soft budget constraint.

Benefits of Competition

In a system of competitive federalism, sub-federal jurisdictions can experiment with new economic policies. This could be efficiency-enhancing for the federal system as a whole since efficient solutions will be followed while unsuccessful policies will not be emulated by the competing jurisdictions. Oates (1999) speaks of 'laboratory federalism' and points out that the reform of welfare in the US in 1996 followed these considerations (see Inman and Rubinfeld 1997a).

Principal-Agent Problems

In democracies, voters (the principals) delegate the power over public spending and taxes to elected politicians (the agents). The principal-agent relationship implies that politicians can extract rents from being in office unless subjected to strict rules by the voters. The uncertainty and complexity of economic and political institutions imply that it may not be possible to write complete contracts that can eliminate all rents. The principal-agent relation resembles an 'incomplete contract' leaving politicians with considerable residual powers (Seabright 1996; Persson et al. 1997; Persson and Tabellini 1999a, 1999b, 2000; and Tabellini 2000). In many studies, the claims of the principal-agent theory have been tested by comparing public finances under representative democracy and direct democracy, which gives voters more opportunities to indicate their preferences and more direct control over politicians, leaving less residual powers to politicians (Pommerehne 1978 and 1990; Matsusaka 1995; Kirchgässner et al. 1999; Feld and Kirchgässner 1999; Buchanan and Musgrave 1999; and Feld and Matsusaka 2003).

Common Pool Problems

Another political economy aspect of fiscal federalism extensively discussed in the literature is the common pool problem (von Hagen and Harden 1996) which arises when politicians can spend money from a general tax fund on targeted public policies. In this case, the group of those who pay for specific targeted policies (the general taxpayer) is larger than the beneficiary group. This implies a divergence between the net benefits accruing to the targeted groups and the net benefits for society as a whole. This divergence induces the targeted groups and the politicians representing them to demand more spending on such policies than what is optimal for society as a whole. The common pool problem results in excessive levels of public spending, often financed by excessive fiscal deficits and government debts (Velasco 1999; von Hagen and Harden 1996). Kontopoulos and Perotti (1999) point out that this tendency for excessive spending, deficits, and debt increases with the number of politicians drawing on the same general tax fund. Division of society on an ideological, ethnic, linguistic, and religious basis increases the tendency of people on one side to neglect the tax burden falling on the other side, making the common pool problem more severe. This has been empirically demonstrated in a number of studies (Roubini and Sachs 1989; Alesina and Perotti 1995; Alesina et al. 1997; and Annett 2000).

The common pool perspective also provides an understanding of vertical fiscal relations within countries. Transfers from the central to local governments imply that residents in one region benefit from taxes paid by residents in other regions. Bailouts of over-indebted local governments are a special form of such transfers. Careaga and Weingast (2000) show how vertical transfers distort local decisions towards excess spending and a bias in favour of public consumption. Various studies included in Rodden et al. (2003) confirm the empirical relevance of bailouts in many countries.

The adverse consequences of the principal-agent problem and the common pool problem can be mitigated by institutions governing the decisions over public finances. Three types of fiscal institutions are particularly relevant in this context: (i) ex-ante rules such as constitutional limits on deficits, spending, or taxes, (ii) electoral rules encouraging political accountability and competition, and (iii) procedural rules regarding the budget process. Studying the effects of these three types of fiscal institutions has been the subject of extensive research in the past two decades, stimulated by the need to constrain excessive spending and deficits in the Organisation for Economic Co-operation and Development (OECD) countries as well as developing countries.

Soft Budget Constraints

Soft budget constraints play a particularly important role in the research-related political economy aspects of fiscal federalism. When an entity such as a state government faces a soft budget constraint, it means that it can implicitly or explicitly pass on its liabilities to other entities, such as the federal government. Much of the research focuses on bailouts in debt crises. It is argued that when the central government plays a significant role in financing provincial governments it is difficult to credibly commit to not bail out the provinces in the event of a debt crisis (Rodden et al. 2003). This creates weak incentives for fiscal discipline on the part of state governments. In particular, it provides incentives for state governments to overspend, under-tax, over-borrow, and under-provide services in the hope that local public expenditures will ultimately be subsidized by tax-payers in other jurisdictions. Instead of implementing politically painful expenditure cuts or tax increases, local politicians might choose not to adjust fiscal policy in the belief that ultimately they will be bailed out by the central government. This kind of dynamic fiscal irresponsibility is one possible manifestation of the fiscal accountability argument in favour of tax decentralization.

A debt-servicing crisis is not the only type of crisis that the states can use to ask for a bailout. Often state governments ask for grants for funding special welfare schemes which may have remained underfunded and lead to some crisis particularly related to health. The Canadian example of health-care funding, is often cited in this context where the provinces have been asking for more federal money on the basis of a health-care crisis. The structure of political institutions has an important impact on these types of moral-hazard problems. In many federal countries, the structure of the central government includes representation of the sub-national constituent units. Depending on the configurations of such representation, possibilities of logrolling emerge, forcing the central government to provide bailouts to certain states, even though the policy is inefficient for the federation as a whole.

In order to benefit from the discipline of hard budget constraint some fiscal reform is a must. Fiscal reform efforts in the developing world should focus on (i) restructuring systems of intergovernmental grants, to reduce the extent of financing that is provided to decentralized levels of government, particularly removing the perverse incentives that they often embody for fiscal behaviour on the part of recipients, (ii) re-designing revenue systems to provide decentralized levels of government a much-expanded access to own -revenues to finance their budgets and thereby reduce their dependence on transfers from above, and (iii) re-viewing the use and restrictions on debt financing to ensure that debt is-sues are not a ready way to finance deficits on the current account. All these three avenues of reform contribute in important ways to the estab-lishment of a hard budget constraint.

The analysis of debt sustainability led the Twelfth and Thirteenth Finance Commissions to recommend the enactment of fiscal responsi-bility legislation in the current or modified forms. One of the key require-ments for a market-preserving federalism is a hard budget constraint. The adherence of the governments to borrowing norms helps to impart a hard budget constraint. Limits on borrowing also imply limits on interest payments, which facilitate the design of more robust transfer systems without generating perverse incentives. Hard budget constraints induce state governments to respond to market signals better, as discussed in the next section. This is why transfer arrangements have a clear link with borrowing limits and mechanisms, particularly whether the central gov-ernment intermediates or borrows on behalf of the state governments.

Market-Preserving Federalism

Market-preserving federalism is an alternative approach to federalism, related to the 'new institutional economics'. It sees political decentraliza-tion in terms of its capacity to sustain a productive and growing market economy. From this perspective, Weingast (1995), McKinnon (1997) have explored the institutional structure of a system that promises to provide a stable framework for a market system (McKinnon et al. 1997; Qian and Weingast 1997). Weingast has highlighted a 'fundamental pol-itical dilemma of an economic system', namely that, 'a government strong enough to protect property rights and enforce contracts is also strong enough to confiscate the wealth of its citizens' (Weingast 1995, p. 1). McGuire and Olson (1996) show that even a self-aggrandizing autocrat has powerful incentives for supporting an economically efficient system.

Weingast has laid out a set of three conditions for a federal system that characterize market-preserving federalism. These conditions require that (i) decentralized governments have the primary regulatory responsibility over the economy, (ii) the system constitutes a common market in which there are no barriers to trade, and (iii) decentralized governments face 'hard budget constraints'. The last condition implies that lower-level governments have neither the capacity to create money nor access to unlimited credit and the central government does not bail them out in instances of fiscal distress. In a federal system, if the central government controls the common currency, then lower-level governments will be limited to fiscal instruments and will not have access to the 'soft' option of monetized debt. McKinnon (1997) points out that state and local governments in the US engage in extensive debt financing for capital projects. This makes good economic sense in terms of spreading the payments for long-lived capital projects over their useful life. But they have no recourse to public sources for funding this debt. They operate in private credit markets just like private borrowers. These markets themselves, through credit ratings and other forms of monitoring fiscal performance, create an environment in which the fiscal authorities are required to behave in responsible ways. These markets, by creating a hard budget constraint in terms of debt finance, have imposed a discipline on decentralized fiscal behaviour. Hard budget constraints imply that decentralized governments must place a basic reliance on their own sources of revenues and not be overly dependent on transfers from above. It is especially important that intergovernmental grants are not so flexible that recipients can turn to the grant system to bail them out of fiscal difficulties (Wildasin 1998).

Fiscal Decentralization and Economic Development

Considerable empirical work has been done to show a strong link between fiscal decentralization and economic development. This relationship depends among other things on the extent of fiscal decentralization. There is a sharp contrast in the extent of fiscal decentralization in industrialized and developing countries. In a study by Oates (1985), in a sample of forty-three countries it is observed that the average share of central government spending in total public expenditure is 65 per cent in the sub-sample of eighteen industrialized countries, as compared to 89 per cent in the sub-sample of twenty-five developing nations. In terms of total public revenues, the central government share for this same sub-sample of developing countries was over 90 per cent. There is clear evidence that developing countries are characterized by relatively high degrees of fiscal centralization (Zhang and Zou 1998).

In this context, the key question is whether fiscal decentralization is a cause or a result of economic development. Bahl and Linn (1992), for example, argue that as economies grow and mature, economic gains from fiscal decentralization emerge, contending: 'Decentralization more likely comes with the achievement of a higher stage of economic development' (p. 391). Beyond a 'threshold level of economic development', fiscal decentralization becomes attractive. From this perspective, it is economic development that comes first and fiscal decentralization then follows. Oates (1999) observes that we may regard intergovernmental structure as part of a larger political and economic system that both influences and is determined by the interplay of a variety of political and economic forces. Fiscal decentralization 'itself' has a real contribution to make to improve economic and political performance at different stages of development. On traditional grounds of efficiency, there is a case for a significant degree of decentralization in public-sector decision-making in developing nations. This case is based both on the potential economic gains from adapting levels of public outputs to specific regional or local conditions and on the political appeal of increased participation in governance. Development policies that are sensitive to particular regional or local needs for infrastructure and human capital are likely to be more effective in promoting economic growth than centrally determined policies that largely ignore these geographical differences. Some observers like Prud'homme (1995), argue that the case for fiscal decentralization has been much exaggerated. Prud'homme claims that many of the premises of the fiscal federalism vision are typically not satisfied in the developing-country setting. Decentralized government bodies, he argues, are frequently unresponsive to the needs of their constituencies and manifest widespread corruption.

Huther and Shah (1996) provide a large and diverse set of indices for eighty nations to empirically examine the relationship between decentralization and growth. These indices encompass a wide variety of measures of economic and political structure and performance: quality of governance, political freedom, political stability, debt-to-GNP (gross national product) ratios, measures of income, and the degree of equality in the distribution of income. In examining the statistical associations among these indices, they find in nearly every case a statistically significant and positive correlation between increased decentralization and improved performance (either in political or economic terms). Kim (1995) uses international panel data to estimate a Barro-type growth model. In addition to the usual explanatory variables, he included a measure of fiscal decentralization that, in most of his estimated equations, has a significant and positive partial association with the rate of economic growth. Kim's findings support the contention that fiscal decentralization enhances economic performance. In contrast, in two studies, one examining a sample of forty-six countries over the period 1970–89 (Davoodi and Zou 1998) and the other a study of the growth of provinces in China (Zhang and Zou 1998), a negative relationship between economic growth and fiscal decentralization has been reported.

Environmental Federalism

The issues of environmental federalism arise because of inter-jurisdictional externalities that are related to the environment. Local jurisdictions do not have full control over the level of environmental quality within their own boundaries. Pollution originating in other jurisdictions affects their citizens through air, water, and land.

Two types of instruments can be used to correct inter-regional environmental externalities. First, there is a regulatory approach where the central government may set common standards to be followed in all jurisdictions. Following efficiency considerations, the central government should set a standard for environmental quality that satisfies the basic Samuelson condition, ensuring that the marginal benefits (that is, benefits from a unit of improvement in environmental quality summed over everyone in the nation) equal marginal abatement cost.

Another approach is to use environmental taxes and/or subsidies to control pollution. These taxes or subsidies can aim to internalize the social damage of pollution. However, in an intergovernmental setting, there may be a role for the central government which can specify differentiated taxes directly on polluting sources across the nation, or offer an appropriate and differentiated subsidy to local governments to induce them to internalize the inter-jurisdictional benefits from pollution control. Leaving the choice entirely to the sub-national governments may lead to suboptimal choices as they may often settle for less than desirable tax rates on polluting inputs and outputs in order to attract investment and economic activities to their jurisdictions.

Oates and Schwab (1988), Wilson (1996), and Oates (2001) have discussed this issue at length and they argue that since more stringent environmental measures raise costs to firms and deflect capital elsewhere, there is an incentive for local governments to choose excessively lax standards for local environmental quality.

There is also the related concern that local decision-making may ignore the inter-temporal or inter-generational implications of environmental decisions. The argument is that local decision-making may be myopic and fail to consider appropriately the interests of future generations. The argument is that with high mobility, current residents have a limited concern with the future quality of the local environment. Not only may they move elsewhere but their children may also not remain in the same jurisdiction. Thus, local residents are likely to undervalue measures that promise to protect or enhance the local environment in the more distant future. This can be overcome by centralized decisions which will tend to internalize such concerns for the future.

In all these cases theoretical considerations show that under certain conditions regional cooperation can be a substitute for central intervention. But often regions are in such conflict among each other, that the best framework may be coordination between central and state governments. A good example is the spate of disputes among Indian states concerning rivers and their flowing across more than one state and the right to water. Oates (2001) argues that some kind of 'Coasian' cooperation among regional governments may be an alternative to central intervention, which by itself is often not effective.

In practice, the case where polluting activities affect environmental quality in neighbouring jurisdictions presents a difficult challenge for environmental management and in many cases issues remain unresolved.

In a political economy context, policymakers in one jurisdiction are concerned with the voters only of their jurisdictions and have little incentive to take into account the costs that their actions impose on their neighbours. While central interventions are an answer, even this often does not work.

Oates (2001) notes that the first-best policy measure is an economic instrument like an effluent charge per unit of waste emissions equal to the marginal external damages. In general, this would need to be a differentiated tax that would depend on the location of the source and the people affected. Such differentiated tax rates are not easy for a central authority either to determine or, politically, to impose. Also, centrally determined, uniform ambient standards for environmental quality are not an efficient policy response in such cases. An alternative approach is for the central authority to set emissions limitations on polluting activities with spillover effects. But even here, uniform regulations are unlikely to be very satisfactory. A fully efficient system of pollution control must take into account the particular patterns and magnitudes of the flows of pollutants across multiple borders. Revesz (1996) shows that in the context of air quality management, federal measures in the US have not been very effective in addressing the issue of inter-state externalities.

Considering the Indian context, the issues of environmental federalism have become quite important in view of the inter-regional externalities of pollution and inter-state claims on natural resources, particularly water. The constitution has also provided considerable scope for central intervention. Under the Indian Constitution, the legislative power is specifically and exclusively reposed in Parliament under Article 262 to enact a law providing for the adjudication of any dispute or complaint concerning the use, distribution, or control of waters of, or in, any inter-state river or river valley. In the exercise of this power, under Article 262, the Indian Parliament enacted 'The Inter-State Water Dispute Act' of 1956. The jurisdiction of all courts, including the Supreme Court, is barred with respect to such disputes, which are to be settled by the Tribunal set up under The Inter-State Water Dispute Act, 1956.

Under Article 249 of the Constitution, Parliament is also empowered to legislate in the 'national interest' on matters covered by the State list. Also, if there is any inconsistency between the law made by Parliament under Article 249 and the law made by the state legislature, the law made by Parliament shall reign supreme. Parliament can enact laws on state subjects for those states whose legislatures have consented to such central legislation. Thus, though 'water' is a state subject, The Water [Prevention and Control of Pollution] Act of 1974 was enacted by Parliament, pursuant to consent resolutions passed by twelve state legislatures. In order to legislate on environmental matters, the Indian Parliament has relied upon two other constitutional provisions. These provisions are Article 253 and Article 51(c). Article 253 empowers Parliament to make laws for implementing any treaty, agreement, or convention with any other country/countries or for implementing any decision made at any international conference, association, or other body. Article 51(c) mandates that the State shall endeavour to foster respect for international law and treaty obligations. These two articles, therefore, provide that Parliament can open up the State List and enact laws on any entries contained in it.

Two major and vital Indian environmental laws, namely the Air [Prevention and Control of Pollution] Act of 1981 and the Environmental [Protection] Act of 1986, have been enacted under these Constitutional provisions. The Constitutional (42nd Amendment) Act of 1976 also resulted in the inclusion of Article 48A and Article 51A(g) in the Constitution. Article 48A casts an obligation on the Indian state not only to protect but, more importantly, to improve the environment and to safeguard the forests and wildlife of the country. Article 51A(g) imposes a fundamental duty on the Indian citizen to protect and improve the natural environment, including forests, lakes, rivers, and wildlife, and to have compassion for living creatures. Therefore, the duty to protect and enhance the quality of the environment in India is the duty of the union, the states, and the citizens.

2

Evolution of Fiscal Federalism in India

The Indian federation has, apart from a central government, twenty-eight states (with three newly created ones), two Union Territories (UTs) with legislatures, five UTs without own legislatures, several autonomous regions within states, a three-tiered structure of rural local bodies, and three levels of urban local bodies.* The three new States—Uttarakhand, Chhattisgarh, and Jharkhand—which came into existence in November 2000, have been carved out from the parent states of Uttar Pradesh, Madhya Pradesh, and Bihar, respectively. The Twelfth Finance Commission had indicated that there were 3,723 urban and 243,685 rural local governments in India as per information provided by the state governments. The system provides for a relatively favourable economic treatment of special category states. As per the classification of the Planning Commission, ten states are categorized as special while the remaining states are considered as non-special or general category states.

All the three parent states are large and low-income states, and the three new states represent regions that are relatively poorer or otherwise disadvantaged, within the parent states. The process of creation of new states, and demands from other regions in other states for separate statehood, have gathered strength in the context of growing inter-regional disparities in the country Chelliah (2006). It is clear that the organizational structure of the federation in terms of sub-national governments has not stabilized.

The focus of this study is on the role of fiscal transfers from the centre to sub-national governments in ameliorating or accentuating disparities in the levels of publicly provided services and overall growth

---

* This chapter is based partly on a study entitled 'Review of Trends in Fiscal Transfers in India', undertaken for the Thirteenth Finance Commission, co-authored by D.K. Srivastava and Bhujanga C. Rao, brought out as Monograph 8/2010, Madras School of Economics, Chennai.

Federalism and Fiscal Transfers in India, Second Edition. C. Rangarajan and D.K. Srivastava, Oxford University Press.
© Rangarajan and Srivastava 2024. DOI: 10.1093/9780198930426.003.0002

across regions and states within India. In this chapter, we propose to review the main developments in the economic and fiscal spheres in the 1990s. We shall highlight the main features of economic reforms that were initiated in the early 1990s and their implications for regional growth. We shall examine the pattern of growth and sectoral profiles of the Gross Domestic Product (GDP), for all-India as well as individual states and also the fiscal profiles of central and state governments. We also propose to analyse the immediate and underlying causes that have led to the continued deterioration of the public finances in the country.

Although the normal periodicity of the Finance Commission is five years, the periods of recommendations have been implemented sometimes for a lesser period (Third and Fourth Finance Commissions) and only once for a longer period (Ninth Finance Commission). Table 2.1 gives the details of the respective years covered by the successive Finance Commissions from the First to the Twelfth. In the overview of trends in fiscal transfers undertaken here, Commission-period averages will refer

Table 2.1 Years Covered under Different Finance Commission Recommendations

Finance Commission	Period for Which Recommendation Was Implemented	No. of Years
First	1952–3 to 1956–7	5
Second	1957–8 to 1961–2	5
Third	1962–3 to 1965–6	4
Fourth	1966–7 to 1968–9	3
Fifth	1969–70 to 1973–4	5
Sixth	1974–5 to 1978–9	5
Seventh	1979–80 to 1983–4	5
Eighth	1984–5 to 1988–9	5
Ninth	1989–90 to 1994–5	6
Tenth	1995–6 to 1999–2000	5
Eleventh	2000–1 to 2004–5	5
Twelfth	2005–6 to 2009–10	5
Thirteenth	2010–11 to 2014–15	5

Source: Fifty Years of Fiscal Federalism, 2003, Report of the Twelfth Finance Commission (2005–10), Thirteenth Finance Commission 2010–15 Volume I: Report, and Thirteenth Finance Commission 2010–15 Volume II: Annexes.

to the averages over these respective periods except for the Twelfth where the reference is for the period from 2005–6 to 2007–8 up to which revised estimates are available.

Evolution of Tax Revenue-Sharing Criteria

In reviewing the inter-se distribution of the aggregate share of states in central tax revenues, the approach of the Finance Commissions can be summarized in terms of three distinct phases. Up to the Seventh Finance Commission, the distribution formulae used for determining the income tax shares were clearly distinct from those for the Union excise duties, and were given under two separate articles of the Constitution, that is, Article 270 and Article 272. Article 270 had provided for the mandatory sharing of income tax which Article 272 had provided for in sharing of the Union excise duties at the discretion of the centre. This may be considered as Phase I. After this, a process of convergence between the two sets of formulae began. A full convergence was arrived at with the recommendations of the Eleventh Finance Commission, after a major amendment to the Constitution, that is, the 80th amendment. The period from the Eighth to the Tenth Finance Commission before the alternative scheme of devolution was implemented may be considered as Phase II. Phase III is for the period of the Eleventh Finance Commission onwards.

Phase I: Separate Criteria for Income Tax and Union Tax Duties

Population and collection/assessment were the only two criteria used for determining the inter-se shares of the states in the case of income tax up to the Seventh Finance Commission. In respect of the Union excise duties, the criteria, as they evolved over time, had placed greater and greater emphasis on factors relating to economic backwardness and fiscal weakness of the states. However, population continued to be the largest determining factor up to the Sixth Finance Commission, although its weight went down from 100 to 75 per cent. The Seventh Finance Commission further reduced this weight to 25 per cent (a fall of 50 percentage points from the preceding Commission). The changes in the relative weights to factors, as recommended by different Finance Commissions, are summarized in Tables 2.2 and 2.3.

In respect of the Union excise duties, the importance of population went down with successive Finance Commissions, while that of factors

Table 2.2 Inter-se Sharing of Income Tax: Phase I

Finance Commission	Percentage Weight Assigned to	
	Population	Collection
First, Third, and Fourth	80	20
Second	90	10
	Population	Assessment
Fifth, Sixth, and Seventh	90	10

Source: Reports of Finance Commissions, Government of India.

Table 2.3 Inter-se Sharing of Union Excise Duties: Phase I

Finance Commission	Relative Weights (per cent)			
	Population	Other Factors		
First	100			
		Discretionary Adjustments		
Second	90	10		
	Population used as Major Factor	Financial Weakness and Economic Backwardness		
Third	(Weight unspecified)	Weight Unspecified Social and Economic Backwardness		
Fourth	80	20 Index of Backwardness		
Fifth	80 + 16.66*	3.33 Distance		
Sixth	75	25		
		Inverse-Income	Poverty Ratio	Revenue Equalization
Seventh	25	25	25	25

Source: Reports of Finance Commissions, Government of India.
Note: *Among states with per capita income below the all-state average.

reflecting poor resource bases continued to increase (Table 2.3). For the sharing of income tax up to the Ninth Finance Commission, the principle of derivation was given some consideration and collection/assessment was given some weight in the sharing of income tax, which was subject to Article 270. This principle was not, however, applied to the distribution of Union excise duties, which was a matter of 'discretionary' sharing (under Article 272).

Phase II: Towards Convergence: Eighth to Tenth Finance Commissions

Beginning with the Eighth Finance Commission, two changes occurred. First, there was a move towards unifying the formulae for the inter-se distribution of both income tax and Union excise duties and, secondly, a portion of the Union excise duties was kept aside for distribution according to 'assessed deficits'. The unified formulae used by the Eighth, Ninth, and Tenth Finance Commissions are given in Table 2.4. The weight to the factor of population ranged between 20 to a little less than 30 per cent for different Finance Commissions.

The sharing of portions that were kept out of the unified formula was implemented as follows. In the case of income tax, 10 per cent of the share recommended for the states was to be shared on the basis of assessment of income tax (Eighth and Ninth Finance Commissions). In the case of Union excise duties, a portion of the shareable proceeds for devolution was kept aside for distribution among states on the basis of assessed deficits. The share kept aside for this purpose also gradually increased. It was five percentage points out of 45 per cent of the shareable proceeds of Union excise duties which formed the states' share, in the case of Eighth and the first report of the Ninth Finance Commission. It was raised to 7.425 percentage points in the case of the second report of the Ninth Finance Commission and subsequently to 7.5 percentage points out of 47.5 per cent of the shareable proceeds of the Union Excise duties by the Tenth Finance Commission.

The Tenth Finance Commission recommended an 'Alternative Scheme of Devolution' whereby after a constitutional amendment proceeds of all central taxes were to be shared with the state governments.

Table 2.4   Inter-se Sharing of Income Tax and Union Excise Duties: Phase II: Eighth, Ninth, and Tenth Finance Commissions

A. Sharing of 90 per cent of Divisible Pool of Income Tax and Specified portion of Divisible Pool of Union Excise Duties According to Common Criteria

	Criteria				
Finance Commission	Population	Distance	Inverse Income	Poverty Ratio	Index of Backwardness
Eighth	25	50	25		
Ninth (1)	25	50	12.5	12.5	
Ninth (2)	25	50	12.5		12.5
	29.94	40.12	14.97		14.97
			Area	Index of Infrastructure	Tax Effort
Tenth	20	60	5	5	10

B1. Income Tax: sharing of balance amount.

Eighth and Ninth Commissions: Sharing of 10 per cent of divisible pool of income tax: According to assessment/contribution. Tenth: The balance 10 per cent was also distributed according to criteria given in Part A of the Table.

B2. Union Excise Duties: Sharing of balance of divisible amount.

Eighth and Ninth (First Report): 5 percentage points out of 45 per cent of Union Excise Duties, which formed the States' share, according to assessed deficits.

Ninth: Second Report: 7.425 percentage points out of 45 per cent according to assessed deficits.

Tenth: 7.5 percentage points out of 47.5 per cent according to assessed deficits.

Source: Reports of Finance Commissions, Government of India.

This was meant to give a significant revenue interest to the central government in all taxes that it was levying and also to facilitate tax reforms by distributing more evenly the burden of adjustment (in terms of any initial revenue loss) between the centre and the states. In the original scheme suggested by the Tenth Finance Commission, gross proceeds of the central taxes were to be shared excluding cesses and surcharges. Articles 268/269 taxes were also kept outside of the purview of such sharing. The alternative scheme was accepted by the central government and implemented through the 80th constitutional amendment. However, sharing was to be with reference to the net proceeds (net of cost of collections) rather than gross proceeds, as originally recommended. With the 80th amendment, states' share of the central taxes also ceased to be part of the Consolidated Fund of India. It is implied in Article 270 that the same percentage share will apply to all central taxes that are to be shared.

Prior to the 80th amendment, apart from the two main taxes of income tax and the Union excise duties, two other arrangements for transfers were in vogue: grant in lieu of tax on railway passenger fares and additional excise duties in lieu of sales tax on specified commodities (cotton textiles, tobacco, and sugar). Both of these arrangements were tax rental arrangements in the sense that the original power to levy the tax was vested with the state governments but was transferred to the centre for the sake of uniformity across states among other reasons. With the 80th amendment to the Constitution, the separate identity of these arrangements was also abolished.

Phase III: Full Convergence: From the Alternative Scheme of the Tenth Finance Commission

Under the global sharing agreement, only one set of shares is to be determined replacing four distinct sets, which were needed prior to the 80th constitutional amendment, relating respectively to: (i) portions of income tax and Union excise duties subjected to common criteria, (ii) portion of devolution according to assessed deficits, (iii) grant in lieu of tax on railway passenger fares, and (iv) additional excise duties in lieu of sales tax on cotton textiles, tobacco, and sugar. The criteria followed by the Tenth Finance Commission (Alternative Scheme), and the subsequent Commissions relate to these generalized sharing arrangements. These criteria jointly reflect four considerations: (i) vertical transfers, (ii) equity, (iii) incentives for efficiency, and (iv) cost disadvantages.

Two core criteria, which have been used by the Finance Commissions for horizontal equity, providing higher per capita transfers to lower per capita fiscal capacity states, are distance and inverse-income formulae. In the case of the Eighth Finance Commission, the combined weight given to these two criteria was 75 per cent. In the case of the Ninth Finance Commission (Second Report), the combined weight for these two criteria was 62.5 per cent for income tax. An additional equity-related criterion was used in the form of the index of backwardness (replacing the index of poverty used in the First Report), which was given a weight of 12.5 per cent. The weight of these three equity-related criteria added to about 70 per cent in the case of Union excise duties. The Tenth Finance Commission had decided to use only one of these criteria, namely, the distance formula, and gave it a weight of 60 per cent. The Eleventh Finance Commission had kept the weight to this criterion at 62.5 per cent.

While computing distance-based shares of states, the Eleventh Finance Commission introduced some changes. The practice followed by the Ninth and Tenth Commissions was that of measuring the distance of the per capita income of a state from that of the highest per capita income. But for this purpose, Goa, being a very small state, was not considered a representative state, and distances were measured from the per capita income of Maharashtra. Maharashtra and Goa were exogenously given the same distance as that for Punjab. As a result, three states—Punjab, Maharashtra, and Goa—obtained the same distances, and consequently the same per capita shares. Instead of taking a single high-income state as the 'representative' highest-income state, the Eleventh Commission had taken a three-state weighted average of per capita Gross State Domestic Product (GSDP) of Punjab, Maharashtra, and Goa as the benchmark from which distances were measured. The distances of these three states were then worked out as a fraction of the distance of Haryana from the representative benchmark. These fractions were obtained by taking the ratio of Haryana's per capita GSDP to the per capita GSDP of these states. The three-state average was taken to be more 'representative'. A similar method was followed by the Twelfth Finance Commission. Table 2.5 gives the different criteria and related weights followed by the Tenth (alternative scheme), Eleventh, and Twelfth Finance Commissions.

The Eleventh Finance Commission had also endeavored to evolve a structure of incentives in the mechanism of fiscal transfer. The Tenth Finance Commission had utilized an index of tax effort made by the states. The Eleventh Finance Commission utilized an index of tax effort and an index of fiscal discipline, and gave these a combined weight of 12.5 per cent. In the index of fiscal discipline, the improvement is measured by considering the ratio of the measure of fiscal discipline in a reference period in comparison to a base period. For the base period, the average for the three years from 1990–1 to 1992–3 was taken. For the reference

Table 2.5 Criteria and Relative Weights for Determining Inter-se Shares of States: Phase III: Tenth (Alternative Scheme), Eleventh, and Twelfth Finance Commissions

Criteria	Relative Weight (per cent)			
	Tenth (Alternative Scheme)	Eleventh	Twelfth	Thirteenth
Population	20.0	10.0	25.0	25.0
Distance/capacity distance	60.0	62.5	50.0	47.5
Area	5.0	7.5	10.0	10
Index of Infrastructure	5.0	7.5	–	–
Tax Effort	10.0	5.0	7.5	–
Fiscal Discipline	–	7.5	7.5	17.5

Source: Reports of Finance Commissions, Government of India.

period, the average of three years from 1996–7 to 1998–9 was taken. Higher own revenues or lower revenue expenditures or any combination of the two can bring about an improvement in fiscal self-reliance. Further, the state-specific improvements are related to the corresponding all-state improvement to neutralize factors that commonly affect all states. The comparison of the performance of a state with the all-state performance reflected the consideration that if the revenue performance of states is deteriorating in general, the state that accomplishes a relatively lower deterioration is to be rewarded relatively more than average. Similarly, if all revenue balance profiles are improving, the state where improvement is relatively more than average is rewarded relatively more.

Cost variations are brought into consideration through the criteria based on area and index of infrastructure: the larger the area (per crore population), the higher the per capita cost; similarly, the lower the index of infrastructure, the higher the per capita cost. In the case of area, which was introduced first by the Tenth Finance Commission, a 'censored' distribution of area was used where a floor and a ceiling were prescribed. The floor reflected the considerations that certain fixed establishment costs are to be incurred even if the state is extremely small. The ceiling reflected the consideration that beyond a limit, additional costs at the margin for providing services become negligible. In the case of the

Eleventh and Twelfth Finance Commissions, the concept of ceiling was dropped. Thus, the three main considerations in the selection of criteria used, in Phase III with full convergence of criteria, by the Tenth (Alternative Scheme), Eleventh, and Twelfth Finance Commissions relate to: (i) resource deficiency, (ii) higher cost of providing services, and (iii) fiscal discipline.

Revenue-Sharing Criteria: Basic Principles

As indicated earlier, there has been a gradual attempt in the dispensation of the Finance Commissions in India, to move away from conventional devolution towards revenue-sharing which is guided by three main principles: (i) capacity equalization, (ii) efficiency promoting incentives, and (iii) allowance for cost disabilities.

The principle of horizontal equity is guided by the consideration that as a result of revenue-sharing, the fiscal resource deficiencies across states arising out of systemic and identifiable factors, and under normative revenue effort, are evened out. Thus, the revenue-sharing exercise is supposed to provide the states resources complementary to their own, so that they may all be enabled to provide an agreed common set of public services at comparable standards in terms of quality and quantity to all citizens living in the different states. Thus, a citizen of India, no matter which state they reside in, becomes entitled to and is provided with the same level of services (state-level public goods and merit goods of high priority) throughout the country. This also calls for the recognition of valid cost differentials in providing a service in different states. The principle of equity, however, is a compensatory principle as it makes up for resource deficiencies. As such, it also creates a vested interest in continuing with the resource deficiency, rather than making efforts to improve own revenue bases, thereby reducing the differences in revenue per unit of resource base across states. To neutralize this adverse incentive, it needs to be complemented by criteria that either neutralize the effect of deficiencies of tax effort relative to average and/or reward 'efficiency', that is, efforts to improve the resource bases and deliver services at minimum (efficient) costs. The latter is useful when the overall tax effort is also required to be improved to improve the average level of public services.

Core Revenue-Sharing Criteria: Analytical Overview

Income-Based Formulae: Criteria Reflecting Fiscal Deficiency

The criteria that have received the highest weights in the dispensation exercises of recent Finance Commissions are the income-based criteria. Income, however, is proxied by per capita State Domestic Product (SDP) (net or gross). Per capita income or per capita GSDP is taken as a proxy for per capita fiscal capacity. Two main criteria have been used in this context. One is based on the distance of per capita income of a state from the highest per capita income among all states. The other is based on the inverse of per capita income of a state (see Srivastava and Aggarwal 1994 for a detailed analysis of the properties of these two criteria). These criteria attempt to reduce post-transfer differences in the fiscal bases of the states through progressive dispensation. The difference between them is that while the distance criterion looks at the absolute resource gaps, the inverse income criterion looks at the relative gaps. Since, in the context of the provision of services at equal standards across states, it is the absolute costs (and absolute gaps) that are relevant, successive Finance Commissions (Eighth, Ninth, and Tenth) have given increasing weight to the distance criterion. The inverse criterion was given a weight of 25 per cent by the Seventh and Eighth Commissions. The Ninth Commission reduced this weight to 12.5 per cent. The Tenth Commission dropped it altogether. In the Twelfth Finance Commission award, the full weight of the income-based criterion was loaded on the distance criterion.

Different Commissions have used the distance criterion with some variations (Vithal and Sastry 2001). The term 'distance' refers to the excess of the per capita income of a state (measured by per capita National State Domestic Product (NSDP) or GSDP) of the highest per capita income among all states over that of an individual state. If per capita income (hereinafter referred to only as income), of the different states is indicated by y_i, and states are arranged in non-descending order of income, y_1 will refer to the per capita income of say, Bihar, and y_{28} will refer to the per capita income of Goa. In general,

$$y_1 \leq y_2 \leq \cdots \leq yn$$

Standard Distance Formula (SDF)

In this version, the share of the ith state can be written as:

$$a_i = N_i(y_n - y_i) / \sum N_i(y_n - y_i) \qquad i = 1, \ldots, 28$$

The per capita share of the ith state

$$a_i^* = (y_n - y_i) / \sum N_i(y_n - y_i)$$

The share of the highest per capita income state will be zero in this standard version.

The SDF can be diagrammatically represented by a straight line falling to the right, where per capita share of a state is represented on the y-axis, and per capita income on the x-axis.

Writing
$$\sum N_i(y_n - y_i) = 1 / \alpha$$
$$a_i^* = \alpha(y_n - y_i)$$
$$a_i^* = \alpha y_n - \alpha y_i$$

If the total amount distributed under the distance criterion is WT, it can be interpreted as equivalent to a mechanism of delivering fiscal capacity equalization payments subject to the assumption that the benchmark income is y_n. Given average tax effort as θ, per capita entitlement of state 'i' is $\theta (y_n - y_i)$.

Total equalization payments are

$$\theta \sum N_i(y_n - y_i) = \alpha \sum N_i a_i^* (y_n - y_i)$$

This determines the required amount under the distance criterion of

$$WT = \theta / \alpha$$
$$W = \theta / T\alpha$$

The distance formula provides higher per capita shares to lower-income states. It attempts to bring in the principle of horizontal equity under the assumption of a normative (common) revenue effort. It can be interpreted as a fiscal capacity equalizing formula, where fiscal capacity (y_i) is measured by the (per capita) income (NSDP or GSDP) of a state. If each state makes a revenue effort of the same degree (say, θ), its revenue capacity is given by θy_i. The revenue capacity of the highest income state is θy_n. The difference between these revenue capacities is $\theta (y_n - y_i)$. This gap is filled, in the distance formula, as a result of which, the post-devolution fiscal capacities are equalized. However, the limiting assumption is that fiscal capacity is reflected in per capita income.

Modified Distance Formula (MDF)

The standard version of the distance formula was modified by some of the Finance Commissions with two considerations in mind. First, in the SDF, the highest income state does not get any share, and secondly, a state other than Goa should be chosen as the highest income state for purposes of measuring distances. Goa has a small population and high income, and the Commissions have opined that this is not 'representative' of a typical high-income state. These two considerations were brought into the formula by measuring distances from Punjab rather than Goa, giving 'notional distances to both Punjab and Goa equal to the distance between Punjab and Maharashtra'. Thus, three states get the same distance in the formula, that is, Punjab, Maharashtra, and Goa.

Dividing the shares can derive the per capita shares under MDF by the respective populations. The modified formula implies a 'kink' in the dispensation line because the per capita shares of the three states at the higher income end become equal. It also implies a higher per capita income share for a few states at the low-income end, as compared to the SDF.

The Eleventh Finance Commission further modified this formula. Rather than measuring the distances from the per capita income of any single state, it has defined the benchmark income from which distances are to be measured as the weighted average of the per capita

GSDPs of the three highest-income states, that is, Goa, Maharashtra, and Punjab. Once the benchmark income is available (say, y^*), the distances of each state outside the highest-income group are calculated as,

$$d_i = y^* - y_i \qquad i = 1, \ldots, 22$$

Here y^* is the population-weighted average of the three highest-income states.

Thus

$$y^* = (N_{23} \cdot y_{23} + N_{24} \cdot y_{24} + N_{25} \cdot y_{25}) / (N_{23} + N_{24} + N_{25})$$

The notional distances of the three highest-income states are calculated as fractions of the distance of the next highest-income state (y_{22}) of Haryana in the following way

$$(y^* - y_j) \cdot (y_j / y_i) \, j = 22; \qquad i = 23, 24, 25$$

Here, y^* is the average of the per capita income of the three highest-income states and y_n is the per capita income in the highest state. The Twelfth Finance Commission followed a similar modification using the average of the three highest per capita GSDP (Goa, Maharashtra, and Punjab) except that we now have 28 states and $j = 25$ and $i = 26, 27, 28$ in the above formula.

Augmented Distance Formula (ADF)

The consideration of giving a positive share to the highest-income state can also be taken care of by measuring distances from a level higher than the y_n, the highest per capita income. Let this point of reference be $y_n + z$ where z is a positive amount. In this case, the 'augmented' distance formula can be written as

$$a_i^* = (z + y_n - y_i) / \sum N_i (z + y_n - y_i)$$

The ADF requires determination of the value of z. The Eleventh Finance Commission has used this criterion while determining shares of states in the context of grants for local bodies. The value of z has been taken as half the standard deviation of the per capita GSDP of states.

Censored Distance Formula (CDF)

In this case, a censored income distribution may be derived as follows:

$$\text{Actual distribution } y_1 \leq y_2 \leq y_i \leq y_i + 1, \leq y_n$$
$$\text{Censored distribution } y^* \leq y_2 \leq y, y = y = y^*$$

Inverse Income Formula (IIF)

The inverse income formula looks at 'relative' fiscal deficiencies. If the revenue capacity of a common revenue effort is θy_n, relative to it, the revenue capacity of a state i, is θy_i, and the relative deficiency is given by $\theta y_n / \theta_i (= y_n / y_i)$. The share of a state under this formula is given by

$$b_i = (N_i / y_i) / \Sigma(N_i / y_i) \qquad i = 1,...,n$$

Let $\Sigma(N_i / y_i) = 1/\beta$ Then, per capita shares can be written as

$$b_i^* = \beta / y_i \text{ or } b_i^* y_i = \beta$$

The inverse income formula can be thus represented in a diagram by a rectangular hyperbola where per capita share is represented on the y-axis and per capita incomes on the axis.

Population Formula: Criterion Providing Equal Per Capita Transfers

The population criterion provides equal per capita transfers to all states. A scheme of equal per capita transfers is a valid scheme if there are no resource and cost differentials across states. It can be shown that the (standard) distance criterion will converge to the population criterion, as the per capita incomes of the states become more and more equal (see Srivastava and Aggarwal 1994). Since the population criterion provides equal per capita transfers, it is indifferent (or neutral) to differences in the fiscal capacities of states. It is, therefore, useful as a benchmark for considering the departures from this neutrality in other criteria. For this

reason, dispensation under the population criterion is often used for purposes of comparison.

Distribution according to population means that the share of a state
in tax devolution would be equal to the share of the population of this
state in the total population of all states. Indicating the population of a
state i by N_i, where i varies from 1 to n where n is the number of states,
the shares of individual states (q_i) in the population formula can be
written as

$q_i = N_i / \sum N_i$ and the per capita shares are given by
$q_i^* = 1/\sum N_i = $ Constant

Criteria Reflecting Cost Disadvantages

Indices relating to area and infrastructure reflect cost disadvantages to
state governments in providing services to its citizens. The larger the area
of a state, the higher the per capita cost of providing services. Similarly,
the weaker the infrastructure of a state, the larger the costs of providing
services. This index is used to indicate a relative deficiency in infrastructure. A state which is relatively more deficient in infrastructure has
been given a higher share in per capita terms by the Tenth and Eleventh
Finance Commissions. The deficiency in infrastructure indicates (i) extra
costs in providing governmental services and (ii) extra resource requirements to improve infrastructure and delivery systems. In the measurement of infrastructure, social infrastructure (e.g., health and education)
expenditure has a large revenue component.

An index of infrastructure was specially constructed for the Twelfth
Finance Commission by a commissioned study carried out by a team of
experts (T.C.A. Anant and K.L. Krishna). This study was updated for the
Eleventh Finance Commission as well as the Twelfth. In these studies,
the aggregate infrastructure index is a weighted combination of economic and social infrastructure indices. In turn, the economic infrastructure index and social infrastructure index are weighted combinations of
a number of sub-indices. For economic infrastructure, the main sectors
are agriculture, communication, banking, electricity, and transportation

including roads. For social infrastructure, the main sectors are health and education. The sectoral indices are in turn constructed by weighted combinations of the sub-indices. Given the series of infrastructure indexes (I_i), the shares of states may be worked out from

$$s_i = \frac{N_i(I_h - I_i)}{\sum_i N_i(I_h - I_i)}$$

where I_h is the highest reading of index among the states, and I_i is the index value for state i. The Eleventh Commission used the weighted average of I_i's for the three highest index states and used the indices for deriving shares of individual states in a manner similar to one used for the distance formula.

Criteria for Performance/Incentives

Two Fiscal performance indicators have been used by the recent Finance Commission: (i) index of tax effort, and (ii) index of fiscal discipline. The index of tax effort was meant to serve as an incentive for improving tax effort. In this scheme, a state, which shows higher tax revenue per unit of tax base, gets a higher share in tax devolution. The basic conceptual issue is that of measurement of tax effort. Tax effort needs to be measured by relating tax revenues to tax potential. Measurement of tax potential (taxable capacity) usually requires an elaborate econometric exercise. Since many of the determinants of taxable capacity are not directly observable or adequate data regarding which are not readily available, often dummy variables and proxy measures are necessitated in such an exercise. As already noted, in criteria-based revenue-sharing, criteria should be based on information compiled on a comparable basis. The approach of the Finance Commission has been to let the tax base of states be proxied by GSDP. Using the ratio of per capita tax revenue (r) to per capita GSDP (y), as reflecting tax effort, the share of a state was defined as:

$$s_i = N_i w_i (r_i / y_i) / \left[\sum N_i w_i \left(\frac{r_i}{y_i} \right) \right] \qquad i = 1, \ldots, n$$

The weight w_i was set equal to $1/y_i$ by the Tenth Finance Commission, and $1/\sqrt{y_i}$ by the Eleventh Finance Commission. Substituting these weights, the two formulae can be written as

$$s_i = [N_i r_i (/y_i^2)]/\Sigma(N_i r_i / y_i^2) \qquad \text{(Tenth Finance Commission)}$$

$$s_i = [N_i r_i (/y_i^{1.5})]/\Sigma(N_i r_i / y_i^{1.5}) \qquad \text{(Eleventh and Twelfth Finance Commissions)}$$

The weights were set as related to the inverse of income, arguing that if two states show the same tax effort, the poorer state of the two is the more constrained and should get a relatively higher share. Factors which constitute genuine constraints in the exploitation of the tax base can in general be used to set these weights. Such constraints could be a below-average level of development and distribution of income, which may favour the consumption of a basket of necessities that bear low rates of taxes. In general, the weighting scheme can be a function of income and parameters reflecting the distribution of income.

Criterion Related to Improvement in Fiscal Performance

The criterion for tax effort looks only at the tax revenues. However, to bring expenditures into analysis, the Eleventh Finance Commission constructed an index of fiscal discipline for use within the devolution formula. The index of improvement in fiscal performance was defined with reference to achieving improvement in revenue balance. The ratio of revenue receipts to revenue expenditure may be called z_i for the state i in the reference year. In the base year, this may be referred to as Z_i^0. The corresponding ratios for the all-state average may be called Z_a and Z_a^0. The index of improvement in fiscal performance is given by

$$I_i = [z_i / z_i^0]/[Z_a / Z] \qquad i = 1, 2, \ldots, n$$

The better the performance of a state in achieving revenue balance relative to others, the higher its share in devolution. The respective shares are determined by

$$s_i = N_i I_i / \Sigma N_i I_i$$

Aggregate Share of States in Central Taxes: First to Twelfth Finance Commissions

Comparing changes in the shares of individual states for the entire period from the First to the Twelfth Finance Commissions is difficult because of the shift from the earlier practice of sharing the revenues of individual taxes to the present practice of sharing all central tax revenues subject to some adjustments. To make such a comparison we need to settle on a common denominator and rework the share of states with respect to this. For this purpose, it is appropriate to take the centre's gross tax revenues as the common denominator. Since the actual shares whether for individual taxes or a divisible pool of central taxes are given as shares and not absolute amounts, we need to rework the absolute amounts and then determine the shares as a percentage of the centre's gross revenue tax receipts. Here, there are two options. One, we may take the estimated absolute amounts of the states' tax shares as provided by the Finance Commissions themselves. These would amount to a weighted share of the shared taxes as envisaged in the Commission's scheme of distribution. The second option is to take the actual share of states in the central taxes in absolute amounts. There would continue to be some difficulty in comparison over time because of the reorganization of states from time to time.

Table 2.1 gives a comparative picture of shares in central taxes from the First to the Twelfth Finance Commission, based on the estimated absolute amounts given by the Commissions themselves. Looking at individual shares it will be observed that there are some stable patterns and some volatile patterns. The share of the general category states, which used to be as high as 97.3 per cent, came down to about 86.5 per cent in the award period of the Tenth Finance Commission, and has risen to about 91.8 per cent for the Twelfth Finance Commission period. Correspondingly, the share of special category states has also changed. It was at the highest for the Tenth Finance Commission period at 13.5 per cent but fell to a range of 7–8 per cent during the Eleventh and Twelfth Finance Commission periods. The larger shares for the Eighth, Ninth, and Tenth Finance Commission periods out of tax devolution were because of the practice of earmarking a certain percentage of the states' share of the Union Excise duties for distribution among states in the proportion of 'assessed' deficits. This practice amounted to giving grants through tax devolution and was given up by the Eleventh Finance Commission, particularly because with the 80th amendment and pooling of central taxes for sharing with the states, Union excise duties could not be treated differently. These changes do not, however, necessarily reflect any erosion in their share of total transfers, because the assessed deficits of the special category states were to be fully given as grants. This is discussed further in Chapter 2.

For individual states some observations can be made as below:

1. For Andhra Pradesh the share in gross central tax revenues has ranged between 7.2 and 8.2 per cent.
2. For Bihar the share has been stable from the period of the Fifth Finance Commission in the range of 10.4 to 11.7 per cent, with the exception of the Eleventh Finance Commission period, when it increased to 14.6 percentage points.
3. For Gujarat there was a steady erosion in its share from a peak of 6 per cent in the Third Finance Commission period to a low of 2.8 per cent by the Eleventh Finance Commission. In the Twelfth Finance Commission period it increased to 3.6 per cent.
4. A similar pattern is observed for Maharashtra. Its share has fallen from 12.9 per cent in the Second Finance Commission period to a low of 4.6 per cent by the time of the Eleventh Finance Commission. It was increased to 5 per cent in the Twelfth Finance Commission period.
5. The share of Uttar Pradesh, was around 16.7 per cent in the Second Finance Commission period. It remained around this level up to the Ninth Finance Commission period and increased to above 19 per cent in the period covered by the Eleventh and Twelfth Finance Commissions.

Apart from tax revenue-sharing, the main alternative channel of fiscal transfer available to the Finance Commission is grants-in-aid of revenues of the states under Article 275 of the Constitution. Under the provisions of the article, grants that have come to be known in the literature as 'revenue-gap' grants are given. The determination of these grants follows from two exercises carried out by the Finance Commissions: (i) assessment of expenditures of each state on the non-plan revenue account, and (ii) assessment of own revenues. Once tax devolution to each state has been determined, grants-in-aid are determined as a residual which is the difference between the assessed expenditure and the sum of the projected own revenues, and the projected amounts arising from their individual shares in central taxes. In other words, grants-in-aid under the Finance Commission are meant to fill a 'gap' which represents expenditure not covered either by own revenues or share in central taxes. The main issue here is whether this gap should be projected based on historical trends or by an assessment of expenditures and revenues on a normative basis. It is clear that if the historical basis is followed it will give rise to strong adverse incentives, where it will be to the benefit of each state to maximize their histories of expenditures and minimize their histories of raising revenues. On the other hand, if the gap were to be determined strictly on a normative basis, such an adverse incentive would not be present.

Constitutional Provisions

In relation to grants, there are two duties cast upon the Finance Commission conjointly by Articles 280(3)(b) and 275. Article 280(3) (b) requires the Commission to make recommendations as to the 'principles' which should govern such grants-in-aid. Following Article 275(1), specific 'sums' are to be recommended to be paid to the states which are assessed to be in 'need of assistance'. It is significant to note that while Article 270 (for division of taxes) speaks of percentage share, Article 275 refers to specific 'sums'. The Constitution prescribes that these grants are to be 'charged' to the Consolidated Fund of India and have to be recommended by a Finance Commission.

The First Finance Commission had considered the 'principles' of determining grants at length and had opined that both unconditional and specific purpose grants can and should be considered by the Finance Commission under Article 275 read with Article 280(3)(b). They had observed that the scope of these articles should not be limited solely to grants-in-aid, which are completely unconditional, and that grants that could be directed to well-defined purposes can also reasonably be considered as falling within the scope of Article 275. The First Finance Commission recommended specific purpose grants for primary education. The Second Commission had observed that grants-in-aid should be a residuary form of assistance given in the form of general and unconditional grants.

However, they also agreed that grants for broad purposes may be given, and in respect of these, states should be under obligation to spend the whole amount in furtherance of the broad purposes indicated. The Third Finance Commission gave specific purpose grants for improvement in communications.

Most of the subsequent Commissions generally agreed to the principles listed by the First Commission but they all proceeded to recommend unconditional revenue gap grants primarily. In addition, some earmarked grants were recommended for special problems, up-gradation of services, and local bodies. However, as most resources are fungible, and even if purposes are specified, states may continue to spend according to their own priorities by reducing normal allocations on the specified heads.

The Seventh Finance Commission, 1978, while recommending grants-in-aid for the up-gradation of standards of administration, felt that grants should be made for meeting capital expenditure as well. The Commission noted that the grants made under the revenue account did not make adequate provision for administrative and residential buildings. As this expenditure has to be on the capital account, the Commission felt that capital expenditure also should be provided for. Accordingly, the Seventh Finance Commission noted that it should recommend capital grants also, and found that there was an implicit and inherent provision for making capital grants, even though the proviso was specifically outside the reach of the Commission, under the terms of reference. The Commission stated:

We have given careful consideration to the scope for grants-in-aid under Article 275 for meeting capital expenditure. The operative part of this article speaks of 'sums'. There is no restriction or bar in the article against making grants for capital expenditure. The first proviso of the article expressly speaks of grants of capital sums. This goes to show that the expression grants-in-aid of revenues do not limit grants to revenue expenditure only. We are fortified in this view by the Note of the Chairman of the Fourth Finance Commission appended to its Report on the interpretation of Article 275. Further, it seems unreasonable to hold that the operative part of the article enables the Commission to make grants for revenue expenditure only, while the proviso enables grants being made for revenue as well as capital nature. It is quite clear therefore that it is open to us to recommend grants for capital expenditure also, apart from grants for revenue expenditure under Article 275. (paragraph 8 of Chapter 10 of the Seventh Finance Commission Report)

The grants recommended by the Seventh Finance Commission for capital purposes amounted to Rs 908.80 crore, while those for revenue purposes aggregated to Rs 1,490.65 crore for fifteen states for the five years of its Report, that is, a significant portion of total grants was for capital expenditures. These recommendations were accepted. It is important to mention that all the grants recommended by a Finance Commission are under the substantive portion of Article 275(1).

In principle, Article 275(1) makes no restriction as to whether needs should be considered only on the revenue account, and further only on the non-plan revenue account. There has been a running debate for quite some time as to whether the whole revenue account or only the non-plan revenue account should be considered by the Finance Commission. There is no restriction in the constitutional provision in this regard. In fact, the term 'grants-in-aid of the revenues' does not imply that consideration should only be of revenue expenditures, that is, current expenditure. Revenues of the states are meant to be spent both on current and capital needs, and there is no constitutional restriction as to what needs should be considered and not considered by the Finance Commission. Further, the distinction between plan and non-plan expenditures has not been made anywhere in the Constitution. Article 112 refers to expenditure on the 'revenue' account to be distinguished from 'other' expenditures.

Within the domain of grants, another critical issue relates to the possibility and desirability of recommending conditional/specific purpose grants, and determining the appropriate proportion between the conditional and unconditional grants. For conditional grants the relevant purposes and associated conditions also need to be specified, along with an effective monitoring mechanism.

The distinction between non-plan versus plan revenue expenditure became material with a minute of dissent from the Member-Secretary of the

Third Finance Commission (1961). The Third Finance Commission took into account the needs of the states for the Third Five-Year Plan and recommended by a majority that the quantum of grants-in-aid should be fixed in such a way as to enable the states, along with any surplus out of devolution, to cover 75 per cent of the revenue component of their plans. In determining the revenue component, the Commission deducted the amount of additional tax to be raised by each state as incorporated in the plan itself. The Commission also recommended special grants to ten states for the improvement of road communications. The recommendations on the first item were not accepted by the president, but those on the second were accepted. Asok Chanda, Chairman of the Third Finance Commission, observed:

> the Planning Commission did not take kindly to the basic scheme or suggestions of the Commission. It was not unexpected therefore that the Member-Secretary of the Commission who was an official, should take the unusual step of appending a note of dissent, nor was it strange that government used this note for rejecting this particular recommendation (Chanda 1965: 222).

Later, the consideration of the needs of revenue expenditure on the plan account was excluded from the purview of the Finance Commission by stipulations in the Terms of Reference (ToR). The Fourth Finance Commission was asked in their ToR to consider 'the requirements of those States to meet the committed expenditure on maintenance and upkeep of plan schemes completed during the Third Plan'. The ToR of Fifth Finance Commission provided that 'the requirements on revenue account of those States to meet expenditure on administration, interest charges in respect of their debt, maintenance and upkeep of plan schemes, transfer of funds to local bodies and aided institutions and other committed expenditure' should be a relevant consideration. A similar reference was made to the Sixth Finance Commission, except that they were also asked to take into account the provision for emoluments of Government employees, teachers, and local body employees. The word 'non-plan' was entered in the ToR of the Finance Commission for the first time in the ToR of the Seventh Finance Commission. *Para 5(iv) of their ToR made reference to 'the requirements on revenue account of those States to meet the expenditure on administration and other non-plan commitments or liabilities ...'* A similar reference was made in the ToR of the Eighth Finance Commission. The ToR of the Ninth Finance Commission was so framed that the option was open for the Commission to take the plan revenue requirements if the Commission so desired. The ToR of the Tenth Finance Commission again restricted the ambit of consideration to the non-plan account. In the case of the Eleventh Finance Commission, both non-plan and plan revenue requirements were referred to explicitly. However, the Commission considered the revenue requirement only on the non-plan account. For the Twelfth Finance Commission, reference was made to the entire 'revenue' account in Paragraph 6 (iv), which specifies the 'objective of not only balancing the receipts and expenditure on revenue account of all the states and the centre, but also generating surpluses for capital investment and reducing fiscal deficit'. This clause corresponds to the relevant clause in the ToR of the Ninth Commission but not to comparable clauses in the ToR of the Tenth and the Eleventh Commissions.

It was open to the Twelfth Finance Commission to take into account the entire 'revenue expenditure' of the centre and the states. The methodology of assessment of expenditures could be determined including the issue as to whether non-plan and plan expenditures are derived separately or in sequence or the total revenue expenditure on an expenditure head is derived with reference to some objective criterion, standard, or benchmark.

Considerations Arising from the Terms of Reference

Paragraph 6(i) and (ii) of the ToR of the Twelfth Finance Commission referred, respectively, to the resources of the central government and the demands on those resources. Resources of the central government have to be assessed based on 'levels of taxation and non-tax revenues likely to be reached at the end of 2003–04'. The 2003–4 tax and non-tax revenues could therefore serve as the base for assessment of resources for the period from 2005–6 to 2009–10. However, the reference to 'levels' of taxation and non-tax revenues requires further analysis. Levels in absolute terms may not mean much in the present context. Levels in relation to respective tax and non-tax bases imply a certain relationship.

If the tax and non-tax bases grow, tax and non-tax revenues would also grow, if this relationship is held constant. However, these would also grow because of additional revenue effort, modification of tax rates, withdrawal of exemptions, and other reforms. Paragraph 6(ii) of the ToR of the Twelfth Finance Commission referred to the demands on central resources by the central government. Particular reference has been made to expenditures on civil administration, defence, internal and border security, debt servicing, and other committed expenditures and liabilities. As already noted, a reference of this nature has been made to successive Commissions since the Fifth Finance Commission. In relation to the previous references, the mention of the need on account of 'internal' security was new for the Twelfth Finance Commission. The items listed for particular reference related mainly to interest payments and pensions as committed liabilities and other general services including defence and border security. The structure and pattern of growth of central expenditure needed to be studied, including that of social and economic services. This is also required in terms of the paragraph on the review and restructuring of the finances of the Union and the states referred to the Twelfth Finance Commission.

Although most of the recent Commissions have attempted not to simply use historical growth rates of revenues or expenditures in their assessments, the assessments are still driven by a number of historical parameters, which are often subjected to modifications to introduce an element of prescriptive benchmarks or norms. An explicit reference as to the use of a normative approach was made for the first time in the Ninth Finance Commission by including in their ToR the following text:

In making its recommendations, the Commission shall:

1. adopt a normative approach in assessing the receipts and expenditures on the revenue account of the States and the Centre and, in doing so, keep in view the special problems of each State, if any, and the special requirements of the Centre such as defence, security, debt servicing and other committed expenditure or liabilities,

2. have due regard to the need for providing adequate incentives for better resource mobilization and financial discipline as well as closer linking of expenditure and revenue raising decisions,

3. take into account the need for speed, efficiency and effectiveness of Government functioning and of delivery systems for Government programme and

4. keep in view the objective of not only balancing the receipts and expenditure on revenue account of both the States and the Centre, but also generating surpluses for capital investment ...

A direct reference to a normative approach in the ToR has not been made for the subsequent Commissions. Economists have frequently criticized the determination of transfers based on gaps derived from historical trends of expenditures and revenues due to their adverse incentives, where states find that it is to their advantage to maximize this gap by having a history of low revenue effort and profligate expenditures. Such an approach has been referred to as the 'Gap Filling Approach' (GFA). In this context, the Commission has to deliberate on the general principles of assessment and the application of norms or prescriptive parameters and the considerations on which these may be based.

There were a few important additions/alterations in the subclauses of Clause 6 of the ToR of the Twelfth Finance Commission. One new subclause related to the taxation efforts of the central and individual state governments as against 'targets' and 'potential' to improve the tax-GDP and the tax-GSDP ratios, respectively, for the central and the state governments. Measurement of 'potential' tax revenue requires a proper methodology to ascertain the relevant tax bases and establish relationships between tax revenues and tax bases. Available methodological frameworks can be evaluated to identify a suitable methodology. There was a reference to the maintenance and upkeep of capital assets, with the stipulation that this should relate only to the non-salary component. In the case of maintenance expenditure on plan schemes to be completed by 31 March 2005, only non-wage related expenditure was to be considered. In the subclause related to irrigation, power projects, departmental commercial enterprises, and public sector enterprises, there was a reference to 'commercial viability' in the ToR of the Twelfth Commission instead of ensuring 'reasonable returns on investment' as referred to in the Eleventh Commission.

Determining Revenue Gap Grants: Overview of Methodology

The revenue gap grants are the key grants given under Article 275. Here we undertake an overview of the methodology of estimating the revenue gap grants for the Ninth, Tenth, Eleventh, and Twelfth Finance Commissions. Given that the ToR of the Commissions themselves indicate the base year, the methodology involves the estimation of the relevant variables for the base year, which are then taken forward for the recommendation years using different growth rates.

The broad methodology can be described as below. The following symbols are used:

g_i^t = Revenue gap grant for state 'i' and period 't'
otr_i^t = Own tax revenue for state 'i' in period 't'
$ontr_i^t$ = Own non-tax revenue for state 'i' in period 't'
e_i^t = Revenue (non-plan revenue) expenditure of state 'i' in period 't'
scr_i^t = Share in central taxes of state 'i' in period 't'

Revenue gap grant for period 't' can be defined as follows:

$$g_i^t = e_i^t - otr_i^t - ontr_i^t - scr_i^t$$
$$e_i^t = e_i^0(1+g_i^e)(1+g_i^e)^t \qquad [g_i^{tr} = b_i^{tr}.g_i]$$
$$otr_i^t = otr_i^0(1+g_i^{tr})^k$$
$$ontr_i^t = ontr_i^0(1+g_i^{ntr})^k$$
$$scr_i^t = [s_i][ctr]^t \qquad [g^{etr} = b^{ctr}.g]$$
$$(ctr)^t = (etr^0)(1+g^{ctr})$$

Methodologically, to estimate the revenue gap grants two steps are involved. First, to estimate the relevant quantities of expenditure, own tax revenue, own non-tax revenue, and state's share in central taxes. For the base year itself, available information may relate to budget or revised

estimates of the concerned state governments and also projections submitted by the concerned state governments. Calculation of the revenue
gap based on this information amounts to subscribing to the existing
pattern of expenditures and revenues. Should the Finance Commission
accept the numbers given by the state budget/revised estimates and/or
projections, the likely gap would be too large and the implied incentives
would be extremely adverse. Finance Commissions had therefore followed a methodology which adjusts the concerned variables in the base
year itself by application of some norms for states' revenue effort as well
as expenditure needs.

The second step is to apply relevant growth rates both for tax and non-
tax items and also for the expenditure heads. Finance Commissions had
undertaken detailed exercises not only to bring about comparability
across states but also to impose norms such that no state can effectively
hope to gain by a less-than-average tax effort by undertaking or by creating histories of excessive expenditures by borrowing in the historical
period and claiming grants in the recommendation period of the Finance
Commissions. We consider below some of the methodologies followed
by the Ninth to Twelfth Finance Commissions.

Ninth Finance Commission

Own Tax Revenues
Among the four recent Commissions, it was only the Ninth Commission
which was asked specifically to follow a normative approach in determining grants in the presidential terms of reference. The Commission
did follow a normative methodology with several adjustments. Some of
the main steps are summarized below.[1]

For determining own tax revenues in the base year, the Commission
followed in its Second Report a modified representative tax system approach. Own tax revenues were divided into six categories: sales tax,
stamp duties and registration fees, tax on motor vehicles and goods and
passengers tax, entertainment tax, and other taxes. For the first five taxes,
a panel model approach was followed with the assumption that the inter-
cepts and slope parameters for each of the explanatory variables are
common across the states. However, time dummies were used to capture

any inter-temporal shifts. Table 2.6 describes the explanatory variables for each of the tax functions so estimated.

The base year for these taxes was 1984–5 except for motor vehicles and passenger taxes, which was 1985–6. For these years, the taxable capacity

Table 2.6 Modified Representative Tax System Approach

Dependent Variable		Explanatory Variables	
Sales tax (high income states) and (low income states)	SDP at factor cost	Proportion of income from non-primary sector	
Sales tax (middle income states)	Road/railway length for 1,000 sq. km area	Per capita energy sales to ultimate consumers	
Stamp duties and registration fees (high income states) and (middle income states)	SDP at factor cost	Road/railway length for 1,000 sq. km area	
Stamp duties and registration fees (low income states)	SDP at factor cost	Road/railway length for 1,000 sq. km area	Proportion of income from non-primary sector
Motor vehicles and passenger goods tax (high income states) and (middle income states)	Total registered motor vehicles	Proportion of heavy vehicles to total vehicles	
Motor vehicles and passenger goods tax (low income states)	Total registered motor vehicles		
State excise duties*(high income group)	Consumption of country spirit	Road/railway length for 1,000 sq. km area	
State excise duties*(low income group)	Consumption of country spirit	SDP at factor cost	
Entertainment tax**	SDP at factor cost	Seating capacity in cinema halls	Proportion of urban population in total population

Source: Report of the Ninth Finance Commission.

Note: *States divided into two groups only: high income and low income

**This was applied to all major states excluding Kerala.

of each state was obtained by substituting the values of independent variables for these years and also the coefficient of the time dummy for this year. These were then projected forward to 1989–90 respectively from 1984–5 and 1985–6. The method of projection was as follows:

Growth rate of tax = Buoyancy of the concerned tax (high, middle, and lower income groups) * state-specific SDP trend growth rate.

Agricultural tax and other tax only trend growth rate was used. From the 1989–90 base numbers, one more projection exercise was carried out for the recommendation period 1990–1 to 1994–5. In this period the SDP growth rate was taken by combining the 6 per cent real growth rate and the 5 per cent inflation rate, giving 11.5 per cent per annum of normal growth. Individual taxes were projected forward based on their past behaviour and adjusted pro-rata to conform to the aggregate.

Some of the features of this exercise may be noted as follows:

1. Basic data for the projection exercises were quite dated and had to be brought forward by steps of projections.
2. Dividing the state into three income groups reduced the sample size for the panel models considerably. Generally, in each sample there were only five observations and five time periods and seven to eight coefficients were to be calculated.
3. The exercise amounted to an estimation of buoyancy for different income groups rather than an application of a common tax effort for all the states.
4. Projections based on such equations required independent projections of all the explanatory variables for the period from 1985–6 to 1989–90 and ideally even further up to 1994–5. Instead of using the estimated equations, projections were eventually made only by using buoyancy growth rates.

Non-tax Revenues

Non-tax revenues were divided into various categories and ad hoc norms of rates of return were used as has been done by most other Commissions.

Non-Plan Revenue Expenditure

Expenditure needs of the states were estimated for the base year and then projected forward. For this purpose, expenditures were classified into three categories:

1. Items where expenditure depends on a relevant stock variable such as interest payments or maintenance expenditure on roads, buildings, and irrigation works.
2. Items of regular and recurring expenditure.
3. Other items where engineering norms are relevant.

Following are some of the item-wise details:

1. Interest payments for 1990–1 were taken based on actual stock of 1989–90 and then a growth rate of 12 per cent was applied for the recommendation period years.
2. Maintenance of capital assets. Various maintenance norms used by relevant central ministries were applied.
3. For regular and recurring expenditures relating to other general, social, and economic services a normative approach was followed. Expenditure needs were derived by estimated cost functions. A distinction was made between cost factors within the control of state governments and those beyond their control. Estimates were prepared for the base year of 1996–7. These estimates represented the required expenditure to provide average standards of services for the different states. Additional allowances were made for the revision of pay scales.
4. Projections were then made from 1986–7 to the adopted base of 1989–90 by using historical growth rates adjusted partially for periodic revision of salaries by the states.
5. These were then projected for the recommendation period of 1990–1 to 1994–5 by allowing a growth rate of 7 per cent. Further year-wise adjustments were made to phase out expenditure by restricting the difference between the actual and normative estimates by 50 per cent in 1989–90 and then by phasing the expenditure growth to reach the targeted level in 1994–5.

Note

1. The Commission for the one year report for 1989–90 followed a panel data modelling approach to estimate taxable capacity for a normative determination of own tax revenues. This was applied to fourteen major states. The explanatory variables were per capita SDP, the proportion of non-primary SDP to total SDP, and the Lorenze ratio of consumer expenditure distribution based on 32nd (1977–8) and 38th (1983–4) rounds of consumer expenditure data which were interpolated for the intervening years. The sample period was from 1980–1 to 1984–5. The tax effort was captured by a dummy variable (fixed effects). The application of the norm for the base year (1984–5) was done as follows. States were divided into three groups: high income, middle income, and low income. Instead of the actual values of the state dummy, the average value of the dummy variable of the group was substituted for each member of the group. This was to ensure that every state has the tax effort equal to the group average. The other explanatory variables for 1984–5 were put at their actual values.

3

Fiscal Federalism in Practice

Canada and India[*]

Canada became a federation in 1867. Over time, Canada has developed a comprehensive system of intergovernmental transfers to address issues both of vertical and horizontal imbalances. The heart of the Canadian system of fiscal transfers consists of a set of equalization grants, which are enshrined in the Canadian Constitution. These, together with the Canadian Health and Social Service Transfers (CHST), ensure the provision of health and other social services at comparable standards across provinces. This chapter examines the basic features of the Canadian system of sharing responsibilities and resources between the federal and provincial governments, particularly the Canadian system of intergovernmental transfers, with the objective of considering its relevance and applicability in the Indian case.

This chapter is divided into six sections. The first section reviews the basic features of the institutional arrangements in Canada in deciding about the principles and volume of transfers. The second section examines the assignments of tax powers including the system of sharing tax bases. The third section looks at the profile of vertical imbalance before and after transfers. The fourth section examines the system of transfers in Canada with a focus on the principles and practices in regard to equalization transfers and the related profile of horizontal imbalance before and after transfers. The fifth section looks at the management of debt in Canada drawing comparisons with India. The sixth section provides concluding observations, particularly in the context of the applicability of the Canadian system of fiscal transfers to India. An addendum to this

---

[*] Originally published as 'Fiscal Transfers in Canada: Drawing Comparisons and Lessons', *Economic and Political Weekly*, Vol. 39, No. 19, 8 May 2004, pp. 1897–1909.

Federalism and Fiscal Transfers in India, Second Edition. C. Rangarajan and D.K. Srivastava, Oxford University Press.

chapter provides an overview of recent developments in the Canadian system of fiscal transfers.

Institutional Framework and Some General Features

Canada is a federal country with ten provinces and three special territories. The provinces are Alberta, British Columbia, Manitoba, New Brunswick, Newfoundland and Labrador, Nova Scotia, Ontario, Prince Edward Island (PEI), Quebec, and Saskatchewan. The territorial governments are Nunavut, Yukon, and the North West Territories. Alberta, because of its mineral wealth, is the richest province. Ontario is the second highest in terms of per capita GDP. Canada's total population is only about 31.5 million, with a high degree of concentration of population and economic activities in a few provinces.

In Canada, federal fiscal relations have evolved through a non-constitutional process, except for the equalization transfers, which have a constitutional status. Most arrangements derive from a series of negotiations between the two tiers of government. Some provinces like Quebec, more recently Alberta and, to some extent, British Columbia have been asking for greater fiscal autonomy. These demands have so far been resolved by a series of discussions and negotiations. It is generally recognized that the evolution of federalism in Canada has been driven to a large extent by Quebec, which is a large and linguistically distinct province. In 1995, the House of Commons adopted a resolution affirming the distinct character of Quebec. Among continuing issues in Canada, there are demands for further reforms in funding health services. Quebec set up the Commission on Fiscal Disequilibrium, known as the Senguin Commission, which gave its report in 2002.

Some of the contentious issues, particularly relating to the interpretation of the Constitution Act of 1867, are often referred to the courts. Under the Supreme Court Act, the federal government can refer questions to the Supreme Court for advisory opinions. The provinces can also secure a ruling from the Supreme Court of appeal after the provincial court has rendered its decision on the appeal under the Provincial Court Act.

In contrast, in India, the institutional arrangements are quite different. The core arrangements regarding the sharing of resources and responsibilities are built into the Constitution itself. The sharing of resources between the central and state governments has been entrusted to the Finance Commission. In addition, resource transfers also take place through the Planning Commission and other central ministries. Other institutions of importance in India are the National Development Council and the Inter State Council. These bodies may broadly compare with the Premiers' or First Ministers' Conference in Canada. In Canada, transfers are calculated on a year-to-year basis, the calculations for any one year remain 'open' for four years, and entitlements are revised as fresh data become available. The relevant data are procured by an independent organization, Statistics Canada. There have not been any significant issues regarding the authenticity or comparability of data. In India, the Finance Commission awards remain valid for five years. Data used are generally authenticated by a body like the Central Statistical Organization (CSO) or the Registrar General of India. But data pertaining, for example, to GSDP are usually dated by several years relative to the years for which the award is made. Unlike Statistics Canada, which is an independent organization, the CSO in India is an organization belonging to the central government. In the absence of any mandate calling for the collection of data on individual tax bases and bases of non-tax revenues of different states, it does not do so.

Some important features of the economy having a bearing on the Canadian system of intergovernmental transfers may also be noted. First, nearly 85 per cent of the population and a little more than 87 per cent of the GDP are located in just four provinces: Ontario, Alberta, Quebec, and British Columbia. Secondly, disparities in per capita incomes, as indicated by per capita GDPs are also within a narrow range. The coefficient of variation ranged between 27 and 35 per cent from 1999 to 2002. Figure 3.1 shows the per capita provincial GDPs considering the three-year average over 2000–2.

In India, in contrast, not only are there considerable disparities in per capita state GDP but also the share in population of the poorer states requiring transfers is relatively large as compared to the share in population of the richer states. In Canada, since the population in the better-off provinces is large, the task of redistribution can be more easily handled.

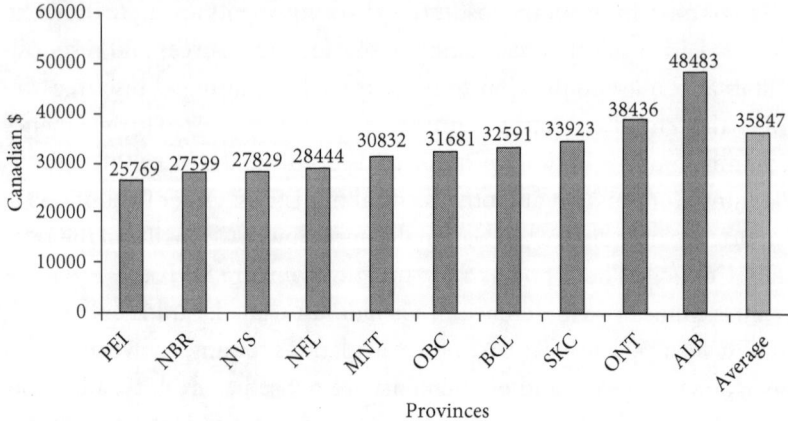

Figure 3.1 Provinces in Canada Arranged in Ascending Order of Per Capita GDP (in Canadian $)

PEI = Prince Edwards Island   NBR = Nebraska   NVS = Nova Scotia
NFL = Newfoundland and Labrador   MNT = Manitoba   QBC = Quebec
BCL = British Columbia   SKC = Saskatchewan   ONT = Ontario
ALB = Alberta

Table 3.1 gives data for Canada regarding the province-wise share in population and all-province GDP. Ontario alone has nearly 38 per cent of the population and a little more than 41 per cent of the all-province GDP. The ratio of the highest per capita GDP, pertaining to Alberta, to that of the lowest per capita GDP for Prince Edward Island in 2002, for example, was 1.9. In India, this ratio between the per capita GDPs of Goa and Bihar, for example, is close to 9. Even for larger states like Maharashtra or Punjab, the ratio with the per capita GDP of Bihar is close to 4.5. The coefficient of variation was a little more than 50 per cent in 1999–2000 and 2000–1.

Allocation of Tax Powers: Tax Base Sharing

The federal government in Canada has, in theory, unlimited powers of taxation. The constitution allows the federal government to raise revenues 'by any mode or system of taxation' under Section 91(3). Section 92(2) gives provinces the right to 'direct taxation within the province in order to the raising of revenues for provincial purposes'. By a court

Table 3.1 Share in Population and All-Province GDP in Canada

Share in Population	(%)				Share in All-Province GDP			
	1999	2000	2001	2002	1999	2000	2001	2002
Newfoundland and Labrador	1.75	1.72	1.68	1.66	1.24	1.29	1.28	1.43
Prince Edward Island	0.45	0.44	0.44	0.44	0.32	0.31	0.31	0.32
Nova Scotia	3.07	3.04	3.01	2.98	2.35	2.30	2.35	2.35
New Brunswick	2.47	2.45	2.42	2.39	1.94	1.88	1.88	1.83
Quebec	24.09	23.97	23.85	23.73	21.46	20.94	21.01	21.27
Ontario	37.85	38.08	38.35	38.57	41.65	40.99	40.91	41.41
Manitoba	3.76	3.74	3.71	3.68	3.25	3.18	3.19	3.21
Saskatchewan	3.34	3.28	3.22	3.17	3.13	3.13	3.03	3.00
Alberta	9.71	9.79	9.85	9.93	11.92	13.37	13.65	12.99
British Columbia	13.19	13.16	13.15	13.12	12.31	12.19	11.93	11.74
Yukon	0.10	0.10	0.10	0.10	0.11	0.11	0.11	0.11
NWT	0.13	0.13	0.13	0.13	0.23	0.23	0.26	0.26
Nunavut	0.09	0.09	0.09	0.09	0.08	0.08	0.08	0.08
	100.00	100.00	100.00	100.00	100.00	100.00	100.00	100.00

Source: Statistics Canada.

decision, 'direct taxation' has been interpreted to include commodity taxes such as sales tax or taxes on goods and services.[1] In practice, therefore, federal and provincial governments have concurrent jurisdiction on the same tax bases, and both tiers collect personal and corporate income taxes as well as taxes on goods and services or some form of sales tax (Value Added Tax-VAT). It is only the customs duties and some excises that are used exclusively by the federal government. Provinces have exclusive rights over mineral resources in their jurisdiction. In fact, it is this right over mineral resources which enables a province like Alberta to raise considerable finances from oil and gas. It also makes Alberta the province with the highest per capita GDP. In India, all the major minerals belong to the Union government although the states get a royalty. Minerals listed as minor minerals belong to the concerned states.

Concurrent jurisdiction over common or almost common tax bases implies that although the tax rates of the two jurisdictions can be independently fixed, there has to be coordination. If one level of government taxes the base excessively, it will adversely affect the base not only for itself but also for the other jurisdictions. This phenomenon of 'vertical externality' in the shared tax bases has been noted by many authors (see, e.g., Boadway et al. 1998 and Keen 1998). The federal and provincial governments generally come to an agreement as to the tax room they can occupy with respect to a given tax base. When the federal government vacates some tax room in terms of reducing the federal rate, enabling the provinces to correspondingly raise their rates, it amounts to a transfer of resources.[2] These transfers are referred to as tax points.

Personal and corporate income taxes are levied by the federal government and all the provinces.[3] Yukon and the North West Territories also levy these income taxes. Corporate income tax is levied by the federal and all provincial governments, but not in Yukon and the North West Territories. Customs and excise duties are levied only by the federal government. Until recently, the federal government collected the provincial personal income tax (PIT) in all provinces except Quebec. The provinces are free to determine their own rates, but they have to use federal levels of exemptions, deductions, and the rate structure. In 1999, the federal government agreed to collect provincial PITs at any rates imposed by them as long as they use the federal tax base as the base for provincial PIT. However, they can now have their own tax schedules with different degrees of progressivity. Using this provision, Alberta has imposed a 10 per cent flat tax. Other provinces have also adopted schedules of tax rates that are different from those of the federal PIT.

Sales tax in the form of Goods and Services Tax (GST) is levied by the federal and provincial governments. The GST is a multi-stage VAT. The federal rate for most goods and services was at 7 per cent for many years. It has been reduced to 5 per cent. For goods that bear an excise tax, GST applies on values inclusive of the excise tax.

At the provincial level, three commodity taxation systems prevail, that is, Harmonized Sales Tax (HST), Retail Sales Tax (RST), and the GST. The Atlantic Provinces excluding PEI have the harmonized sales tax along with the federal GST. The federal government administers the harmonized GST with a 7 per cent federal rate and an 8 per cent provincial rate. Provinces with HST are New Brunswick, Nova Scotia, and Newfoundland. Quebec has a provincial GST at 7.5 per cent which is applied on top of the federal GST at 7 per cent, making the overall rate of provincial GST 8.025 per cent. Quebec administers its provincial GST as well as the federal GST. Prince Edward Island has a provincial GST at the rate of 10 per cent which is applied on top of the federal rate of 7 per cent making the overall rate, 10.7 per cent. Alberta does not have a provincial GST. Only the federal GST is levied at 7 per cent. The rates of provincial GST in British Columbia are 7.5 per cent, in Saskatchewan 6 per cent, and in Manitoba 7 per cent. These rates relate to the situation when the federal GST rate was 7 per cent. Subsequently, it was reduced to 5 per cent. In these cases it is not levied on top of the federal GST. The federal government collects its own GST as well as the provincial GST in the case of British Columbia, Saskatchewan, Manitoba, and PEI. Quebec collects provincial GST as well as the federal GST. In Ontario, the provincial government collects its RST while the federal government collects its GST.

In contrast, in India, there is no direct 'tax-base' sharing. The Constitution assigns tax bases clearly either to the Union or to the states. Union Excise duties and State sales taxes may, however, be considered as sharing the tax base up to the stage of manufacturing in the sphere of commodity taxation. However, there are no explicit arrangements as to the rates that the central government can charge on the Union Excise Duty items or the sales tax rates that the states can charge on the same items. Instead of the 'tax-base' sharing, in India, there is a constitutionally provided system of 'tax-revenue' sharing, which now encompasses nearly all the central tax revenues. There are many countries where some form of tax revenuesharing with the sub-national governments (i.e., provincial or local) is in vogue, such as in Germany, Switzerland, Belgium, Hungary, Brazil, Colombia, and Russia (see e.g., Ter-Minassian 1997, for a discussion).

Vertical Imbalance

The main federal responsibilities in Canada relate to foreign affairs, defence, international trade, airlines and railways, money and banking, and employment insurance. Some important responsibilities being handled by both tiers of government relate to pensions, immigration, agriculture, and industry. Some of the main provincial responsibilities relate to education, health, municipal institutions, social welfare, police, natural resources, and highways. However, as has happened in India, the federal government is assuming increasing responsibilities in areas that are in the domain of the provinces. In Canada, this has been achieved through what has been described as 'spending power'.

Since a majority of the resource-intensive expenditure responsibilities rest with the provinces, in spite of their access to considerable financial resources, there is still a vertical imbalance between the revenue capacity and expenditure responsibilities of the provinces vis-à-vis the federal government. One set of transfers, the Canadian Health and Social Transfers, serve to correct the vertical imbalance. Although conditional and for a specific purpose, these grants can be treated as correcting the vertical imbalance since these are provided to all provinces on a per capita basis.

Vertical imbalance can be measured in a number of ways. A vertical imbalance inheres in the relationship of revenues relative to expenditure responsibilities. The federal government, prior to the transfers, had more revenues relative to expenditures and the provincial governments less. The degree of pre-transfer excess or deficiency can be measured relative to a suitable denominator. Similarly, the 'correction' in imbalance can also be measured by looking at the post-transfer figures. Table 3.2 looks at the extent of vertical imbalance in alternative ways. Two of these, P1 and P2, provide a provincial perspective, while C1 and C2 give a federal perspective. These are described below:

P1: This is defined as provincial expenditure minus own revenues divided by provincial expenditure. It indicates the built-in imbalance in terms of the assignment of resources and responsibilities. Actual expenditures are treated here as appropriate and desirable.

P2: This term is defined as the ratio of provincial expenditure minus own revenues plus the federal transfers divided by the provincial expenditure. This ratio indicates the vertical imbalance that is left after the transfers.

C1: This is defined as the centre's expenditure inclusive of transfers minus the centre's gross revenue receipts divided by the centre's expenditure inclusive of transfers.

C2: This term indicates the centre's expenditure net of transfers minus the centre's revenue net of transfers divided by the centre's expenditure net of transfers.

It is clear from P1 in Table 3.2 that the provincial expenditure in Canada is far larger than the own revenues indicating that expenditure responsibilities are assigned largely to the provincial governments. However, it can also be seen that over the years this ratio has come down from the peak of a little more than 33 per cent in 1986–7 to as low as 8.5 per cent in 2000–1. P2 in Table 3.2 indicates that in recent years provincial expenditures have been met almost fully by own revenues and transfers, implying that the vertical imbalance in the assignment of functions and resources is almost eliminated after transfers. A positive sign of P2 indicates that some of the expenditures remain uncovered by transfers, which must therefore be financed through borrowing. A negative sign indicates a surplus which could be used for retiring debt.

The issue can also be examined from the perspective of the federal government. It is clear from C2 in Table 3.2 that since 1997–8, as indicated by the negative sign, federal revenues have exceeded expenditures net of transfers enabling them to retire debt. Thus, there is no imbalance after transfers for either of the two tiers.

Table 3.3 draws a corresponding picture for India. The P1 column indicates that more than half of the states' expenditures remain uncovered from their own resources. The time profile since 1980–1 does not indicate any significant inter-temporal variation in this built-in vertical imbalance. P2 in Table 3.3 indicates that considerable correction is made after transfers, but there are uncovered expenditures as indicated by the positive sign, which necessitates borrowing. It is also indicated that post-transfer imbalance increased sharply after 1997–8. The centre's position is not in surplus even prior to transfers. The centre's own expenditures exceed its revenues excluding transfers by a larger margin in relation to its own expenditures.

Table 3.2 Measuring Vertical Imbalance in Canada

Year	Provincial		Federal	
	(Expenditure–own revenue)/ expenditure	(Expenditure–own revenue+ transfers*)/ expenditure	(Expenditure–revenue)/ expenditure	(Exp net of transfers* –revenues net of transfers*)/ exp net of transfers*
	P1	P2	C1	C2
1980–1	28.39	6.64	22.95	28.70
1981–2	26.26	4.86	20.63	25.48
1982–3	31.57	11.64	32.38	39.22
1983–4	31.68	9.37	33.88	42.03
1984–5	31.08	8.89	35.10	42.93
1985–6	31.09	10.04	31.02	38.02
1986–7	33.32	13.14	26.35	32.09
1987–8	27.57	7.36	22.16	26.91
1988–9	24.96	4.60	21.66	26.38
1989–90	23.39	3.58	20.28	24.53
1990–1	26.66	7.50	21.14	25.59
1991–2	33.07	15.32	21.97	26.44
1992–3	35.22	16.20	25.42	31.13
1993–4	30.89	12.95	26.59	32.37
1994–5	28.50	10.06	23.30	28.53
1995–6	25.90	7.45	18.01	22.16
1996–7	20.24	4.63	5.94	7.11
1997–8	16.66	2.02	−2.55	−3.03
1998–9	16.54	0.96	−2.04	−2.46
1999–2000	13.49	−1.67	−8.29	−10.05
2000–1	8.54	−7.58	−11.24	−13.74
2001–2	18.43	1.14	−5.42	−6.79

Source: Fiscal Reference Tables: Department of Finance, Canada.

Note: *Transfers refer to federal cash transfers.

Table 3.3 Vertical Imbalance in India

Year	State Governments		Central Government	
	(State exp-own revenue)/ state exp	(State exp-own rev I transfers/ expenditure)	(Cent exp inc of trans cent gross rev rec)/ centre exp inc of transfers	(Centre exp net of trans-centre rev net of trans-fer)/ Centre. Exp net of transfer
	P1	P2	C1	C2
1980–1	56.43	22.45	35.32	47.48
1981–2	52.39	19.68	30.86	41.27
1982–3	52.77	20.13	32.71	43.38
1983–4	54.88	22.05	35.16	46.55
1984–5	55.91	24.06	37.75	48.86
1985–6	56.31	19.66	38.64	51.19
1986–7	56.42	20.66	39.88	51.77
1987–8	56.05	20.67	37.75	50.34
1988–9	54.59	19.73	37.10	48.80
1989–90	54.31	22.35	36.30	46.14
1990–1	57.05	22.82	39.76	52.34
1991–2	53.61	19.55	33.47	45.41
1992–3	54.98	19.37	33.84	46.23
1993–4	51.87	16.48	40.20	54.53
1994–5	49.81	18.79	35.28	47.05
1995–6	50.60	19.54	31.56	42.00
1996–7	52.20	20.36	29.42	39.48
1997–8	56.66	21.33	29.50	39.99
1998–9	56.55	30.26	34.97	44.91
1999–2000	56.34	31.28	32.48	41.53
2000–1	56.91	27.68	34.48	40.90
2001–2	55.06	28.87	35.21	40.57

Source: Indian Public Finance Statistics (IPFS).

Notes: Expenditures are net of loan recoveries. Transfers are as given in IPFS Table 3.4.

Central expenditure and revenues net of transfers are derived by deducting grants as tax devolution is already deducted in expenditure and revenue data.

System of Transfers and Horizontal Imbalance

Aggregate Transfers

There are three main avenues of resource transfers from federal to provincial governments in Canada: (i) equalization grants, (ii) Canada Health and Social Transfers (CHST), and (iii) Territorial Formula Financing (TFF). In addition, there is a small and new facility called the Health Reform Fund (HRF). CHST are for the provinces as well as the Territorial governments. Equalization transfers are intended for selected provinces and TFF for the Territories.

Table 3.4 looks at the volume of total transfers from the federal to subnational governments and how these have changed over time relative to GDP. Way back in 1961–2, total transfers amounted to 1.6 per cent of GDP. The transfers steadily increased over time to reach a peak of 4.2 per cent in 1976–7 and again in 1983–4. Transfers relative to GDP have since gone down to reach a level of 2.4 per cent in 2001–2.

In comparison, in India transfers to the state governments relative to GDP were close to 5 per cent of GDP during the award periods of the Eighth and Ninth Finance Commissions covering the years 1984–9 and 1988–95 respectively. In India also, transfers relative to GDP declined since then but they have remained above 4 per cent of GDP except in two years in the recent period.

Relative to federal revenues, transfers in Canada reached a peak level in 1983–4 and 1984–5 when these were more than 26 per cent. Since then, transfers in Canada declined relative to the federal revenues. In Canada, federal revenues relative to GDP were 17.8 per cent in 1991–2. Since then they have come down to 15.4 per cent in 2001–2.

In contrast, in India, transfers to the state governments have been larger relative to the centre's gross revenue receipts, varying broadly in the range of 35–8 per cent, considered as averages for periods covered by the seventh and later Finance Commissions (Table 3.5). Because of this higher proportion, transfers in India relative to GDP are higher even though the centre's gross revenue receipts constitute a lower proportion of GDP than that in Canada.

Table 3.4 Major Transfers* to Other Levels of Governments: Canada

Year	Amount	Amount relative to federal revenues	Relative to GDP		Amount	Amount relative to federal revenues	Relative to GDP
	($million)	(per cent)	(per cent)		($million)	(per cent)	(per cent)
1961–2	642	9.90	1.6				
1962–3	737	11.06	1.6	1982–3	14,177	23.37	3.7
1963–4	798	11.24	1.7	1983–4	17,125	26.69	4.2
1964–5	918	11.17	1.7	1984–5	18,548	26.10	4.1
1965–6	841	9.28	1.4	1985–6	18,879	24.54	3.9
1966–7	1,016	10.30	1.6	1986–7	19,569	22.77	3.8
1967–8	1,464	13.62	2.1	1987–8	20,518	21.02	3.7
1968–9	1,813	15.05	2.4	1988–9	22,145	21.28	3.6
1969–70	2,237	15.54	2.7	1989–90	23,417	20.59	3.6
1970–1	2,954	19.72	3.3	1990–1	22,928	19.21	3.4
1971–2	3,610	21.72	3.7	1991–2	24,865	20.38	3.6
1972–3	4,134	21.53	3.8	1992–3	26,544	22.05	3.8
1973–4	4,585	20.44	3.5	1993–4	26,947	23.23	3.7
1974–5	5,884	20.12	3.8	1994–5	26,313	21.34	3.4
1975–6	6,874	21.71	4.0	1995–6	26,076	20.01	3.2
1976–7	8,399	24.41	4.2	1996–7	22,162	15.73	2.6
1977–8	8,512	24.58	3.8	1997–8	20,504	13.36	2.3
1978–9	9,551	25.83	3.9	1998–9	25,523	16.37	2.8
1979–80	10,601	25.22	3.8	1999–2000	23,243	13.99	2.4
1980–1	11,578	23.69	3.7	2000–1	24,724	13.77	2.3
1981–2	13,088	21.70	3.6	2001–2	26,616	15.36	2.4

Source: Statistics Canada.

Note: *Only major cash transfers are included.

In comparison, in India transfers to the state governments relative to GDP were close to 5 per cent of GDP during the award periods of the Eighth and Ninth Finance Commissions covering the years 1984–9 and 1988–95 respectively. In India also, transfers relative to GDP declined since then but they have remained above 4 per cent of GDP in except in two years in the recent period.

Table 3.5 Central Transfers in India Relative to Centre's Gross Revenue Receipts and GDP

Year	Total transfers as per cent of						
	Centre's gross revenue receipts	GDP at market prices	CGRR as per cent of GDP mp		Centre's gross revenue receipts	GDP at market prices	CGRR as per cent of GDP mp
1970–1	33.37	2.99	8.97	1985–6	39.67	5.24	13.20
1971–2	36.91	3.75	10.16	1986–7	37.96	5.21	13.73
1972–3	35.68	3.73	10.46	1987–8	39.18	5.31	13.55
1973–4	34.03	3.24	9.52	1988–9	37.23	4.92	13.22
1974–5	29.35	2.95	10.04	1989–90	32.66	4.51	13.82
1975–6	29.85	3.47	11.62	1990–1	38.97	4.89	12.56
1976–7	31.76	3.69	11.62	1991–2	38.62	5.05	13.08
1977–8	32.43	3.70	11.41	1992–3	39.62	5.14	12.97
1978–9	34.80	4.17	11.98	1993–4	42.84	5.03	11.74
1979–80	39.45	4.81	12.20	1994–5	37.86	4.46	11.77
1980–1	39.64	4.58	11.56	1995–6	35.55	4.28	12.04
1981–2	35.92	4.23	11.77	1996–7	35.40	4.28	12.10
1982–3	36.40	4.39	12.07	1997–8	38.90	4.86	12.49
1983–4	37.48	4.40	11.73	1998–9	32.25	3.73	11.57
1984–5	36.46	4.48	12.28	1999–2000	30.23	3.79	12.52
				2000–1	34.93	4.26	12.19

Source: Indian Public Finance Statistics.

Composition of Transfers

Table 3.6 indicates the relative importance of CHST and equalization transfers in Canada for four recent years covering 2000–1 to 2003–4. While the CHST transfers including tax points—that is, a reduction in the federal rate and a corresponding increase in the provincial rate—have accounted for a share of 72 to 74 per cent of the total transfers, equalization has accounted for 21 to 25 per cent. This is so when some equalization implicit in the CHST is counted on the side of equalization. TFF accounts for a small share.

Table 3.6 Canada: Composition of Transfers

				($ millions)
	2000–1	2001–2	2002–3	2003–4
Canada Health and Social Transfer				
Cash	15,500	18,300	19,100	20,800
Tax Points	16,415	16,153	16,150	16,958
Total CHST	31,915	34,453	35,250	37,758
Health Reform Fund				1,000
Equalization	10,861	10,372	10,290	10,499
Territorial Formula Financing	1,205	1,458	1,344	1,655
Total Major Transfers adjusted for Equalization implicit in Tax Points Transfers*	42,688	44,778	45,422	49,407
CHST (excluding implicit equalization) as per cent of Adjusted Total)	71.73	73.58	74.39	73.38
Equalization (including implicit equalization) as per cent of Adjusted Total	25.44	23.16	22.65	21.25

Source: www.fin.gc.ca

Notes: *Equalization associated with CHST tax transfer is included in both CHST (under 'Tax Points') and Equalization. Totals have been adjusted to avoid double counting.

Equalization Grants

The equalization grants aim at equalizing fiscal capacities. The 'equalization' payments have been mandated in the constitution since 1982, although these were being made earlier also. Section 36(2) of the *Constitution Act* commits the federal government to the 'principle of making equalization payments to ensure that provincial governments have sufficient revenues to provide reasonably comparable levels of public services at reasonably comparable levels of taxation'. The case for equalization has been made on the grounds of equity (see, e.g., Graham (1964)) as well as of efficiency (see, e.g., Boadway and Flatters (1982); Boadway and Hobson (1993); Dahlby (2008)). Fiscal inefficiency arises when decisions regarding the location of economic activity are influenced by net fiscal benefits, that is, the level of public services relative to cost. Fiscal equity requires that the public sector treats individuals equally who are in equal circumstances, implying that comparable individuals are entitled to the same net benefits from the public sector, that is, to the same level of public services if they are taxed in the same way. The equalization grants aim at achieving these results. As Boadway (2001) observes: 'fiscal equity does not conflict with fiscal efficiency: both depend on NFBs [Net Fiscal Benefits] being equalized across jurisdictions'.

The equalization transfer to a province in absolute amount is determined by applying the average revenue effort to the difference between the standard base and the actual base for that province with respect to the various revenue sources. This produces an estimate of revenue, which is higher than the actual revenue for provinces that have 'below-average' capacity. This exercise is carried out for all revenue bases used by the provinces. At present, there are thirty-three such revenue bases (listed in Appendix 3A.1), which include tax revenues, royalties, and user charges. This system of calculating the 'notional' revenue performance is called the 'Representative Tax System' (RST), where each tax or revenue source is considered individually and the 'average' or 'representative' tax effort is applied to the difference between the standard revenue base and the actual base. Let the provinces be indicated by subscript i and revenue sources by superscript j. In specifying the equalization grant formula the following symbols may be used:

N_i: population of province i

R_i: revenue of the ith province from a given source

b_i: per capita revenue base (total base: $B = N_i * b, B = N_i * b_i$) of a given source

a_x: all-province average tax rate for a given revenue source

r_i: actual per capita revenue of the ith province from a given source

b_s: Per capita standard tax base

The subscripts x and s are kept different to emphasize that, as in Canada, in calculating the average tax rate and the standard tax base, the provinces included in the respective exercises may not constitute the same set.

The average tax rate, considering the ten provinces is defined as

$$a_x = \Sigma R_i / \Sigma B_i = \Sigma N_i r_i / \Sigma N_i b_i \quad (i = 1,...10) \quad (3.1)$$

A benchmark revenue base is derived from the revenue bases of five selected provinces. At present this list excludes Alberta and the four Atlantic provinces. The per capita benchmark revenue base for a given revenue source may be defined as below.

$$b_s = \Sigma B_i / \Sigma N_i \quad [i = 1,...5] \tag{3.2}$$

Where b_s may be considered as the per capita benchmark revenue base.

The total equalization entitlement with respect to an individual revenue source is determined by

$$\begin{aligned} E_i &= a_x[b_s - b_i]N_i & if\,(b_s - b_i) > 0 \\ E_i &= 0 & if\,(b_s - b_i) \leq 0 \end{aligned} \tag{3.3}$$

Total equalization payment for all sources for the ith province will be the summation of such terms for all the revenue sources. Equalization operates as a 'gross' scheme, that is, provinces with a positive entitlement receive their entitlement, but nothing is taken away from those that have a negative entitlement. It can also be seen that the per capita entitlement in respect of any one source can also be written as

$$a_x(b_s - b_i) = a_i(b_s - b_i) + (a_x - a_i)(b_s - b_i)[a_x - a_{i>0}, b_s - b_{i>0}] \tag{3.4}$$

The first term indicates the required correction if only the lack of capacity is made up. The second term indicates the correction where the shortfall in the rate is also corrected in respect of the additional fiscal capacity. If $a_i = a_x$, equalization makes up only for the differences in fiscal capacities. If $a_i < a_x$, it not only corrects for the differences in capacity but also provides for the shortfall in the rate in relation to the additional capacity. If, however, $a_i > a_x$, the benefit from the adjustment in capacity is only to the extent of the average rate.

Some of the important characteristics of the RTS approach to equalization may be noted, as below.

1. The equalization approach requires that for a given tax the relevant tax bases are comparable across provinces. This requires that the relevant bases are identifiable and easily measurable.
2. The benchmark per capita revenue base is to be determined with reference to selected provinces. In Canada, rather than using the average of all provinces, a five-province average is being used. The

ten-province benchmark revenue base emerges to be higher than the average of the selected provinces. The ten-province benchmark revenue base would bring even Ontario, which has the second highest per capita provincial GDP, among the entitled provinces and it would also raise the volume of grants to the present beneficiaries.

3. In its pure form, the total amount of equalization payments could change significantly from year to year, not only in absolute amounts but also in relation to GDP. Also, the federal government would not have any control over the total equalization payments. In Canada, until recently, this pure version was not being applied. Rather, the overall entitlements were subject to a ceiling and when in any one year estimated aggregate entitlement exceeded the ceiling, actual payments were reduced pro-rata for each of the entitled provinces. The ceiling was determined at $10 billion with a built-in formula linked to the growth rate of the national GNP. The ceiling was removed with effect from 2002–3. There is however a floor, which protects provinces from sudden reductions in entitlements.[4]

4. The objective of equalization is to make up for the deficiencies in fiscal capacities at the average all-province tax rate. The Canadian 'equalization' is not intended to result in equal per capita expenditures across provinces. Actual expenditures could be higher than the average in provinces where the revenue effort is higher and lower in provinces where the tax effort is lower. A province may, however, choose to have a lower tax rate, relying more on private sector participation for the provision of services. The levels of expenditure of individual items as well as the aggregate also depend on the preferences of the provinces.

5. Although equalization grants are enshrined in the constitution, and a methodology has also been developed for determining normative revenues from multiple revenue bases by applying the average revenue effort, as Boadway observes 'leading constitutional scholars have argued that the provisions are probably too vague, and too political to be justiceable in the courts'.

Table 3.7 shows the share of equalization payments in total transfers, including tax points for each of the provinces over the period 2000–1

Table 3.7 Share of Equalization Payments in Total Transfers

Provinces	2000–1	2001–2	2002–3	2003–4
Newfoundland and Labrador	71.3	69.2	64.7	61.3
Prince Edward Island	70.3	67.3	64.4	62.3
Nova Scotia	62.4	59.2	55.8	53.9
New Brunswick	65.9	62.6	61.6	59.7
Quebec	42.4	38.1	37.6	34.6
Ontario	0.0	0.0	0.0	0.0
Manitoba	54.3	53.4	52.2	49.5
Saskatchewan	18.4	20.5	18.3	24.4
Alberta	0.0	0.0	0.0	0.0
British Columbia	0.0	5.9	12.4	15.0

Source: www.fin.gc.ca

to 2003–4. Ontario and Alberta are the only two provinces that do not qualify for the equalization grants. British Columbia has been getting a grant since 2001–2. Provinces where equalization payments account for more than half of their transfers are Newfoundland and Labrador, PEI, Nova Scotia, New Brunswick, and Manitoba. For Quebec, Saskatchewan, and British Columbia, equalization payments accounted for 35, 24, and 15 per cent of their respective transfers in 2003–4.

One clear trend that characterizes all the beneficiary provinces is that the share of equalization grants in total transfers has generally gone down between 2000–1 and 2003–4. This is in large part due to the imposition of a ceiling on the growth of equalization transfers. It has also been noted that equalization payments have not necessarily contributed to reducing the volatility of provincial revenues nor have they made the transfers more predictable.[5]

Several problems have been noted in the literature in the actual working of the system of equalization payments. We can group these issues into the following broad categories: (i) problems related to perverse incentives, (ii) problems related to ad hoc adjustments which make the system opaque, (iii) issues related to non-consideration of needs and costs, (iv) measurement difficulties in relation to the revenue bases, (v) compensation for lack of revenue effort, and (vi) faulty indicators of capacity. These are discussed below.

Perverse Incentives

In spite of the normative design of the formula, it has some built-in perverse incentives. It is said that a province can increase its equalization entitlement by raising its tax rate and reducing its tax base. However, for this to happen the tax base should be small and the elasticity of the tax base to the tax rate should be high. If its tax base is sensitive to the tax rate increase, its base will fall and its entitlement will increase, particularly if neither the average tax rate nor the standard tax base are affected significantly.[6] Conversely, a province with a large tax base can reduce its tax rate, thereby reducing the overall tax rate, which will lead to a fall in the equalization entitlements of all other provinces. This may be particularly attractive if the concerned province is not a recipient of the equalization entitlement. Though there would be a loss in its own revenue, the citizens of the province would gain correspondingly in their disposable incomes. This is not an unrealistic situation. One apprehension that the beneficiary provinces currently have is that the equalization standard will fall significantly if Alberta and Ontario continue to reduce their tax rates. These provinces can easily vary their effort to affect the national average tax rate and affect the entitlement of other provinces.[7]

Ad Hoc Adjustments

The federal government sometimes controls the total amount of equalization transfers by including only a part of the base of some revenue sources. For example, in the case of oil and gas revenues, only half of the provincial revenues were included in the 1970s and early 1980s. The inclusion of these revenues fully would have raised the benchmark and thereby raised the equalization payments. The evolution of a five-province standard is also part of this consideration where, by excluding Alberta, the federal government is able to reduce the aggregate equalization payments. In addition, until recently, there has been an externally imposed ceiling on the growth of total equalization payments.

Non-consideration of Needs and Costs

Canada focuses mainly on equalization with respect to the revenue-raising capacities of the provinces. It does not give any consideration to differences in expenditures that arise due to differences in needs or costs.

For example, differences in needs may arise due to demographic composition while costs of providing services may differ due to geographic features. Some have argued that only needs should be taken into account as neutralizing costs would affect location efficiency. In a comprehensive system of equalization, some correction for differential needs as well as costs becomes necessary.

Measurement Difficulties

The compilation of thirty-three revenue bases across provinces, which may not all have the same statutory definition for a given revenue source, is also a problem. There are serious measurement difficulties with respect to some. The property tax is one example where the tax bases are significantly different across provinces. Different provinces use different property evaluation techniques.[8] Further, larger urban centres have relatively high per capita property values. Applying the national average to determine equalization entitlements would work in favour of provinces that are less urbanized and which have lower costs of service provision. Similar issues arise in the case of user charges. Since these are in the nature of benefit taxes, there may not be any need to equalize user charges. Using a standard tax base when some provinces levy the relevant taxes and others do not is also a problem. Lotteries and gambling also pose such questions. Further, the legality of different forms of gambling can differ across provinces.

Compensation for Lack of Revenue Effort

In spite of the elaborate design, the equalization formula also appears to provide some correction for lack of effort. As per the constitutional provision, if a province does not make comparable effort, it should be entitled to a level of public service which is less than the standard. It may be a conscious choice by the province that it taxes less and leaves more role for the private sector to provide the service. The difference in the capacity alone needs to be corrected and not in the effort. Accordingly, the per capita entitlement, for a province which makes both less effort ($a_i < a_x$) and lower capacity ($b_x < b_i$), should be given per capita entitlement equal to $a_i (b_x - b_i)$. Since the actual per capita entitlement is $a_x (b_s - b_i)$, there is an extra payment amounting to $(a_x - a_i).(b_s - b_i)$, as indicated in equation 3.4. This results in some compensation for lack of effort.

Faulty Indicators of Capacity

Yet another issue is whether the tax bases that enter into the RTS are legitimate indicators of fiscal capacity. The provinces have the option to vary the tax rates and thereby influence the tax base. As Barro (2002) observes,

> If two provinces have identical budget constraint but one exerts greater fiscal effort than the other, the former will have lower taxable sales and residential property per capita, and so will appear incorrectly to have lower capacity as measured by the RTS method. Thus, the RTS has a built in tendency to underestimate the capacities of high effort provinces and to overestimate the capacities of low effort provinces, even apart from any tax induced change in private sector economic behavior (p. 10).

In the context of the impact of tax rate changes on the tax bases and the related feedback mechanisms, Barro (2001) identifies three main channels as (i) spatial shifting of economic activity, (ii) changes in levels or hikes of spending in respect of differential tax rates, and (iii) capitalization of taxes into asset prices. The first two mechanisms apply mainly to sales tax bases, and the third, particularly to the property tax. While spatial shifting occurs gradually, the other feedback effects can occur quickly. The distorting effect of feedback on capacity indicators is likely to be stronger for the RTS index, which is based heavily on sales and property tax bases than for the macroeconomic measures of capacity.

Macro Approaches to Equalization

In view of some of the conceptual and practical problems, macro approaches to equalization have often been discussed in Canada as an alternative. For example, Barro (2001) observes, 'The RTS indicator now used in Canada has serious theoretical flaws, as a result of which the provinces' fiscal capacity scores undoubtedly are distorted, but to an as yet unmeasured degree. The macroeconomic approach is better grounded in positive economic theory ...' (p. 16). It has been argued that a macro approach can avoid most of the incentive problems, as one-to-one links with individual tax bases are avoided. The complexity[9] of the current system and the difficulties in defining the standard tax bases can also be avoided. The success of a macro approach depends on defining a suitable macro indicator of the revenue base.

Quite a number of alternative macro formulae have been suggested. Way back in 1984, Courchene (1984) suggested a macro formula of the following form:

$$E_i = (\Sigma_j \, TR_j)[(N_i/N_c) - (MB_i/B_c)] \qquad (3.5)$$

where, MB_i/MB_c denotes province i's share in the macro base (MB). TR_j is total tax-revenue for all provinces from all sources, where j refers to all individual sources. N_i indicates the total population of the ith province. This formula indicates that the entitlements of a province i from all revenue sources are determined by the excess of its share in population over its share in the macro base.

The formula suggested by Coucherene can be rewritten in the following way. Let

$$\Sigma_j \, TR_j/MB_c = a_c$$

This indicates the average all-province tax rate relative to the macro base. The per capita macro base of the ith province can be written as

$$MB_i/N_i = mb_i \qquad (3.6)$$

The expression given in (3.5) can be written as[10]

$$E_i = N_i . a_c [mb_c - mb_i] \qquad (3.7)$$

From the above it can be seen that the attempt is to compensate for the deficiency in the macro base of a province. This is equivalent to equation 3.3 except that b_s is replaced by mb_c and b_i by mb_i. Courchene had considered two potential macro bases, that is, personal income excluding certain items and provincial gross domestic product at factor cost. Apart from per capita personal income, per capita gross domestic product and per capita net domestic product, other broader measures have also been suggested like Total Taxable Resources (TTR), which was proposed by the US Treasury Department and is in limited use for allocating certain US federal grants. The TTR is defined as 'the unduplicated sum of the income flows produced within a state and income flows received by its residents that a state can potentially tax' (see Compson and Navratil (1997), Barro (2001), for a discussion). The concept of TTR takes into account income produced in the state and received by its residents and adds to it income produced outside the state but received by its residents after netting out income produced in the state but received by residents outside the state. The concept has considerable relevance in India as remittances add to the tax base of some states in a significant way. The macro approach, as brought out by equation 3.7, has a close resemblance to the 'deviation' criterion used for allocating central assistance by the Planning Commission in India. In both cases, provinces above the average level are not entitled to any allocation.

The literature (e.g., Barro 2001) also discusses the adjustment that should be made to the macro aggregates that may be used as indicators of fiscal capacity. An important issue discussed is tax exportation, which occurs when a province is able to collect revenues from non-resident persons or businesses. In fact, Statistics Canada has identified fourteen problems which vitiate the usability of GDP as a macro indicator of taxable capacity.[11]

Canada Health and Social Transfers

Apart from equalization grants, two other channels of transfers in Canada are the Canada Health and Social Transfer (CHST) and Territorial Formula Financing (TFF). There is also the recently created Health Reform Fund (HRF). The CHST is the largest federal transfer to the provinces and territories. It was instituted in 1996–7 by replacing two earlier transfer programmes: Established Programs Financing (EPF) and Canada Assistance Plan (CAP). Though these transfers take the form of a specific purpose grant, they may be treated as correcting the vertical imbalance in as much as every province receives a share in these transfers. The CHST transfers are meant to support health care, boost secondary education, and support social assistance and social services including early childhood development. These transfers imply a degree of equalization since the determining principle for the CHST transfers effectively becomes the per capita amounts.

The CHST has two forms: cash and tax transfer points. The tax transfer arrangements were introduced in 1977 under EPF when the federal government agreed with the provincial and territorial governments to reduce its personal and corporate income tax rates by the margin of 13.5 percentage points and correspondingly allow the provinces to raise their tax rates by an equal margin. This has been called the transfer of tax points or the vacation of tax room by the federal government in shared tax bases. This has allowed the provinces to directly obtain the revenues from the relevant tax bases that would otherwise have accrued to the federal government.

The CHST cash transfers are computed as a residual by subtracting the equivalent value of the tax points from provincial per capita total entitlements. The richer provinces gain larger amounts from the tax point transfers because their tax bases are larger. The cash transfers are estimated broadly on a per capita basis adjusted for the amounts calculated under the transfer of tax points. Ontario receives the lowest cash transfer under CHST, since its own-source fiscal capacity exceeds the fiscal capacities of all other provinces inclusive of equalization in the case of recipient provinces. Hobson (2001) refers to the portion of other provinces' cash transfers, which raises them to a common standard, as a sort of 'super-equalization'.[12] Such super-equalization is paid to both Alberta and British Columbia.

The CHST is a general-purpose transfer which gives the provinces and territories the flexibility to allocate payments among social programmes according to their own priorities, subject to upholding the principles of the Canada Health Act and the condition that no period of minimum residency is required with reference to the social assistance.

In a recent meeting of the First Ministers or Premiers of the Provinces in 2003, there was an agreement on an action plan for renewing health care. This would result in an increase in federal support for health care relative to the 2003 levels by $17.3 billion over three years and by $34.8 billion over five years. It has also been agreed to restructure the CHST w.e.f. 1 April 2003 by dividing it into two separate transfers. The new system comprises Canada Health Transfers (CHT) in support of health, and Canada Social Transfers (CST) in support of post-secondary education, social assistance, and social services including early childhood development. In this restructuring, the existing CHST consisting of cash as well as tax transfers will be apportioned between CHT and CST. The percentage of cash and tax points apportioned to CHT will reflect the percentage of provincial health spending within the overall provincial spending supported by the CHST. The remaining cash and tax points will be allocated to the CST.

As derived in endnote 12, the CHST formula for cash transfers can be written as

$$c_i = [c^* - zq_0] + z[q_0 - q_i] \qquad (3.8)$$

The various terms used in this equation are explained below:

c_i is the per capita cash transfer to the ith province
c^* is the normative per capita expenditure on health and social services
z is the tax points transfer (13.5 percentage points) applicable to personal and corporate income tax bases
q_i is the tax base of the ith province (covering personal and corporate income taxes)
q_0 is the corresponding tax base of Ontario

The term $[c^* - zq_0]$ is a constant, z is a fraction and $[q_0 - q_i]$ gives the distance of the per capita revenue base of the ith province from the highest per capita base among provinces. This formulation once again has a close resemblance to the distance criterion used by the Finance Commissions in India for deciding the horizontal distribution of shareable taxes. In the formulation used by the Finance Commissions, states with lower per capita incomes benefit more as the distance is measured from the highest per capita income or the average of three states with the highest per capita incomes. In the Canadian formulation, the distance is measured from the tax base of Ontario which has the highest tax base in this context. However, the weight attached to this criterion is differently determined.

Territorial Formula Financing

The North-West Territories and the territorial governments of Nunavut and Yukon receive a portion of their funds through TFF, which is meant to compensate them for the higher per capita costs of providing services which arise due to the small size of the population, the large area, and the extreme weather conditions. In 2003–4, total TFF amounted to $1,655 million. For the governments of the territories, TFF accounts for more than 90 per cent of their respective total transfers. The other major source, CHST, accounted for only 8, 5, and 8 per cent of total transfers in 2003–4 respectively, for the North-West Territories, Nunavut, and Yukon.

The TFF is a 'gap-filling' formula, which takes into account the difference between the expenditure needs and the own resources of the territorial governments. The formula uses on the expenditure side the concept of Gross Expenditure Base (GEB). The GEB is indexed to provincial spending so that the growth rates in provincial spending and territorial government spending can match. There is a further adjustment for territorial population growth relative to that of Canada as a whole. On the revenue side, territorial revenues are derived by applying the average provincial tax effort to the territorial revenue bases. Some adjustment is made in these estimates in recognition of the special circumstances of the North. In addition, a financial incentive is also provided to the Territories to encourage economic activity and greater self-sufficiency. Agreements regarding federal financing of territorial expenditures are generally arrived at for a five-year period. The present arrangements, for example, took effect on 1 April 1999.

Horizontal Imbalance

Revenues
The outcome of the Canadian Transfer System is to reduce both vertical and horizontal imbalances. As already noted, provinces differ from each other in terms of area and size of population, natural endowments, and economic base. These differences result in considerable horizontal imbalance, which is addressed through 'equalization grants' in Canada. As long as there is enough vertical imbalance in the system with the federal government transferring sufficient funds to all provinces, it could always structure them so that horizontal equalization is achieved. We can examine how effective the system has been in reducing horizontal

imbalances by looking at the per capita revenues of provinces relative to average provincial revenues before and after transfers.

Table 3.8 shows that the range of the difference between the minimum and the maximum in 2000–1 was 80.7 before transfers and 47.1 after

Table 3.8 Horizontal Fiscal Imbalance: Revenue Before and After Transfers: Canada

Provinces	Before			After		(per cent)
	1999–2000	2000–1	2001–2	1999–2000	2000–1	2001–2
Newfoundland and Labrador	74.5	73.2	87.3	113.2	111.5	124.3
Prince Edward Island	79.2	76.7	83.2	111.8	110.1	117.4
Nova Scotia	66.3	65.2	73.9	92.8	90.3	96.6
New Brunswick	79.2	76.2	82.6	109.1	103.1	113.5
Quebec	110.7	107.4	110.2	109.6	109.5	112.3
Ontario	97.9	92.3	93.1	92.6	87.4	88.1
Manitoba	73.7	74.8	78.4	93.9	92.9	96.7
Saskatchewan	90.4	107.5	95.9	97.7	105.8	100.1
Alberta	123.9	145.8	128.6	115.7	134.5	119.0
British Columbia	94.7	96.8	98.8	92.2	93.9	93.6
All provinces	100.0	100.0	100.0	100.0	100.0	100.0
Minimum	66.3	65.2	73.9	92.2	87.4	88.1
Maximum	123.9	145.8	128.6	115.7	134.5	124.3
Range (% points)	57.6	80.7	54.7	23.4	47.1	36.2
Coefficient of variation	20.3	26.4	17.6	9.5	13.4	11.8

Source: Fiscal Reference Tables, Department of Finance, Ontario, Canada.

transfers. The coefficient of variation prior to transfers was 17.6 in 2001–2 which fell to 11.8 after transfers. Table 3.9 shows the corresponding picture for India. Three sets of three-year averages are given, providing per capita state revenues before and after transfers for the general category states excluding Goa, which is an outlier, and including Assam from among the special category states.

The per capita revenues prior to transfers show a minimum of 28 per cent for Bihar compared to the fifteen-state average and the corresponding ratio of 237 per cent for Haryana being the highest during 1993–4 to 1995–6. The coefficient of variation was 58.3. The range as well as the coefficient of variation prior to transfers decreased subsequently but only marginally. The position improved considerably after transfers as the range dropped to about 102 percentage points in the latest period and the coefficient of variation was also just a little above 30 per cent. However, compared with Canada, the coefficient of variation is about three times in magnitude after transfers, showing that much horizontal difference is left in revenues even after transfers.

Expenditures

The final outcome of transfers is to correct the horizontal imbalance in expenditures, which are affected by own revenues, transfers, and borrowing. An examination of the per capita expenditures of provinces in Canada relative to average provincial expenditure (see Table 3.10) shows that the range of variation is more or less the same as in the case of revenues. This is because the provinces do not resort to any significant borrowing. The range of variation from the average in Canada was 23.2 percentage points in 1999–2000, with 92.6 per cent of the average being the minimum and 115.8 per cent being the maximum. In 2001–2, this range increased to 38 percentage points.

The extent of equalization required in India is much more than that in Canada because of the difference in the revenue bases. In India, states also borrow to a substantial extent and their relative capacities to borrow differ. This adds to horizontal imbalance when expenditures on services are considered. Differences in per capita expenditures arise because of differences in revenues as well as per capita borrowing. One qualification, however, needs to be added, namely that sometimes these differences are

Table 3.9 Per Capita Revenues Relative to 15-State Average Before and After Transfers

(per cent)

States	Before		Average	After		Average
	1993–4 to 1995–6	1996–7 to 1998–9	1999–2000 to 2001–2	1993–4 to 1995–6	1996–7 to 1998–9	1999–2000 to 2001–2
Andhra Pradesh	82.53	91.93	106.74	89.55	97.89	108.28
Assam	42.98	39.94	44.17	94.67	91.36	87.35
Bihar*	27.90	28.00	27.28	49.00	48.30	48.83
Gujarat	142.48	150.44	149.76	121.92	128.17	128.28
Haryana	236.88	205.89	168.07	183.20	163.55	134.02
Karnataka	115.89	123.35	121.60	105.80	113.94	115.59
Kerala	110.68	126.17	121.35	107.41	119.81	114.26
Madhya Pradesh*	66.43	68.12	65.09	75.63	78.16	75.23
Maharashtra	145.21	148.94	154.97	121.49	122.97	123.40
Orissa	46.85	44.42	47.43	74.07	69.93	76.44
Punjab	179.87	173.34	186.67	145.64	140.38	150.41
Rajasthan	82.53	75.52	74.52	93.66	84.78	86.23

Tamil Nadu	117.97	130.53	135.63	110.96	120.14	121.73
Uttar Pradesh*	46.35	41.50	44.91	62.42	57.07	61.09
West Bengal	55.45	51.90	51.80	64.59	63.55	68.84
Total 15 States	100.00	100.00	100.00	100.00	100.00	100.00
Minimum	27.90	28.00	27.28	49.00	48.30	48.83
Maximum	236.88	205.89	186.67	183.20	163.55	150.41
Range	208.97	177.89	159.40	134.19	115.25	101.58
Coefficient of Variation	58.26	55.41	52.29	34.71	33.29	30.06

Source: Finance Accounts of State Governments and Population Census 1991 and 2001.

Note: *refers to the pre-divided states.

Annual Population figures are calculated on the basis of monthly compound average growth rates and the mid-year October figures are taken to calculate per capita figures.

Table 3.10 Horizontal Fiscal Imbalance in Expenditure: Canada

			(per cent)
Provinces	1999–2000	2000–1	2001–2
Newfoundland and Labrador	115.8	120.8	124.8
Prince Edward Island	114.7	119.8	117.8
Nova Scotia	103.3	99.0	100.4
New Brunswick	110.8	106.8	109.7
Quebec	111.4	114.6	113.0
Ontario	92.6	89.5	86.8
Manitoba	97.0	97.9	95.5
Saskatchewan	98.0	99.8	103.4
Alberta	101.3	107.5	111.6
British Columbia	95.3	94.4	101.0
All provinces	100.0	100.0	100.0
Minimum	92.6	89.5	86.8
Maximum	115.8	120.8	124.8
Range (per cent points)	23.2	31.3	38.0
Coefficient of variation	8.19	10.21	10.51

Source: Fiscal Reference Tables, Department of Finance, Ontario.

not just due to differences in capacities but also to differences in provincial preferences in providing services by government where the private sector can also participate.

In India, looking at per capita expenditures, the range appears to be much larger, showing that even after transfers considerable horizontal imbalances remain uncorrected. The inter-state per capita expenditure on general, social, and economic services relative to the average per capita expenditure shows that disparities have been large and have increased over time. Table 3.11 gives three-year averages of per capita expenditures for the period 1987–8 to 2001–2, covering fifteen states that include all the general category states except Goa, which is an outlier, and Assam, which is the largest among the special category states. Bihar has the minimum per capita expenditures, which amounted to more than 62 per cent of the average per capita expenditures but have fallen to about 50 per cent of the average in recent years. Maharashtra and more

Table 3.11 Horizontal Imbalance: India

| Per Capita Expenditure of States Relative to Average (Three Year Averages) | | | | | (in Rupees) |
States	1987–8 to 1989–90	1990–1 to 1992–3	1993–4 to 1995–6	1996–7 to 1998–9	1999–2000 to 2001–2
Andhra Pradesh	99.9	98.3	108.6	109.8	111.9
Assam	107.6	100.9	96.4	79.3	85.5
Bihar	67.7	62.9	52.7	50.7	50.1
Gujarat	139.1	136.9	130.1	143.7	152.7
Haryana	148.3	136.3	194.9	181.6	140.9
Karnataka	110.9	114.0	117.0	115.8	118.0
Kerala	108.4	109.2	121.1	134.2	127.3
Madhya Pradesh	88.6	84.1	81.5	83.0	75.4
Maharashtra	138.7	129.8	137.3	134.4	148.6
Orissa	90.3	90.8	89.2	89.2	91.6
Punjab	172.2	174.3	179.2	168.9	173.2
Rajasthan	100.1	104.2	112.5	104.2	96.0
Tamil Nadu	111.0	130.4	119.4	128.7	120.8
Uttar Pradesh	76.2	82.3	74.8	73.1	66.9
West Bengal	80.8	75.9	77.2	83.6	99.5
Total 15 States	100.0	100.0	100.0	100.0	100.0
Minimum	67.7	62.9	52.7	50.7	50.1
Maximum	172.2	174.3	194.9	181.6	173.2
Range	104.5	111.4	142.2	130.9	123.1
Coefficient of Variation	26.6	26.7	33.8	32.8	31.2

Source: Finance Accounts of State Governments.

recently Punjab have had the largest per capita expenditures. The range of variation between the minimum and maximum was 105 percentage points in the late 1980s. This increased, reaching a peak of 142 percentage points, during 1993–4 to 1995–6 and has fallen since then to 123 during 1999–2000 to 2001–2. The coefficient of variation shows a similar pattern. In terms of magnitude, the coefficient of variation is about three times that in Canada.

Federal and Provincial Debt

The resource gap that remains unmet by fiscal transfers leads to borrowing by the provincial governments. In Canada, however, provinces do not borrow from the central government. Total government debt in Canada excluding government employee pension liabilities went up to as high as 99.5 per cent of GDP in 1995. However, since then there has been a decline in government debt relative to GDP. It was 83.2 per cent in 2001. The overall debt-GDP ratio of the central and state governments considered together in India, at 75 per cent at the end of 2002–3, is less than that of Canada. However, while in Canada it has been falling in recent years, in India it has been rising. Canada appears to have solved its debt-fiscal deficit problem by having a fiscal surplus for several years, which resulted in the fall of the debt-GDP ratio. It may also be noted that the sustainable threshold of the debt-GDP ratio is much lower in India because it has a much lower revenue-to-GDP ratio. As already noted, while this ratio is about 17 per cent in India, it is more than 40 per cent in Canada.

Provinces in Canada can borrow from the domestic market or even from abroad. However, they do not borrow from the federal government. Their ability to borrow from the market depends entirely on the assessment by the markets and the credit ratings that they might receive. This, itself, serves as an instrument of fiscal discipline. In India, states are heavily indebted to the central government. Part of the assistance that the central government extends to the states for their plans is in the form of loans. The borrowing that the states are able to do on the basis of small savings is fully backed by the central government. The protection and the implicit guarantee that the central government provides to the borrowings by the states serve to dilute the discipline that the markets may otherwise impose.

* * *

While comparing the Canadian System of intergovernmental transfers with the system of fiscal transfers in India, the following features may be highlighted:

1. The heart of the Canadian transfer system is equalization. Apart from equalization grants, the CHST also serves the objective of equalization as provinces are able to spend in per capita terms close

to each other. Together, these transfers are able to eliminate to a considerable extent both vertical and horizontal imbalances. While the CHST is based almost entirely on per capita expenditures, equalization grants utilize an elaborate system of normative determination of capacities.

2. Vertical imbalance is corrected in most federations through tax-base sharing, revenue sharing and grants. India follows all three routes while in Canada the emphasis is on tax-base sharing and grants. Revenue sharing becomes necessary where tax assignment is inadequate. Unlike in India, in Canada, almost all tax bases are common to both levels of government. It is notable that some vertical imbalance is corrected through a special purpose grant, that is, CHST. In India, the vertical imbalance is sought to be corrected by revenue sharing, and the horizontal imbalance through the formula of distribution of the shareable revenues among states supplemented by grants.

3. Incomes as well as population are concentrated in just a few provinces in Canada, namely Ontario, British Columbia, Alberta, and Quebec. This facilitates a transfer system aimed at equalization. However, redistribution in India is more difficult because the share of the population in states which have a high per capita income is smaller than the population in the states with low per capita incomes, which require transfers.

4. The normative determination of capacities is done by utilizing a system called RTS which requires equalization of the bases of thirty-three revenue sources. In the RTS system, only the revenue capacities are determined and no account is taken of relevant cost differentials in the provision of services or differences in needs. Apart from other limitations, this calls for an elaborate mechanism for collecting and updating data. In Canada, this task is facilitated by an independent statistical agency. The Indian system, in correcting horizontal imbalances, uses macro variables at the state level. An attempt is also made to correct for some cost differentials.

5. Even after the determination of the actual transfers in any given year, calculations remain open in Canada for four years where amounts are adjusted in view of the revision of the relevant data. In

the Indian case, this option is not open in general, particularly for the Finance Commission transfers although amounts of tax devolution automatically adjust with reference to the actual realizations of the central taxes. Most grants are fixed in nominal terms well in advance of the years for which those grants are to be given. These are also derived on the basis of data which are dated by several years.

6. In the Canadian system, there is no autonomous body like the Finance Commission. In their case, most decisions are arrived at through consultations and discussions. In the Indian case, apart from the constitutionally mandated body like the Finance Commission, there are other institutions also dealing with different aspects of federal-state relations like the Planning Commission, and various central ministries and departments. Changes in some components of transfers, like those under the Gadgil Formula, require endorsement by the National Development Council. Thus, in India, the system of transfers is fragmented with several bodies being responsible for the transfers.

Even though the modalities of equalization may appear to be different in Canada and India, the use of the distance factor in the Finance Commission formula for distribution is not very different from the way cash transfers are determined under CHST in Canada. Similarly, the use of the deviation criterion by the Planning Commission is not very different from the equalization principle of Canada if the macro base is substituted for the multiple individual bases.

Determining equalization entitlements based on a source-by-source approach, as adopted by Canada, is less practical in the case of India simply for want of comparable and reliable information required for applying the method. Even on theoretical grounds, that approach has been questioned extensively. A more practical alternative is the macro approach, which is adopted in India. However, the Canadian system brings home the point that a good indicator of fiscal capacity will have to go beyond using the per capita GSDP. Account has to be taken not just of production in a state but rather of the incomes that accrue to its citizens. Also, the concept of ensuring that resources are available for maintaining the per capita expenditure of select basic services at certain levels among states, as attempted in Canada, is worth exploring.

Addendum to Chapter 3: Recent Developments in the Canadian System of Fiscal Transfers

Some important changes have taken place in the Canadian system of fiscal transfers, including the determination of equalization payments following the recommendations of an Expert Panel in 2006. Some of the main changes are discussed below.

Changes in the calculation of equalization payments

The earlier equalization standard pertained to five provinces. This has now been replaced by an equalization standard based on the average fiscal capacity of all ten provinces. This includes Alberta. Since Alberta's fiscal capacity is relatively high because of its oil resources, the effect of broadening the coverage of provinces in the measurement of the benchmark standard has been to uplift it. As a result, the magnitude of equalization entitlements has gone up for the provinces that are now entitled to them.

Further, the fiscal capacities are now based on just five tax bases: personal income tax base, the business income tax base, the property tax base, the sales tax base, and 50 per cent of natural resource revenues. The earlier measurement covered thirty-three revenue sources. This change has considerably simplified the measurement of provincial fiscal capacities.

A third change relates to the treatment of natural resources. Instead of using the revenue base, it is the revenues that are directly taken into account. Fifty per cent of revenues from natural resources are used for this purpose. The resource revenues taken into account cover fourteen different natural resources, including hydroelectricity, oil and gas, and forestry. These changes have helped bypass the problems associated with the measurement of revenue bases and also broadened the overall coverage of natural resources.

One more change in the calculation of fiscal capacity relates to the use of market values in measuring the residential property tax base. Earlier, some proxy for the property tax base was used in which some economic indicators were utilized. This has now been replaced by market values, which has resulted in a substantial increase in the fiscal capacity of some provinces such as British Columbia while there has been a reduction in the fiscal capacity of Quebec, where property values are relatively low.

In the new system, equalization entitlements are calculated based on a three-year weighted moving average of measured fiscal capacities with a two-year lag. The weights associated with the first two years in this calculation are 25 per cent each while for the final year, it is 50 per cent.

One important provision in the computation of equalization payments in the new system is to introduce a fiscal capacity cap. This is meant to ensure that a recipient province's fiscal capacity does not exceed that of any non-recipient province.

Changes in the Overall System of Fiscal Transfers

The overall system of fiscal transfers in Canada covering its provinces and special territories consists now of four main channels: Canada Health Transfer, Canada Social Transfer, Equalization Payments, and Territorial Formula Financing. In addition, some other channels of transfers are also used, such as Offshore Offsets and payments under the Fiscal Stabilization Program. Based on this system of transfers, we can look at the vertical and horizontal dimensions of the Canadian system of fiscal transfers.

Vertical Dimension

In terms of the total amount of transfers, just a little less than one-fourth of the Canadian federal revenues are being transferred to the provinces and the territories. In terms of the relative importance of the main types of transfers, health transfers are the largest in terms of magnitude followed by equalization transfers and social transfers respectively (Addendum Table 3.1).

Canada's health transfers have been increasing in terms of its relative share in total transfers, crossing 50 per cent in 2016–17. Equalization transfers have accounted for a little more than 25 per cent of total federal transfers. Canada's social transfers as well as other transfers have fallen in terms of their relative importance since 2009–10.

Addendum Table 3.1 Federal Support to Provinces and Territories

Major Transfers[1]	2014–15	2015–16	2016–17	2017–18	2018–19	2019–20	2020–1	2021–2	2022–3	2023–4
Magnitude of transfers (in dollar million)										
Canada Health Transfer[2]	32,113	34,026	36,068	37,150	38,584	40,373	41,870	43,126	45,208	≤9,421
Canada Social Transfer	12,582	12,959	13,348	13,748	14,161	14,586	15,023	15,474	15,938	16,416
Equalization	16,669	17,341	17,880	18,254	18,958	19,837	20,573	20,911	21,920	23,963
Offshore Offsets[3]	196	125	44	36	-72	2	86	44	48	–
Territorial Formula Financing[4]	3,469	3,561	3,603	3,682	3,785	3,948	4,180	4,380	4,553	4,834
Total - Federal Support	**65,029**	**68,013**	**70,943**	**72,870**	**75,416**	**78,746**	**81,732**	**83,935**	**87,667**	**94,634**
Per Capita Allocation (dollars)	1,832	1,899	1,959	1,997	2,038	2,098	2,149	2,197	2,258	2,397
Population (in million derived)	35.5	35.8	36.2	36.5	37.0	37.5	38.0	38.2	38.8	39.5
Relative shares of different types of federal transfers (%)										
Canada Health Transfer[2]	49.4	50.0	50.8	51.0	51.2	51.3	51.2	51.4	51.6	52.2
Canada Social Transfer	19.3	19.1	18.8	18.9	18.8	18.5	18.4	18.4	18.2	17.3

(*continued*)

Addendum Table 3.1 Continued

Major Transfers[1]	2014–15	2015–16	2016–17	2017–18	2018–19	2019–20	2020–1	2021–2	2022–3	2023–4
Equalization	25.6	25.5	25.2	25.1	25.1	25.2	25.2	24.9	25.0	25.3
Offshore Offsets[3]	0.3	0.2	0.1	0.0	-0.1	0.0	0.1	0.1	0.1	0.0
Territorial Formula Financing[4]	5.3	5.2	5.1	5.1	5.0	5.0	5.1	5.2	5.2	5.1
Total - Federal Support	100.0	100.0	100.0	100.0	100.0	100.0	100.0	100.0	100.0	100.0

Source (Basic data): Department of Finance, Government of Canada; https://www.canada.ca/en/department-finance/programs/federal-transfers/major-federal-transfers.html (Accessed on 23 September 2023)

Notes:

[1]The Fiscal Stabilization payments to Newfoundland and Labrador ($31.7 million) and to Alberta ($251.4 million) for 2015-16 are not included. The Fiscal Stabilization payments to Alberta ($251.4 million) and Saskatchewan ($20.3 million as well as a $18.6 million ex gratia payment) for 2016-17 are also not included.

[2]Canada Health Transfer (CHT) includes transition protection payments to Newfoundland and Labrador and Nunavut in 2014–15. This excludes one-time top-ups to the CHT of $500 million in 2019–20, $4 billion in 2020–1 and $2 billion in 2021–2.

[3]Offshore Offsets to Nova Scotia include cash amounts from the 2005 Arrangement (including the extension until 2022–3). They also include Cumulative Best-of Guarantee payments/recoveries to Nova Scotia until 2019–20.

[4]Territorial Formula Financing (TFF) payments include an additional $67 million to Yukon ($16 million), Northwest Territories ($24 million), and Nunavut ($26 million) in 2016–17, stemming from the legislative amendments to enhance the stability and predictability of the program.

TFF includes transition payments to Yukon ($1.3 million) and Northwest Territories ($1.7 million) for five years starting in 2019–20.

Horizontal Dimension

In considering the horizontal dimension of transfers in Canada, it is useful to note the large differentials in the share of GDP across provinces. The largest province, Ontario, accounts for 38.1 per cent of national GDP, followed by Quebec at 20.1 per cent. Alberta and British Columbia account for 14.9 per cent and 14 per cent of national GDP respectively. Thus, these four provinces, all sharing borders with the US, together accounted for 87.1 per cent of the national GDP (Addendum Chart 3.1). The remaining six provinces and three special territories accounted only for 12.9 per cent of GDP.

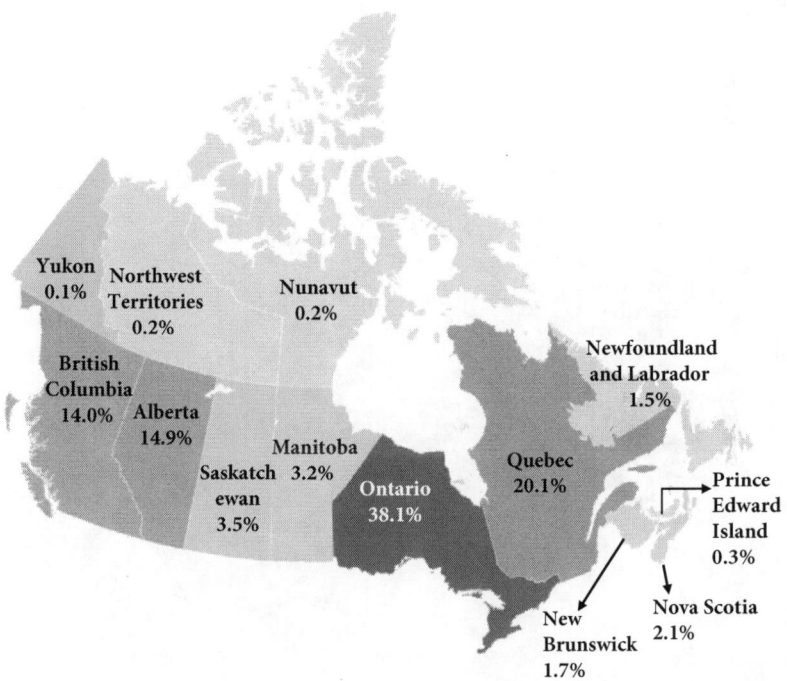

Addendum Chart 3.1 Share in Nominal GDP (%, 2021)

Source (Basic data): Statistics Canada and Authors' creation

Notes: (1) Map created by using Microsoft Excel (GeoNames).

(2) Not to scale and indicative only

Shares in population also show a corresponding pattern. These four provinces also accounted for 86.5 per cent of the total population in 2021 (Addendum Chart 3.2).

All the Canadian provinces receive health and social transfers but only a subset of provinces receives equalization transfers. In particular, Newfoundland and Labrador, Saskatchewan, Alberta, and British Columbia did not get any equalization transfer from 2014–15 to 2023–4 (Addendum Table 3.2). The largest equalization transfer in per capita terms is being provided to Prince Edward Island followed by New Brunswick. These are low-population Atlantic provinces. Among the relatively larger provinces, Manitoba gets the highest per capita

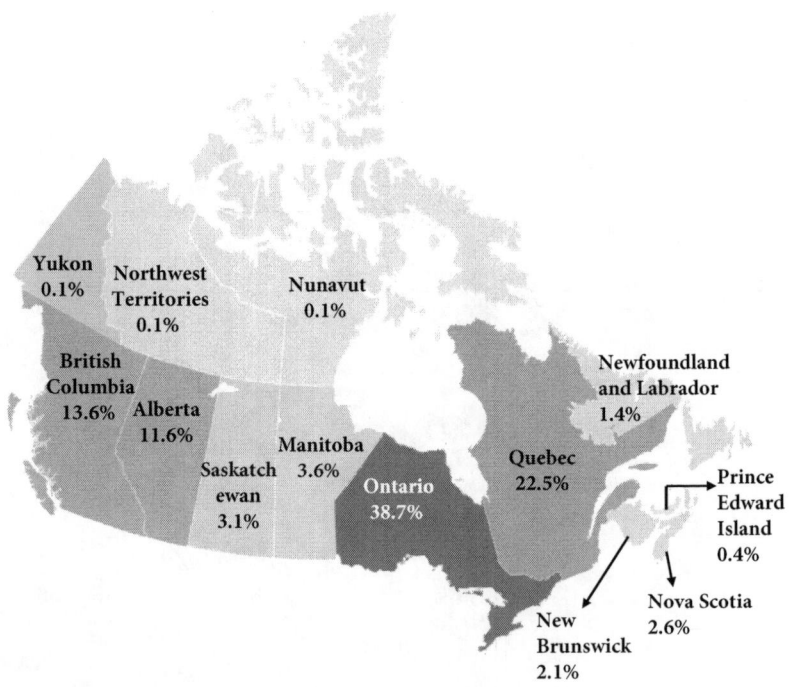

Addendum Chart 3.2 Share in Population (%, 2021)

Source (Basic data): Statistics Canada and authors' creation

Notes: (1) Map created by using Microsoft Excel (GeoNames)

(2) Not to scale and indicative only

Addendum Table 3.2 Distribution of Per Capita Equalization Transfers (in dollars): Canadian Provinces and Territories

Province/Territory	2014–15	2015–16	2016–17	2017–18	2018–19	2019–20	2020–1	2021–2	2022–3	2023–4
Newfoundland and Labrador	0	0	0	0	0	0	0	0	0	0
Prince Edward Island	2463	2465	2545	2594	2738	2667	2819	2946	2959	3185
Nova Scotia	1718	1792	1817	1873	2019	2081	2187	2341	2420	2688
New Brunswick	2207	2213	2256	2297	2433	2606	2824	2881	2917	3171
Atlantic Provinces	**834**	**864**	**881**	**906**	**977**	**1003**	**1063**	**1137**	**1175**	**1304**
Quebec	1132	1154	1207	1337	1400	1546	1545	1526	1574	1602
Ontario	145	171	165	101	67	0	0	0	0	27
Manitoba	1369	1343	1320	1365	1507	1650	1818	1954	2085	2468
Saskatchewan	0	0	0	0	0	0	0	0	0	0
Alberta	0	0	0	0	0	0	0	0	0	0
British Columbia	0	0	0	0	0	0	0	0	0	0
Core Provinces	**445**	**459**	**468**	**473**	**482**	**497**	**507**	**509**	**524**	**560**
Total provinces	**470**	**484**	**494**	**500**	**512**	**529**	**541**	**547**	**565**	**607**

Source (Basic data): Department of Finance, Government of Canada https://www.canada.ca/en/department-finance/programs/federal-transfers/major-federal-transfers.html (Accessed on 23 September 2023)

equalization transfer followed by Quebec. For Ontario, only marginal per capita equalization entitlements are given.

The formula for Canada's health transfers has evolved in a manner such that, subject to minor adjustments, similar per capita amounts are given to each province (Addendum Table 3.3). However, over time, a certain growth is provided in the magnitude of per capita health transfers.

In per capita terms, Canada's health transfers have been increasing with a growth rate ranging from 2.2 per cent to 7.5 per cent from 2015–16 to 2023–4, averaging 3.7 per cent, as shown in Addendum Chart 3.3.

Canada's social transfers cover payments towards support for children, post-secondary education, and social programmes. Subject to minor adjustments, Canada's social transfers have also been given in broadly equal per capita amounts to different provinces (Addendum Table 3.4). In this case also, a certain growth over time has been provided, as shown in Addendum Chart 3.4.

Growth in per capita social transfers has been in the range of 1.3 per cent to 2.6 per cent during the period 2015–16 to 2022–3 with an average growth of 1.8 per cent.

Thus, the Canadian system of fiscal transfers, and especially its equalization component, has been streamlined in recent years. The largest transfers in per capita terms received by all provinces and territories pertained to Canada's Health Transfers. The next in order of relative importance are the Equalization Payments although these are not received by all provinces.

Addendum Table 3.3 Distribution of Per Capita Health Transfers (in dollars): Canadian Provinces and Territories

Province/Territory	2014–15	2015–16	2016–17	2017–18	2018–19	2019–20	2020–1	2021–2	2022–3	2023–4
Newfoundland and Labrador	927.2	949.0	994.7	1018.3	1043.1	1074.6	1101.4	1128.4	1163.6	1252.9
Prince Edward Island	903.1	949.1	998.1	1017.7	1045.7	1075.7	1099.2	1126.1	1164.9	1249.0
Nova Scotia	904.2	950.0	995.8	1018.1	1042.2	1076.0	1100.7	1129.4	1163.9	1251.3
New Brunswick	903.6	950.9	996.1	1017.9	1042.4	1075.7	1100.4	1129.0	1164.2	1252.2
Atlantic Provinces	**909.1**	**950.0**	**995.8**	**1018.1**	**1042.7**	**1075.6**	**1100.7**	**1128.8**	**1164.0**	**1251.8**
Quebec	904.1	950.3	995.9	1018.1	1042.8	1075.5	1100.8	1129.0	1164.1	1251.7
Ontario	904.1	949.9	996.2	1018.0	1042.9	1075.5	1101.0	1128.9	1164.4	1251.8
Manitoba	904.1	949.6	995.8	1017.8	1042.9	1076.0	1100.8	1129.1	1164.5	1251.5
Saskatchewan	903.9	950.4	995.3	1018.8	1042.3	1075.4	1100.8	1128.7	1164.7	1252.0
Alberta	904.5	950.2	995.6	1018.2	1042.3	1075.3	1101.1	1128.9	1164.4	1252.0
British Columbia	904.5	950.1	995.5	1018.0	1042.4	1075.5	1101.0	1128.8	1164.4	1252.1
Core Provinces	**904.2**	**950.0**	**995.9**	**1018.1**	**1042.7**	**1075.5**	**1101.0**	**1128.9**	**1164.4**	**1251.8**
Total provinces	**904.5**	**950.0**	**995.9**	**1018.1**	**1042.7**	**1075.5**	**1100.9**	**1128.9**	**1164.3**	**1251.8**
Yukon	896.3	937.5	1000.6	1011.1	1037.4	1063.6	1091.1	1137.8	1166.5	1261.7
Territories	910.6	951.0	985.3	1023.7	1039.9	1065.6	1101.4	1138.1	1162.4	1252.6
Nunavut	942.3	959.9	996.8	1014.5	1052.9	1062.9	1101.5	1135.1	1159.4	1253.7
Total territories	**915.9**	**949.5**	**993.7**	**1016.8**	**1043.1**	**1064.1**	**1098.0**	**1137.1**	**1162.8**	**1256.0**
Total provinces and territories	**904.6**	**950.0**	**995.9**	**1018.1**	**1042.7**	**1075.5**	**1100.9**	**1128.9**	**1164.3**	**1251.8**

Source (Basic data): Department of Finance, Government of Canada; https://www.canada.ca/en/department-finance/programs/federal-transfers/major-federal-transfers.html (Accessed on 23 September 2023)

Addendum Table 3.4 Distribution of Per Capita Social Transfers (in dollars): Canadian Provinces and Territories

Province/Territory	2014–15	2015–16	2016–17	2017–18	2018–19	2019–20	2020–21	2021–22	2022–23	2023–24
Newfoundland and Labrador	353.8	361.1	369.3	376.7	381.9	387.5	394.6	405.6	411.4	415.1
Prince Edward Island	355.8	361.9	368.4	379.1	385.6	388.3	397.4	407.8	411.8	414.4
Nova Scotia	354.5	361.6	368.2	376.9	382.2	388.3	395.4	405.4	410.6	416.1
New Brunswick	353.8	362.0	368.6	377.2	382.9	389.1	394.9	405.5	410.3	415.8
Atlantic Provinces	**354.2**	**361.6**	**368.6**	**377.1**	**382.6**	**388.3**	**395.2**	**405.7**	**410.7**	**415.7**
Quebec	354.3	361.9	368.6	376.7	382.7	388.6	395.0	405.1	410.5	415.8
Ontario	354.4	361.7	368.7	376.7	382.7	388.5	395.0	405.1	410.5	415.8
Manitoba	354.3	361.6	368.7	376.5	383.1	388.4	394.7	405.4	410.2	415.5
Saskatchewan	354.2	361.6	368.7	377.1	382.7	388.6	395.2	405.3	410.3	416.0
Alberta	354.5	361.8	368.4	376.8	382.7	388.4	395.1	405.1	410.6	416.0
British Columbia	354.5	361.9	368.5	376.8	382.6	388.5	395.0	405.0	410.4	415.9
Core Provinces	**354.4**	**361.8**	**368.6**	**376.8**	**382.7**	**388.5**	**395.0**	**405.1**	**410.5**	**415.8**
Total provinces	**354.4**	**361.8**	**368.6**	**376.8**	**382.7**	**388.5**	**395.0**	**405.1**	**410.5**	**415.8**
Yukon	353.1	375.0	368.6	379.2	370.5	386.8	403.2	394.7	411.7	405.5
Territories	364.2	362.3	358.3	378.3	376.1	399.6	396.5	415.9	416.7	417.5
Nunavut	360.3	356.5	377.2	373.8	394.8	388.9	384.2	403.6	419.3	409.9
Total territories	**359.5**	**364.5**	**367.4**	**377.2**	**380.0**	**392.0**	**395.0**	**405.0**	**415.8**	**411.1**
Total provinces and territories	**354.4**	**361.8**	**368.6**	**376.8**	**382.7**	**388.5**	**395.0**	**405.1**	**410.5**	**415.8**

Source (Basic data): Department of Finance, Government of Canada; https://www.canada.ca/en/department-finance/programs/federal-transfers/federal-transfers/major-federal-transfers.html (Accessed on 23 September 2023)

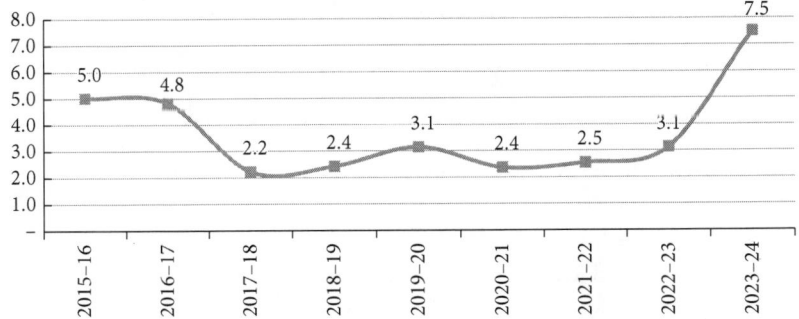

Addendum Chart 3.3 Growth in Per-Capita Health Transfer (%)

Source (Basic data): Department of Finance, Government of Canada and Authors' calculations

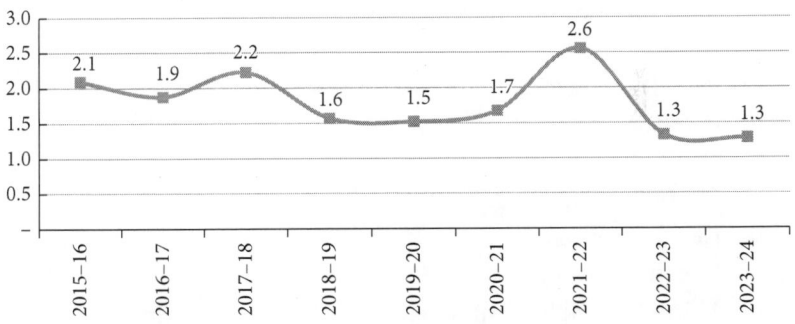

Addendum Chart 3.4 Growth in Per-Capita Social Transfer (%)

Source (Basic data): Department of Finance, Government of Canada and Authors' calculations

APPENDIX 3A.1

Revenue Sources

1. Personal Income Tax Revenues
2. Business Income Revenues
3. Capital Tax Revenues
4. General and Miscellaneous Sales Taxes
5. Tobacco Taxes
6. Gasoline Taxes
7. Diesel Fuel Taxes
8. Non-Commercial Vehicle Licences
9. Commercial Vehicle Licences
10. Alcoholic Beverage Revenues
11. Hospital and Medical Insurance Premiums
12. Race Track Taxes
13. Forestry Revenues
14. New Oil Revenues
15. Old Oil Revenues
16. Heavy Oil Revenues
17. Mined Oil Revenues
18. Third-Tier Oil Revenues
19. Heavy Third-Tier Revenues
20. Natural Gas Revenue
21. Sales of Crown Leases
22. Other Oil and Gas Revenues
23. Total Mineral Resources
24. Water Power Rentals
25. Insurance Premium Revenues
26. Payroll Taxes
27. Provincial Local Property Tax Revenues
28. Lottery Revenues
29. Other Games of Chance Revenues
30. Misc. Provincial-Local Property Tax Revenues
31. Shared Revenues: Offshore Activities/NFLD
32. Shared Revenues: Offshore Activities/N.S.
33. Shared Revenues: Preferred Share Dividend

Notes

1. The Court's interpretation is based on the notion that retailers are the collection agents of the governments and that they are merely collecting taxes that governments intend to impose directly on the consumers of the taxed goods. This interpretation has been extended to include VAT although the tax liability can occur well before the retail stage on the basis that ultimately the tax is intended to apply to consumers.

2. The arrangement regarding transfers of tax-points arrangement came when the old EPF system was operative.

3. This is as the system exists now. The fiscal system in Canada has undergone many changes. The pendulum has swung from excessive centralization, as was seen during the World War II period, to the present situation of more balanced distribution of assignment of taxes. Both in the political and economic spheres, Quebec has been responsible for pushing for more powers for the provinces.

4. In February 2003, the federal government agreed to permanently remove the equalization ceiling on a going-forward basis, starting with 2002–3. It remains in effect for earlier years. The floor is meant to protect provinces from undue fluctuations in the equalization payments.

5. Boothe (2001) finds using data for Saskatchewan over 1987–2001 that equalization payments increased the volatility of total revenues of the province as compared to the volatility of own revenues, and that there is little evidence to say that equalization improved the predictability of the Saskatchewan government revenues over the period.

6. Usher (2001) gives an example of taxation of Potash in Saskatchewan. He observes 'It is in the interest of that province not to tax that base at all because it could lose dollar for dollar. This is known as "rate tax-back problem". The federal government has adopted special rates to modify the disincentive from the rate tax-back and the base tax back problem. But such rules drive the equalization problem further and further away from the ideal section 36 (2) of the Canadian constitution.'

7. In the context of royalty of petroleum, Usher (2001) observes: 'Whenever additions to provincial revenue—for example, from royalties on petroleum— are dissipated through the loss of equalization payments, the province acquires an incentive to convert the additional revenue into a new form with less impact on equalization payments. It is said that the government of Newfoundland is anxious to have the Aluminum from Voisey Bay processed within Newfoundland not because it is efficient to do so, but because direct revenue from Aluminum production would accrue to the federal government through a reduction in Newfoundland's entitlement to equalization payments under the current Canadian formula. This is known as the base tax back problem.'

8. Usher (2001) observes: 'Property tax may be high or low depending in part on how the provincial government's services to the property are financed. Property tax is high to the extent that the cost of public expenditure on roads, water and electricity is covered by the revenue from the property tax'.

9. One aspect for which the Canadian equalization system has sometimes been criticized is its complexity. The system is actually simple for those who handle it, but their number is limited. The complexity arises from various ad hoc adjustments and special provisions that are made to make the numbers look 'right'. Usher (2001) observes 'Complexity in the equalization formula is a recipe for negotiation, compromise and conflict among the provinces that stand for gain or lose according to how the final formula is chosen'.

10. The expression in equation (3.5) can be written as

$$Ei = [\textstyle\sum_j TR_j][N_i / MB_c][MB_c / N_c - MB_i / N_i]$$

The term a_c in equation (3.7) is equal to $[\textstyle\sum_j TR_j]/[MB_c]$, which is the effective tax rate with respect to the macro-base.

11. The thirteen problems listed by Statistics Canada (see Aubut and Vaillancourt (2001)) in using GDP as a macro indicator of taxable capacity are:

 (i)   classification of some government activities as intermediate of fiscal production
 (ii) inappropriate method of valuing services and output of banks
 (iii) treatment of interest on the public debt as transfer rather than fiscal expenditure
 (iv) mix of units in the personal and unincorporated business sector
 (v)   treatment of consumer durables as fixed assets
 (vi) non inclusion of capital gains and losses
 (vii) non inclusion of non reproducible natural resources
 (viii) treatment of trusted pension funds. While these are considered theoretical problems with the concept of GDP itself there are some problems that are considered measurement problems
 (ix) difficulty of data reconciliation for establishments and enterprises
 (x)   lack of real income estimation
 (xi) inaccurate estimates of consumption by sector
 (xii) inappropriate treatment of commercial buildings and industrial equipment leasing arrangements
 (xiii) non-inclusion of the underground economy.
       Aubut and Vaillancourt (2001) consider only five of these as relevant in the context of equalization. They suggest some additional items. Their main recommendations relate to: (i) inclusion of value of capital gains and losses, (ii) inclusion of the value of the underground economy, (iii) value of household services, (iv) value of volunteer work, (v) value of non-reproducible resources, (vi) value of revenues of pensions, (vii) value of imputed items, and (viii) income from the population living on reserves. The first four call for additions to the officially estimated GDP and the latter four (items v to viii) require to be subtracted from the official GDP. These changes affect the calculations of equalization entitlements in different ways. The most adversely affected province would be Prince Edward Island and the most important element of adjustment is the imputation for household production.

12. Defining: z = tax points transferred to provinces under the EPF arrangement q_i = per capita tax base of the ith province q_0 = per capita base of Ontario c_i = per capita cash transfer under CHST to the ith province c_0 = per capita cash transfer to Ontario c^* = per capita expenditure on CHST The per capita cash entitlement to the ith province can be written as

$$c_i = c^* - z.q_i c_i = c^* - zq_0 + zq_0 - zq_i c_i = [c^* - zq_0] + z[q_0 - q_i]$$

The second term is zero for Ontario, since in its case. Hence, Ontario gets only as its per capita tax transfer. All other provinces get a positive amount under the second term of the expression given above since $q_i < q_0$ in their case. This leads to equalization implicit in the calculation of CHST transfers linked to the tax points component.

4

Fiscal Federalism in Practice

Australia and India[*]

The working of fiscal federalism in Australia is now more than a hundred years old. It was in 1901 that Australia became a federation, when six separate British colonies came together to form a Commonwealth, becoming its states in consequence. These states are Queensland, New South Wales (NSW), Southern Australia (SA), Victoria, Western Australia (WA), and Tasmania. In addition, there are two territorial administrations, that is, the Northern Territory (NT) and the Australian Capital Territory (ACT). Australia's federal fiscal structure is characterized by a high level of vertical imbalance, an elaborate system of horizontal fiscal equalization (HFE), and numerous specific purpose payments (SPPs). The centrepiece of the Australian system of fiscal transfers is HFE, which looks into both revenue and expenditure sides of the state budgets and calculates revenue and expenditure 'disabilities' that account for departures from a pure equal per capita distribution of the shareable amounts. Australian equalization calculations, cast in terms of 'disabilities' rather than factors, and state 'relativities' rather than the more usual term of state shares, are distinct in their presentational scheme. The Australian fiscal transfer system is also unique in having developed an institutional framework for five-yearly reviews and annual updates of the relativities and also for having developed techniques of micro assessments, particularly on the expenditure side.

Currently, the Australian system of fiscal transfers is going through a major transition with the introduction of a comprehensive Goods and Services Tax (GST), which is in the nature of a Value Added Tax. The

---

[*] Originally published as 'Fiscal Transfers in Australia: Review and Relevance to India', *Economic and Political Weekly*, Vol. 39, No. 33, 14 August 2004, pp. 3709–22.

introduction of GST has had a far reaching influence on the vertical and horizontal sharing of resources among the Commonwealth and the state governments. The GST is collected by the Commonwealth Government and fully passed on to the states. It by itself accounts for almost the entire untied transfers, and since it has come in replacement of several state-level taxes, its distribution significantly affects the availability of resources to the states. The Commonwealth Grants Commission (CGC), which is the main institution that makes recommendations about the horizontal fiscal transfers, has made a new set of recommendations in its 2004 Review for the years covering the period after 2003–4. There is an extensive contemporary debate in Australia about the relevance and implications of the manner in which the principle of HFE has been applied, particularly after the introduction of the GST, and also the way in which the SPPs have proliferated. It is some indication of the disenchantment of some of the states that three states, that is, New South Wales, Victoria, and Western Australia—the so-called better off and 'donor states'—jointly appointed a Review Committee comprising two eminent experts, Ross Garnaut and Vince FitzGerald, to assess the current system of transfers in terms of economic efficiency, equity, simplicity, and transparency. The disenchantment reached such a peak that after the 2004 Review, New South Wales took out an advertisement in the newspapers asking the citizens of the state to send a telegram to the Prime Minister expressing their dissatisfaction. The CGC itself observes in its Report containing the 2004 Review that the Commission 'is supportive of a far reaching review of equalization, including its underlying purposes and objectives' and that the Commission itself did not go into these questions because these were not part of its terms of reference. The transfers system in India is facing similar questions today.

Australia's system of HFE and the related debates are relevant to other fiscal transfer systems including that of India. In this chapter, we examine the working of the Australian system with a view to drawing comparisons with the corresponding Indian fiscal transfer system and deriving appropriate lessons. This chapter begins by looking at the assignment of revenues and responsibilities in Australia. It then summarizes the institutional arrangements in Australia that play a key role in the working of the federal fiscal arrangements. It also looks at the state economies in Australia and their demographic features, drawing appropriate comparisons with India, and then examines the extent of vertical imbalance in Australia as well as India. It attempts to review the arrangements of HFE, highlighting the use of revenue and cost disabilities in deriving the states' shares in the overall untied transfers. A summary of the key features of the Australian system of fiscal transfers focusing on practices that can be adopted with benefit in the Indian context has also been provided.

Assignment of Powers and Functions

In Australia, the functions of the Commonwealth Government relate to foreign affairs, foreign trade, defence, immigration, currency, and banking. The states have responsibilities in respect of public safety, housing, transport, and community and social services. The state governments also have jurisdiction over local governments. Responsibilities such as maintaining the road system, recreational and cultural services, and public services like water supply and sewerage have been delegated to the local governments.

The Commonwealth Government has the power to levy all taxes and the states have concurrent powers except in the case of customs and excise duty. At the inception of the federation, the Constitution was so framed as to give exclusive powers on the customs and excise revenues to the Commonwealth Government. Further, since 1908, the High Court has consistently interpreted these powers more and more in favour of the Commonwealth Government by extending the definition of excises. In particular, states have not been permitted to levy sales taxes. The local bodies depend mainly on property taxes.

Prior to the taking over of the income tax by the Commonwealth Government, states were raising more than 70 per cent of the total income tax revenue collected in Australia, way back in 1938–9. Ceding access to this revenue source to the Commonwealth Government during the war years completely reversed the relative position of the Commonwealth and state governments in revenue-raising powers. With the Uniform Income Taxation Act of 1942 eliminating the role of states in raising income tax, and subsequent court rulings closing sales and excise taxation fields to the states, most of the important taxes on individuals, enterprises, and non-residents stand assigned to the Commonwealth Government. With the GST also being collected by the Commonwealth Government as a result of the Intergovernmental Agreement (IGA) in 2000, its domination of the tax field is near-complete. The states' most important own tax revenue sources are the payroll tax that is levied on company payrolls, taxes on financial and capital transactions, and taxes on gambling, insurance, and motor vehicles. The states also employ franchise fees and taxes on excisable goods converted into service taxes for constitutional reasons. Local governments are given taxes on immovable property at the municipal rates.

The IGA, finalized in 2000, was aimed at achieving a new national tax system which is not distortionary and which also improves the financial position of the state governments. These reforms have led to the implementation of GST, which is presently set at the uniform rate of 10 per cent. There is some ambiguity as to whether the GST should be considered a federal tax or a state tax. The Commonwealth Government itself has argued that the GST should be regarded as a state tax, which it collects on behalf of the state governments and fully returns to them. The Australian Bureau of Statistics treats the GST as a Commonwealth tax. This seems appropriate because the Commonwealth Government is not collecting the GST on behalf of the states and returning it to them on the basis of derivation. The Commonwealth Government has itself given up the wholesale sales tax and it is using the GST revenues for distribution among states on equalization principles. The GST revenue sharing arrangements do not have constitutional force although these are based on the IGA.

Table 4.1 shows that the Commonwealth Government collects 76 per cent of all government revenues. About 20 per cent is collected by the state governments and the remaining by the local governments. This high degree of centralization in raising revenues arises primarily from the fact that more than 50 per cent of all tax revenues are raised as income tax followed by the GST, which contributes about 11 per cent of the total, and excise and levies that contribute a little more than 8 per cent, all being with the Commonwealth Government.

Table 4.2 shows the extent of centralization in expenditures, that is, the situation after transfers. About 52 per cent of expenditures are incurred by the Commonwealth Government in total expenditures. There are several fields that the Commonwealth Government co-occupies with

Table 4.1 Own Source Revenues by Governments, 2000–1

	Commonwealth Government	State Government	Local Governments	Multi-jurisdictional
Total taxes *of which*	76.35	19.73	3.33	0.59
Income taxes	50.59	0.00	0.00	0.00
Payroll taxes	1.50	3.98	0.00	0.00
Taxes on property	0.01	5.20	2.67	0.00
Goods and services tax	10.81	0.00	0.00	0.00
Excise and levies	8.15	0.00	0.00	0.00
Taxes on international trade	1.93	0.00	0.00	0.00
Income from GBEs	1.23	2.24	0.00	0.01

Source: Australian Bureau of Statistics, Taxation Revenue, and Government Finance statistics.

the state governments, particularly those relating to health, housing and community amenities, and some economic sectors like fuel and energy, agriculture, forestry, fishing, mining, manufacturing, construction, and so on.

Table 4.3 shows the corresponding picture for India using 2000–1 data. Apart from defence, the central government has a share higher than states in industries and transport. In most of the social and economic services, it is the states that have the larger shares of expenditures.

Institutional Arrangements

The framework of institutions dealing with financial and other matters between the central and the sub-national governments is critical for the successful functioning of centre-state financial relations. In India, apart from the constitutional provision for a Finance Commission, there are other institutions like the Planning Commission, the Inter-State Council, and the National Development Council. In Australia, there are five

Table 4.2 Australia: Inter-jurisdictional Shares in Expenditures, 2000–1

	Commonwealth Government	State government	Local governments	Multi-jurisdictional*	Total all-government expenditure ($million)
General public services	51	40	9	1	19,046
Defence	100	0	0	0	11,327
Public order and safety	14	82	3	0	10,745
Education	5	69	0	26	35,777
Health	46	53	1	0	41,179
Social security and welfare	91	8	1	0	72,059
Housing and community amenities	28	46	26	0	10,583
Recreation and culture	31	41	29	0	6,592
Fuel and energy	70	30	0	0	3,760
Agriculture, forestry, and fishing	45	55	0	0	3,857
Mining, manufacturing, andconstruction	55	33	12	0	1,876
Transport and communications	15	67	18	0	15,549
Other economic affairs	46	50	3	0	6,586
Total	52	39	5	4	238,936

Source: Australian Bureau of Statistics as quoted in Madden (2002).

Note: *This category includes only universities.

Table 4.3 Relative Share of Centre and States in India: Selected Heads

	Share of		
	Centre (per cent)	States (per cent)	Combined (Amount in Rs crore)
Defence services	100.0	0.0	49,622.0
Fiscal services	46.0	54.0	9,014.9
Administrative services	35.2	64.8	34,897.4
Organs of State	37.6	62.4	4,260.7
Pension and other retirement benefits	36.6	63.4	38,818.7
Education, art and culture	11.1	88.9	63,756.0
Medical and public health, water supply, and sanitation	11.5	88.5	24,360.4
Family welfare	23.5	76.5	2,826.3
Housing	56.6	43.4	4,156.2
Agriculture and allied services	32.4	67.6	35,140.4
Industry and minerals less DCUs	57.8	42.2	6,762.2
Power, irrigation and flood control	11.8	88.2	33,799.2
Transport and communications	51.3	48.7	24,492.2
Public works	17.6	82.4	4,006.6

Source: Indian Public Finance Statistics.

Note: The centre's expenditures are derived by deducting state expenditures from the combined amounts. DCUs stands for Departmental Commercial Undertakings.

bodies that play a key role in the management of the federal fiscal system. These are described below.

Council of Australian Governments

This council consists of the prime minister, state premiers, and chief ministers of the territories. This Council has superseded the Premiers' Conference that earlier decided about the vertical transfers. As now there is an agreement to transfer the full amount of GST to the states, the volume of untied transfers to that extent gets determined automatically.

Ministerial Council for Commonwealth-State Financial Relations

This council, which is also known as the Treasurers' Conference, provides a platform for an annual meeting of the treasurers (finance ministers) of the states and territories to discuss grant allocations to the states (until recently this was done at the Premiers' Conference).

Special Purpose Ministerial Councils

These Councils consist of the Commonwealth and state ministers of a particular portfolio. These Councils look after a wide range of SPPs.

Commonwealth Grants Commission

The main body entrusted with the task of making recommendations regarding the horizontal transfers of sharable resources in Australia is the CGC. The CGC is an advisory body that responds to its terms of reference. It does not have powers to initiate and pursue inquiries on its own. In recent years, the main references have sought advice on per capita relativities for distributing the distributable pool of resources among the states and territories.

The Commission was established in 1933 to assess claims made by the states for financial assistance (special grants) under section 96 of the Constitution. At various times, Queensland, Western Australia, South Australia, Tasmania, and the NT had sought special grants.

Various issues are referred to the CGC under sections 16, 16A, and 16AA of the Commonwealth Grants Commission Act 1973. Although references to the CGC are provided by the Minister for Finance and Administration, their content is usually decided in negotiations between the Commonwealth and state governments, conducted largely through their treasuries. While the resulting Commission reports are provided formally to the Commonwealth Government, they are made available to the states immediately thereafter. The relativities recommended in those reports are considered at the annual Treasurers' Conference.

The CGC defines its own role as 'an independent, impartial, and authoritative arbiter in relation to distributional aspects of fiscal federalism in Australia' (Commonwealth Grants Commission (1983), p. 160). The Commission looks at the state budgets in a comprehensive manner and looks at all needs, whether on current or capital account. There is no fragmentation in approach as is the case in India where expenditures are divided into revenue and capital accounts, and further into plan and non-plan categories, with two bodies, that is, Finance and Planning Commissions looking after different segments of the expenditure requirements.

Unlike in India, where the Finance Commission looks at both the vertical and horizontal dimensions of transfers, the CGC does not look into the issue of vertical imbalance. With the introduction of GST, the vertical transfers are determined by the amount of actual collections of the GST, supplemented by the Health Care Grants (HCGs). Prior to the GST, the pool of transfer consisted of Financial Assistance Grants (FAGs) and the HCGs. In addition, the Commonwealth Government pays SPPs, which are conditional grants aimed at specific sectors. The SPPs are broadly comparable to the centrally sponsored schemes in India.

For the 2004 Review, the terms of reference asked the CGC to review the methods used to determine and report upon the question of the per capita relativities for distribution of GST revenue grants and HCGs which the Commission would regard as appropriate to apply after 2003-4.[1] The Commission was also asked to continue to prepare its assessments on the basis that SPPs quarantined, that is, excluded in the previous terms of reference, should continue to not affect the per capita relativities.[2]

In preparing its assessment, the Commission was asked to have regard for the need to observe policy neutrality in relation to a reduction in the level of an SPP resulting from non-compliance by a state or territory with the conditions of the payment. Any such reductions should not directly influence the Commission's assessments of the per capita relativities. The Commission was asked to prepare its assessments on a basis consistent with the Commonwealth Government's intention that specified components[3] of the Australian Health Care Agreements between the Commonwealth Government and a state should not directly influence the per capita relativities.

The Australian Loan Council

Australia is unique among federations in that it has a mechanism in the form of the Australian Loan Council to coordinate borrowing by the Commonwealth and state governments. Effective control of public sector borrowings is a major concern for all federations as government borrowing is linked with monetary policy and macroeconomic demand management. Unrestrained borrowing can compromise fiscal discipline by softening the budget constraints of governments at all levels. The Loan Council was set up by the Financial Agreement of 1927, as ratified by a constitutional amendment in 1928, to provide an effective control of borrowings by the state governments and state business enterprises Australian Loan Council (1993).

The Loan Council's origins lie in the 1920s when the Commonwealth and state governments competed for funds on the capital markets. The Commonwealth Government wanted to refinance war debt while the states wanted to fund infrastructure programmes. To resolve this and other conflicts, the May 1923 Premiers' Conference agreed to form a voluntary Loan Council. The Loan Council is formally a Commonwealth-State Ministerial Council comprising the Commonwealth Treasurer as chairman, and State and Territory Treasurers. The *Financial Agreement Act 1928* provided among other things for:

1. the Loan Council to regulate borrowing by the Commonwealth and state governments,
2. the Commonwealth Government to borrow on the states' behalf,
3. limits on the states' borrowing powers,
4. the Commonwealth and state governments to contribute to the National Debt Sinking Fund to redeem debt, and
5. the Commonwealth Government to provide grants to the states to help them meet interest payments and Sinking Fund contributions.

The 1928 Financial Agreement has been altered on a number of occasions to take account of new developments. The 1928 Agreement did not encompass borrowing by Commonwealth and state semi-governmental and local authorities. As the Loan Council's restrictions became stringent, the states found ways of circumventing the Council by using statutory authorities for borrowing. In 1936, a voluntary 'Gentleman's Agreement' was negotiated to bring such borrowing under the supervision of the Loan Council.

A major change in the role of the Loan Council took place in the 1950s when the Commonwealth Government increasingly saw it as an instrument of macroeconomic policy Corden (1997). Early in the 1950s, Australia had faced strong inflationary pressures, and the Commonwealth Treasurer advocated reducing Council-approved borrowing to ease these pressures. The Commonwealth Government's influence over the Loan Council was strengthened by the fact that the Government undertook to provide funds to the states if they were unable to raise, through the issue of securities, any borrowing that the Loan Council had approved. In effect, the Commonwealth Government agreed to underwrite state borrowing.

The Gentlemen's Agreement was also bypassed when some states used 'unconventional' financing techniques such as financial leases to circumvent its restrictions. The states also established borrowing authorities like the New South Wales Treasury Corporation, which was used to circumvent the Loan Council borrowing limits. In 1984, the Loan Council suspended the Gentlemen's Agreement and replaced it with Global Borrowing Limits. This 'global approach', among other things, limited the level of all new borrowings, conventional and unconventional, by Commonwealth and state authorities.

However, the global approach also broke down. A major reason was the increasing use of sophisticated financing techniques that eroded the Loan Council's effectiveness. In December 1992, the Loan Council meeting adopted new arrangements for monitoring and reporting.

Under these arrangements, which came into effect in 1993–4, each jurisdiction nominated a Loan Council Allocation, which was based on its net borrowings as indicated by its deficit/surplus. The arrangements also changed the way in which borrowings were allocated among the states. Previously, the global limit was allocated by a formula based on state population. But this formula did not take account of a state's particular fiscal circumstances. The Loan Council therefore considered the nominations having regard to each jurisdiction's fiscal position and 'reasonable' infrastructure needs as well as the macroeconomic implications of the total nominations.

The *Financial Agreement Act 1994,* which came into effect on 1 July 1995, includes changes agreed at the June 1992 Loan Council meeting. These changes:

1. removed the requirement for Commonwealth and state borrowings to be approved under the Agreement,
2. removed the Commonwealth Government's explicit power to borrow on the states' behalf,
3. abolished the restriction on a state's borrowing through the issue of securities in their own names, and
4. included the ACT and NT as members (they previously had observer status).

These changes, particularly the removal of the requirement for approval of borrowing, constitute a major restructuring of the Loan Council powers. Current arrangements seek to emphasize transparency of public sector finances, through financial market scrutiny of proposed borrowing to restrict borrowing to prudent levels. The Loan Council meets once a year to consider the nominations, having regard to each jurisdiction's fiscal position.

The Loan Council's allocations are not binding in a legal sense. According to its own statement the Loan Council has moved from an approach based on rigid compliance to that of a credible and transparent framework for the allocation of net borrowings. To ensure that borrowings are consistent with the states' fiscal and debt positions and the nation's overall macroeconomic strategy, the Loan Council has implemented a joint Commonwealth/state government forecasting exercise. The National Fiscal Outlook contained nationally agreed debt targets, and states' nominations were considered in that light. This arrangement continued until 1998. Since then, each government's own forecasts have been used to set their targets.

Governments are required to present three-year forward estimates as well as actual outcomes within a uniform presentation framework. Discipline is now exercised by using ratings from international rating agencies, and the majority of states have very good ratings. Most states are now in budget surplus.

Australian States: Population and State Economies

Australia is the world's smallest continent but the sixth largest country, with its population concentrated along the eastern and southeastern coasts. Its arable land is only 6.88 per cent of its total area. Australia is rich in several minerals, particularly, bauxite, coal, and iron ore. In terms of 2001 figures, the share of agriculture in the economy was only 3 per cent, with industry having a share of 26 per cent, and services about 71 per cent. As shown by Table 4.4, New South Wales and Victoria are the two biggest states in terms of population. The total population of Australia is about 20 million. In contrast, India has twenty-eight states and seven Union Territories and its population size is more than fifty times as large as that of Australia.

Table 4.4 Australia: Mean Resident Population: 1997–8 to 2002–3

Share of States and Total Population						(per cent)
Province	1997–8	1998–9	1999–2000	2000–1	2001–2	2002–3
New South Wales	33.89	33.88	33.87	33.87	33.84	33.71
Victoria	24.81	24.78	24.76	24.76	24.74	24.74
Queensland	18.38	18.46	18.55	18.64	18.79	19.00
Western Australia	9.72	9.76	9.78	9.79	9.80	9.81
Southern Australia	7.98	7.94	7.89	7.82	7.76	7.71
Tasmania	2.54	2.51	2.48	2.45	2.42	2.40
Australian Capital Territory	1.66	1.65	1.65	1.64	1.64	1.63
Northern Territory	1.01	1.02	1.02	1.02	1.01	1.00
Australia	100	100	100	100	100	100
Australia (million)	18.61	18.82	19.04	19.28	19.53	19.76

Source: Commonwealth Grants Commission, 2004 Review, supporting information.

Table 4.5 Australia: Gross State Product at Current Prices

	1997–8	2002–3	1997–8	2002–3
Province	$ Per Capita	$ Per Capita	Relative to Average	
New South Wales	31,837	40,127	105.65	105.18
Victoria	30,433	39,058	100.99	102.38
Queensland	26,623	33,782	88.35	88.55
Western Australia	33,939	42,269	112.63	110.79
Southern Australia	26,297	32,294	87.27	84.65
Tasmania	22,467	27,100	74.56	71.03
Australian Capital Territory	36,389	47,438	120.76	124.34
Northern Territory	32,208	45,870	106.88	120.23
AustraliaRatio of Max pcGSP to Minimum	30,134	38,151	100.00	100.00
Among states only	1.51	1.56		
Among states and territories	1.62	1.75		

Source: Commonwealth Grants Commission, 2004 Review, supporting information.

In terms of per capita gross state product (GSP), the richest states, leaving out the territories, are Western Australia followed by New South Wales and Victoria. While economic activities are more concentrated in NSW and Victoria, Western Australia is richer in mineral resources. The relatively less well-off states are South Australia, Queensland, and Tasmania. Table 4.5 shows the state-wise per capita GSP. The ratio of the highest per capita GSP to lowest per capita GSP among states (Western Australia/Tasmania) is only 1.5. This ratio, when the territories are included is 1.6. The corresponding ratios in India's case are far higher, showing that difference in fiscal capacities is much lower in Australia compared to that in India.

The main states which serve as 'donor' states in the exercise of redistribution through the fiscal transfer mechanism are NSW and Victoria (see Table 4.5). Such redistribution is relatively easier to handle as most of the population is concentrated in these two states. In contrast, the recipient states have lower populations. Such redistribution is far more difficult in

India where a large proportion of the population is concentrated in the low fiscal capacity states. Recognizing this feature in Australia, Mathews (1993) observed, 'Fiscal equalization is achieved more easily if the states with low fiscal capacity also have relatively small populations, because transfers involving small per capita payments from the federal (or other granting) government are translated into large per capita grants for the recipient governments.'

Vertical Transfers and Vertical Imbalance

Unconditional general revenue assistance as well as specific purpose grants are given to the states according to Section 96 of the Constitution. General revenue assistance is given for recurrent as well as for capital purposes. Specific Purpose Payments in the form of recurrent or capital grants are given for specific state functions like social services, including health, education, social security and welfare, economic services (roads, transport, industry assistance, water resources), and other services (housing and urban renewal, regional development, disaster relief, and debt charges). Three types of payments can be distinguished: (i) payments to states for funding direct state outlays, (ii) payments through the states to be passed on to other bodies or individuals, and (iii) direct payments to local governments.

The evolution of the extent and shape of vertical transfers in Australia in more recent years can be seen in terms of four distinct phases, that is, prior to 1976 when general revenue assistance was given to states, 1976 to 1985 when revenue-sharing arrangements were put in place, 1986 to 1997 when the system of FAGs was reintroduced, and after the IGA in 2000, which provides for the sharing of the GST revenues.

Phase 1: Up to 1976: General Revenue Assistance

Prior to 1976, general revenue assistance in the form of FAGs was given to each state, determined largely by a formula subject to variation through Commonwealth-state government negotiations. Financial assistance grants were increased annually (from 1959 to 1976) by a formula stressing for each state three factors: population changes, average wage increases, and a so-called betterment factor designed to allow the states to expand their relative level of services.

Phase 2: 1976–85: Revenue-Sharing Arrangements

In 1976, as part of the Fraser Government's 'New Federalism' policy, the untied FAGs were replaced by 'tax sharing entitlements', whereby the states received a fixed percentage of Commonwealth Government personal income tax receipts, distributed on the basis of existing per capita relativities. Access to personal income taxation was reopened to the states. However, the states declined to impose personal income taxes of their own and the Commonwealth Government did not make room for them by reducing Commonwealth personal income tax. A state that took up the option would have had to impose an additional tax or surcharge.

Sharing was first adopted for the income tax alone. The pool was formed by applying first a fixed proportion and later an increasing proportion of the tax proceeds collected in the states. This led to the states' revenues being determined by factors similar to those used for FAGs before. Later, revenue sharing was extended to federal tax receipts as a whole, which somewhat lowered the rate of growth of the states' revenue pool.

Phase 3: 1986–97: Reintroduction of FAGs

Financial Assistance Grants were reintroduced in 1986. The size of pool was determined by the percentage growth rate set to reflect specified real changes in assistance, which could be negative when fiscal restraint is called for. Since 1990, the Commonwealth Government has agreed to maintain the real value of such grants in order to provide greater certainty in the funding of the state budgets.

The extent of vertical fiscal imbalance between revenue powers and expenditure responsibilities in the Federation increased substantially in 1997, when the states lost the capacity to impose business franchise fees on liquor, tobacco, and petroleum products. This resulted from a High

Court decision which held that such fees are in the nature of excises and reserved for the Commonwealth Government. The Commonwealth Government compensated the states for their lost revenue by increasing its own excise on those products and returning the revenue to the states in the form of a new component of untied grants.

Phase 4: GST Sharing and the IGA, 1999

The Intergovernmental Reform Agreement (IGA) on the Reform of Commonwealth-State Financial Relations was signed in April 1999. It dealt with the GST-based reforms in the tax system. This agreement was revised in May 1999 as a result of negotiations between the federal government and the Democrats. The final agreement provided for the levy of GST at the uniform rate of 10 per cent. Concurrently, the federal government abolished the wholesale sales tax and the state governments abolished the financial institutions duty, bed taxes (in NSW and NT), stamp duty on quoted marketable securities, and the debits tax. It was also agreed that several remaining stamp duties would be taken up for review in 2005.

The IGA also provided for the replacement of the FAGs by GST revenue sharing. The overall package of transfers now consists of the GST revenues to the extent of 100 per cent, HCGs, and SPPs.

The GST and related arrangements have increased the vertical imbalance in raising revenues because some state taxes have been abolished while increasing the scope of fiscal equalization because the overall amount of untied transfers is larger. In order to smoothen the transition, particularly for the states who lose more from the abolished taxes than gain from the larger divisible pool, provision has been made for giving a Guaranteed Minimum Amount (GMA) in the form of Budget Balancing Assistance (BBA), consisting of interest free loans and grants to cover the difference between the share in GST revenue and the GMA. Accordingly, the CGC has been asked to calculate two sets of relativities, one based on the sharing of the GST-HCG pool, and the other on the earlier FAGs on the assumption that the old system continued. Appendix 4A.1 gives the difference between FAG and GST relativities as assessed in the 2004 Review. The relativities differ

Table 4.6 Vertical Fiscal Imbalance in Australia: Selected Years

	1993–4	1995–6	1996–7	1997–8	1999–2000	2000–1
Own Source Revenue (%) Relative Shares						
Commonwealth	72.6	73.6	73.1	73.1	74.8	76.4
States and Local governments	27.4	26.4	26.9	26.9	25.2	23.7
Own Purpose Expenditures (%) Relative Shares						
Commonwealth	56.4	57.8	57.1	55.6	55	52.0
States and Local Governments	43.6	42.2	42.9	44.4	45	48.0
Vertical Fiscal Imbalance Ratio						
Commonwealth	1.29	1.27	1.28	1.31	1.36	1.47
States and Local Governments	0.63	0.63	0.63	0.61	0.56	0.49

Source: Adapted from Collins (2000) for 1993–4 to 1997–8, Searle (2002) for 1999–2000, and Madden (2002) for 2000–1.

Note: Vertical fiscal imbalance ratio is equal to the ratio of share of own source revenue to share of own purpose expenditure. This is an appropriate measure of vertical imbalance in countries where expenditures equal revenue and there is little borrowing.

because, among other things, states have given up some resources as part of the IGA and the amount under distribution through GST is larger. Analysing the impact of the IGA, Collins (2000) observes: 'Since the new arrangements will involve the application of newly calculated GST relativities to a GST funds pool that will be in the order of 35 per cent higher than the FAG pool, any inequities in the HFE process will tend to be magnified over time.'

Table 4.6 looks at the vertical fiscal imbalance at the level of raising resources in Australia. The Commonwealth Government raised nearly 29 per cent more revenues than what it required to spend in 1993–4. This vertical imbalance in raising revenues increased after the introduction of GST. In 2000–1, the Commonwealth Government raised nearly 40 per cent more revenue than it required to spend on its own. This vertical imbalance has been accompanied by high degree of centralization in expenditures, with the Commonwealth Government spending about 56–7 per cent of total expenditure up to 1999–2000, and 52 per cent after the

Table 4.7 Vertical Fiscal Imbalance in India: Selected Years

	1993–4	1995–6	1996–7	1997–8	1999–2000	2000–1
Revenue Receipts: Relative Share of Centre and States in Accrual (%)						
Centre	60.65	60.67	62.81	60.80	61.60	59.24
States	39.35	39.33	37.19	39.20	38.40	40.76
Expenditures: Relative Share of Centre and States after Transfers (%)						
Centre	42.52	42.80	42.47	43.49	43.17	41.67
States	57.48	57.20	57.53	56.51	56.83	58.33
Vertical Imbalance Ratio						
Centre	1.43	1.42	1.48	1.40	1.43	1.42
States	0.68	0.69	0.65	0.69	0.68	0.70

Source: Indian Public Finance Statistics, Government of India.

Note: In the case of receipts from the total interest receipts paid by the states to the centre are netted out. The relative share of the centre and the states in the total expenditure is also influenced by their respective shares in borrowing.

introduction of GST. The share of Commonwealth expenditure in total expenditure has come down in 2000–1 to 52 per cent.

In contrast, as indicated in Table 4.7, in India, nearly 60 per cent of total revenues are raised by the central government and its share in the combined total expenditure of the centre and states is about 43 per cent. Thus, both in raising revenues and incurring expenditures India is less centralized than Australia.

Horizontal Transfers: System of Fiscal Equalization

The main task of the Commission is to advise the Commonwealth Government on the distribution among the states and territories of the revenue from the GST and CHGs. The Commission operates such that a full Review of state shares including the methods used to calculate them is undertaken every five years, and in the intermediate years shares are updated annually, using the latest available figures and the methods of the last Review. The Reviews have been carried out in 1981, 1982, 1985, 1988, 1993, 1999, and 2004. The most recent Review was undertaken in 2010. The review process is aimed at ensuring that the relativities reflect changes over time in the circumstances of the states, developments in public administration, and trends in service delivery.

The heart of the horizontal transfers system is fiscal equalization, which is defined by the CGC as follows: 'State governments should receive funding from the pool of goods and services tax revenue and HCGs such that, if each made the same effort to raise revenue from its own sources and operated at the same level of efficiency, each would have the capacity to provide services at the same standard.' The Australian equalization differs from the Canadian equalization due to the reference to efficiency and standard of services. The Canadian system makes reference only to equalization in fiscal capacity. In Australia, fiscal equalization looks at both the revenue and expenditure sides.

The CGC makes reference to 'three pillars' supporting and guiding the application of equalization. These are capacity equalization, internal service standards, and policy neutrality. Policy neutrality refers to the consideration that a state's own policies or choices about services should not directly influence the level of grants it receives. The CGC's calculations are based on all-state averages so that these may reflect average efficiency. These are also treated as ensuring policy neutrality, being the result of policy decisions of all states. There is a comprehensive coverage of the services provided by the states and the revenues raised by them.

Equalization: From Disabilities to Relativities

The CGC recognizes that since states have differential fiscal capacities and different demographic, economic, and physical circumstances, there will be differences in their revenue-raising capacities and relative costs of providing services. Relative differences that are beyond the control of individual state governments are called 'disabilities'. Standards of services as well as the disabilities are measured relative to the all-state position.

The first step in the equalization exercise is the preparation of the standard budget. The standards are equal to all-state averages in expenditures as well as revenues. The Commission does not consider any exogenous targets or norms. Any departure from the average per capita expenditure needs to be justified on account of cost disabilities.

The equalization budget brings together all expense and revenue categories of state budgets. The per capita expense for each service that the state would incur if it were to provide the Australian average standard of service is calculated. On the revenue side, the per capita revenue each state would raise if it applied the average revenue effort to its revenue base is calculated. Expenditure assessment adjusts the standard expenses to allow for the effects of disabilities. Disabilities are broadly classified as use disabilities and cost disabilities, according to whether they affect the rate of use or the cost of each unit of service. Use disabilities reflect differences between states in the use of services as a result of factors such as population characteristics and the availability of private services. Cost disabilities are influences that affect the cost per unit of service provided to particular groups or places, for example, large cities or remote areas. Cultural and communication factors can increase the costs of providing some services to people from culturally and linguistically diverse backgrounds. Some cost disabilities arise due to variation in inter-state prices and diseconomies of scale.

On the revenue side, tax bases are generally measured using the value of transaction in each state that would be taxed under the average tax policy. For example, the value of the payroll tax is the estimated annual value of payrolls above a threshold level paid by the private sector businesses and most public trading enterprises. Table 4.8 gives some of the major revenue and expenditure side factors taken into account in the assessment of disabilities.

A mathematical presentation of the equalization methodology can be provided, using symbols defined as below:

e_i = standardized per capita expenditure of state i; γ_i = expenditure disability of state i

r_i = standardized per capita revenue of state i; ρ_i = revenue disability of state i

o_i = per capita special purpose payment of state i

d_s = per capita budget surplus; $d_i = d_s$ for all states

N_i = population of state i; $\sum N_i$ = population of all states

Subscript 's' indicates corresponding numbers for the all-state averages.

Table 4.8 Main Factors Affecting Revenue and Cost Disabilities

Revenue Bases	Factors Affecting Expenditures
GSP per capita	Share of Australian population
Payrolls of large businesses	Proportion of population aged 65 years or over
Sales of real estate	Proportion of population who are indigenous
Value of commercial/ industrial land	Proportion of population resident in centres of 50,000 or more
Value of mining production	Proportion of population resident in remote areas
	Proportion of population enrolled in government schools
	Proportion of population with low income
	Relative average weekly earnings
	Relative length of arterial roads

Source: Commonwealth Grants Commission, 2004 Review.

The per capita all-state average grant is given by

$$g_s = e_s - r_s + d_s - o_s \tag{4.1}$$

The per capita grant to state i is given by

$$g_i = e_i - r_i + d_i - o_i \tag{4.2}$$

Here, e_i and r_i refer to standardized expenditure and revenue for state i, d_i is the standard budget surplus, which is common for all states and o_i is the given SPP. All standardizations are made in relation to corresponding all-state averages which provides the standard, and the relevant expenditure and revenue terms can be written as

$$e_i = \gamma_i e_s, \, r_i = \rho_i r_s \tag{4.3}$$

For a given state the standardized expenditure and revenue will be the summation of standardized expenditures on different categories and standardized revenues from different sources. The SPPs are considered exogenously determined. The CGC determines first the total grants and derives the untied grants by deducting the SPPs (o_i) that are treated by inclusion. Grants inclusive of the SPPs may be written as g^* and per capita untied grants as g, where

$$g_i^* = g_i + o_i \qquad (4.4)$$

There are three ways in which the derivation of the share in GST-HCG transfers can be presented: the standardized model version, the needs version, and the normative gap version. For this purpose, we focus on g_i^*, from which g_i is derived by deducting the SPP grants.

Standardized Model Version

In this version, we write the state-specific terms as ratios to the all-state averages. Substituting the terms in equation (4.3) in equation (4.2), we have

$$g_i^* = \gamma_i \, e_s - \rho_i \, r_s + d_s \qquad (4.5)$$

and
$$g_i = g_i^* - o_i \qquad (4.6)$$

Thus, the financial assistance to a state is the excess of assessed expenditure over assessed revenues, both written as fractions of the all-state averages plus a budget surplus which is common for all states, minus the SPPs treated by inclusion.

Needs Version

Substituting $r_s - e_s = d_s$ in (4.5), we can write what is known as the needs version of the grant equation. Thus,

$$g_i^* = [(\gamma_i - 1)e_s + (1 - \rho_i)r_s] \qquad (4.7)$$

This indicates that the essence of the exercise is the departure of the disabilities γ_i and ρ_i from 1. Further, total grants can be seen as the sum of expenditure disabilities and revenue disabilities. This equation also makes clear the difference between the Australian and Canadian systems. In the Canadian system only the second term, that is, revenue disability is operative and no consideration is given to the expenditure side disability. This implies that implicitly γ_i is put equal to 1. The revenue disability

(ρ_i) in Australia (p. 350 of the CGC 2004 Review, supporting information) is measured by the ratio of states i's revenue base (b_i) and the average per capita revenue base (b_s). Thus, $\rho_i = b_i / b_s$. Substituting this in equation 4.7 and setting $\gamma_i = 1$, we have

$$g_i^* = r_s - \rho_i \ r_s = ab_s - ab_i \qquad (4.8)$$

This describes the method of determining untied transfers in Canada (see Rangarajan and Srivastava (2004a) for a discussion).

A third way in which the determination of grants can be written is what might be called the normative gap version. This would facilitate comparison with the Indian system also.

Normative Gap Version

The term $\gamma_i e_s$ can also be written as

$$e_s \gamma_i = e_s + (\gamma_i - 1)e_s \qquad (4.9)$$

From equation (4.5)

$$g_i^* = e_s - \rho_i \ r_s + (\gamma_i - 1)e_s + d_s \qquad (4.10)$$

Substituting $a.b_i$ for $\rho_i \ r_s$, we can write

$$g_i^* = e_s - a \ b_i + \beta_i e_s + d_s \qquad \text{[where } \beta_i = (\gamma_i - 1)]$$

The term e_s can be written as az where z is a constant $[e_s / a = z]$

$$g_i^* = a[z - b_i] + \beta_i e_s + d_s \qquad (4.11)$$

The first term is the term comparable to the distance criterion used in the tax-sharing formula in India. The expenditure term is also comparable to the supplementary factors representing factors accounting for more than average costs like area and infrastructure. The term d_s is a constant and therefore reflects the population term in the devolution formula. Thus, the Australian formula is comparable to the Indian tax-sharing formula, although the relative weights to different terms are determined and derived differently.

Total Grants and Relativities

Deriving g from g^*, the total CGC grant for a state can be written as:

$$G_i = N_i \, g_i \qquad (4.12)$$

The per capita relativity of state i gives its per capita grant relative to the all-state per capita grant, g_s. Thus,

$$f_i = g_i / g_s \qquad (4.13)$$

The relativities can be converted into shares:

$$s_i = G_i / \textstyle\sum G_i = g_i N_i / g_s \sum N_i = f_i [N_i / \textstyle\sum N_i] \qquad (4.14)$$

A relativity of below 1 means that a state requires less than an equal per capita share of the divisible pool. A relativity above 1 means that a state requires more than equal per capita share. No state can have its relativity increased without the relativity of one or more states being reduced. The relativities are based on the average of the assessments for the five most recently completed years. Each state's relativity for a grant year is the average of its per capita requirement for a share of the pool in each of the five most recently completed financial years.

Table 4.9 gives relativities and corresponding shares with respect to the GST assessments in the 2004 review. It is clear that redistribution is from NSW and Victoria to the other states in comparison to an equal per capita distribution. Table 4.10 describes how the relativities have moved over time between the 1999 Review and the 2004 Review. Between the two review years, the per capita relativities of NSW and the NT have both gone down. There is a major change in the status of Western Australia, whose share had remained below 1 until the 2003 update. It has become a net recipient in the 2004 Review with a relativity of more than 1.

Issues of Endogeneity

The expenditure assessment methodology in Australia raises some issues of endogeneity. In particular, grants depend on expenditures and unless expenditures are incurred, grants cannot be determined. However,

Table 4.9 Australian States: Population, Income, and 2004 Relativities

States	PCGSP*	Population#	Share in all-state GSP	Assessed GST relativity	Share in transfers**	Excess of share of transfers over share of population
New South Wales	36,505	33.8	35.5	0.86750	29.322	−4.479
Victoria	35,810	24.7	25.4	0.86534	21.374	−3.326
Queensland	30,727	18.8	16.6	1.05504	19.835	1.035
Western Australia	38,664	9.8	10.9	1.03054	10.099	0.299
Southern Australia	29,286	7.8	6.6	1.20407	9.392	1.592
Tasmania	25,024	2.4	1.7	1.55939	3.743	1.343
Australian Capital Territory	42,549	1.6	2.0	1.12930	1.807	0.207
Northern Territory	41,472	1.0	1.2	4.26538	4.265	3.265
Australia	34,769	100.0	100.0	1.00000	99.836	−0.164

Source: Tables C-11, E-5, and E-8, Report on State Revenue Sharing Relativities, 2004 Review, Commonwealth Grants Commission.

Note: *Average of 1998–9 to 2002–3; # 2001–2 based on data from 2001 census; **based on GST relativities (average over 1998–9 to 2002–3).

expenditures cannot be incurred unless grants are already provided. The way out in the Australian methodology is to use past expenditures and other data considering the average over five years as a predictor of current levels of expenditures, revenues, and budget outcomes. Grants are determined by using past levels of these variables, converted into shares, which are reconverted into absolute amounts when actual GST revenues are known. The implicit assumption is that all components of the equalization calculations can be scaled up or down by the same fraction by which GST revenues are larger or smaller than the average of those in the earlier years, data of which are used for the equalization calculations.

The issue is whether equalization calculations remain valid when the sum of total grants under the CGC formula is different from the GST

Table 4.10 Australia: Per Capita Relativities: 1999–2004 Review

States	1999 Review	2000 Update	2001 Update	2002 Update	2003 Update	2004 Review
New South Wales	0.89948	0.90913	0.92032	0.90631	0.89117	0.86750
Victoria	0.86184	0.87049	0.87539	0.86824	0.8701	0.86534
Queensland	1.00687	1.0183	1.00269	1.01174	1.01902	1.05504
Western Australia	0.94793	0.98365	0.97516	0.97592	0.96946	1.03054
Southern Australia	1.2068	1.18258	1.17941	1.19447	1.21215	1.20407
Tasmania	1.60905	1.51091	1.50095	1.55419	1.59948	1.55939
Australian Capital Territory	1.1027	1.11289	1.14633	1.15216	1.14979	1.12930
Northern Territory	4.84429	4.16385	4.02166	4.24484	4.38638	4.26538

Source: Report of Commonwealth Grants Commission, 2004 Review.

amount that is to be distributed. According to the equalization calculations, the total distributable amount is,

$$G^* = [(e_s - r_s + d_s - o_s) \Sigma N_i] \tag{4.15}$$

This amount can be less than or more than the actual GST collections. Suppose that GST is a proportion λ of G^*, where λ can be equal to or different from 1.

$$GST = \lambda. \, G^* \tag{4.16}$$

If $\lambda = 1$, the equalization calculations remain valid. However, unless it can be established that standardized expenditures, revenues, and budget outcomes would fall or rise in the same proportion in which actual GST is lower or higher than the estimated G^*, actual grants may not be consistent with required equalization entitlements. In a recession, when GST is lower, salaries and other cost elements are not likely to fall in the same proportion as the fall in revenues. The equalization formula assumes that, the equalization formula is homogenous of degree one with respect to λ. In practice, such a condition may rarely be met. In a recession, budget deficits may adjust far more than expenditures. In an expansionary phase, revenues may adjust faster than other components.

Some Features of Revenue Assessment

The main revenue categories analysed are payroll tax, land revenue, stamp duty on conveyances, financial transactions taxes, stamp duties on shares and marketable securities, gambling taxation, insurance taxation, heavy vehicle registration fees and taxes, light vehicle registration fees and taxes, stamp duty on motor vehicle registrations and transfers, other tax revenue, mining revenue, and contributions by trading enterprises. A list of the assessed revenue sources is given in Appendix 4A.2. For each category, the relevant revenue base for each state is taken up. The actual revenues from all states are added up. Dividing these revenues by the aggregate revenue base of all states gives the average tax rate.

Thus, the average tax rate for any revenue head is given by

$$a = r_s / b_s \qquad (4.17)$$

where $r_s [=\Sigma R_i / \Sigma N_i]$ and $b_s [= \Sigma B_i / \Sigma N_i]$ indicate all-state per capita revenue and expenditure from the relevant category.

The standardized per capita revenue of a state for a given category is given by

$$r_{ij} = a_j {}^* b_{ij} \qquad (4.18)$$

where i refers to the state and j refers to the revenue categories.

Summation of all such terms over the revenue categories gives per capita standardized total revenue of a state

$$r_i = \rho_i r_s = ab_i \qquad (4.19)$$

where a is a weighted average of the individual all-state average tax rates.

The CGC observes that apart from ACT and the NT, the GSP provides a broad approximation of the relative revenue-raising capacities of the states. For the two exceptions, the capacity is assessed to be lower, although the per capita GSP is higher because of 'Australian government activities (which they cannot tax) and the general government activities of the states (which do not add to their revenue raising capacity)' (CGC Review 2004, p. 27).

Some Features of Expenditure Assessment

On the expenditure side also, assessment is undertaken in a disaggregate way. Techniques of expenditure assessment are recognized to be the unique part of the CGC methodology of determination of relativities. It is also that component of the methodology that is often criticized for its complexity and lack of transparency.

The overall methodology can be seen in three steps. Aggregate expenditures are the sum of category expenditures. Each category of expenditure consists of a weighted sum of components. Each component is a function of one or more disability factors. The main expenditure categories that are separately assessed relate to education, health and community services, law, order and public safety, culture and recreation, and economic activities. A full list of the expenditure items that were separately assessed in the 2004 Review is given in Appendix 4A.3. Expenditures are considered net of user charges. The expenditure relativity $[\gamma_i]$ therefore gives a weighted average of the relativities of the individual expenditures categories. Many of the disability factors like wages, administrative scale, socio-demographic composition and so on are common for several components in different categories of expenditures, and general methodologies have been developed for treating these disabilities. Appendix 4A.4 provides an illustration of the application of the assessment methodology in the case of the expenditure category of 'Inpatient Services'.

Some Important Common Disability Factors

A discussion of the disability factors also makes it clear that the CGC has to resort to judgments at various places, particularly in regard to weights of different factors affecting expenditure levels where expenditures are considered net of user charges.

Wages Input Costs

Wages and salaries are major costs incurred by the states, which differ significantly between states. In the 1999 Review, this disability was measured by considering the inter-state differences in average weekly earnings in the non-state sector. This was considered relevant as these differences were not likely to be affected by state policies. The Commission averaged the assessments over ten years and halved the inter-state differences on the basis of judgment. In the 2004 Review also, the Commission found that there were significant wage differentials between states. The underlying wages were well above average in NSW and below average in Queensland, South Australia, and Tasmania. The Commission undertook an analysis of the underlying causes of the wage differential on the basis of an econometric model but considered that the analysis did not 'provide a fully adequate basis to estimate disabilities for the smaller states' (CGC, 2004, p. 40). Specific adjustments were then made to the model results on the basis of judgment.

Socio-demographic Composition

Factors like age, sex, income, and location account for differences in per capita expenditures. The Commission in its 1999 Review assessed socio-demographic composition disabilities by applying the Australian average use and unit cost weights to the number of people in each state in different groups characterized by age, sex, income, location, non-English background, and indigenous status. Use and cost weights were calculated from national data sets, wherever possible. Judgment was used when data were not available, particularly in regard to cost weights for indigenous people living in remote locations and for people having low English ability. A similar method was applied in the 2004 Review, except that additional costs were provided on account of cultural and linguistic diversity.

Administrative Scale

Some fixed costs are incurred in all states for providing basic services regardless of the size of population. In per capita terms, these costs are higher for less populous states. The administrative scale factors therefore result in higher relativities for less populous states and lower relativities for the more populous states. Here again, the Commission had to resort to some judgment. The Commission observes, 'Some data for fixed costs are available for most expense categories or groups of categories but comprehensive estimates call for the use of judgment' (2004 Review: 45).

Specific Purpose Payments

The SPPs are grants from the Commonwealth Government to the states for specified services, such as health, education, roads, and the environment. Section 96 of the Constitution provides the legal basis for SPPs and other Commonwealth grants. It stipulates that 'the [Commonwealth] Parliament may grant financial assistance to any state on such terms and conditions as the parliament thinks fit'.

The Commonwealth Government uses SPPs for a number of reasons. In particular, SPPs are given to:

1. introduce programmes reflecting Commonwealth Government's wishes in areas of state constitutional responsibility (the majority of SPPs),
2. impose or encourage national standards (e.g., free public health and vocational training standards),
3. pay states for the delivery of Commonwealth programmes (there are only a few examples of this, such as funding legal aid for federal law cases),
4. compensate states for the cost of Commonwealth initiatives (e.g., the cost to the states of increased access to pensioner concessions), and
5. comply with international obligations (e.g., payments to help manage World Heritage areas).

The SPPs were introduced in the 1920s to provide assistance for road construction and debt costs. These remained limited in scope until after World War II. Following the war, there was a gradual increase in the number of tied grants programmes, including those for housing, education, agriculture, some health programmes, and infrastructure development. The SPPs increased markedly in the mid-1970s under the Whitlam Government, with comprehensive funding for education and public hospitals and the provision of general purpose grants for local governments. Since then, SPPs have continued to increase slowly as a proportion of total Commonwealth funding to the states.

The specific purpose grants are administered by the Statutory Commissions appointed by the Commonwealth Government. These constitute about 20 per cent of the total expenditure of the states. The distribution of SPPs hinges on several factors, including the historical distribution, which was often arbitrary or reflected the Commonwealth Government's policy priorities. In applying the equalization principle, the CGC takes into account all operating revenues available including the SPPs, except those quarantined, that is excluded, before calculating its relative need for revenue from the GST-HCG pool.

The SPPs are subject to individual agreements, which include a variety of terms and conditions applicable to the grants. They are also usually classified as either payments to the states for programmes administered by the states, or payments 'through' the states, which are payments to be passed on to other bodies, principally non-government schools and local governments.

The SPPs have grown substantially in importance over time, increasing from 22 per cent of total Commonwealth payments in 1942–3 to 51 per cent of total Commonwealth payments in 2001–2. Over time, the SPPs have also proliferated. The Commonwealth Government identified over 120 separate SPPs, many of which consist of a number of sub-programmes. Questions have often been raised about the efficiency of maintaining a large number of small SPP programmes. Since many of the SPPs are in areas in which the states have sole responsibility under the Constitution, questions arise as to whether it is efficient and appropriate for the Commonwealth Government to be determining priorities in such areas. Commonwealth conditions on SPPs show substantial variation. Some of the largest SPP programmes (e.g., funding for government schools and hospitals) have a limited set of conditions and provide the states with a relatively high degree of flexibility to provide services consistent with the general objectives of these SPPs, whereas small SPP programmes can involve substantial Commonwealth oversight and micromanagement. In its assessment exercise, the CGC divides the SPPs into three main categories: SPPs considered out of scope for the assessment exercise, SPPs treated by exclusion, and SPPs treated by inclusion in the assessment exercise. Most of the major SPPs are considered by inclusion. The effect of the CGC's method of inclusion is to neutralize allocation priorities of the SPPs as higher SPP allocations would result in lower untied grants and vice versa. Garnaut and FitzGerald (2002a: 11) observe in their Review Final Report: 'The CGC effectively overrides the assessments that underlie most SPP allocations, which are determined under direct legislative and ministerial authority.'

Horizontal Imbalance

The outcome of such a comprehensive equalization exercise in Australia is to reduce the horizontal imbalance in state expenditures. Table 4.11 shows that this objective is successfully achieved. If the territories are excluded, the actual expenditures are within a narrow range from the all-state mean.

The difference between the minimum and maximum per capita expenditure relative to the all-state average is in the range of 19–22 percentage points. However, the per capita expenditure in the NT is more than double the all-state average. This is the outcome primarily of the additional costs of providing services in this region. The coefficient of variation of the expenditures relative to the average is limited in the range of 7–10 per cent if the territories are excluded. In contrast, the outcome of the overall transfer process in India still leaves a considerable horizontal imbalance in the system. It is also clear that states which receive larger grants have larger per capita expenditures, implying larger public sectors in these states.

Some Issues in Assessment

Several issues in the context of CGC's assessment procedures regarding HFE have been raised from time to time, particularly those related to its impact on efficiency. These issues have become even more important in the context of the transition from sharing the FAG pool to sharing a GST-HCG pool. Some of these issues are discussed below. The extent of redistribution can also be measured in terms of the amount the donor states would have received on a per capita basis.

Table 4.11 Australia: Horizontal Fiscal Imbalance Per Capita Expenditure
Relative to All-State Average

			(per cent)
Provinces	1999–2000	2000–1	2001–2
New South Wales	98.27	95.39	96.30
Victoria	90.85	91.01	88.93
Queensland	90.79	98.22	104.44
Western Australia	113.01	111.91	107.17
Southern Australia	112.68	106.67	106.29
Tasmania	111.10	112.19	108.31
Australian Capital Territory	119.56	126.62	115.38
Northern Territory	265.84	266.36	249.00
Australia	100.00	100.00	100.00
Minimum	90.79	91.01	88.93
Maximum excl. territories	113.01	112.19	108.31
Range	22.22	21.18	19.38
Coefficient of Variation (excl. territories)	10. 5	8.7	8.5

Source: Commonwealth Grants Commission, 2004 Review, supporting information.
Note: Expenditures are compiled from the equalization budget.

Extent of Redistribution

The main outcome of the exercise of HFE is the redistribution of resources among states. The CGC itself calculates the extent of redistribution compared to a situation of equal per capita allocations. Table 4.12
shows that the extent of redistribution has ranged from 11.4 per cent
in 1981–2 to a low level of 6 per cent in 2001–2. It is also shown that
the extent of redistribution has come down over the years. The extent of redistribution can also be measured in terms of the amount the
donor states would have received on a per capita basis. For example, in
2002–3, on a per capita basis, NSW and Victoria together would have
received $21,951 million, and the amount redistributed is 11.3 per cent
of their share.

Table 4.12 Total Pool over the Years and Extent of Redistribution (1981–2005)

Year	Based on review/ update of	Total pool ($ million)	Amount redistributed ($ million)	Proportion redistributed (per cent)
1981–2	1981 Review	8,202.9	932.4	11.37
1982–3	1982 Review	9,217.9	1,023.5	11.10
1985–6	1985 Review	11,826.3	1,205.7	10.20
1988–9	1988 Review	16,019.9	1,265.0	7.90
1993–4	1993 Review	17,315.7	1,632.0	9.42
1999–2000	1999 Review	23,064.6	1,692.1	7.34
2000–1	2000 Update	30,506.3	1,961.0	6.43
2001–2	2001 Update	33,209.7	1,988.5	5.99
2002–3	2002 Update	37,555.7	2,472.4	6.58
2003–4	2003 Update	38,825.2	2,747.5	7.08
2004–5	2004 Update	41,594.1	3,213.7	7.73

Source: Commonwealth Grants Commission, 2004 Review.

Revenue and Expenditure Side Equalizations: Relative Roles

The distinguishing feature of the Australian fiscal equalization exercise is the importance given to expenditure side equalization. Revenue-side equalization is also practiced in Canada, and the two systems in their mechanics are quite similar. While in Canada, in the general purpose grant calculation, only revenue-side equalization is undertaken, in Australia, not only the expenditure side equalization is undertaken, but also, as Table 4.13 indicates, it is the stronger influence since the redistribution through expenditure requirement at $2,521.4 million is greater than that due to revenue raising capacity at $1,880.7 million. It can also be seen that NSW loses more because of its higher revenue raising capacity than on account of assessment of expenditure requirements. On the other hand, Victoria suffers only because of expenditure equalization.

Table 4.13 Relative Contribution of Revenue, Expenditure, and SPP Disabilities in the 2004 Review

				($ million)
	Revenue raising capacity	Expense requirements	SPPs	Total redistributed
New South Wales	−1,159.6	−625.5	69.6	−1,715.50
Victoria	488.6	−1,871.9	97.9	−1,285.40
Queensland	262.6	132.4	21.2	416.20
Western Australia	−721.2	840.8	0.6	120.20
Southern Australia	668.8	−9.4	−49.9	609.50
Tasmania	327.5	226.3	−37.8	516.00
Australian Capital Territory	102.1	−13.7	−6.0	82.40
Northern Territory	31.1	1,321.9	−95.6	1,257.40
All States*	1,880.7	2,521.4	189.4	4,591.50

Source: Report of Commonwealth Grants Commission, 2004 Review.
Note: *sum of positive amounts.

Revenue Equalization: Relevance of a Macro Approach

As far as the revenue-side equalization is concerned, the approaches in Canada and Australia are quite similar. In both cases, a tax-by-tax approach is followed with the average all-state tax rate being applied to the actual tax base of each state. The difference is in the nature of taxes themselves. While in Canada, most of the major taxes are used by the provinces (including income and corporate taxes and also the GST), in Australia, states are left with a very limited and specialized set of taxes. This also has a bearing on the issue of whether a macro approach rather than a tax-by-tax approach would be better. In the Canadian case, the individual tax bases are more likely to be highly correlated to a macro base than in Australia where the taxes under consideration are small and specialized. Nevertheless, the issue of substituting a macro base for the tax-by-tax approach has also been discussed in Australia. In the macro or global approach each state is free to choose any combination of utilization of the tax bases available to it as long as it produces the same overall revenue result. The CGC recognizes the importance of the global approach when it observes:

> A global approach assumes that, whatever the legal incidence of a particular form of revenue, its ultimate effective incidence would fall on income or be reflected in the value of production ... The type of tax base adopted has implications for the nature of equalization. The use of global (and sub-global) bases tends to imply that equalization is about the capacity of State to pay tax. The use of tax bases tends to imply that equalization is about the capacity of state governments to raise revenues (CGC 1999).

Collins (2000: 49–54) shows that the use of a global approach leads to results that are quite different from those of a tax-by-tax approach. He lists the following arguments against using partial measures, that is, a tax-by-tax approach in measuring fiscal capacity:

1. Individual tax bases are not necessarily related directly to state taxpayers' ability to pay.
2. It is possible for the states to adjust their calculated taxable capacities by varying tax mixes and tax policies.
3. Partial measures are not policy neutral, for example, improvement in the rail network of a state might reduce its motor vehicle tax capacity; on the other hand, improvement in suburban transport facilities might lead, through higher land prices, to higher land tax capacity.
4. Federal tax policies can affect states' taxable capacities, for example, reduction in capital gains tax rate may, through raising property prices and property turnover, increase revenues from land taxes and stamp duties.

Collins argues that significant data problems exist in Australia in measuring global tax bases. He observes (ibid: 53) that there are serious data difficulties with state national account statistics. The narrow tax bases left with the Australian states is also an issue as they are poorly correlated with global measures of fiscal capacity. Favouring the adoption of global measures of fiscal capacity in the longer run, he observes (p. 53), 'While the balance of the argument might lie with the use, in the long run, of global rather partial measures of States' taxable capacities, it does not appear possible at this stage to mount conclusive arguments in favour of either approach.' Given the narrow tax base of the states in Australia, a tax-by-tax approach may have more relevance. The Indian situation is quite different as the tax base of the states is much wider.

Equity Issues

While the CGC methodology has successfully equalized access to resources to the states provided they make comparable revenue effort, the effect of the scheme of transfers on equity objectives has often been questioned. Horizontal equity refers to 'equal treatment of individuals in equal circumstances'. Garnaut (2002), Garnaut and FitzGerald (2002a) in their Review note: 'There are well known systematic regional differences in the quality of service available to Australians (for example, between metropolitan, provincial, rural and remote areas. Some differences are inevitable, reflecting differences in costs of provision of services, while others are amenable to policy change.' They argue that 'the CGC's approach has equalized States' capacity to provide services, not service provision'. In particular, they argue that it is possible to base an HFE distribution on monitoring and evaluating outcomes without prescribing them.

In theory, equalization has always been about equalizing fiscal capacities. Actual outcomes may yet differ because of differences in policies and preferences as well as efficiency in different states. There is, however, some evidence of convergence in the provision of services as the proportion of redistribution of the total pool of distribution (see Table 4.12) has steadily come down.

Efficiency Issues

In their Review of Commonwealth-State Funding, Garnaut and FitzGerald (2002a) have summarized in their Final Report several types of efficiency-reducing effects of the transfer arrangements. They argue that equalizing transfers tend to

1. reduce the incentives for resources to locate in higher productivity locations,
2. reduce the capacity for investment in human resource development in low productivity regions to enhance national economic potential,
3. increase the overhead and transactions costs of managing the system,
4. discourage the attraction and retention of high-value mobile resources in an international market,
5. lead to duplication, lack of coordination and game playing by officials,
6. unduly enlarge the role of the public sector
7. encourage grant-seeking behaviour, particularly where states have the capacity to influence the CGC's assessed standard budget
8. dilute incentives for cost reducing reforms, and
9. discourage growth-promoting policies if the benefits of growth are mostly transferred to others.

Garnaut and FitzGerald observe that most of these efficiency-reducing effects arise from the expenditure side of equalization: 'It is common to perceive the efficiency costs as arising principally from compensation for disabilities on the expenditure side, through their tendency to discourage movement of people out of high cost locations.' They also note that states that are larger recipients of equalization grants have noticeably larger public sectors. Thus, they observe, 'there are signs that the exceptionally large role of the public sector and exceptionally small role of the private sector in some states that are large recipients of transfers, notably Tasmania and South Australia, have changed the political orientation in ways that are unfavorable to growth.'

The theoretical literature on equalization (particularly the contributions by Buchanan (1950), Scott (1950), Buchanan and Wagner (1971), Graham (1964), and Mathews (1993)) has looked at the issue of the implications of equalization, especially expenditure side equalization, on efficiency in detail. While Scott had argued way back in 1950 that equalization is detrimental to efficiency because it impedes the mobility of factors of production to locations where they would be most productive, Buchanan and Wagner have argued that efficiency would be impeded if migration is fiscally induced by states providing more public goods at lower tax costs. They argued that rich states can induce migration by providing higher fiscal surpluses but eventually, due to the existence of congestible goods, the fiscal surpluses will fall. As too many people migrate to the richer states, there will be a loss of efficiency in the economy as a whole. This incentive towards excessive migration in their view ought to be neutralized through fiscal equalization. As such, equalization is consistent with equity and efficiency.

Gramlich (1989) particularly questioned expenditure side equalization by arguing that this removes any disincentives for people to move from high-cost areas to low-cost areas and therefore raises the overall costs of service provision. He favoured that no allowance should be made for expenditure disabilities. In response, Mathews (1985) argued that expenditure side equalization was an essential ingredient of overall equalization. Grewal and Mathews (1983) also showed that locational choice is usually influenced by private production and consumption activities rather than by fiscal and other activities of the governments.

While cost disabilities due to structural and exogenous factors need to be neutralized, policy-induced disabilities should not be neutralized. However, in practice, it is often difficult to separate one from the other and measure their impact.

* * *

As compared to Australia, India has not only a larger number of states and a larger population but also a greater concentration of population in low fiscal capacity states. Fiscal transfers aimed at horizontal equalization therefore call for larger redistribution in India Grewal (1999). The differences in the size, heterogeneity, and scale of problems notwithstanding, the conceptual basis of the transfer system in Australia has much relevance for India. At the same time, serious difficulties have also been noted with the Australian system. Some of the important differences, similarities, and essential lessons in respect of the vertical and horizontal dimensions of transfers are summarized below:

1. The Australian system is characterized by a high degree of vertical imbalance and centralization of expenditure. In raising

revenues, the Indian system is also characterized by high vertical imbalance but somewhat lower than that in Australia. Also, the centralization of expenditure after transfers in Australia is higher than that in India. In the context of Australian vertical imbalance, Mathews (1993) observed, 'It is a paradox that Australia has combined the world's finest system of HFE with one of the most vertically unbalanced fiscal systems. The threat to HFE in Australia arises not from any inherent defects in fiscal equalization, but from pressures which are being placed on it by continuing failure to restore vertical fiscal balance. It is the Commonwealth tax monopoly that needs to be dismantled and not the system of fiscal capacity equalization.' Since Mathews wrote this in 1993, with the GST arrangement, the vertical fiscal imbalance has gone up rather than down.

2. In Australia, the determination of the vertical share of resources to be transferred to the states is not in the hands of the CGC. It is determined automatically by the amount of revenues collected under the GST supplemented by the SPGs, which are also in the hands of the Commonwealth Government. In India, the Finance Commission determines a large part of the transfers in the form of tax devolution under global sharing and grants, requiring it to determine in some way the vertical imbalance. The Finance Commission transfers are supplemented by the Planning Commission grants and other discretionary grants determined by the central government. Global tax-sharing may have some merits over the sharing of a single tax as in Australia, where the collecting agency, namely the Commonwealth Government, has no revenue interest. Deciding about vertical transfers facilitates horizontal equalization and to that extent India has an institutional advantage.

3. Australia has one of the most elaborate systems of determining equalization transfers. The Australian equalization payments are based on explicit principles that aim at enabling states to provide their citizens services at comparable standards if they are willing to make comparable revenue efforts and are able to operate at comparable levels of efficiency. The overall approach to equalization is with reference to entire transfers as most SPPs are integrated into

the equalization calculations. The Australian system is sound in principle, but the methodology adopted, particularly with respect to equalizing expenditure disabilities, has made the system unduly complex. The system is still grappling with issues of efficiency. From the Indian perspective, the major lesson to be drawn from the Australian experience is the need for a clearer enunciation of the equalization objective and its translation in practice. It may be practical to consider a macro base for revenue-side equalization and focus on expenditure equalization in select services where mobility is limited.

4. The working of the Australian Loan Council has relevance for India where consideration of sub-national borrowing in a framework of sustainability and macroeconomic stability is desirable. There is a need for an institutional arrangement for keeping the growth of central and state debt within prudent limits and consistent with the requirements of macroeconomic stability. In fact, as in Australia, states should be allowed to raise loans in the market subject to agreed limits and there is no need for the central government to intermediate. Over time, market-based discipline would become more and more effective.

In conclusion, in India, there is a need to modify the transfer mechanism so as to make it consistent with the equalization principle. Consideration of cost disabilities, particularly those that are structural in nature, should also be taken up, focusing first on select social services like education and health.

Addendum to Chapter 4: Recent Developments in the Australian System of Fiscal Transfers

In the case of Australia, it is the GST revenues that are distributed among states using their equalization methodology. This methodology was changed substantially in 2018 on the basis of a legislation passed by the Commonwealth Parliament. The key elements of the new equalization methodology are summarized below.

Australia's New Equalization System

First, a new equalization benchmark has been defined that is linked to the fiscally stronger states of New South Wales or Victoria. Second, a GST relativity floor has been established. Third, some top-ups to the GST pool are being funded by the Commonwealth Government. Further, certain transitional arrangements were introduced to ensure that no state becomes worse off in the new equalization framework.

In the new equalization arrangement, the standard state would be one of the two fiscally stronger states, New South Wales or Victoria. The GST relativity of each state is calculated with reference to the standard state. In the new arrangement, each state's GST relativity is uplifted to equal the fiscal capacity of the standard state. Thus, no state receives less GST per person than the standard state.

The concept of a GST floor sets a relativity below which any state's GST share cannot fall. It creates a minimum per person GST share that each state receives, irrespective of its fiscal circumstances. In 2022–3 and 2023–4, the floor was fixed at 0.70. It is to be uplifted to 0.75 in 2024–5. If it becomes necessary to activate the floor, the resultant financing will occur from the GST pool with Commonwealth top-ups.

The Commonwealth Government topped up the GST pool by $600 million in 2020–1. This arrangement is being continued with some indexation in the succeeding years. In 2024–5, the GST pool is to be supplemented with a further $250 million with indexing of both amounts continuing in subsequent years.[4]

In moving to the new system, a six-year transition system has been provided for from 2021–2 to 2026–7. In this transition period, GST relativities would remain a blend of the old and new arrangements. For 2021–2, each state's GST relativity was based on 5/6 of its GST relativity under the old arrangements and 1/6 of its relativity under the new arrangements. For 2022–3, the split will be 4/6 and 2/6, and so on. By 2026–7, GST distribution will fully reflect the new equalization benchmark. A 'no worse off' guarantee will continue to apply during the transitional period.

Addendum Table 4.1 summarizes the different components of transfers during the transition period and 2027–8.

Addendum Table 4.1 Summary of the Transition by Year[1]

Year	2021–2	2022–3	2023–4	2024–5	2025–6	2026–7	2027–8
GST pool							
Pool top-up	$600m	$600m + indexation	$600m + indexation	$250m + ($600m + indexation)	$850m + indexation	$850m + indexation	$850m + indexation
GST revenue	Yes	Yes	Yes	Yes	Yes	Yes	Yes
Relativity floor	External[2]	0.70	0.70	0.75	0.75	0.75	0.75
Relativity ratio transition							
Full	5/6ths	4/6ths	3/6ths	2/6ths	1/6th	0/6ths	0/6ths
Reasonable	1/6th	2/6ths	3/6ths	4/6ths	5/6ths	6/6ths	6/6ths
No worse off guarantee	Yes	Yes	Yes	Yes	Yes	Yes	No

Source: Treasury Laws Amendment (Making Sure Every State and Territory Gets Their Fair Share of GST) Act 2018; https://www.aph.gov.au/Parliamentary_Business/Bills_Legislation/Bills_Search_Results/Result?bId=r6203#:~:text=Gives%20effect%20to%20the%20elements%20of,Commission%20(CGC)%20inquiry%20into%20how (Accessed 19 September 2023)

1 2027–8 is the first year following the completion of the transition period.

2 The Commonwealth Government is directly funding the cost of the floor in 2021–2. After this, the floor will be funded from within the GST pool.

Equalization Transfers in Australia in Recent Years

As discussed before, Australia has six states, and two territorial governments referred to as the Australian Capital Territory and the NT. In terms
of share in GDP, New South Wales is the largest province followed by
Victoria, Queensland, and Western Australia. Addendum Table 4.2 shows
the share of each state/territory in the Australian GDP. In Australia's case
also, four states—New South Wales, Victoria, Queensland, and Western
Australia—together accounted for 89.4 per cent of Australia's total nominal GDP in 2022

Their share in population was 88.1 per cent of Australia's total population in 2022, as shown by Addendum Chart 4.1.

In terms of per capita GDP, the richest state is Western Australia, primarily due to its mineral resources. In terms of territories, the NT has the
highest per capita GDP also because of its mineral resources and large
per capita general revenue assistance. This is followed by per capita GDP
in the ACT due to its small population and the location of most of the
Commonwealth Government offices. Among the states, Tasmania has
the lowest per capita GDP (Addendum Table 4.3).

Addendum Table 4.2 State's Share in Nominal GDP (%)

State/ Year	2016	2017	2018	2019	2020	2021	2022
New South Wales	32.7	32.7	32.5	32.1	31.6	31.2	30.2
Victoria	23.8	23.7	23.9	23.7	23.7	22.8	22.3
Queensland	18.2	18.6	19.0	18.8	18.2	17.7	19.4
Western Australia	14.3	14.1	13.9	14.7	15.8	17.6	17.5
South Australia	6.0	5.8	5.7	5.6	5.6	5.7	5.6
Australian Capital Territory	2.1	2.1	2.1	2.1	2.1	2.1	2.0
Tasmania	1.7	1.6	1.6	1.6	1.7	1.7	1.7
Northern Territory	1.3	1.3	1.3	1.3	1.3	1.2	1.3
Australia total	100.0	100.0	100.0	100.0	100.0	100.0	100.0

Source (basic data): Australian Bureau of Statistics; https://www.abs.gov.au/ (Accessed 19
September 2023)

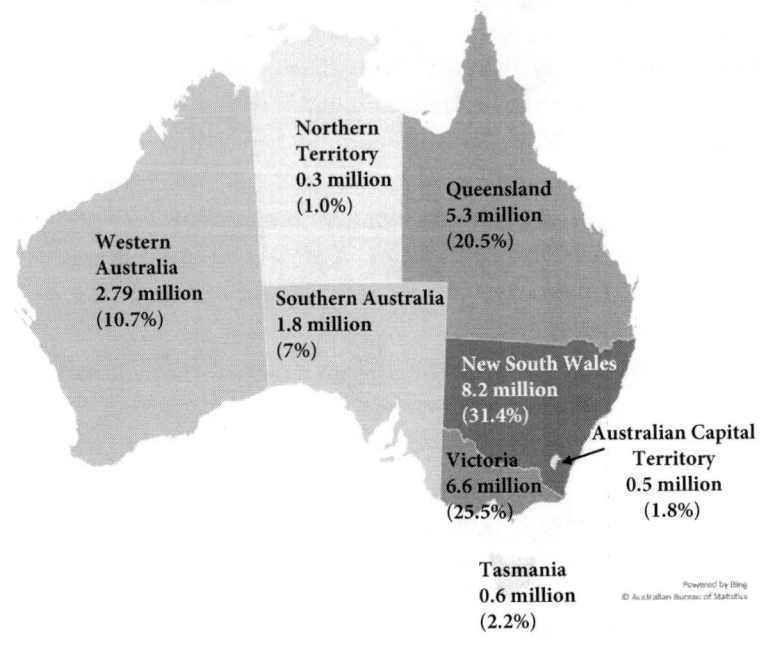

Addendum Chart 4.1 State-Wise Population of Australia (2022)

Source (Basic data): Australian Bureau of Statistics; https://www.abs.gov.au/ (Accessed 19 September 2023) and authors' creation.

Notes: (1) population numbers are in person terms and state's share in total population is indicated in the parenthesis

(2) Map created by using Microsoft Excel (GeoNames)

(3) Not to scale and indicative only

Following the new approach, the relativities in 2022–3 and 2023–4 are shown in Addendum Table 4.4, along with the corresponding GST shares of different states. Using these, the distribution of GST magnitudes is also shown.

In addition to the transfers based on GST relativities, there are other components of transfers in Australia's overall system of general revenue assistance. These include various components which have changed from time to time. Addendum Table 4.5 shows the amounts involved in the general revenue assistance consisting of four main elements other than the GST entitlement for the period from 2022–3 to 2026–7.

Addendum Table 4.3 State-wise Per Capita GDP (in Australian dollars)

State/Year	2016	2017	2018	2019	2020	2021	2022
Western Australia	92,769	95,937	97,668	107,726	115,151	133,087	144,891
Northern Territory	89,996	93,447	96,748	101,505	106,427	100,302	124,092
Australian Capital Territory	85,278	87,251	89,218	92,447	94,971	98,308	101,537
New South Wales	70,069	73,257	75,290	77,730	77,026	80,174	85,393
Queensland	62,144	66,530	69,890	72,019	69,867	70,591	84,103
Victoria	63,848	66,203	68,545	70,559	70,964	72,438	77,711
South Australia	57,778	59,168	60,623	62,016	61,765	65,611	70,613
Tasmania	53,912	54,463	56,048	58,316	58,912	62,046	67,372
Australia	**68,519**	**71,519**	**73,814**	**76,835**	77,175	**80,996**	**88,765**

Source (basic data): Australian Bureau of Statistics; https://www.abs.gov.au/ (Accessed 19 September 2023) and authors' calculations

Addendum Table 4.4 Relativities, Shares, and Illustrative GST Distribution, 2022–3 and 2023–4

State	Relativities		GST shares		GST distribution	
	2022–3	2023–4	2022–3	2023–4	2022–3	2023–4
			%	%	$m	$m
New South Wales	0.95065	0.92350	29.7	28.8	24,717	24,870
Victoria	0.85861	0.85169	21.9	21.8	18,175	18,796
Queensland	1.03377	1.03118	21.1	21.1	17,547	18,220
Western Australia	0.70000	0.70000	7.5	7.5	6,228	6,482
South Australia	1.28411	1.39463	9.0	9.8	7,477	8,420
Tasmania	1.85360	1.79080	4.1	4.0	3,404	3,409
Australian Capital Territory	1.09250	1.19540	1.9	2.1	1,609	1,831
Northern Territory	4.86988	4.98725	4.8	4.9	3,965	4,219
Total	**1.00000**	**1.00000**	**100.0**	**100.0**	**83,122**	**86,248**

Source: Commonwealth Grants Commission – GST revenue sharing relativities – 2023 Update (released on March 2023); https://www.cgc.gov.au/sites/default/files/2023-03/2023%20Upd ate%20of%20GST%20revenue%20sharing%20relativities_0.pdf (Accessed 19 September 2023)

Addendum Table 4.5 Per Capita General Revenue Assistance (Australian dollars, millions)

	2022–3	2023–4	2024–5	2025–6	2026–7
GST entitlement	82,346.0	86,620.6	90,207.6	95,494.9	101,287.7
HFE transition payments*	4,112.4	4,915.5	5,349.6	5,666.8	3,481.1
Other general revenue assistance *of which*	1,562.5	934.3	788.2	620.6	492.7
ACT municipal services	42.5	44	45.4	46.4	47.3
Royalty payments	1,520.00	890.3	742.8	574.2	445.4
Total	88,020.9	92,470.4	96,345.3	101,782.3	105,261.5

Source: Government of Australia; https://budget.gov.au/content/bp3/download/bp3_13_par t_3.pdf (Accessed 19 September 2023)

Note: *Estimates of the HFE transition payments for 2024–5 and later years are based upon the 2023–4 GST relativities and adjusted to take into account the transition to the new HFE system. The 2026–7 HFE transition payment is assumed to be half of that implied using the 2023–4 relativities.

Addendum Table 4.6 shows the inter-state distribution of the general revenue assistance for different states and territories for 2021–2. The main recipients of the HFE transition payments are New South Wales, Victoria, Queensland, Southern Australia, and the ACT.

Addendum Table 4.6 General Revenue Assistance Payments to the States, 2021–2 (Australian dollars, millions)

Items	NSW	VIC	QLD	WA	SA	TAS	ACT	NT	Total
GST entitlement*	22,248.6	17,409.8	16,028.8	3,331.9	6,995.5	3,211.3	1,514.9	3,440.0	74,180.8
Transitional GST top-up payments	–	–	–	2,115.2	–	–	–	–	2,115.2
HFE transition payments	64.3	55.7	33.0	–	2.7	–	2.1	–	157.7
Other general revenue assistance *of which*	–	–	–	1,033.2	–	–	41.7	2.1	1,076.9
ACT municipalservices	–	–	–	–	–	–	41.7	–	41.7
Compensation forreduced royalties	–	–	–	89.1	–	–	–	–	89.1
Royalty payments	–	–	–	944.1	–	–	–	2.1	946.1
Total general revenue assistance	22,312.9	17,465.5	16,061.7	6,480.3	6,998.2	3,211.3	1,558.7	3,442.0	77,530.7

Source (basic data): Final Budget Outcome 2021–2; https://archive.budget.gov.au/2021-22/fbo/download/01_part_1.pdf (Accessed on 19 September 2023)

Notes: *The 2021–2 GST outcome will be finalized following a Determination by a Treasury portfolio minister. This figure reflects the most recent data received from the Australian Taxation Office.

APPENDIX 4A.1

Difference between GST and FAG Relativities

Table 4A.1 provides a comparison between GST and FAG relativities as assessed in the 2004 Review. Although the CGC was not asked to provide estimates in the 2004 Review for the FAG relativities, that is, relativities calculated with the assumption that the old system of financial grants continued. A comparison with the 2004 GST relativities shows that NSW and Victoria gain in the GST relativities as compared to the FAG relativities. Their FAG relativities have gone down considerably compared to the corresponding relativities in 1999–2000.

APPENDIX 4A.2

State Taxes in Australia

Payroll tax
Stamp duties
On contracts and conveyances of property (other than shares and marketable securities)
On unlisted shares and marketable securities
On motor vehicle registration and transfers
On cheques
Financial transactions taxes
Debits tax
Deed of settlement
Agreements under seal
Stamp duties on mortgages and loan securities
Stamp duty on leases
Other duties
Hiring arrangements duty (rental duty) Land taxation
Gambling taxation
Motor taxation
Registration fees

Table 4A.1 Comparison of GST and FAG Relativities

	GST relativities 2004	FAG relativities 2004	GST 2004–FAG 2004		Net aggregate loss(−)/ gain (+) (per cent points)	FAG relativities 1999 Review	2004 FAG relativities-1999 review FAG relativities
New South Wales	0.86750	0.80363	0.06387	33.71	2.153	0.89948	−0.09585
Victoria	0.86534	0.83480	0.03054	24.74	0.755	0.86184	−0.02704
Queensland	1.05504	1.10104	−0.04600	19.00	−0.874	1.00687	0.09417
Western Australia	1.03054	1.00781	0.02273	9.81	0.223	0.94793	0.05988
Southern Australia	1.20407	1.30402	−0.09995	7.71	−0.770	1.2068	0.09722
Tasmania	1.55939	1.74908	−0.18969	2.40	−0.456	1.60905	0.14003
Australian Capital Territory	1.12930	1.16529	−0.03599	1.63	−0.059	1.1027	0.06259
Northern Territory	4.26538	5.22706	−0.96168	1.00	−0.964	4.84429	0.38277

Source: Report of Commonwealth Grants Commission, 2004 Review (Tables 3-1, 4-2, D-11).

Motor vehicle weight/engine capacity tax
Driver licence fees
Surcharge on motor vehicle third party insurance
Energy resource levies
Public authority income

APPENDIX 4A.3

Australia: Main State Expenditure Categories

A. Education
  1 Pre-school education
  2 Government schools education
  3 Non-government schools education
  4 Vocational education and training
  5 Higher education
  6 Transport of rural school children

B. Health and Community Services
  7 Inpatient services
  8 Non-inpatient and community health services
  9 Population and preventive health
  10 Family and child services
  11 Aged and disabled services
  12 Homeless and general welfare
  13 Housing
  14 First Home Owners Scheme
  15 Services to indigenous communities

C. Law and Order and Public safety
  16 Police
  17 Administration of justice
  18 Corrective services
  19 Public safety

D. Culture and Recreation
   20   Culture and recreation
   21   National parks and wildlife services

E. Economic activities
   22   Electricity and gas
   23   Water sanitation and protection of the environment
   24   Non-urban transport
   25   Urban transit
   26   Roads
   27   Primary industry
   28   Mining, fuel, and energy
   29   Tourism
   30   Manufacturing and other industry
   31   Subsidies—petroleum products
   32   Subsidies—alcohol products

F. General Public services
   33   Superannuation
   34   GST administration costs
   35   General public services
   36   Debt charges
   37   Depreciation

APPENDIX 4A.4

Inpatient Services: Example of Expenditure Assessment Techniques

We look at this category as an illustration of the Australian expenditure assessment techniques. The Inpatient Services category expenditure is obtained as a weighted sum of five components: scale-affected expenditure, hospital acute inpatient services, hospital non-acute inpatient services, patient transport, and isolation. Costs in respect of each of these

Table 4A.2 Hospital Services Assessment Structure: 2004 Review

Component weight	Disability factors					
	Administrative scale	Input costs	Socio-demographic composition	Hospital costs	Cost of patient transport	Cost of isolation
Fixed costs/scale affected expenditure	0.44	*	A			
Hospital acute inpatient services	84.71		B	*	*	
Hospital non-acute inpatient services	13.23		B	*	*	
Patient transport	1.49					*
Isolation	0.12					*

Basis of calculation; weights in parenthesis

Input costs(A)	General method with wages (80%), accommodation (2%), electricity (1%)
Input costs(B)	General method with wages (70%), accommodation (2%), electricity (1%)
Administrative scale	General method
Socio-demographic composition	Cost-weighted utilization rates by age, Aboriginality, income, region, and low English fluency
Hospital costs dispersion,	Based on the average cost of treatment by region to account for service delivery scale and research and use complexity
Cost of patient transport	Dispersion factor: based on general dispersion method for air travel, inter-regional travel, and local travel
Isolation	Isolation factor: general method

Source: Draft Assessment Paper CGC 2003/28, Inpatient Services Assessment, Commonwealth Grants Commission.

components are individually affected by a set of disability factors like administrative scale, input costs, hospital costs, costs of patient transport, and costs related to isolation. On the use side, costs depend primarily on the socio-demographic composition, which affects the individual component costs. Table 4A.2 provides the components and their determinants for the Inpatient expenditure category. The component weights were determined from national average cost data for acute, non-acute, and mental health inpatients. The cost of the patient transport component was determined from the national average cost from state data returns and from cost of patient transport data based on the 2000–1 Australian Hospital Statistics Report from the Australian Institute of Health and Welfare.

Administrative scale refers to fixed costs and generally covers head office expenses. This is a component of expenditure which is present in all expenditure categories considered by the CGC. Fixed costs for each state under the hospital inpatients category were assessed to be $8.16 million for each state in the 2004 Review. An extra fixed cost of $0.69 million was assessed for the NT for dual policy development tasks that it has to perform due to the high proportion of the indigenous population. The input costs factor covers costs of labour, office accommodation, and electricity. For scale-affected cost components, those factors were applied with the following proportions of standard expenses: wages and salaries (80 per cent), accommodation (2 per cent), and electricity (1 per cent).

The acute inpatients services component considers three disability factors relating to socio-demographic composition, hospital costs, and input costs. The socio-demographic composition factor is assessed to reflect the use and unit cost influences of different population groups on the total cost of acute inpatient services. This factor is based on Australian standard hospital use rates and Diagnosis Related Groups (DRG) cost weights for different population groups. The socio-demographic composition factor takes account of use rates and costs in respect of groups distinguished by age, sex, indigeneity, low English fluency, population location, and socio-economic status. Use rates measure the standard use of inpatient services. DRG weights measure the relative costs of treating patients. Data on the use and cost of services by different population groups were derived from the National Hospital Morbidity Dataset in the 1999

Review. Data on the number of people in state populations were from the Census of Population and Housing. The 2004 Review also used data from the ABS National Health Survey and the National Hospitals Inpatients Data. The 2004 Review also worked out an extra cost weight for the disability factor related to Culturally and Linguistically Diverse (CALD) groups. There was also a socio-economic status (SES) weight to account for the greater use of public hospital inpatient services by people from low socio-economic groups.

The non-acute inpatient component was assessed in the same way as the inpatient component, using socio-demographic composition, hospital costs, and input costs as factors. Since the cost of treating a private patient in a public hospital is less than the cost of treating a public patient in a public hospital, a cost discount was applied. This discount was 12 per cent in the 1999 Review, which was reduced to 9 per cent in the 2004 Review. The availability of private sector hospital facilities in a state reduces the burden on public hospitals. This also called for adjustments. Table 4A.2 gives the component weights. In each case, the contribution of a component to category expenditure is calculated as the component weight multiplied by the component factor. The component factor is the term given in brackets and is a function of the disability factors in the formulae described below. The symbols are defined as below:

Fixed costs (scale) = SAE
Acute Inpatients Component = AINP
Non-acute Inpatients Component = NAINP Cost of Patient
   Transport = CPT
Isolation Component = ISO
Fixed costs input costs factor = ic_sae
Administrative scale factor = s
Hospital costs factor = hc
Socio-demographic composition acute inpatients = sdc_anmp
Socio-demographic composition non-acute inpatients = adc_naimp
Input costs acute inpatients = input costs non-acute inpatients = ic_oth
Cost of patient transport (dispersion factor) = cpt
Isolation factor = iso

The component contribution equations are given by

$$SAE = w1 * (ic\_sae * s)$$
$$AINP = w2 * [(hc + sdc\_ainp - 1) * ic\_oth$$
$$NAINP = w3 * [(hc + sdc\_nainp - 1) * ic\_oth$$
$$CPT = w4 * (cpt)$$
$$ISO = w5 * (iso)$$
$$w1 + w2 + w3 + w4 + w5 = 1$$

The related calculations are given in Table 4A.3.

Expenditures are considered net of user charges. An important part of the assessment exercise is to assess the user charges. This assessment is based on national average use rates of private patients in public hospitals, adjusted for age, sex, region, indigeneity, and income. Patient fees derived from inpatients, non-inpatients, and same-day patients in all public hospitals are covered. The standardized number of private patients by the different categories multiplied by the standard user charges gives the assessed user charge.

Table 4A.3 Inpatient Service Costs Derivation of the Service Factor

Factors	NSW	VIC	QLD	WA	SA	TAS	ACT	NT
Fixed costs	0.44	%						
Administrative scale factor	0.340	0.463	0.615	1.178	1.487	4.774	7.000	18.945
Fixed costs input costs factor	1.035	0.990	0.974	0.982	0.971	0.920	1.013	1.090
Component factor	0.352	0.458	0.600	1.156	1.445	4.392	7.092	20.648
Contribution to category factor	0.002	0.002	0.003	0.005	0.006	0.019	0.031	0.091
Acute inpatients	84.71	%						
Hospital costs factor	0.994	0.999	0.992	1.023	1.006	0.977	1.018	1.122
Socio-demographic composition	0.992	0.971	1.014	0.995	1.063	1.112	0.754	1.436
Input costs: acute inpatients	1.031	0.991	0.977	0.984	0.975	0.929	1.011	1.090
Component factor	1.016	0.961	0.983	1.003	1.041	1.011	0.782	1.698
Contribution to category factor	0.861	0.814	0.833	0.849	0.882	0.857	0.662	1.438
Non-acute inpatients	13.23	%						
Hospital costs factor	0.994	0.999	0.992	1.023	1.006	0.977	1.018	1.122
Socio-demographic composition	0.982	1.021	0.976	0.914	1.216	1.257	0.564	0.774
Input costs: acute inpatients	1.031	0.991	0.977	0.984	0.975	0.929	1.011	1.090
Component factor	1.007	1.011	0.947	0.923	1.191	1.146	0.589	0.977
Contribution to category factor	0.133	0.134	0.125	0.122	0.158	0.152	0.078	0.129

Cost of patient transport	1.49	%						
Dispersion factor	0.9339	0.6145	1.5586	1.1956	0.8497	0.7798	0.1912	3.3280
Component factor	0.9339	0.6145	1.5586	1.1956	0.8497	0.7798	0.1912	3.3280
Contribution to category factor	0.0139	0.0092	0.0232	0.0178	0.0127	0.0116	0.0028	0.0496
Isolation	0.12	%						
Isolation factor	0.051	0.107	0.178	0.748	0.565	3.495	1.518	68.272
Component factor	0.051	0.107	0.178	0.748	0.565	3.495	1.518	68.272
Contribution to category factor	0.000	0.000	0.000	0.001	0.001	0.004	0.002	0.082
Category factor	1.0098	0.9591	0.9843	0.9951	1.0594	1.0433	0.7759	1.7899

Source: Commonwealth Grants Commission, Draft assessment Paper CGC 2003/28.

Notes

1. The terms of reference called for:

   An inquiry into and report upon, by 25 February 2004 at the latest, the question of per capita relativities which the Commission would regard as appropriate to apply after 2003–4 for the distribution of the combined pool of GST revenue grants and health care grants among the states, the Northern Territory, and the Australian Capital Territory.

   A review as to whether the allowances for special circumstances granted to the Australian Capital Territory continue to be necessary and, if so, make appropriate assessments.

   Preparation of a work programme for improving methods of assessment and consultation with the states and the Commonwealth Government in deciding the priorities for the work programme.

2. These payments include but are not necessarily limited to (a) National Competition Payments; (b) states' contribution the Commonwealth's deficit reduction strategy; (c) payments to the states to reimburse them for revenue lost as a result of the establishment of a national scheme of companies, securities, and future regulation; (d) payments which are funded from the National Heritage Trust of Australia and the Regional Telecommunications Infrastructure Fund; (e) payments for the Fringe Benefit Tax Transitional Grants for the public and not-for-profit hospitals; (f) payments for Building IT Strengths—Tasmanian 'Intelligent Island'; (g) payments for Connecting Tasmanian Schools; (h) payments for the Extension of the First Home Owners Scheme; (i) payments for the Roads to Recovery programme; and (j) Commonwealth payments made to the Sinking Fund on State Debt.

3. These components are (a) payments in relation to mental health; (b) payments in relation to the National Health Development Fund; (c) payments in relation to the Pathways Home Initiative; (d) all payments under an adjustment module, including those related to the Critical and Urgent Treatment (CUT) Waiting List Initiative; and (e) Compliance payment arrangements (in this case including the maximum available compliance payments in the assessments).

4. Treasury Laws Amendment (Making sure every state gets their fair share of GST) Act 2018, Section 8A.

5

Resolving Vertical and Horizontal Imbalances in India*

With the recent constitution of the Thirteenth Finance Commission, issues of resolving vertical and horizontal imbalances in the system of fiscal transfers in India have once again come to the fore. The Twelfth Finance Commission (TFC) submitted its Report[1] at the end of 2004 with the backdrop of severe fiscal stress affecting government finances, particularly states' finances in India. The Report contained, apart from the recommendations concerning the core tasks of the Finance Commission regarding tax devolution and grants, a detailed roadmap for the restructuring of India's public finances, including an incentive-linked debt-relief scheme for the states. Government finances showed significant improvements since then, prior to the recent economic slowdown. The targets for achieving fiscal deficit and revenue deficit under the restructuring programme seemed well within reach for the central as well as the state governments. Many states have enacted their fiscal responsibility legislations and others are following suit. In spite of these achievements, the fiscal transfers system in India requires further reforms concerning both its vertical and horizontal dimensions. These concerns primarily revolve around the following main questions:

1. Stability in Vertical Transfers: Vertical transfers should be stabilized around an appropriate level. These should not continuously be changed in favour of one side or the other. The question assumes importance also because of the likely impact of the proposed Goods and Services Tax (GST) on the vertical imbalance in India.

* Originally published as 'Reforming India's Fiscal Transfer System: Resolving Vertical and Horizontal Imbalances', *Economic and Political Weekly*, Vol. 43, No. 23, 7 June 2008, pp. 47–60.

2. Composition of Transfers: The composition of transfers should be changed towards grants as compared to tax devolution and within grants, larger emphasis should be on statutory grants as recommended by the Finance Commission (FC), rather than grants at the discretion of the centre.

3. Gap-filling Approach to Determining Transfers: In the case of horizontal transfers, the long-term criticism of the Indian approach has been the so-called gap-filling approach in the assessment of needs and resources by the FC, because of the implicit adverse incentives.

4. Measurement of Fiscal Capacity: In applying the equalization principle, the measurement of the fiscal capacity of states is a key requirement. The measurement of state-level fiscal capacity in India is proxied by estimates of the Gross State Domestic Product (GSDP) at factor cost. This provides an incomplete indicator of fiscal capacity although the Central Statistical Organization prepares comparable estimates of GSDP. We need a more comprehensive indicator of fiscal capacity.

5. Determination of Relative Weights of Sharing Criteria: The revenue-sharing criteria used by the FC account by far for the largest share of transfers. However, the relative weights assigned to different criteria remain by and large ad hoc. There is a need to develop a more objective framework for determining suitable weights for the alternative revenue-sharing criteria.

6. Bailouts and Controls on Borrowing: In a system where states have been borrowing heavily from the centre, there is a built-in expectation that the centre will provide a bailout from time to time. This leads to strong adverse incentives for the states to finance current expenditures through borrowing from the centre and other sources and they expect that either a gap-filling grant or a debt-service write-off will bail them out in future.

7. Growing Centralization of Expenditure on State Subjects: This is an issue concerning the relative ambits of assignments of the two tiers of governments. There is clearly a noticeable trend of central government getting involved in progressively spending more and more on subjects that are under the Concurrent List or the State List in the Constitution, sometimes through the state governments and sometimes bypassing them.

This chapter attempts to discuss the following: (i) the evolving fiscal scenario since the recommendations of the TFC, (ii) the issue of resolving vertical imbalance in the context of the proposed GST, and (iii) the horizontal dimension of transfers, particularly the equalization methodology and its adaptation in India in an axiomatic framework guiding tax revenue-sharing. It also highlights the extent of equalization achieved by the TFC recommendations by decomposing recommended transfers into vertical, equalizing, and special needs components, (iv) the considerations relevant for determining suitable weights for the revenue sharing criteria used by the FC, (v) the equalizing health and education grants recommended by the TFC and the need for strengthening these, and (vi) the steps relative to borrowing by the states in the wake of the TFC recommendations.

Fiscal Developments Since the Recommendations of the Twelfth Finance Commission

Empirical Backdrop

The TFC deliberated on fiscal transfer issues in the background of severe fiscal imbalances affecting both central and state finances. To reverse these trends, the TFC recommended a scheme that provided for a major restructuring of government finances including the borrowing and on-lending regimes for the states. These changes were aimed at limiting the borrowing levels of both tiers of government to sustainable levels, removing the adverse incentives in the on-lending mechanism, and maximizing growth by keeping the revenue account in balance and augmenting the saving rate. The evident progress towards lower revenue deficits since 2004–5 also led to the elimination of public sector dis-saving. This was accompanied by moderate interest rates and an increase in investment thereby leading to higher growth. During 2001–2 to 2006–7, the aggregate saving rate went up from 23.5 per cent to 32 per cent. Nearly half of this increase comes from the turnaround in the public sector saving, which increased from (–) 2.0 per cent to 2.0 per cent, a turn about of more than 4 percentage points coming from the reduction in government's dis-saving. This corresponds to a fall in the combined revenue deficit from about 7 per cent of GDP to a little over 2 per cent during the same period.

Table 5.1 shows the profile of fiscal imbalance of the central and state governments, as indicated by revenue, fiscal, and primary deficits from 1990–1 to 2006–7. Consistent with the restructuring plan suggested by

Table 5.1 Fiscal and Revenue Deficits of Centre and States

					(per cent to GDP)	
	Fiscal Deficit		Revenue Deficit		Primary Deficit	
	Centre	States	Centre	States	Centre	States
1990–1	7.76	3.27	3.23	0.92	4.02	1.76
1991–2	5.50	2.86	2.46	0.86	1.47	1.20
1992–3	5.31	2.76	2.45	0.68	1.20	1.01
1993–4	6.93	2.37	3.76	0.44	2.71	0.55
1994–5	5.63	2.70	3.03	0.60	1.33	0.81
1995–6	5.01	2.62	2.47	0.68	0.85	0.79
1996–7	4.82	2.69	2.36	1.16	0.52	0.84
1997–8	5.78	2.87	3.02	1.06	1.51	0.91
1998–9	6.44	4.22	3.80	2.48	2.01	2.18
1999–2000	5.35	4.67	3.45	2.75	0.74	2.36
2000–1	5.64	4.25	4.04	2.54	0.93	1.79
2001–2	6.18	4.21	4.39	2.59	1.47	1.47
2002–3	5.92	4.17	4.40	2.25	1.11	1.31
2003–4	4.47	4.46	3.56	2.22	−0.03	1.50
2004–5	4.00	3.49	2.51	1.16	−0.06	0.68
2005–6	4.11	3.20	2.59	0.48	0.39	0.70
2006–7	3.71	2.58	2.03	0.04	0.15	0.16

Source: RBI and Central Statistical Organization.

GDP figures relate to the 1999–2000 base series. Figures prior to 1999–2000 have been adjusted by a conversion factor.

State fiscal data are taken from RBI and follow RBI coverage and definitions. 2006–7 data for the centre is RE and for the states, BE.

the TFC, there were clear signs that both the central and state govern-ments would meet the fiscal responsibility targets of reducing the fiscal deficit to GDP ratio to 3 per cent. In 2006–7, the revenue deficit of the states relative to GDP fell to a near zero level.

The fiscal deficit of the states had also fallen to below 3 per cent of GDP. These changes indicated that the revenue deficit and fiscal def-icit targets relative to GDP set out by the TFC for 2008–9 were well within reach. With the fall in the fiscal deficit ratio, the debt-GDP had also started falling. For the centre, after reaching a peak at 63.8 per cent in 2004–5, it had fallen to an estimated level of 60.3 per cent in 2006–7. The state debt relative to GDP also fell in the corresponding period from 33.4 per cent to 30.8 per cent. The combined debt-GDP ratio has fallen by nearly 6.6 per centage points from 82.4 per cent to 75.8 per cent. Thus, although the fiscal deficit to GDP ratio has fallen, the fall in the debt-GDP ratio is slower and it will take some more years to reach the target of 56 per cent of GDP as set out by the TFC. That is why, it is important to continue to adhere to the suggested re-form path beyond 2008–9. As shown in Rangarajan and Srivastava (2005), the adjustment period for reaching the debt level relative to GDP at which it should be stabilized could extend beyond the mid-2030s of the current century while maintaining the fiscal deficit of 6 per cent of GDP throughout the period. It can be advanced by a few years by achieving a higher growth rate, but the broad message is that fiscal responsibility targets will have to be adhered to for a long period.

Resolving Vertical Imbalance

An excess of federal revenues relative to its responsibility and a cor-responding deficit in the state accounts where expenditures exceed own revenues is referred to as the vertical fiscal gap. The notion of a vertical gap conceptually contrasts with a benchmark situation in which responsibilities and resources perfectly match for the two tiers of government. In federal systems, a vertical gap is often deliberately created for efficiency gains that result from the relative assignments and fiscal transfers that are used to close the gap or convert it into a balance. The main justification for such transfers may be listed as follows:

1. Transfers may be purely passive responses to the asymmetric decentralization of expenditure and revenue-raising authority (vertical transfers).
2. These may be used to equalize the fiscal capacity of the regions to avoid inefficient migration of persons and businesses among regions and to foster horizontal equity in the federation as a whole (Boadway et al. 2002).
3. These may also be used in conditional forms to neutralize fiscal externalities imposed by regional governments on other regions, as well as to achieve national standards in social programmes and to induce efficiency in the internal economic union of the federation (Dahlby 1996).
4. These may be used as instruments for insuring regions against shocks to their fiscal capacities (Lockwood 2002).

Some Analytical Considerations

The terms vertical gap, vertical imbalance, and vertical fiscal imbalance are often used interchangeably in the literature. However, in the more recent literature, following a normative approach, a distinction is made between vertical gap, optimum vertical gap, and vertical fiscal imbalance. Boadway and Tremblay (2005) and Dahlby and Wilson (1994) define vertical fiscal imbalance in revenue-raising as a deviation from the optimum vertical gap, where the optimum vertical gap is a situation in which the marginal cost of public funds is equalized across the levels of government. In many studies, the allocation of spending responsibilities is taken as predetermined, and the issue is how revenue-raising and federal-regional transfers should be designed to achieve the second-best optimum in a decentralized setting, given that taxes are distortionary.

In Boadway and Tremblay (2005), the notion of imbalance is related to the inability to achieve the second-best optimum in a decentralized federation, and the distinction between the vertical fiscal gap and Vertical Fiscal Imbalance (VFI) reflects that inability. Specifically, the vertical fiscal gap is taken to be the optimal level of transfers when the second best is achieved by a hypothetical central planner, or equivalently a unitary national government that can take coordinated decisions for both levels of government. A VFI is then defined as any deviation whether positive or negative from the optimal vertical fiscal gap. These deviations will occur in a decentralized setting because regional governments emit fiscal externalities on one another (Keen 1998) and are unable to coordinate their decisions. The existence of a VFI will be an optimal response of the federal government to this coordination failure between regional governments, and will be efficiency-enhancing.

Empirically, separating VFI from the Horizontal Fiscal Imbalance (HFI) is quite difficult although it is attempted here in the context of the TFC transfers. Bird and Tarasov (2002, p. 2) observe that

> it is important to understand that the two concepts of fiscal balance ... —VFI and HFI— cannot be cleanly separated. One way to think of VFI, for example, is that it might be considered to be eliminated—that is vertical fiscal balance is achieved ... when expenditures and revenues (excluding transfers) are balanced for the *richest* local government, measured in terms of its capacity to raise resources on its own. Even if this is achieved, fiscal gaps or VFI will of course still remain for all poorer local governments. Generally ... it is common to discuss such gaps instead as HFI ...

Later in this chapter, we will follow the approach of taking the per capita transfer to the richest state as the benchmark for calculating the vertical transfers.

India: Long-term Stability in Vertical Imbalance

As shown in the TFC Report, in India there has been long-term stability in the vertical distribution of resources after transfers. It is remarkable that while the relevant ratios and shares have been adjusted from time to time, there is a perceptible stability of the relative shares of the centre and states in the combined revenue receipts and combined revenue expenditures. The main features of the resultant vertical distribution of resources may be highlighted since the period of the Seventh Finance Commission as follows:

1. Prior to transfers, the centre collects on average about 63–4 per cent of the combined revenue receipts; after transfers, the states get nearly 64 per cent of the combined revenue receipts.
2. This enables the states to spend nearly 57 per cent of the combined expenditure on average on revenue account. The centre spends about 43 per cent of the combined revenue expenditure by retaining 36 per cent of revenues after transfers by borrowing relatively more.

The Eleventh Finance Commission (EFC) had suggested for the first time an indicative benchmark of 37.5 per cent covering all transfers from the centre to the states, with a view to achieving stability in the overall transfers from the centre to the states. Given the historical trends and the current relatively high buoyancies of the central taxes, particularly the direct taxes and service tax, the TFC suggested a marginally higher benchmark of 38 per cent. The TFC also recommended an increase in the share of states in central taxes to 30.5 per cent of the divisible revenues. There has been an argument that this share should be fixed in nominal terms for a few decades or so. It can be argued that the objective of stability will not be served by fixing the share of states in the central taxes in nominal terms as long as the central and state taxes are growing with different buoyancies. In particular, some upward adjustment is needed if central taxes are growing more than that of the states. At the present juncture this was justified as the centre's tax buoyancy is expected to be relatively higher due to their exclusive power to tax the base of growing services while for some time states will be undergoing adjustments on account of moving to the state-level VAT.

As detailed in Appendix 5A.1, it can be shown that between any two periods, the share of states in the total tax revenue of the centre and states after transfers will be constant only if the share of states in the central taxes is increased by the margin by which the buoyancy of central tax revenues exceeds the buoyancy of the combined tax revenues. This result can also be stated in terms of the buoyancies of the central and state taxes.

Table 5.2 Share of States in Combined Revenues

			(per cent)
Average (Award Period)	Revenue Receipts		Revenue Expenditure
Finance Commissions	Before Transfer	After Transfer	
Seventh	35.3	61.4	58.0
Eighth	34.6	62.0	55.7
Ninth	37.5	64.7	56.9
Tenth	38.6	63.0	56.8
Eleventh	39.0	63.9	57.1

Source: Indian Public Finance Statistics.

Representing the respective buoyancies of state, central, and combined tax revenues as b, c, and d, and the share of states in central taxes and t and t' between two periods, it can be shown that the share of states (or centre) in total tax revenues after transfers will be constant between the two periods if

$$t' - t = (c - d)g \qquad (5.1)$$

where g is the GDP growth rate. If α is the share of the states' own revenues in total tax revenues, this condition can also be written as

$$t' - t = (c - b)\,\alpha.g \qquad (5.2)$$

This also implies that for stability, there should be no change in the share of states if the buoyancy of central taxes is equal to that of the states.[2] Adjustments are also needed if the central government changes the size of the divisible pool by additional surcharges and cesses that are not divisible.

A scheme of assignment of resources, heavily in favour of the centre purely for efficiency reasons, is always prone to lead to a centralization of expenditures in direct and indirect ways. There is a noticeable tendency in India for various expenditures in the Concurrent List, and often even if they belong to the State List, to be incurred by the central government.

Vertical Imbalance and GST

Considering some important forthcoming tax reforms in India, it is important also to recognize that the vertical imbalance would be affected depending on the way the GST is implemented in India. In Australia, the implementation of GST led to a substantial increase in the vertical imbalance because the states agreed to forego a number of taxes assigned to them in favour of a national GST. In India, the 2007–8 budget has mentioned the plan for implementing a National GST by 1 April 2010. This target date has subsequently been shifted. The exact contours of the plan for GST, which are still being debated, would have a significant bearing on the vertical imbalance in the system. In this context, the following three issues are of importance.

Nature of GST Regime

First, it is important to determine whether the proposal is for a central GST, or state GST, or a concurrent or dual GST. In the first two cases, the pre-transfer vertical imbalance would increase substantially. The options may be as follows:

Central GST: In this case the GST is levied by the central government and state VATs are all subsumed in this central levy. This would be like the Australian model. This option would deliver harmonization by definition as only uniform rates will prevail. The whole country would be one common market and there would be no problems related to inter-state trade. But this would increase vertical imbalance tremendously. States would have to forego their power to levy a sales tax. A provision would have to be made for distribution of the centrally collected VAT. Although a similar arrangement has been implemented in Australia, it would have a significant impact on the nature of fiscal federal relations. States would lose their autonomy to fix rates and collect their own revenues. It is doubtful that states would agree to such an arrangement. The scheme of redistribution would also be required to follow a principle different from the one normally used by the FC so that states are adequately compensated for the revenues that they would have otherwise earned through the existing system of state VAT or sales taxes.

Concurrent or Dual GST: This seems the most practical route as it can be implemented while maintaining the current pre-and post-transfer profiles of vertical imbalance. It would require that states be enabled to tax services and the service tax rate should be the same as that for goods. Alongside, the central government should be enabled to tax value added in the case of goods up to the retail stage. These changes would lead to a comprehensive and unified system of taxation of goods and services. The major problem in this case would be the handling of inter-state transactions. In the literature, three main solutions have been suggested, (a) a system of compensating VAT (CVAT); (b) dual VAT; and (c) Viable Integrated VAT (VIVAT). The system of compensating VAT (CVAT) is also known as the Versano proposal. McLure Jr (2000) suggested a modified version of the CVAT. In CVAT, uniform definitions and laws for the tax base in all jurisdictions are needed. States are allowed, however, to have their own tax rates with the proviso that all inter-state transactions are zero-rated for state VAT. In addition to the central VAT, the central government levies a compensating VAT for all inter-state transactions. The rate of compensating VAT is common across states. For inter-state imports, a system of deferred payment of state VAT and credit for compensating VAT is then put in place. The compensating VAT is an additional federal-level tax to ensure the tax revenues that might otherwise be lost to cross-border tax evasion are captured. One alternative to CVAT in concurrent tax regimes is the dual VAT as practiced in Canada (see Bird and Gendron (2000)). In dual VAT, central and state VAT rates are applied. States have the autonomy to determine the state VAT rates. The central VAT is included in the tax base of the state VAT. States therefore have an incentive to collect the central component, if they are asked to collect it. The VIVAT system pertains to the exclusive state-level VAT system.

State-level VAT: This option takes one to the other extreme where the GST/VAT is levied exclusively by the state governments. This also changes the vertical balance equations drastically although in favour of the states. The centre will then largely lose power to undertake transfers for purposes of horizontal transfers. Even to provide centrally provided public goods, it may need to save some sumptuary excises for itself. Otherwise, it may have to depend on reverse transfers. The problem of inter-state harmonization and inter-state transactions will remain. For the case of an exclusive state VAT regime, Keen and Smith (1999) suggested the system of Viable Integrated VAT (VIVAT). In this case, for all intermediate purchases, that is, sales between dealers, a uniform tax rate regime is advocated. This would be applied to transactions within a state as well as across states. There is no central VAT or GST.

If the vertical imbalance in the system is not to be drastically altered, the concurrent or dual VAT regime seems to be most relevant in the current fiscal conditions of India. Subsequent deliberations and models currently being discussed in India suggest that it is concurrent GST which may be adopted in India.

Determining the Overall Rate

The second issue is to determine a suitable GST rate. At present goods are taxed at the core rate of Cenvat at 16 per cent and state VAT of 12.5 per cent. This together would be very high although it would be less than 28.5 per cent as the 16 per cent rate applies to value added only up to the manufacturing stage and the GST will have a larger base. The service tax rate is 12 per cent. The suggestion of the Kelkar Committee to aim at a 20 per cent combined GST rate seems to be a suitable target as it compares well with some of the international GST rates. The highest GST rates are in Sweden and Denmark at 25 per cent. At the lower end, Switzerland, Japan, Thailand, and Singapore have GST/VAT rates at 5 per cent or marginally above.

Determining the Central and State GST Rate Components

The third issue relates to decomposing the overall GST rate into its central and state components making sure that the relative pre-transfer revenue levels are not disturbed. To achieve a 20 per cent composite rate, both tiers of government have to jointly bring down the overall tax rate, which at present amounts to 16 per cent and 12.5 per cent on the respective tax bases of the Cenvat and state VAT as far as manufacturing and sales of goods are concerned. While the tax rate on goods can come down, that on services, which is at 12 per cent, may have to be incrementally raised to bring it closer to the long-term desired norm. In the medium term, to preserve our federal structure, a system of dual taxation consisting of a State GST (SGST) and a Central GST (CGST) seems to be a viable option. The Kelkar Committee had suggested a division of the overall rate of 20 per cent into a 12:8 ratio in favour of the centre. This may need to be re-examined with current levels of revenues under Cenvat and service taxes and the SGST and other related taxes that may be subsumed in the GST.

Resolving Horizontal Imbalance: Towards Equalizing Transfers

In theory as well as practice, a system of equalization transfers is considered desirable as it is consistent with both equity and efficiency. The efficiency implications follow from two considerations:

1. Locational inefficiencies that can result from inefficient migration induced by fiscal surpluses are neutralized by equalization transfers; and
2. The redistribution implied by equalization transfers from the richer to poorer states gives a return also to the richer states by avoiding congestion resulting from excessive migration in the context of services provided by these states that are in the nature of 'congestible' goods.

Courchene (1984 and 1992) argued that the efficiency case of equalization depends on the existence of fiscally induced migration. If there is no fiscally induced migration, there is no efficiency case for equalization. Dahlby and Wilson (1994) made a case for equalization on efficiency grounds even in the absence of fiscally induced migration. They examine the role of equalization grants as an instrument for maximizing a social welfare function or minimizing the 'excess burden' of taxation. Optimal tax theory suggests that the social cost of raising revenues depends not only on the size of the tax base but also on the responsiveness of the tax base to tax rate changes. They argue that it is important to use 'responsiveness' (or buoyancies in the formula for equalization) rather than just the tax rate. The higher the demand and supply elasticities to tax rate changes, the larger the marginal cost of public funds. On this basis they show that differences in fiscal capacities, even in the absence of fiscally induced migration, are sound grounds for arguing for equalization.

Equalization: Some International Practices

In Canada, the 'equalization' payments have been mandated in the constitution since 1982, which commits the federal government to the 'principle of making equalization payments to ensure that provincial governments have sufficient revenues to provide reasonably comparable levels of public services at reasonably comparable levels of taxation'. This has been discussed in detail in Chapter 3. The equalization transfer to a province in absolute amount is determined by applying the average revenue effort to the difference between the standard base and the actual base for that province with respect to the various revenue sources. This produces an estimate of revenue which is higher than the actual revenue for provinces that have 'below-average' capacity. This exercise is carried out for all revenue bases used by the provinces (see e.g., Rangarajan and Srivastava (2004b), for a discussion). In the Canadian system, there is no reference to cost differentials and the states are free to use their equalized capacities in providing any mix of public goods and merit goods. The equalization grants are supplemented by health and social sector transfers that are equally important in volume and are also of an equalizing nature.

The Australian system of equalization transfers as discussed in Chapter 4 (see Rangarajan and Srivastava (2005)) goes into the question of cost differentials relevant for comparison with some notion of equal efficiency in the provision of goods and services by the provincial authorities. The guiding principle of the horizontal transfers system is fiscal equalization, which is defined by the Commonwealth Grants Commission (CGC) as follows: 'State governments should receive funding from the pool of goods and services tax revenue and health care grants such that, if each made the same effort to raise revenue from its own sources and operated at the same level of efficiency, each would have the capacity to provide services at the same standard'. The Australian equalization differs from the Canadian equalization due to the reference to efficiency and standard of services. The Canadian system makes reference only to equalization in fiscal capacity. In Australia, fiscal equalization looks at both the revenue and expenditure sides. It may be noted that the typical methodology for determining equalization transfers is not devoid of adverse incentives, as discussed in some recent literature (e.g., Garnaut and FitzGerald 2002b) on the subject.

The ground conditions in India are different from Canada or Australia in two critical respects. First, the extent of difference in the resource bases is far larger than in Australia or Canada. For example, the ratio of maximum per capita GSDP to minimum is 1.6 to 1 between Ontario (leaving Alberta as a special case) and Prince Edwards Islands; in Australia, the ratio of per capita GSDP of New South Wales to Tasmania is 1.5 to 1. In India, this ratio between Maharashtra or more recently Haryana (leaving Goa as a special case) and Bihar is close to 6 to 1. The second difference is that the population that resides in the main 'donor' states as compared with the main recipient states is much larger in Canada and Australia. In India, it is the other way round. As a result, the amount of redistribution implicit in the equalizing scheme is far larger when the recipients are more than donors, making it extremely difficult to achieve full equalization. Thirdly, there are large inter-state differences in cost conditions in India due to differences in density and composition of population, nature of terrain, and other such factors.

In India, the horizontal imbalance is resolved through a combination of tax devolution and revenue-gap grants. In Canada, this is done by grants. In Australia, this is done by sharing the revenue under the GST topped up by the Health Care Grants. The Australian system has switched from grants to revenue-sharing and back from time to time. Some economists consider grants as the right means of transfers. States themselves overwhelmingly prefer revenue-sharing. The transfer system in India has evolved in a manner that relies on both modes of transfer. Finding a suitable combination is the relevant problem.

India: Tax Revenue-Sharing under an Axiomatic Framework

An explicit equalization methodology was not developed or followed in India. Instead, an elaborate framework of tax revenue-sharing was developed supplemented by revenue-gap grants. This methodology can also lead to an equalizing system of transfers if some basic principles are followed. The evolution of criteria-based tax revenue-sharing as recommended by the Finance Commission can be interpreted in an axiomatic framework. Fully equalizing transfers are a special case under this axiomatic framework. The following five axioms may be proposed as desirable axioms for criteria-based revenue-sharing: (i) Normalization 1, (ii) Normalization 2, (iii) Horizontal equity, (iv) Comprehensiveness, and (v) Neutrality. The two normalization axioms and horizontal equity can give rise to a system of fully equalizing transfers.

Axiom 1: Normalization 1
If two states have the same criterion values, their shares should be proportional to their populations.[3]

Axiom 2: Normalization 2
The sum of the shares of all states should add to 1.

Axiom 3: Horizontal Equity
Between any pair of states, the state with a lower per capita fiscal capacity should have a higher per capita share, and per capita shares should be equal for states with equal per capita fiscal capacity.

Axiom 4: Comprehensiveness
In determining the share of any one state, information on all states should be used. A corollary of this is that under each criterion, every state should get a positive share.

Axiom 5: Neutrality
The allocation criterion should be neutral with respect to the organization of states. There should not be an incentive to bifurcate states with a view to benefiting from the allocation mechanism.

These axioms are discussed in Appendix 5A.2. It may be noted that the FCs have endeavoured to meet these criteria even though they were not explicitly stated. The same cannot be said, for example, of the dispensation criterion for determining grants under the Gadgil formula. Under their deviation formula, states with per capita GSDP above the national per capita GDP or average per capita GSDP get a zero share thereby not satisfying the comprehensiveness criterion. Similarly Assam, with a lower per capita GSDP, may sometimes get a per capita grant which is lower than Meghalaya, thereby violating the horizontal equity criterion. Since shares under the individual criteria under the Gadgil formula are not made public, it is not possible to subject these to a critical review.

Measuring the Extent of Equalization:
TFC Recommendations

For broad issues like those of resolving vertical and horizontal imbalances, the fiscal transfer scheme needs to be analysed in terms of the combined effect of all components of transfer. The total recommended transfers to states may be calculated based on the projections of the TFC regarding tax devolution and adding to these the grants already specified in nominal terms. The grant profile tends to give larger grants in the initial years, and to get a better picture of the inter-state distribution of the recommended transfers, we have given the average annual transfers by dividing total transfers by 5 and considering the average annual transfers as centred in 2007–8. These are given in Appendix Table 5A.1 in per capita terms using the state-wise population of the 2001 Census.

The issue of determination of revenue-gap grants as 'gap-filling' has been raised by many authors from time to time. The concern arises from the implicit adverse incentive for a state to create a history of expenditure in the expectation of getting a grant later. For the period covered by the recent FC, except for a very limited number of general category states and for some years, the revenue-gap grant is given mostly only for the special category states. The fact that the special category states get a large share of the revenue-gap grant follows from their large committed expenditures linked to the large plan assistance that they have obtained in the past.

Let the per capita income (GSDP) of the states arranged in ascending order of per capita GSDP be denoted by $y_1, y_2, ..., y_n$ and the corresponding population be denoted by $N_1, N_2, ..., N_n$. If the vertical fiscal transfer is measured with reference to the richest state, in per capita terms, it may be defined as $[e - a.y_n]$ (assuming that $e > a.y_n$), where e is per capita expenditure norm, a is the average tax-effort, and y_n is the per capita fiscal capacity of the highest income state. If e is exogenously or normatively determined, the total transfer to the highest income state is given by

$$N_n.[e - a.y_n]$$

Since every state gets at least the amount $[e - a.y_n]$ in terms of per capita transfers, we may write total vertical transfer as

$$\sum N_i [e - a.y_n] = [e - a.y_n] \sum N_i \qquad (5.3)$$

All other states have a lower fiscal capacity and would get an amount, in per capita terms, higher than that obtained by the highest-income state in a progressive scheme of transfers under the axiom of horizontal equity. The transfers to these states can be seen as consisting of the vertical component equal to the per capita transfer to the highest income state, an 'equalizing' component due to deficiency in fiscal capacity and a residual which reflects cost disabilities and other special need considerations.

Thus, for any state i, the per capita transfer can be decomposed into three components reflecting (a) transfers made on account of vertical imbalance, (b) transfers on account of equalization transfers, and (c) the residual component. Thus, per capita transfers to a state can be written as:

$$t_i = (e - ay_n) + (ay_n - ay_i) + res_i \quad \text{for a state where } res_i \geq 0 \qquad (5.4)$$

Here, e is permitted per capita expenditure norm, a is average tax effort, and 'res' is the residual reflecting other cost and special need considerations. The term $(ay_n - ay_i)$ represents equalization transfers. The states may be divided into two groups: one where the per capita recommended transfer consists of three components: vertical, equalizing, and special needs as given above. There may be other states where, after vertical transfers are taken out, the balance falls short of equalization entitlement and there is nothing left for special needs. Let the shortfall in such cases be def_i. In their case, we may write per capita transfers as

$$t_i = (e - ay_n) + (ay_n - ay_i) - def_i \qquad (5.5)$$

In both cases, we can multiply the per capita transfers by respective populations to get total transfers. By adding up the two sets, we get the total transfers (TT) as

$$TT = \sum N_i t_i = \sum N_i (e - ay_n) + [\sum N_i (ay_n - ay_i) - \sum N_i def_i] + \sum N_i res_i$$

Here, $def_i > 0$ is for states that get less than their equalization entitlement and $res_i > 0$ is for states that get more than their equalization entitlement.

The total transfers can thus be divided into three components, the respective shares of which in total transfers may be written as:

1. Share of vertical transfers in total transfers: $A1 = \sum N_i (e - ay_n) / TT$
2. Share of equalizing transfer in total transfers: $A2 = [\sum N_i (ay_n - ay_i) - \sum N_i def_i] / TT$
3. Share of transfers for special needs: $A3 = \sum N_i res_i / TT$

We calculate below these shares for the TFC recommended transfers. In making these calculations, the following qualifications apply:

1. Average per capita comparable GSDP at current prices for 1999–2000 to 2001–2, as used by the TFC, is taken as a macro proxy of the state base for own tax revenues.
2. Population according to the 2001 census is used wherever population is required to be used for conversions of aggregates into per capita terms or vice versa. It may be noted that wherever relevant, the TFC had used 1971 population data.
3. The estimated per capita transfer of Maharashtra is used to determine the vertical transfers. Maharashtra has the minimum per capita transfer among all states.

4. The all-state average tax-GSDP ratio is taken as 6.54 per cent, as given in the TFC Report.

5. Comparisons are made for transfers centred in 2007–8, which is the mid-year of the TFC award period. Tax devolution is taken as projected by TFC for different years and grants as spread out for different years and the total is divided by 5 to obtain transfers centred in 2007–8.

It is shown that the per capita transfers for the highest benchmark state, that is, Maharashtra is Rs 746.67. This multiplied by the total population of all states in 2001 at Rs 101.209 crore gives a total vertical transfer of Rs 75,570 crore. The total transfer recommended by TFC consists of Rs 6,13,112 crore of estimated devolution and Rs 1,42,640 crore of grants for five years. Thus, the per year transfer is Rs 1,51,150.4 crore. As shown in Table 5.4, vertical transfers constitute about 50 per cent of total transfers. We calculate below the degree of equalization achieved and the share of transfers devoted to equalization.

The equalization transfer is calculated and added for each state as determined by $[N_i * (a) * (y_n - y_i)]$, where symbols have meaning defined as earlier. In particular ' a ' is the average tax price, which is equal to the average own tax revenue to GSDP ratio of the states, equal to 6.54 per cent (as given in Annexure 7.9 of the TFC Report). The details of the calculations and the related decomposition are given in Appendix Tables 5A.1 and 5A.2. A comparison of equalizing transfers plus vertical transfers, called benchmark transfers, with the TFC recommended transfers is depicted in Figure 5.1.

In Figure 5.1 the general category states (leaving Goa) are arranged in ascending order of per capita income. It will be seen that the TFC-recommended transfers are progressive and follow the same pattern as equalization transfers determined at the average tax price. It can be said that for the general category states that, except Goa, the pattern of transfers follows an equalizing approach and not a gap-filling approach. This is because, in their case the effective determinant of transfers is tax devolution supplemented by equalizing grants on health and education that supplement the equalizing content of tax devolution. At the same time, vertical transfers are taken care of by the larger weight to population

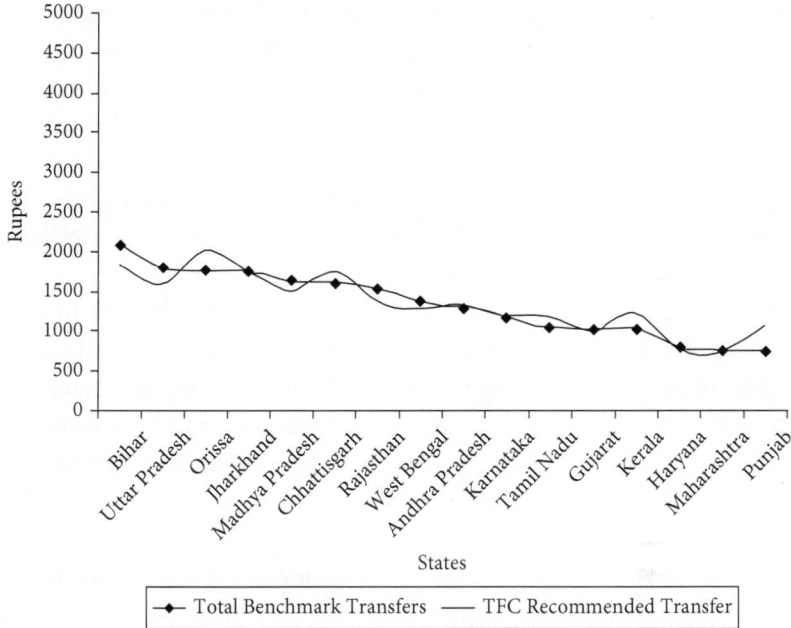

Figure 5.1 Comparing Equalizing Benchmark Transfers with Twelfth Finance Commission Recommended Transfers: General States

Table 5.3 Twelfth Finance Commission Recommended Transfers: Vertical and Horizontal Components

	(Rs crore)
Total Transfers (average per year centred in 2007–8)	151150.4
Amount used for vertical transfers	75570
Share of vertical transfer	50.00
Amount for equalization transfers	58738
Share of equalizing transfers in total transfers	38.86
Amount needed for full equalization	66740
Extent of equalization achieved	88.01
Amount used for cost differential and special needs	16843
Share of transfers for cost diff and special needs	11.14

Source: Estimated based on Appendix Tables 5A.1 and 5A.2.

criterion, the weights given to tax effort and fiscal discipline criteria, and a number of grants that relate to maintenance and special needs.

Table 5.3 summarizes the relative shares of the three components in total transfers, that is, vertical, equalizing, and special needs. Details are given in Appendix Tables 5A.1 and 5A.2.

It is thus clear that 50 per cent of total transfers are used as vertical transfers. Despite this large share for vertical transfers, 88 per cent of equalization has been achieved when it is evaluated at the average tax-GSDP ratio. A little more than 11 per cent of transfers are used for special needs that have gone mainly to the special category states. This large degree of equalization could be achieved by introducing the health and equalization grants, which use relatively a small amount of transfer but improve the equalizing content of transfers significantly as they go only to those states that are less than average in the per capita health and education expenditure. The TFC has made a new beginning in this context. However, the gap covered was only 30 per cent in the case of health and 15 per cent in the case of education. These ratios will have to be increased to a larger extent to achieve full equalization.

Several qualifications may be noted in respect of the above comparisons. First, the equalization benchmark is calculated with a revenue side approach and expenditure side considerations are not included. Secondly, a macro base reflecting fiscal capacity like the GSDP is used. Thirdly, the highest per capita GSDP among states, excluding Goa, is used as the benchmark. Fourthly, shortfalls from the equalization benchmarks are equally weighted. Ideally, shortfalls for lower-income states would require a relatively higher weight.

Determining Relative Weights of Tax Devolution Criteria

Considerable time is spent by the FC on determining the relative weights that should be attached to the different tax devolution criteria, yet an explicit analytical framework has not been spelt out for this purpose. Given the preceding discussion, it is possible to develop a framework for determining suitable weights for alternative devolution criteria. Given the benchmark for equalization (such as the highest or mean income), the total amount needed for equalization gets determined. Thus, the amount needed for equalization (horizontal transfer) is given by

$$H = a.\sum N_i(y_n - y_i) \qquad (5.6)$$

Here, a is the average tax effort. The vertical transfer (V) may be determined exogenously as it relates to the overall balance of responsibilities and resources. Both the vertical and horizontal transfers can be given through either route, that is, grants or tax devolution. In the case of both tax devolution and grants, three components can be distinguished: vertical component, horizontal component that is equalizing, and horizontal component reflecting other considerations. Suppose these three components given through grants are referred to as g^v (same for all states), g_i^h, and g_i^o. The latter two are different per capita amounts for different states. The corresponding transfers through tax devolution are, say, d^v, d_i^h, and d_i^o.

Thus, we have the following sets of decompositions:

$$t_i = t_v + t_i^h + t_i^o \text{ (same as equation 5.4 given earlier)}$$
$$g_i = g_v + g_i^h + g_i^o$$
$$d_i = d_v + d_i^h + d_i^o$$

where $t_v = g_v + d_v, t_i^h = g_i^h + d_i^h$, and $t_i^o = g_i^o + d_i^o$ (5.7)

Let a share W of per capita devolution ($= W.d$) be given for (total devolution $D = d.\sum N_i$) equalizing horizontal transfers (using criterion like the distance criterion), a share $W1$ of d for vertical transfer (under population or similar criterion). The remaining part of devolution constitutes a share $W2$, which is given for other considerations (like cost differentials), where the three weights add to 1. $W2$ may be taken as exogenously determined. Putting together the equalizing horizontal transfers under grants and through tax devolution, the following condition should be satisfied:

$$W.D + \sum N_i g_i^h = a.\sum N_i(y_n - y_i)$$

This can be solved to yield,

$$W.D = a.\sum N_i(y_n - y_i) - \sum N_i g_i^h \qquad (5.8)$$

Or,

$$W.d = a.(y_n - \mu) - g^h \qquad (5.9)$$

Where, d is per capita devolution, y_n is benchmark per capita income, μ is mean income $(= \sum N_i y_i /(\sum N_i))$, and g^h is mean per capita equalizing transfers given as a grant. For the vertical transfer, we have

$V = (\sum N_i)[g^v + d^v]$ or the per capita vertical transfer is, $v = [g^v + d^v]$.
Per capita vertical transfers given through devolution is

$$(1 - W - W2)d = d^v \qquad (5.10)$$

Using equations (5.9) and (5.10), we have,

$$(1 - W - W2)/W = d^v/[a.(y_n - \mu) - g^h]$$

This can be solved to yield,

$$W = (1 - W2)^*[(a.(y_n - \mu) - g^h]/[d^v + a.(y_n - \mu) - g^h] \qquad (5.11)$$

Correspondingly

$$d = [d^v + a.(y_n - \mu) - g^h]/(1 - W2) \qquad (5.12)$$

This indicates that given

1. the exogenously determined average per capita equalizing grant (g^h),
2. weight to be given to considerations other than vertical or equalizing transfer in devolution ($W2$),
3. the benchmark (y_n) and average per capita fiscal capacity (μ),
4. the average tax-GSDP ratio (a), and
5. the exogenously determined per capita vertical devolution (d^v),

the weight that needs to be given to horizontal equalizing devolution (under the distance or similar criteria) and the total amount of per capita devolution may simultaneously be determined in order to achieve full equalization.

In practice, in applying this to India, the tax devolution criteria in India may be considered in three parts: those meant for vertical transfers (population, and a large component of transfer under tax effort, fiscal discipline criteria), those meant for equalizing horizontal transfers (distance), and those reflecting cost disabilities (like area). The effort and fiscal discipline criteria are efficiency-promoting modifications of the population criterion and should be taken as part of the group of tax devolution criterion meant for vertical transfers and the deviations may be counted as part of the 'other' considerations.

Illustrating these considerations, with the TFC per capita amounts, centred in 2007–8, subject to some approximations, Table 5.4 provides the relevant numbers. State-wise details are given in Appendix Table 5A.3. The numbers are derived in a manner consistent with the decompositions given in equation 5.7.

It may be noted that the actual weight given to the distance formula in the TFC was 50 per cent. However, since even in the devolution formula an amount is given to the highest-income state, there is a vertical component. The actual weight to the equalizing horizontal component is estimated to be 45 per cent, obtained by dividing d^h by d. The desired weight as derived for full equalization weight is marginally more at 47 per cent. In addition, this is associated with higher per capita devolution amounting to Rs 1,275 instead of the actual amount of Rs 1,212. It may be also noted that increasing the amount of equalizing horizontal grants would reduce the total amount needed for devolution almost by the same margin since the term g^h occurs in the numerator. This would also affect the weight to the equalizing component of the devolution formula, but the effect operates through both numerator and denominator. In general, increasing the equalization component of grants makes it easier to achieve full equalization through devolution. That is why, the equalization grants given in respect of education and health, which was a new type of grant given by the TFC, but where equalization was limited only to 30 per cent, needs to be strengthened.

Table 5.4 Illustrative Derivation of Weight for Equalization

			(Amounts in Rs)
g^v	g^h	g^o	g
114.2	38.5	129.2	281.87
d^v	d^h	d^o	d
632.5	541.91	37.18	1,211.58
v	h	o	t
746.7	580.4	166.4	1,493.4
a. $(y_n - \mu)$	641.20		

Weight to horizontal equalizing devolution and per capita devolution

	Desired	Actual (as per TFC)
W	0.47	0.45
d	1,274.34	1,211.58

Source: *TFC Report*, 2004, Variables defined as in text amounts are in per capita terms.

Equalization Grants for Health and Education

In devolution formulae, it is difficult to use the mean income as the benchmark as states with per capita incomes higher than the mean income will get a zero share in tax devolution. The practice followed by the FCs in India has been to allocate a positive share to all states. It is easier to use benchmarks with reference to the mean of per capita incomes or service levels in determining grants for selected services. In this context, the TFC introduced equalization grants for education and health to augment the equalization content of fiscal transfers, focusing on two high-merit services.

In devising a grant that is specific-purpose and aimed at given sectors, it is important to make up for the deficiency in resources but not to underwrite the deficiency in priority accorded to the sector by the concerned state government. The TFC methodology entailed the following steps: (i) derivation of the average preference for allocation to health and education (say a) and (ii) derivation of the gap of the state-specific expenditure on the concerned service (education/health) from the corresponding group average (general category/special category states) evaluated by applying the average preference to the state's aggregate expenditure. Thus for, any service, suppose that the group average per capita expenditure is z and state-specific expenditure for a state, z_i.

Here,
$$z = \Sigma z_i N_i / \Sigma N_i \qquad (5.13)$$

Subscript i varies over the states belonging to the relevant group. The per capita capacity of a state is given by r_i and the average capacity is given by

$$r = \Sigma r_i N_i / \Sigma N_i \qquad (5.14)$$

The average budgetary allocation for the given service is given by

$$a = \Sigma z_i N_i / \Sigma r_i N_i$$

Thus,
$$z = a.r \text{ and } z_i = a_i.r_i.$$

The actual gap in expenditure between a state and the group average can be seen as the sum of two components: one due to deficiency in fiscal capacity and the other due to giving the concerned sector less than average preference. It is only the first part, that is deficiency in expenditure due to lack of capacity, that is taken into account, while the deficiency that results from giving less than average preference in budgetary allocation is ignored. Thus, the actual gap may be written as:

$$z - z_i = (z - ar_i) + (ar_i - z_i) \qquad (5.15)$$

or,
$$z - z_i = a(r - r_i) + (a - a_i)r_i \text{ [where } a_i = z_i / r_i \text{]} \qquad (5.16)$$

Thus, the relevant gap is reflected in the first term, which is due to the deficiency in the fiscal capacity, given the average allocation to the concerned sector. The second term is the difference due to allocating less than the average share given the capacity of the state, and this difference does not require to be made up under the equalization principle. Thus, the total grant should be determined by $N_i a(r - r_i)$. In estimating the resources, r was proxied by resources devoted to expenditure excluding interest payments and pensions. In the TFC scheme, only 30 per cent of the equalizing grants were provided. Clearly, there is a need for providing larger equalizing transfers as this would ease the pressure on tax revenue-sharing to accommodate a large share of equalizing transfers.

Discontinuance of Further Debt Relief

Recommendations regarding debt relief were formulated in the context of the overall programme for restructuring government finances in the country. Debt relief was linked to the state governments meeting a set of conditionalities including the enactment of fiscal responsibility legislation. According to available information, all state governments, except two, have already enacted their respective fiscal responsibility legislations.

Two major recommendations regarding the state-level borrowing from the centre were: (i) to delink grants and loans in plan assistance, and (ii) to discontinue the centre's intermediation for state borrowing. Once the centre's intermediation is discontinued, the moral hazard of expecting periodic bailouts would also be eliminated or at least significantly reduced. There is now no case for including a 'debt-relief' clause in the terms of reference for future Finance Commissions. The Reserve Bank of India (RBI) has recommended that states should go more and more for the auction route as it leads to price discovery, promotes market discipline, and improves secondary market liquidity. With some degree of flexibility in borrowing from the National Small Saving Fund (NSSF), the states should be able to adapt to the new market-oriented regime without much difficulty. Regarding the NSSF, the obligatory share of the states has been reduced to 80 per cent with effect from 2007–8. The RBI has made arrangements so that State Development Loans (SDLs) are eligible for repo transactions under the liquidity adjustment facility, and it has been decided to introduce the non-competitive bidding facility in respect of the primary auctions of SDLs. While the centre's intermediation has been discontinued, loans and grants have not been delinked in plan assistance except in the case of external assistance. This linking requires re-examination on the part of the Planning Commission particularly when the assistance is for social sector projects or for poverty alleviation where the capacity to service the loan is not created as a result of assistance.

The TFC had also recommended the constitution of a loan council, which may decide the overall annual borrowing limits for the state governments. While a fully-fledged loan council has not been constituted, some steps have been taken towards achieving the related objectives. In particular, the RBI has moved to set up a Standing Technical Committee (STC) with representation from the central and state governments and the RBI. The STC will make annual projections of borrowing requirements of the state governments, build alternative scenarios, and suggest alternative strategies and instruments for raising state resources. It will also advise a mechanism for the annual allocation of market borrowings among the states. It will take note of actual and budgeted borrowings of the state governments, develop a suitable database, assess fiscal risks from issuances of guarantees, and advise state governments on various issues relating to their borrowings.

It is useful to note that the reference to the debt relief clause has now been withdrawn from the terms of reference to the Thirteenth Finance Commission. This follows from the discontinuance of centre's intermediation in state borrowing and on-lending to states subject to limited exceptions like the external assistance, which is also being passed on back-to-back terms.

* * *

This chapter has reviewed the fiscal transfer arrangements in India in the context of resolving the vertical and horizontal imbalances. The main conclusions may be summarized as follows:

Vertical Imbalance

In the literature, a distinction has been made between the concepts of vertical gap, optimum vertical gap, and vertical fiscal imbalance. In the context of the Indian transfer system, in resolving the vertical fiscal imbalance, the following points have been made:

1. In India, there has been long-term stability in the share of the centre and states in the combined tax revenues of the system after tax devolution. It may be considered desirable to continue to maintain

this stability as long as there are no basic changes in the division of responsibilities between the centre and the states. It is further shown that maintaining such stability would require an upward adjustment in the share of states in the divisible pool of taxes in periods where the expected buoyancy of central taxes is higher than that of the states.

2. The proposed move to a national GST will have significant implications for vertical imbalance. For maintaining the existing extent of vertical imbalance, a concurrent system of GST is recommended. The GST rates for the two tiers should be determined taking into account the present level of revenues of the two tiers from the concerned taxes. If, however, a central GST is adopted, the vertical imbalance of resources prior to transfers will shift excessively in favour of the centre, and the resultant vertical gap will have to be resolved by a corresponding increase in transfers. This will also have significant implications for the horizontal distribution of transfers.

3. For operational purposes, 'vertical gap' is measured in this chapter as the total transfer to all states. This reflects the division of resources between the two tiers of government without looking into the inter se distribution of the share of states among the states. With a view to examining the inter se distribution, the transfers recommended by the Finance Commission are further decomposed into: (i) the vertical component of transfers (as distinct from the vertical gap) indicating per capita transfers to all states including the highest-income state, (ii) equalizing transfers indicating the component of transfers only to the states with a fiscal capacity less than the defined benchmark capacity, and (iii) a residual reflecting special needs and ad hoc components.

Horizontal Imbalance

In respect of the horizontal dimension of transfers, the equalization approach to transfers, which is followed by some of the important federal systems like Canada and Australia, is suitable for India also. While in Canada, attention is focused on equalizing revenue capacities only, in Australia, this is complemented by a comprehensive expenditure side equalization covering all services. In this context, the following points are made:

1. Subject to certain assumptions, tax revenue-sharing under an axiomatic framework will result in transfers that will be consistent with the concept of revenue side equalization used in Canada. The difference is that in the Indian case, a macro base rather than a tax-by-tax approach is followed on the revenue side. While using a macro approach, there is a need to obtain a better measure of fiscal capacity as GSDP at factor cost is an incomplete indicator for this purpose. The Central Statistical Organization, which prepares comparable estimates of GSDP for the Finance Commission should be asked to prepare a more comprehensive indicator of fiscal capacity, taking GSDP at market prices and providing supplementary information on remittances and other influences that add to the spending capacity in different states.

2. A suitable methodology can be developed to objectively determine the relevant weights in the tax-devolution formulae, given the large share of tax devolution in total transfers, which it is not easy to scale down and substitute by grants.

3. Using available information, it has been shown that contrary to the contention made by several economists, transfers in India have not been necessarily 'gap-filling' in nature in the recent past, at least for the general category states subject to the exception of one or two states for some years. Taking the TFC recommended transfers, it is shown that, under specific assumptions, systematic elements of transfers constitute a high proportion of transfers: 50 per cent of transfers are used as the vertical component of transfers and nearly 40 per cent are equalizing in nature, consistent with the revenue side equalization approach. The remaining is for assessed special needs and goes mainly to the special category states.

4. It is shown that for achieving full equalization, subject to various assumptions, the weight-to-distance formula should have been 47 per cent combined with a higher amount of devolution. It is advisable to increase the amount of per capita equalizing grants to reduce the necessity for using devolution to perform this task.

5. In the present exercise, equalization has been viewed in terms of fiscal capacity equalization only, which is the approach followed in Canada. Considerations of cost differentials and efficiency will modify the results.

6. Equalizing grants may be extended particularly in services like health and education. These also provide cases where revenue side equalization should be supplemented by expenditure side equalization where cost and use disabilities should be fully neutralized, extending the methodology suggested by the TFC.

Others

7. If GST is levied and collected as a central levy, the principles of distribution of transfers to states may need to keep divisible revenues of GST as a separate category. States would need to be compensated on the basis of 'return' requiring estimation of revenue foregone on account of sales and related taxes.

8. As on-lending to states from the centre has been discontinued, there is no case for including a debt-write-off clause in the terms of reference of the future FCs, as has been done in the case of the Thirteenth Finance Commission.

APPENDIX 5A.1

Vertical Stability and Relative
Tax Buoyancies

We examine the conditions under which the share of the centre (or states) in the combined revenues of the centre and states remains constant over time. The following symbols are used:

Central tax revenues prior to transfers: R_C
State tax revenues prior to transfers: R_S
Total Revenues: $R = R_C + R_S$

The buoyancies of central, states, and combined tax revenues are given by c, b, and d, respectively.

Thus,

$$c = [\Delta R_C / R_C].[Y/\Delta Y] \text{ or } \Delta R_C = c.R_C.\Delta Y/Y = c.R_C.g$$

where $g = \Delta Y/Y$ is the growth rate between the relevant periods.

Similarly $\Delta R_S = b.R_S.g$ and $\Delta R\, d.R.g$

Let transfers (T) be a fraction t of central revenues in the initial period.

$$T = t.R_C$$

Share of centre after transfers in total revenues

$$\text{Share (centre)}_0 = (R_C - t\,R_C)/(R) = [R_C(1-t)]/[R]$$

After a given period let the ratio of transfer be t'. The new share of Centre in total revenues will be

$$\text{Share (centre)}_n = [(R_C + \Delta R_C) - t'(R_C + \Delta R_C)]/[R + \Delta R]$$
$$= [(R_C + \Delta R_C)(1 - t')]/[R + \Delta R]$$

$$= [(R_C + R_C.c.g)(1-t'')]/[R+R.d.g]$$
$$= [R_C(1+cg)(1-t')]/[R(1+d.g)]$$

The relative shares of the centre and states between the two periods is a constant of

$$[R_C(1-t)]/[R] = [R_C\{(1+cg)\}(1-t')]/[R(1+dg)]$$

Or,

$$1-t = \{(1+cg)(1-t')\}/(1+dg)$$
$$(1-t)(1+dg) = (1+cg)(1-t')$$

Ignoring 2nd order terms, $t'-t = (c-d)g$

Thus, if the buoyancy of the central taxes is higher than the combined tax revenues, the ratio of transfer to the states will need to go up between two periods in order to keep the relative share of the centre and states stable after transfers. The extent of the increase will depend on the growth rate and the difference between central and combined tax buoyancies. This condition can also be written in terms of the buoyancy of state tax revenues.

We have,
$$\Delta R = \Delta R_C + \Delta R_S$$
$$d R.g = cR_Cg + bR_S.g$$
$$d.R = cR_C + bR_S$$
$$d = [c.R_C]/[R] + [b.R_S]/[R]$$
$$= c[R - R_S]/R + b[R_S/R]$$

Let the share of states' own revenues in total revenues be

$$\alpha = R_S / R$$

We have

$$d = c(1-\alpha) + b\alpha$$

the condition of stabilization is

$$t' - t = [c - \{c(1 - \alpha) + b\alpha\}]g$$
$$= [c - c(1 - \alpha) - b\alpha]g$$
$$= [c - c + c\alpha - b\alpha]g$$
$$t' - t = (c - b)\alpha g$$

Thus, an increase in the share of transfer is warranted provided the central tax buoyancy exceeds that of state taxes for keeping the share of the two tiers in total tax revenues stable.

APPENDIX 5A.2

Criteria-Based Tax Revenue Sharing: Axiomatic Basis

In discussing this axiomatic framework, the following additional symbols will be used:

N_i = Population of state i

y_i = per capita tax base of state i

s_i = share of the i th state

s_i^* = corresponding per capita share

S_i = total transfer in absolute amount received by a state under a criterion

S_i^* = per capita transfers received by a state in absolute amount by a state

Let the number of states be 'n'. States are arranged in ascending order of per capita tax base, that is,

$$y_1 \leq y_2 \leq \ldots \leq y_n$$

The per capita macro tax base (y_i) is approximated by the comparable per capita GSDP in determining FC transfers. We can write the state shares and per capita shares under the well-known population and distance criterion as given below:

Population criterion: share of i th state = q_i (say) = $N_i / \Sigma N_i$ and per capita share as $q_i^* = 1 / \Sigma N_i$

Distance criterion: share of ith state = a_i (say) = $N_i(y_n - y_i) / \Sigma N_i \cdot (y_n - y_i)$ and per capita share as $a_i^* = (y_n - y_i) / \Sigma N_i \cdot (y_n - y_i)$. The state shares and per capita shares can be written in a more general form as follows.

Let the per capita share of a state in an allocation mechanism be a function of per capita income (tax base) and a set of other variables. The set of variables used in a criterion is referred to in a general way by $f(.)$. Let this be normalized by a function written as θ. Thus, the per capita share of the i th state is

$$s_i^* = \theta f_i(.) \tag{5A.1}$$

Correspondingly, the share for the state as a whole is given by

$$s_i = \theta f_i(.) N_i \tag{5A.2}$$

The total and per capita transfers in absolute amounts can be written as

$$S_i = \theta . f_i(.) N.T \quad \text{and} \quad S_i^* = \theta . f_i(.) T \tag{5A.3}$$

where T is the total amount of transfers.

Axiom 1: Normalization 1

If two states have the same criterion values, their shares should be proportional to their populations.

The entitlement of a state under any criterion should be determined in per capita terms. If two states have the same value of the allocation variable, but different sizes of population, the share of the state with the larger population should be larger by the ratio by which its population is larger compared to the other state. The basic consideration here is that all transfers are aimed at citizens residing in the state, because all services are meant for the citizens. Population is the appropriate scaling factor in this context. This axiom means that, for two states i and j,

$$s_i/s_j = N_i/N_j \text{ if } \theta.f_i(.) = \theta.f_j(.) \tag{5A.4}$$

Axiom 2: Normalization 2

The sum of the shares of all states should add to 1.

Under any criterion, the share of all states should add to 1. This axiom ensures that the entire sum to be transferred to the states as a whole would be precisely exhausted among the states. If the total amount of transfer is T, we require that the sum of transfers received by each state should be equal to the total amount T, that is, the transfer received by each state is equal to $\left(s_i.T\right)$

Therefore,

$$s_1.T + s_2.T + \ldots + s_n.T = T \tag{5A.5}$$

$$\Sigma s_i T = T \text{ or } \Sigma s_i = 1$$

Thus, $$\Sigma \theta.f_i(.)N_i = 1 \text{ or } \theta = 1/\Sigma f_i(i)N_i \tag{5A.6}$$

For a given set of N_i, and values of variables entering $f(.)$, θ could be taken as given. This axiom also ensures that all allocation criteria satisfying it would be indifferent with respect to scalar changes in population. If population of all states increase by a factor 'k', we have the new set of shares, given as indicated below:

$$f_i(.)(kN_i)/\Sigma f_i(.)kN_i = fi(.)N_i/\Sigma fi(.)N_i = s_i,$$

so long as population is not a variable entering $f_i(.)$

Axiom 3: Horizontal Equity

Between any pair of states, the state with lower per capita fiscal capacity should have a higher per capita share, and per capita shares should be equal for states with equal per capita fiscal capacity.

The allocation mechanism should be consistent with horizontal equity. Horizontal equity requires that the allocation mechanism should treat equally two states if their criterion values are the same. It should treat them differently if their criterion values are different. This implies that if two states have the same per capita fiscal capacity, they would receive the same per capita share, and if the two states have different per capita fiscal capacities, states with the lower fiscal capacity would get a higher share. A criterion that satisfies this characteristic may be referred to as a progressive transfer mechanism, which ensures that a poorer state receives a higher per capita transfer according to the specified criterion. The poorer the state, the lower the fiscal capacity to raise its own resources if these are assessed at a common tax effort. This condition requires that for a pair of states, b_i and b_{i+1}, where they have been arranged in an ascending order of per capita income if,

$$b_i < b_{i+1}, s_i^* > s_i^* + 1$$

and if
$$b_i = b_{i+1}, s_i^* = s_{i+1}^*.$$

Considering the case where no two per capita incomes are equal, we require, for progressivity,

$$\theta f_i(.) > \theta f_{i+1}(.).$$

or
$$f_i(.) / f_{i+1}(.) > 1 \text{ or } f_i(.) - f_{i+1}(.) > 0 \qquad (5A.7)$$

Since $f_i(.)$ among other variables is also a function of per capita income, we may write

$$s_i^* > s_{i+1}^*, \quad \text{if} \quad \partial s_i^* / \partial y_i = \theta \partial f(.) / \partial y_i < 0, \text{ for a given value of } \theta.$$

Axiom 4: Comprehensiveness

The Finance Commissions have followed the practice that under no criterion, any state is given a zero share. This implies that information on all states is always considered together. The shares of any subsets of states are not to be determined independently, ignoring relevant information pertaining to the remaining states. Suppose that some state (j) receives a zero share in the allocation mechanism. In this case,

$$s_j^* = \theta f_j(.) = 0$$

and $\qquad s_j = \theta f_j(\ )N_j = 0 \text{ or } f_j(.)N_j - 0 \text{ since } \theta \neq 0$

The normalization axiom indicates that

$$1/\theta = f_i(.)N_i + \ldots + f_n(.)N_n \qquad (5A.8)$$

If for some j, $f_j(.)N_j = 0$, it will not enter in the allocation formula. As such no information on the j th state would enter into the allocation formula. Thus, to ensure that information on all states is used in the allocation exercise, we require,

$$s_i^* > 0 \text{ for all } i$$

However if $f(.)$ itself contains the relevant information of the j th state, in the criterion values of all the states, the share of the j th state can still be set at zero.

Axiom 5: Neutrality

The allocation criterion should be neutral with respect to the organization of states. There should not be an incentive to bifurcate states with a view to benefiting from the allocation mechanism. As shown below, all non-linear criteria implicitly give an incentive either for splitting a state into smaller states or for regrouping a state into larger states. All convex and progressive allocation criteria provide an incentive for a poorer region in a state to break off and form a 'new' state. If it does so, with its lower per capita income, it would ensure a higher per capita share in the transfer mechanism. Such fissiparous tendencies can however be neutralized by providing a mechanism of allocation of resources which is neutral to the organization of the states. However, even with such an intra-state mechanism, some of the devolution criteria may not be neutral to the organization of the states under certain conditions. Consequently, they may encourage either the disintegration of states into smaller units or their integration into larger units. It is a desirable property for a devolution criterion to be neutral to the organization of states. The conditions required for this purpose may be stated as below:

If, for any state i, if there are two regions 1 and 2, with per capita income y_i^1 and y_i^2, and population N_i^1 and N_2^2, such that

$$N_i = N_i^1 + N_i^2$$

$$y_i N_i = y_j^1 N_j^1 + y_i^2 N_i^2$$

The neutrality of an allocation formula would require that the sum of transfers received by the two regions as separate states should be equal to the transfer received by the undivided state. We have

$$s_i^1 = \theta f_i^1(.)N_i^1$$

$$s_i^2 = \theta f_i^2(.)N_i^2$$

The total number of states now being $(n+1)$, neutrality thus requires;

$$s_i^1 + s_i^2 = s_i$$

or $$\theta[f_i^1(.)N_i^1 + f_i^2(.)N_i^2] = \theta f_i(.)N_i \qquad (5A.9)$$

An alternative way in which this axiom could be stated is that under the allocation mechanism, no two states should either gain or lose if they joined up to form an integrated state. The neutrality axiom ensures that by itself, the devolution criteria do not give any incentives for states to bifurcate themselves or for two states to join together. The devolution criterion should be neutral to the existing organization of states as a datum.

Considering two important examples of specific criteria in use, namely the population criterion and distance criterion, we can specify the values of θ and $f_i(.)$ for each criterion as given below.

For Population Criterion:

$$s_i = q_i; f(.) = 1; \theta = 1/\sum N_i$$

For Distance Criterion

$$s_i = a_i; f(.) = y_n - y_i; \theta = 1/\sum(y_n - y_i)N_i.$$

Using these axioms to analyse the devolution criteria used by recent commissions it can be ascertained that all criteria used by TFC—namely, population, distance, area, tax effort, and fiscal discipline—meet the two normalization axioms. These also meet the comprehensiveness axiom in the sense that information about all states is used to determine the share of any one state under all the criteria. The distance criterion meets the horizontal equity axiom. The population criterion and the pure form (where the highest per capita income gets a zero share) of the distance criterion also meet the neutrality axiom under certain conditions (see Srivastava and Aggarwal (2000), for a detailed discussion).

It may be noted that tax shares of different states under individual criterion are not published in some of the other transfer exercises such as those under the Gadgil formula. While in some components, the axioms may be satisfied, in other cases, these may not be satisfied. It would be useful if the Planning Commission could make public the state-wise indices under different components of the criteria used under the Gadgil formula for a more informed debate on the subject. Using the notations given above, we can propose a set of axioms and their related properties for considering a desirable criteria-based system of tax revenue-sharing.

The per capita vertical transfer (column 3 of Appendix Table 5A.2) is split between per capita vertical grant (equal to the lowest per capita grant among all states (for Maharashtra) and per capita vertical devolution (equal to the lowest per capita devolution, also for Maharashtra). All states get these amounts. The equalizing components of grants and devolution are calculated in two steps. As a first step, per capita equalizing grants for all states are calculated by applying the ratio of Bihar's per capita horizontal grant (per capita total grant minus vertical component of grant) to benchmark equalizing transfer (column 5 of Appendix Table 5A.1). Per capita devolution is also decomposed into three components: vertical, equalizing horizontal, and residual.

The equalizing component of devolution is taken by comparing two series. The first series is per capita total devolution minus the vertical component of devolution. The other is the excess of the equalizing total per capita transfer (column 4 of Appendix Table 5A.2) over the equalizing grant referred to above. The equalizing component of devolution consists of the lower number of the two series. This gives series 6 of

Table 5A.1 Comparison of Equalization Transfers Based on Available Data with TFC Recommended Transfers

	Average tax ratio		0.0654		Vertical component:746.67	
	Population (2001)	Per capita GSDP (average 1999–2000 to 2001–2)	Equalization transfers based on data centered in 2000–1		Total Per capita benchmark transfers	Actual Per capita recommended transfer
	(Crore)	(Rs)	Per capita gap (Rs)	Per capita transfer (Rs)	(Rs)	(Rs)
States	2	3	4	5	6	7
1						
Bihar	8.300	6,539	20,455	1,337.8	2,084	1,821.5
Uttar Pradesh	16.620	10,798	16,196	1,059.2	1,806	1,605.0
Orissa	3.680	11,234	15,760	1,030.7	1,777	2,006.0
Jharkhand	2.695	11,717	15,277	999.1	1,746	1,754.6
Assam	2.666	12,288	14,706	961.8	1,708	1,824.2
Madhya Pradesh	6.035	13,340	13,654	893.0	1,640	1,534.0
Chhattisgarh	2.083	13,710	13,284	868.8	1,615	1,752.9
Rajasthan	5.651	15,059	11,935	780.5	1,527	1,381.5
Meghalaya	0.232	16,035	10,959	716.7	1,463	3,765.5
Arunachal Pradesh	0.110	16,579	10,415	681.1	1,428	6,419.1
Uttaranchal	0.849	16,998	9,996	653.7	1,400	2,871.7
Manipur	0.217	17,264	9,730	636.3	1,383	6,339.5
West Bengal	8.018	17,377	9,617	629.0	1,376	1,268.2

Jammu & Kashmir	1.014	18,132	8,862	579.6	1,326	4,217.5
Andhra Pradesh	7.621	18,869	8,125	531.4	1,278	1,320.4
Tripura	0.320	18,974	8,020	524.5	1,271	5,260.7
Nagaland	0.199	20,469	6,525	426.7	1,173	7,489.5
Karnataka	5.285	20,703	6,291	411.4	1,158	1,188.0
Sikkim	0.054	20,929	6,065	396.7	1,143	6,759.6
Mizoram	0.089	21,245	5,749	376.0	1,123	10,488.1
Tamil Nadu	6.241	22,587	4,407	288.2	1,035	1,174.9
Gujarat	5.067	22,708	4,286	280.3	1,027	1,010.1
Kerala	3.184	22,824	4,170	272.7	1,019	1,230.7
Himachal Pradesh	0.608	24,762	2,232	146.0	893	4,754.1
Haryana	2.114	26,256	738	48.3	795	760.2
Maharashtra	9.688	26,994	0	0.0	747	746.7
Punjab	2.436	28,030	0	0.0	747	1,057.3
Goa	0.135	56,599	0	0.0	747	2,557.6
Total						

Source: Report of the Twelfth Finance Commission, 2004.

Note: Vertical component is equal to the per capita recommended transfer to Maharashtra. This is the minimum per capita transfer among all states.

Equalization transfers are calculated by applying the average all-state tax-rate to the difference between the three-state average per capita GSDP (Maharashtra, Punjab and Goa) and the per capita GSDP of any given state.

Table 5A.2 Decomposition of Recommended Per Capita Transfers

(Rupees)

States	Actual recomm- ended transfer	Vertical comp- onent	Equali- zation com- ponent	Residual (for special needs and cost disabilities)	Shortfall In equali- zation
1	2	3	4	5	6
Bihar	1,821.5	746.7	1,074.8	0.0	263.0
Uttar Pradesh	1,605.0	746.7	858.3	0.0	200.9
Orissa	2,006.0	746.7	1,030.7	228.7	0.0
Jharkhand	1,754.6	746.7	999.1	8.8	0.0
Assam	1,824.2	746.7	961.8	115.8	0.0
Madhya Pradesh	1,534.0	746.7	787.3	0.0	105.6
Chhattisgarh	1,752.9	746.7	868.8	137.5	0.0
Rajasthan	1,381.5	746.7	634.9	0.0	145.7
Meghalaya	3,765.5	746.7	716.7	2,302.1	0.0
Arunachal Pradesh	6,419.1	746.7	681.1	4,991.2	0.0
Uttaranchal	2,871.7	746.7	653.7	1,471.2	0.0
Manipur	6,339.5	746.7	636.3	4,956.5	0.0
West Bengal	1,268.2	746.7	521.6	0.0	107.4
Jammu & Kashmir	4,217.5	746.7	579.6	2,891.3	0.0
Andhra Pradesh	1,320.4	746.7	531.4	42.4	0.0
Tripura	5,260.7	746.7	524.5	3,989.5	0.0
Nagaland	7,489.5	746.7	426.7	6,316.1	0.0
Karnataka	1,188.0	746.7	411.4	29.9	0.0
Sikkim	6,759.6	746.7	396.7	5,616.3	0.0
Mizoram	10,488.1	746.7	376.0	9,365.4	0.0
Tamil Nadu	1,174.9	746.7	288.2	140.0	0.0
Gujarat	1,010.1	746.7	263.4	0.0	16.9
Kerala	1,230.7	746.7	272.7	211.3	0.0
Himachal Pradesh	4,754.1	746.7	146.0	3,861.5	0.0
Haryana	760.2	746.7	13.5	0.0	34.7
Maharashtra	746.7	746.7	0.0	0.0	0.0
Punjab	1,057.3	746.7	0.0	310.7	0.0
Goa	2,557.6	746.7	0.0	1,810.9	0.0

Source: TFC Report and Estimates.

Note: Equalization component is calculated by comparing actual recommended transfer net of vertical component with benchmark equalization transfer (col. 5 of Appendix Table 5A.1). If the actual transfer net of vertical component is more than benchmark equalization transfer, the benchmark equalization transfer is entered in column 4. The excess becomes the residual given in column 5. If the actual transfer net of vertical transfers falls short of the benchmark equalization transfer, the actual transfer is written in column 4 and the shortfall is given in column 6.

Table 5A.3 Decomposition of Per Capita Grants and Devolution into Vertical, Equalizing Horizontal, and Residual Components

						(Rs Crore)
State	Grants			Devolution		
	Vertical	Equalizing horizontal	Residual	Vertical	Equalizing horizontal (residual)	Residual
1	2	3	4	5	6	7
Bihar	114.2	78.0	0.0	632.5	996.8	0.0
Uttar Pradesh	114.2	69.5	0.0	632.5	788.8	0.0
Orissa	114.2	60.1	112.3	632.5	970.6	116.4
Jharkhand	114.2	102.1	8.8	632.5	897.0	0.0
Assam	114.2	106.1	115.8	632.5	855.7	0.0
Madhya Pradesh	114.2	56.2	0.0	632.5	731.1	0.0
Chhattisgarh	114.2	50.7	26.0	632.5	818.1	111.5
Rajasthan	114.2	50.2	0.0	632.5	584.7	0.0
Meghalaya	114.2	41.8	1,647.6	632.5	674.9	654.5
Arunachal Pradesh	114.2	39.7	3,048.7	632.5	641.4	1,942.5
Uttaranchal	114.2	38.1	1,363.0	632.5	615.6	108.2
Manipur	114.2	37.1	4,139.6	632.5	599.2	816.9
West Bengal	114.2	74.7	0.0	632.5	446.8	0.0
Jammu and Kashmir	114.2	33.8	2,501.7	632.5	545.8	389.6
Andhra Pradesh	114.2	31.0	−8.3	632.5	500.4	50.7
Tripura	114.2	30.6	3,475.5	632.5	493.9	514.1
Nagaland	114.2	24.9	5,729.9	632.5	401.9	586.2
Karnataka	114.2	24.0	15.3	632.5	387.4	14.6
Sikkim	114.2	23.1	1,475.7	632.5	373.5	4,140.6
Mizoram	114.2	21.9	7,053.8	632.5	354.1	2,311.6
Tamil Nadu	114.2	16.8	1.5	632.5	271.4	138.5
Gujarat	114.2	32.2	0.0	632.5	231.2	0.0
Kerala	114.2	15.9	74.3	632.5	256.8	137.0

(continued)

Table 5A.3 Continued

(Rs Crore)

State	Grants			Devolution		
	Vertical	Equalizing horizontal	Residual	Vertical	Equalizing horizontal (residual)	Residual
1	2	3	4	5	6	7
Himachal Pradesh	114.2	8.5	3,578.3	632.5	137.5	283.2
Haryana	114.2	22.6	0.0	632.5	−9.1	0.0
Maharashtra	114.2	0.0	0.0	632.5	0.0	0.0
Punjab	114.2	0.0	289.2	632.5	0.0	21.4
Goa	114.2	0.0	86.8	632.5	0.0	1,724.1
Average (Population weighted)	114.2	46.9	120.8	632.5	533.4	45.7

Source: TFC Report, 2004.

The per capita vertical transfer (column 3 of Appendix Table 5A.2) is split between per capita vertical grant (equal to the lowest per capita grant among all states (for Maharashtra) and per capita vertical devolution (equal to the lowest per capita devolution, also for Maharashtra). All states get these amounts. The equalizing components of grants and devolution are calculated in two steps. As a first step, per capita equalizing grants for all states are calculated by applying the ratio of Bihar's per capita horizontal grant (per capita total grant minus vertical component of grant) to benchmark equalizing transfer (column 5 of Appendix Table 5A.1). Per capita devolution is also decomposed into three components: vertical, equalizing horizontal, and residual.

Appendix Table 5A.3. The residual of the devolution column is calculated as the total per capita devolution minus the vertical component of devolution (column 5 of Appendix Table 5A.3) and the equalizing component of devolution (column 6) of Appendix Table 5A.3.

Since the residual of grants and devolution should add to the overall residual as shown by column 5 of Appendix Table 5A.2, the residual series for grants is derived as the difference between the overall residual and the residual of the per capita devolution series (column 5 of Appendix Table 5A.2 minus column 7 of Appendix Table 5A.3). This gives the residual grant series (column 4 of Appendix Table 5A.3).

Finally, the adjusted equalizing grant series (column 2 of Appendix Table 5A.3) is derived as per capita total grant minus per capita vertical grant minus per capita residual grant. These procedures satisfy the conditions of equation 5.7 in the text.

There are two negative numbers in columns 4 and 7 of Appendix Table 5A.3. These numbers may be adjusted by following a suitable rule in calculating the residuals, but since the magnitudes involved are small, further adjustment has not been done.

Notes

1. The subject of resource sharing in federal systems has important theoretical underpinnings and the TFC Report also evoked a number of responses from economists, an example of which is *Economic and Political Weekly*'s issue of 30 July 2005 that carried contributions of some well-known experts on the subject. Notwithstanding several issues raised, in writing the overview of these contributions, Amaresh Bagchi, member of the Eleventh Finance Commission, observed in the summary of his overview: 'The Twelfth Finance Commission has broken new ground in several key areas and made recommendations which, if fully recommended, will have a far reaching impact on the finances and functioning of government in the country at all levels.'

2. If the power to levy the sales tax in respect of three commodities namely, textiles, sugar, and tobacco is reverted back to states, the states' share in the divisible pool of central taxes would be 29.5 per cent. Until this is done, it will be 30.5 per cent.

3. Sometimes area of a state is considered as a scaling factor, but this is more appropriately taken as a determinant of per capita cost, which may be higher in states where large areas are sparsely populated. It may also be higher if population density is extremely high.

6

Dynamics of Debt
Accumulation in India

Impact of Primary Deficit, Growth, and Interest Rate[*]

Issues of fiscal transfers and debt sustainability are intertwined. Interest payments on accumulated debt are part of committed expenditures, which Finance Commissions take into account in assessing states' resource requirements. The matter of debt relief has also been referred to the Finance Commissions. In this chapter, we look at the evolution of central debt and related issues. In the next chapter, we look at the combined debt of central and state governments. Accumulation of debt can be seen as the result of the balance between cumulated primary deficits and the cumulated weighted excess of growth over interest rate. Decomposing the change in the central government's liabilities relative to GDP since 1951–2, it is seen that but for three recent years, the accretion to debt relative to GDP was due to the cumulated primary deficits. A significant part of the effect of the cumulated primary deficits could be absorbed in the 1960s, 1970s, and 1990s due to the excess of growth over interest rate. However, there were large unabsorbed parts in the 1950s and the 1980s. The cushion provided by the excess of growth over interest rate may not continue to be available for long. For three years, from 2000–1 to 2002–3, the interest rate exceeded the growth rate. This, together with the continuing primary deficits, though at a reduced level, led to an acceleration in the debt-GDP ratio in recent years. For stabilization of the

---

[*] Originally published as 'Dynamics of Debt Accumulation in India: Impact of Primary Deficit, Growth and Interest Rate', *Economic and Political Weekly*, Vol. 38, No. 46, 15 November 2003, pp. 4851–8.

debt-GDP ratio at current or reduced levels, focus on primary balance becomes necessary.

In the analysis of the accumulation of debt, two factors are identified as contributing to the debt-GDP ratio. One is the cumulated primary deficits and the other is the cumulated effect of the difference between growth rate and interest rate. This chapter looks at the relative contribution of cumulated primary deficits and the cumulated effect of the excess of growth rate over interest rate on the accumulation of outstanding liabilities[1] of the central government in India from 1951–2 to 2001–2. The interest rate in this discussion refers to the effective interest rate of the central government, calculated as the ratio of interest payments in a year to the outstanding liabilities at the beginning of the year. This chapter particularly highlights the implications of the sign reversal in the difference between real growth and interest rates, evidenced during the past three years from 2000–1 to 2002–3. Throughout the stretch of forty-five years from 1955–6 to 1999–2000, the real growth rate was in excess of the real interest rate. Since 2000–1, for three consecutive years, the real growth rate has been less than the real interest rate. During the 1990s, even when the GDP growth rate remained in excess of the interest rate, the gap between the two has been narrowing. If the days of large positive differences between growth and interest rates are all but over, there are serious implications for strategies aimed at containing the growth of debt relative to GDP. We are entering into an era where corrections in the primary balance profile of the central government have become imperative.

This chapter is organized as follows. It begins by proposing a methodology for decomposing the accumulation of debt into cumulated primary deficits and cumulated weighted excess of growth over interest rates. It goes on to set out data preliminaries, particularly in relation to data pertaining to the outstanding liabilities of the centre and the related fiscal deficits. It goes on to provide a decade-wise examination of the growth of central debt and assesses the relative importance of cumulated primary deficits and the cumulated impact of the differential between growth and interest rates in explaining the dynamics of debt accumulation. Another section looks at time profiles of growth and interest rates. The pattern of growth of primary deficit relative to GDP and medium-term prospects in regard to the central government's outstanding liabilities relative to GDP are also discussed towards the end.

Decomposing Accumulation of Debt

The standard specification of the equation describing debt dynamics with discrete time periods[2] is given by

$$b_t = p_t + b_t - 1[(1+i_t)/(1+g_t)] \tag{6.1}$$

where b_t = debt-GDP ratio in period t

p_t = ratio of primary-deficit to GDP in period t

g_t = growth rate of GDP in period t

i_t = effective nominal interest in period t

Writing $z_t = b_t - b_{t-1}$, equation (6.1) can also be written as

$$z_i = p_t - b_{t-1}\left[\frac{g_t - i_t}{1 + g_t}\right] \tag{6.2}$$

The increment in debt can be cumulated over any relevant period $t = 1$ to T. Thus

$$\sum_{t=1}^{T} z_t = \sum_{t=1}^{T} p_t - \sum_{t=1}^{T} b_{t-1}[((g_t - i_t)/(1+g_t))] \tag{6.3}$$

Equation 6.3 helps in decomposing the change in the debt-GDP ratio between any two benchmark years into the contribution of the cumulated primary deficit relative to GDP and that of the cumulated effect of the weighted excess of growth over the interest rate. In the Indian case $\sum p_t$ has been much larger than $\sum z_t$ for long stretches of time, and the role of the growth/interest rate differential has been to absorb the impact of the cumulated primary deficits from getting translated into accretion to the debt-GDP ratio. It is, therefore, useful to write equation (6.3) as

$$\sum_{t=1}^{T} p_t = \sum_{t=1}^{T} z_t + \sum_{t=1}^{T} b_{t-1}[((g_t - i_t)/(1+g_t))] \tag{6.4}$$

Of the cumulated primary deficit relative to GDP, that part which was absorbed by the differential of growth rate and interest rate is given by, say $A1$, where

$$A1 = \sum_{t=1}^{T} b_{t-1}[(g_t - i_t)/(1+g_t)]/\sum_{t=1}^{T} p_t \tag{6.5}$$

Correspondingly, the share of the cumulated primary deficit which results in the accretion to the debt-GDP ratio (say $A2$) is given by

$$A2 = \sum_{t=1}^{T} z_t / \sum_{t=1}^{T} p_t \qquad (6.6)$$

Thus, $A1 + A2 = 1$

It might be useful to further decompose the term containing the effect of growth-interest rate differential between the effect of real growth / real interest rate differential and inflation. Writing g^* and i^* for real growth and real interest rates and π for the inflation rate, we have $(g_t - i_t = g_t^* - i_t^*)$ and $1 + g_t = 1 + g_t^* + \pi_t$. We can then write, using the expansion of the term and ignoring second-order terms, with the assumption that $/g_t/ < 1$:

$$(1 + g_t)^{-1} = (1 + g_t^* + \pi_t)^{-1} = 1 - g_t^* - \pi_t \qquad (6.7)$$

Thus, $\displaystyle\sum_{i=1}^{T} b_{t-1}(g_t - i_t)(1 + g_t)^{-1} = \sum_{i=1}^{T} b_{t-1}(g_t^* - i_t^*)(1 - g_t^*) -$

$$\sum_{i=1}^{T} b_{t-1}(g_t^* - i_t^*)\pi_t \qquad (6.8)$$

The relative shares of the two terms on the right-hand side in the factor giving the impact of the growth-interest rate differential can provide the relative contributions of the differential between real growth and interest rates and the inflation rate. It may be noted that the effect of inflation is in a direction opposite to that of the influence of the differential between real growth and real interest rate. Thus, when the real growth rate exceeds the real interest rate, its beneficial effect in containing the process of debt accumulation is partly offset by the influence of the inflation rate, and vice versa.

Some Data Preliminaries

In theory, change in outstanding debt should be equal to the fiscal deficit. Estimating fiscal deficit in this manner and juxtaposing these to the official fiscal deficit figures show discrepancies Chelliah (1996) and Rajaraman and Mukhopadhyay (2000). A comparison is made between the fiscal deficit as reported in the Receipts Budget of the Central Government and the fiscal deficit obtained by taking the change in the year-end outstanding liabilities as shown once again in the Receipts Budget. For this study we have used the figures for 1987–8 to 2002–3. We have noted that the discrepancies between the two series are quite large after 1999–2000. The primary reason for this is the way in which liabilities on account of the National Small Savings Fund (NSSF) are shown in the Receipts Budget since 1999–2000.

The NSSF was established with effect from 1 April 1999 and is maintained in the Public Account of India. The balance of collections into the NSSF over withdrawals is invested in special government securities issued by the central as well as the state governments, that is, central and state governments borrow from the NSSF on the basis of these special securities. Prior to 1998–9, small savings were shown as part of 'other liabilities' of India, where all net borrowings from the public account were shown, whether ultimately lent to the central or state governments. Since 1999–2000, the central borrowings from the NSSF constitute part of the centre's 'internal debt'. However, one component of it continues to be shown as 'other liabilities' which primarily represents the borrowing from the NSSF by the state governments. This component needs to be taken out while showing the centre's outstanding liabilities.

While the outstanding liabilities as shown in the Receipts Budget are overstated because of the 'double counting' on account of the small savings, the fiscal deficit is understated because certain securities issued by the central government are kept off-budget. Important among these are securities issued to oil companies after the winding up of the Oil Pool Account as well as securities issued to Unit Trust of India (UTI), Industrial Investments Bank of India, and the Kudremukh Iron Oil Project. The amount of these securities in some years is quite large. While it may be debated as to whether or not these liabilities should form part of the fiscal deficit, clearly these are accretions to central liabilities and would become a budgetary burden whenever these are redeemed. Therefore, these securities need to be included as part of the outstanding liabilities and must form part of the fiscal deficit. However, the budget documents do not take these securities into account while calculating the fiscal deficit. It may be noted that the outstanding liabilities as reported by the Comptroller and Auditor General (CAG) avoid the overstatement of outstanding liabilities on account of the NSSF and at the same time include the other securities issued by the central government kept off the budget in estimating fiscal deficit. We have, therefore, taken the figures of outstanding liabilities given by the CAG Report on Union Government (2003, No.1: 109) since 1976–7 as the basis for calculating the fiscal deficit. For the earlier years, the figures used are drawn from the series of Indian Public Finance Statistics. The new series of fiscal deficit derived from taking the change in the outstanding liabilities may be referred to as the 'Derived Fiscal Deficit'. The revised outstanding liabilities and the 'Derived Fiscal Deficit' have been worked out since 1950–1 and 1951–2, respectively.[3]

Thus, two modifications are being used in this exercise as compared to the published figures on the outstanding liability and fiscal deficit given in the Receipts Budget. First, the figures for outstanding liabilities are adjusted since 1999–2000 in respect of the NSSF as contained in CAG's Report on Union Finances (2000, No. 1). Secondly, the figures for the fiscal deficit are adjusted to obtain the Derived Fiscal Deficit to take into account some of the liabilities kept off the budget. During 1987–8 to 2001–2, the differences between the official fiscal deficit and the derived fiscal deficit ranged from −0.21 to 1.84 per centage points of GDP. These differences are reflected in the derived primary deficit figures also. These adjustments imply that the figures for outstanding liabilities of the central government are lower (since 1999–2000) than those given in the Receipts Budget, and the fiscal deficit and primary deficit figures are higher.[4]

Accumulation of Central Debt

The debt-GDP ratio at the end of 1950–1 was 28.84 per cent. During 1951–2 to 1959–60 a little less than 10 per centage points was added to the debt-GDP ratio. An additional accretion of about 3 per centage points took place in the 1960s. In the 1970s, and later in the 1990s, there was hardly any change in the debt-GDP ratio. It was only in the 1980s that there was an increase of 13.6 per centage points in the debt-GDP ratio. We examine below how the cumulated primary deficit resulted in large cumulated increases in the debt-GDP ratio over some

Table 6.1   Decade-Wise Decomposition of Debt Accumulation
Relative to GDP

	Cumulated Changes in			Impact of Cumulated Primary Deficit	
	Debt-GDP ratio	Primary Def-GDP ratio	Growth & interest rate differential	Increase in Debt-GDP ratio (per cent)	Absorption by Gr./ int. diff. (per cent)
1951–2 to 1959–60	9.82	20.54	10.72	47.80	52.20
1960–1 to 1969–70	3.08	28.89	25.81	10.66	89.34
1970–1 to 1979–80	−0.19	23.76	23.95	−0.79	100.79
1980–1 to 1989–90	13.61	48.53	34.92	28.05	71.95
1990–1 to 2001–2	0.20	24.56	24.36	0.82	99.18
1951–2 to 2001–2	26.52	146.28	119.76	18.13	81.87

Memo:
Debt-GDP Ratio at the end of–

1950–1	28.84
2001–2	55.36

Source: Indian Public Finance Statistics, Ministry of Finance, Government of India, compilation based on annual issues.

stretches of time and not others. Table 6.1 and Figure 6.1 show the relative effects of the cumulated primary deficits and the factor reflecting the effect of growth-interest rate differential (called $(g-i)$) differential, hereafter) in the process of accumulation of debt of the central government since 1951–2. The Indian experience shows that throughout the period from 1955–6 to 1999–2000, it was the primary deficit that caused the increase in the debt-GDP ratio. Often a significant part of the pressure of primary deficit could be absorbed by the excess of growth over interest rates. Had this cushion not been available, cumulated primary deficits from 1950–1 to 2001–2 would have resulted in a central debt-to-GDP ratio of about 146 per cent (see Table 6.1).

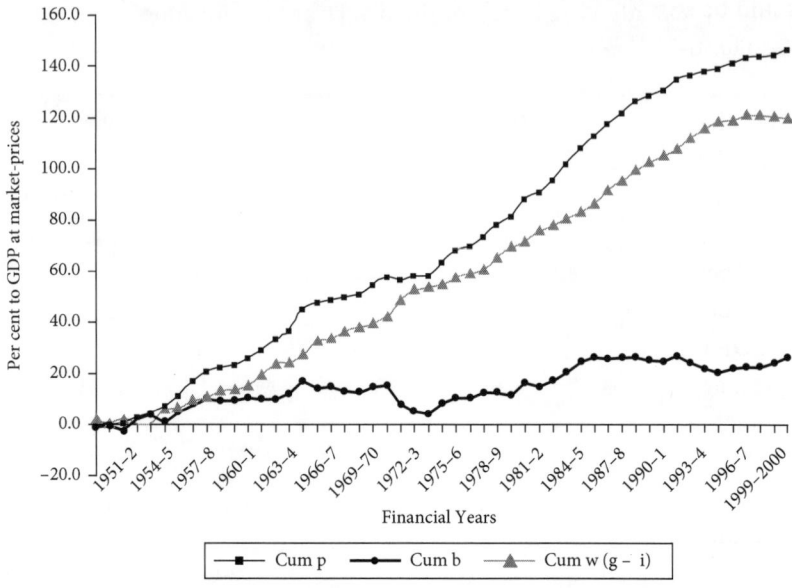

Figure 6.1 Growth of Central Debt Relative to GDP: Relative Roles of Cumulated Primary Deficit and Excess of Growth over Interest Rates
Key:
Cum *p*: Cumulated primary deficit to GDP ratio
Cum *b*: Cumulated debt to GDP ratio
Cum *w* (*g* – *i*): Cumulated effect of weighted excess of growth over interest rate

The decade-wise picture indicates that in the 1950s, 52.2 per cent of the impact of cumulative primary deficit was absorbed by the growth-interest rate differential. Thus, only 47.8 per cent of the cumulated primary deficit of 20.5 per centage points resulted in an increase in the debt-GDP ratio of 9.8 per centage points. In the 1960s, the pressure exerted by the cumulated primary deficit was relatively larger (29 per centage points). However, 89 per cent of this was absorbed by the differential of growth over interest rate, resulting in only a small increase of 3.1 per centage points in the debt-GDP ratio. During the 1970s and again during the 1990s, almost 100 per cent of the impact of primary deficit was absorbed by the growth/interest rate differential leading to a negligible increase in the debt-GDP ratio during these two decades considered as a whole. In the 1980s, only 72 per cent of the pressure of cumulated primary deficit could be absorbed by the $(g-i)$ differential. Using a similar decomposition for the OECD countries, Shigehara (1995, p. 59) observed:

> for the two decades 1974 to 1994, the ratio of net debt to GDP for the OECD area as a whole rose by about 23 per centage points, of which about 18 per centage points can be accounted for by cumulated primary deficits, and 5 per centage points can be attributed to the differential between interest rates and growth rates. However, since 1980 when the debt dynamics became unfavourable for the OECD area, the debt-GDP ratio has risen by about 18 per centage points of which only 8 per centage points can be attributed to primary deficits and 10 per centage points are accounted for by the effect of the interest rate/growth rate differential.

The long-term Indian experience is different in as much as for a stretch of forty-eight years, the single cause of the rise in debt was the cumulated primary deficit. The excess of growth rate over interest rate helped to mitigate the situation. In the case of the OECD countries, while both factors contributed to the rise in debt-GDP ratio, the growth-interest differential had become more important in recent years. In India over the period from 1951–2 to 2001–2, the central debt-GDP ratio rose by 26.5 per centage points. The increase occurred mainly in the 1950s and the 1980s. In the remaining period of thirty years, except for a small rise, all the pressure of cumulated primary deficit was absorbed by the $(g-i)$ differential.

The critical contemporary question relates to whether one can continue to rely on the $(g-i)$ differential to provide a reliable cushion, or whether with interest rates being increasingly market-determined, the situation warrants a fresh examination of the factors behind debt accumulation in India.

Profiles of Growth and Interest Rates

The effective interest rate is derived by dividing actual interest payments during a financial year by the outstanding liabilities at the beginning

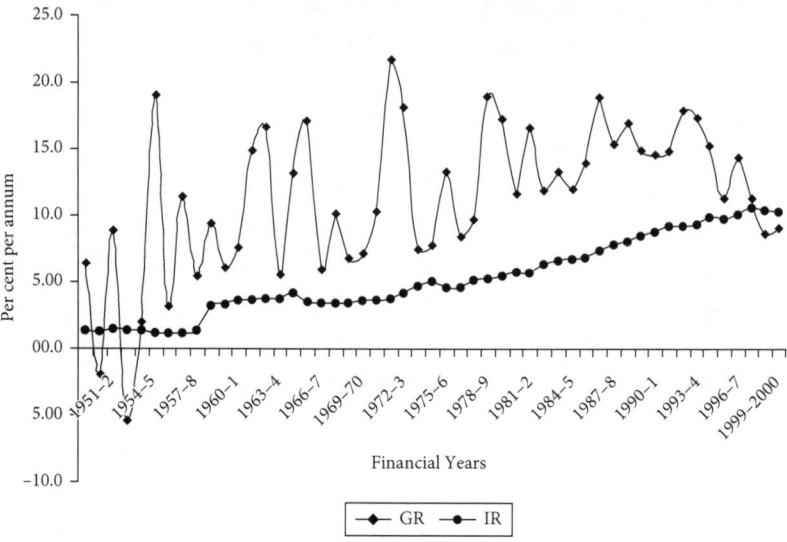

Figure 6.2 Time Profile of Nominal Growth and Interest Rates

of that year. This means that the effective interest rate is the weighted average of past interest rates pertaining to debt that are currently being serviced. It implies that even if current interest rates fall, the effective rate will fall more slowly than the current interest rates. Conversely, it will also rise more slowly, in a period where nominal interest rates are rising. Figure 6.2 shows the steady rise of the effective interest rate until the end of the 1990s, after which it started falling. Until 1959–60, the nominal interest rate was well below 2 per cent per annum. It generally remained in the range of 3.2 to 3.7 per cent up to 1973–4. Rising steadily since then, the peak was attained towards the end of the 1990s with the average rate going above 10 per cent. It is clear that in the long run the nominal growth rate has been far more volatile than the nominal interest rate. As a result, the intra-year variability in the debt accumulation process is largely due to the growth rate volatility.

The real interest rate is derived by deducting from the effective nominal rate, the implicit price deflator of GDP at market prices. There is considerable volatility in the real interest rate because of fluctuations in inflation. However, one trend is clear. As Figure 6.3 shows, except for a few years, the real interest rate has been negative throughout the years

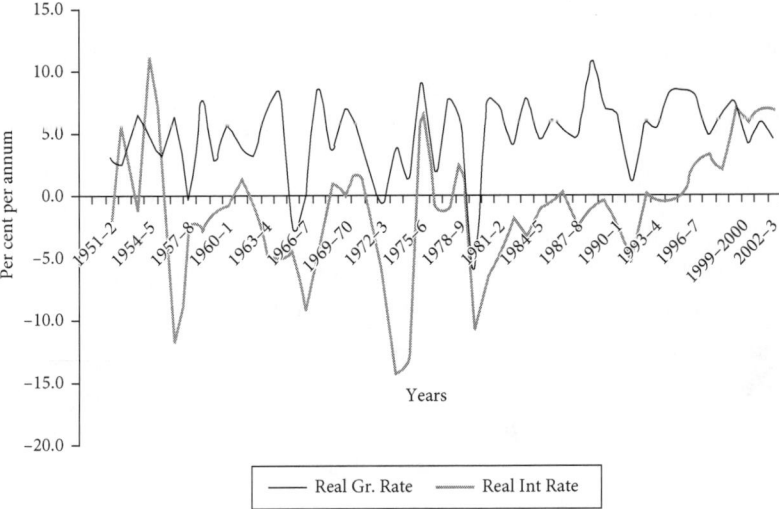

Figure 6.3 Real Growth and Interest Rates

1951–2 to 1994–5. The turning point seems to have occurred in 1995–6 when the real interest rate became positive. Concurrently, the excess of growth over interest rates, whether real or nominal, started falling in magnitude, becoming negative in 2000–1.

Historically, the real interest rates on government securities were kept low as the government was able to borrow from the domestic market at rates much below the market rates due to a variety of banking regulations including requirements for banks to maintain specified statutory liquidity requirements (SLR) and cash reserve ratio (CRR) and by controlling a number of financial institutions.[5] With the liberalization of the financial sector, the government is borrowing at rates which are by and large market determined.

The six years from 1997–8 to 2002–3 require special attention. The 2002–3 figures are available as revised estimates. These estimates put the growth of GDP at factor cost in 2002–3 at 4.3 per cent in real terms and 7.1 per cent at current prices. The effective interest rate on central government liabilities in 2002–3 is estimated to be in the vicinity of 9 per cent. Growth in GDP at market prices is likely to be marginally lower as the buoyancy of indirect taxes continues to be less than one. The central debt-GDP ratio[6] at the end of 2002–3 is estimated to be 57.6 per cent.

Thus, in 2002–3, the interest rate will again be higher than the growth rate. During 1997–8 to 2002–3, the central-debt GDP ratio rose by 8.22 per centage points, at an average rate of 1.37 per centage points per year. This is a rate of growth in the accumulation of debt relative to GDP that is more than three times that of the average increment of 0.44 per centage points per year in the previous forty-six years. If the reversal in the sign of $(g - i)$ is likely to be sustained, it is clear that rather than partially absorbing the impact of cumulated primary deficit, it will add to the accumulation of debt. With the prevailing debt-GDP ratio of around 57 per cent of GDP, every 1 percentage point differential in $(i - g)$ will cause just a little less than 0.57 per centage points of increase in the debt-GDP ratio. Even if the $(g - i)$ differential sometimes turns out to be positive, it is likely that the days of a large excess of growth rate over interest rate are over. Therefore, the likelihood of primary deficits getting converted into a rise in the debt-GDP ratio is stronger now. It may also be noted that the effective interest rate for the central government is lower than the corresponding effective rate for the states. The adverse impact of the changes in the $(g - i)$ differential for the states would therefore be even stronger.

An economy where the condition $g = i$ is met is considered 'dynamically efficient' (see, e.g., Abel et al. 1989). Lahiri and Kannan (2001) and Chrystal and Kevin (1987) provide a discussion of the issue in the Indian context. If interest rates are persistently lower in relation to the growth rate, it is due either to excessive capital accumulation relative to other factors or because the real interest (or profit) rate deviates from the marginal product of capital due to financial repression or other market distortions. Writing early in the 1990s, Buiter and Patel (1992, p. 185) and Buiter (1988) observed, 'We assume in what follows that while the interest rate can be below the growth rate for extended finite periods of time, the Indian economy is not dynamically inefficient, and there are no social free lunches to be earned by increasing the Public debt.' In the context of growing liberalization, it is not expected that the interest rates could be much below the marginal product of capital for sustained periods of time. Under these circumstances, if the debt-GDP ratio is to be stabilized at its current level, a balance would have to be achieved on the primary account. However, if the debt-GDP has to be brought down, as it has already been considered excessively high in some analyses, a reasonable primary surplus will have to be generated.

It is worth exploring whether in India the real interest rate would over-take the real growth rate on a sustained basis in the near future.[7] In some studies, it has been noted that the possibility of growth rate exceeding the interest rate by a significant margin in the near future is limited. Reynolds (2001) specifies a model where in the 'no-change' scenario, the relevant long-term parameters imply that the real interest rate would exceed the real growth rate around 2007–8 on a sustained basis. The World Bank Report (2003: 27) provides for a negligible margin between growth and interest rates in both base and reform scenarios in the period 2003–4 to 2006–7. It is notable that the interest rate at which the central government has been able to borrow is the lowest because of the minimum risk perception as well as indirect returns offered through a plethora of exemptions in central taxes. For state governments, the situation is likely to be more adverse. It is critical therefore to get a better understanding of the process of generation of primary deficits.

Accumulation of Primary Deficit

The profile of the ratio of derived primary deficit to debt from 1951–2 to 2001–2 shows that, except for a few years, the central budget did not have a primary surplus. The primary deficit to GDP ratio was continuously above 4 per cent during 1984–5 to 1990–1 and again in 1993–4.

The primary deficit is the excess of primary expenditure, that is, total expenditure minus interest payments over revenue receipts. Its capacity to adjust to changes in the relativity of growth and interest rates is limited. Figure 6.4 indicates that the primary deficit to GDP ratio is less volatile and more autonomous than the $(g - i)$ differential. It shows that the maximum build-up of primary deficit was in the period from 1979–80 to 1993–4. During this period the primary deficit to GDP ratio remained above 3 per cent except in three years. The peak was reached in 1982–3 when it exceeded 6.5 per cent. However, throughout this period, a build-up of the debt-GDP ratio could be contained because of the excess of growth rate over interest rate. The primary deficit to GDP ratio since 1993–4 remained below 2.5 per cent of the GDP, and the change in the debt-GDP ratio was modest till 1999–2000 because the growth rate also exceeded the interest rate. The debt-GDP ratio started rising from

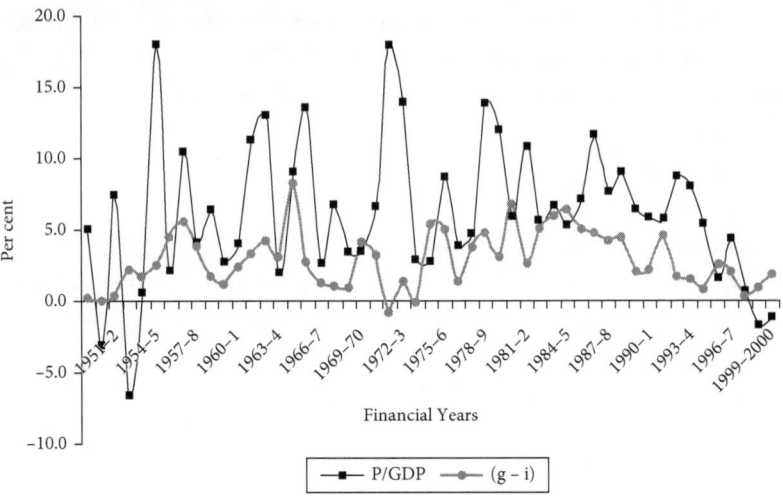

Figure 6.4 Primary Deficit to GDP Ratio and Excess of Growth over Interest Rates

2000–1 because of the combined effect of primary deficit and the negative difference between the growth rate and the interest rate.

Medium-Term Prospects

Although the interest rates have been higher than the growth rates for three consecutive years from 2000–1 to 2002–3, it is possible that in 2003–4, the sign of the $(g - i)$ differential will be reversed again. With the inflation rate expected in the region of 5 to 5.5 per cent, the real interest rate could be in the region of 3.5 to 4 per cent for the central government, given the nominal effective interest rate in the vicinity of 9 per cent. If the growth rate is above 4 per cent, which it is likely to be as the forecasts are in the region of 6 per cent, we should have a positive differential.

In 1996–7, the debt-GDP ratio was about 49 per cent, which was very close to the restructuring target set out by the Eleventh Finance Commission at 48 per cent of GDP (Government of India 2000, EFC

Report: 21). The cumulative departure away from this target has been due to both continued primary deficits and the sign reversal in the growth/ interest rate differential.

A summary of the main findings is given below:

1. Starting with a debt-GDP ratio of about 29 per cent of GDP at market prices in 1950–1 for the central government, by 2001–2, the debt-GDP ratio had reached a level of 55.36 per cent of GDP, an increase of about 26.5 per centage points. Nearly half of this increase occurred in the first three plans.

2. Accumulation of central debt relative to GDP, for an unbroken period of forty-five years since 1955–6, has been due entirely to cumulated primary deficits relative to GDP with the factor of excess of growth rate over interest rate mitigating its impact in a significant way. This trend has reversed itself during the last three years from 2000–1 to 2002–3 when the excess of interest rate over growth rate has also contributed to the growth of debt.

3. A significant part of the potential build-up of debt due to cumulated primary deficits was absorbed by the excess of real growth rate over real interest rate as adjusted for the influence of the inflation rate. Most of the intra-year variability in the process of debt accumulation was due to the volatility of the nominal growth rates.

4. With liberalization and the end of the regime of financial repression, large excesses of growth rate over interest rate may not be expected on a sustained basis. Prospects are that the difference will remain in a narrow range, even if the growth rate remains higher than the interest rate.

5. To stabilize the debt-GDP ratio at current levels, fiscal reforms aimed at attaining a balance on a primary account are imperative. To reduce the debt-GDP ratio, a primary surplus will have to be generated on a sustained basis. Hence the need to focus on primary balances in any effort to control the growth in the debt-GDP ratio becomes unavoidable.

6. The position of state governments would be even more difficult as the effective interest rate is higher in their case.

Notes

1. Outstanding liabilities include all the three major components of debt: domestic non-monetized debt, monetized debt, and external debt. External debt is in terms of historical exchange rates, that is, the rates that prevailed at the time of contracting the debt. Alternative series of external debt evaluated at current exchange rates, that is, rates prevalent at the end of the financial year for which figures are given in both Indian Public Finance Statistics (since 1974–5) and the CAG's Report on Union Finances (since 1991–2). The difference between the two series, which was a little more than 11 per cent of GDP in 1991–2, has come down to about 5.6 per cent of GDP in 2001–2. The difference has been coming down in magnitude in recent years.

2. Let D = end-period outstanding debt, $Y = GDP$ at market prices, g = growth rate, i = effective interest rate, P = primary deficit, F = fiscal deficit, and I = interest payment. The relevant period is indicated by the subscript t. The debt-GDP ratio is given by b and the primary deficit to GDP ratio is given by p. Thus, $b_t = D_t / Y_t$, and $p_t = P_t / Y_t$.

   By definition,

   $$D_t - D_{t-1} = F_t$$

   or,
   $$D_t - D_{t-1} = P_t + I_t \tag{a}$$

   We can write, $I_t = i\, D_{t-1}$, and $Y_t = Y_{t-1}(1+g_t)$
   Dividing (a) by Y_t, we have

   $$b_t - b_{t-1}[1/(1+g_t)] = p_t + i_t\, b_{t-1}[1/(1+g_t)]$$

   or,
   $$b_t = p_t + b_{t-1}[(1+i_t)/(1+g_t)] \tag{b}$$

   or,
   $$b_t - b_{t-1} = p_t - b_{t-1}[1-(1+i_t)/(1+g_t)]$$

   or,
   $$b_t - b_{t-1} = p_t - b_{t-1}[(g_t - i_t)/(1+g_t)] \tag{c}$$

3. It is somewhat surprising that there are large differences in the fiscal deficit figures between the Receipts Budget and the Economic Survey for 1997–8 and 1998–9. For 1997–8, the Economic Survey and the Receipts Budget report the fiscal deficit at Rs 73,205 crore and Rs 88,937 crore, respectively. For 1998–9, the figures are Rs 89,560 crore in the Economic Survey and Rs 1,13,348 crore in the Receipts Budget.

4. There is a small difference between the derived fiscal deficit figures and the CAG's fiscal deficit figures. In the latter case, net borrowing is fiscal deficit minus net draw down from cash balances.

5. The monetized part of debt is reflected in the centre's outstanding liabilities to the RBI. The central government pays interest to the RBI on its outstanding liabilities. Prior to the Agreement in 1997, the government paid the RBI an interest which was significantly lower than that on the market bonds. However, since the

agreement, the government pays the RBI the same rate as for the market. This led to a significant increase in the RBI's profits, which come back to the central government in the form of dividends from the RBI as part of non-tax revenue. As a result, there has been an improvement in the primary deficit. For the earlier years, although some dividends still came to the central government from the RBI, these were of a much lower order. Further, there has been both direct and indirect seignorage in the Indian system in the sense that liquidity is sometimes placed with the banks and financial institutions so as to enable them to lift government bonds.

6. Taking the figure of outstanding liability given as revised estimate for 2002–3 in the Receipts Budget and excluding the figure for small savings shown under 'other liabilities'.

7. Fiscal and primary deficits along with growth and interest rates may be considered as interdependent. Particularly, fiscal deficits may affect interest rates and the level of primary expenditure may affect growth rates. This analysis looks primarily at their historical paths in explaining their relative roles in the process of accumulation of debt. For future projections of the behaviour of debt, the interrelationship among the relevant variables would have to be kept in view. However, this would require detailed modelling to adequately take into account the important interrelationships.

7

Fiscal Deficits and Government Debt in India

Implications for Growth and Stabilization*

Fiscal deficits are like obesity. You can see your weight rising on
the scale and your clothing size increasing, but there is no sense
of urgency in dealing with the problem.

Martin Feldstein
Address to Reserve Bank of India, 12 January 2004

High levels of fiscal deficit relative to GDP, under certain conditions,
not only cause sharp increases in the debt-GDP ratio, but also adversely
affect savings and investment, and consequently growth Seshan (1987),
Rakshit (2000). The usability of fiscal policy as a tool of counter-
cyclical intervention is also compromised when the fiscal deficit is high
and structural in nature. This chapter examines the long-term profile of
fiscal deficits in India, and its impact on growth that arises from its impact on savings and investment, which may occur directly or through
its effects on interest rates and inflation. It also looks at relevant considerations for determining levels of debt and deficit relative to GDP at
which these should be stabilized in India, given the current configuration of key determinants like the revenue-to-GDP ratio and public and
private savings rates consistent with the objective of achieving higher
growth.

* Originally published as 'Fiscal Deficits and Government Debt: Implications for Growth and
Stabilisation', *Economic and Political Weekly*, Vol. 40, No. 27, 2 July 2005, pp. 2919–33.

Federalism and Fiscal Transfers in India, Second Edition. C. Rangarajan and D.K. Srivastava, Oxford University Press.
© Rangarajan and Srivastava 2024. DOI: 10.1093/9780198930426.003.0007

The combined fiscal deficit of the Centre and states stood at 9.3 per cent of GDP in 1990–1. There was a clear improvement in the early 1990s. After falling to 6.26 per cent in 1996–7, the fiscal deficit to GDP ratio started rising again and was around 10 per cent in 2001–2 and 2002–3. Although only marginally higher than that in 1990–1, this level of fiscal deficit was qualitatively much different because it was accompanied by much higher levels of the debt-GDP ratio, the ratio of interest payments to revenue receipts, and the share of revenue deficit in the fiscal deficit. The debt-GDP ratio has risen from 61.7 per cent in 1990–1 to about 76 per cent in 2002–3, when external debt is considered at historical exchange rates and liabilities of states on account of reserves and deposits are not included. When these are included and external debt is evaluated at current exchange rates an upward adjustment of about 9 percentage points of GDP is called for, consisting of 3 and 6 percentage points for the two factors, respectively, taking government liabilities to about 85 per cent of GDP at the end of 2002–3.

This chapter discusses the following: (i) The theoretical perspectives that provide an insight into ways in which fiscal deficits can affect some of the important macro variables of the economy; (ii) the conditions of sustainability of fiscal deficits and its relationship with growth, primary deficits, and interest rate in the context of the dynamics of debt accumulation and examines the growth of the debt-GDP ratio in India in a long-term perspective; (iii) the savings and investment performance in India, empirically investigating certain critical relationships describing the impact of fiscal deficit on savings and investment that have a bearing on the growth prospects in India; and (iv) the differences between structural and cyclical deficits and the role of discretionary policy for macroeconomic stabilization.

Theoretical Perspectives

There is no agreement among economists on analytical grounds or on the basis of empirical results on whether financing government expenditure by incurring a fiscal deficit is good, bad, or indifferent in terms of its real effects, particularly on investment and growth. Among the mainstream analytical perspectives, the neo-classical view considers fiscal deficits detrimental to investment and growth, while in the Keynesian paradigm, it constitutes a key policy prescriptive. Theorists persuaded by Ricardian equivalence assert that fiscal deficits do not really matter except for smoothening the adjustment to expenditure or revenue shocks. While the neo-classical and Ricardian schools focus on the long run, the Keynesian view emphasizes the short-run effects (Barskey, Mankiw and Zeldes (1986) and Bernheim and Bagwell (1988)).

The Neo-Classical View

The component of revenue deficit in fiscal deficits implies a reduction in government savings or an increase in government dis-saving. In the neo-classical perspective (see, e.g., Bernheim 1989), this will have a detrimental effect on growth if the reduction in government savings is not fully offset by a rise in private savings, thereby resulting in a fall in the overall savings rate. This, apart from putting pressure on the interest rate, will adversely affect growth. The neo-classical economists assume that markets clear, in the sense that demand for and supply of goods match in the goods as well as the labour market so that full employment of resources is attained. In this paradigm, fiscal deficits raise lifetime consumption by shifting taxes to future generations. If economic resources are fully employed, increased consumption necessarily implies decreased savings in a closed economy. In an open economy, real interest rates and investment may remain unaffected, but the fall in national savings is financed by higher external borrowing accompanied by an appreciation of the domestic currency and a fall in exports. In both cases, net national savings fall and consumption rises accompanied by some combination of fall in investment and exports. The neo-classical paradigm assumes that the consumption of each individual is determined as the solution to an inter-temporal optimization problem where both borrowing and lending are permitted at the market rate of interest (Kotlikoff 1988, 1995). It also assumes that individuals have finite life spans where each consumer belongs to a specific generation and the life spans of successive generations overlap.

Citing recent evidence in the US context, Gale and Orszag (2002) observed that 'a reasonable estimate is that a reduction in the projected budget surplus (or increase in the projected budget deficit) of one per cent of GDP will raise long term interest rates by between 50 to 100 basis points'. In their view, fiscal discipline promotes long-term growth primarily because budget surpluses are a form of national savings.

Keynesian View of Fiscal Deficits

The Keynesian view (see, e.g., Eisner 1989, Hodrick and Prescott (1981), Eisner and Pieper (1984) and Feldstein (1976)), in the context of the existence of some unemployed resources, envisages that an increase in autonomous government expenditure, whether investment or consumption, financed by borrowing would cause output to expand through a multiplier process. The traditional Keynesian framework does not distinguish between alternative uses of the fiscal deficit as between government consumption or investment expenditure, nor does it distinguish between alternative sources of financing the fiscal deficit through monetization or external or internal borrowing. In fact, there is no explicit budget constraint in the analysis. Subsequent elaborations of the Keynesian paradigm envisage that the multiplier-based expansion of output leads to a rise in the demand for money, and if the money supply is fixed and the deficit is bond financed, interest rates would rise, partially offsetting the multiplier effect. However, the Keynesians argue that increased aggregate demand enhances the profitability of private investment and leads to higher investment at any given rate of interest. The effect of a rise in interest rate may thus be more than neutralized by the increased profitability of investment. Keynesians argue that deficits may stimulate savings and investment even if the interest rate rises, primarily because of the employment of hitherto unutilized resources. However, at full employment, deficits would lead to crowding out even in the Keynesian paradigm. In the standard Keynesian analysis, if everyone thinks that a budget deficit makes them wealthier, it would raise the output and employment, and thereby actually make people wealthier. Unlike the loanable funds theory, the Keynesian paradigm rules out any direct effect on the interest rate of borrowing by the government.

Ricardian Equivalence Perspective

In the perspective of Ricardian equivalence (e.g., Barro 1974, 1976, 1979, 1987, 1989), fiscal deficits are viewed as neutral in terms of their impact on growth. The financing of budgets by deficits amounts only to a postponement of taxes. The deficit in any current period is exactly equal to the present value of future taxation that is required to pay off the increment to debt resulting from the deficit. In other words, government spending must be paid for, whether now or later, and the present value of spending must be equal to the present value of tax and non-tax revenues. Fiscal deficits are a useful device for smoothening the impact of revenue shocks or for meeting the requirements of lumpy expenditures, the financing of which through taxes may be spread over a period of time. However, such fiscal deficits do not have an impact on aggregate demand if household spending decisions are based on the present value of their incomes that takes into account the present value of their future tax liabilities. Alternatively, a decrease in current government savings that is implied by the fiscal deficit may be accompanied by an offsetting increase in private savings, leaving the national savings and therefore investment unchanged. Then, there is no impact on the real interest rate. Ricardian equivalence requires the assumption that individuals in the economy are foresighted, they have discount rates that are equal to governments' discount rates on spending, and they have extremely long-time horizons for evaluating the present value of future taxes. In particular, such a time horizon may well extend beyond their own lives, in which case they save with a view to making altruistic transfers to take care of the tax liabilities of their future generations.

The economic universe of these alternative schools of thought is also characterized by individuals who differ in their behavioural responses in critical respects. The Keynesian world is inhabited by myopic, liquidity-constrained individuals who behave under money illusion, and have a high propensity to consume out of current disposable income. The Ricardian equivalence individuals conceive of a universe of farsighted, fully informed, altruistic individuals. The neo-classical world is inhabited by rational individuals who respond to real changes in their wealth portfolios, and who are farsighted enough to plan consumption over their life cycle. Table 7.1 summarizes the main differences in these alternative paradigms.

Table 7.1   Fiscal Deficits and the Economy: Salient Features of Alternative Paradigms

	Neo-Classical	Ricardian	Keynesian
Consumers	Finite, lifetime horizon	Infinite time perspective through altruistic transfers	Myopic, liquidity-constrained
Effects of a deficit based tax cut on private saving	Overall savings rate would fall	Private saving remains unaffected	Aggregate demand increases
Employment of resources	Full employment	Full employment	Resources not fully employed
Effect on interest rate	Interest rate increases	No effect	Interest rate increases
Contention	Fiscal deficits detrimental	Fiscal deficits irrelevant	Fiscal deficits beneficial

Source: Authors' compilation.

The 'Tax and Spend' Hypothesis

A fourth hypothesis formalized by supply-side economists is sometimes called the 'tax and spend' hypothesis. An exposition of the hypothesis is given in Vedder, Gallaway, and Frenze (1987). In their view, raising taxes to cut down deficits would not work because it would only encourage politicians to spend more. The result would be that while the deficit would remain the same, in the long run the size of the private sector would be cut down. In their view, a tax cut, which puts pressure on the contraction of government spending leaving deficits and national savings unchanged, and which leads to an increase in private consumption, should be considered more desirable. The main problem is that when government expenditure does not fall, it has to run a deficit, which raises interest payments and causes total government expenditure including interest payments to rise as a share of GDP.

Debt and Fiscal Deficits: Issues in the Indian Context

The issue of fiscal deficit assumed importance in India since the late 1980s when the fiscal deficit to GDP ratio rose to levels above 7 per cent. In the early 1990s, it was above 9 per cent, and after some improvement it started rising again, crossing the threshold of 10 per cent of GDP in 2001–2. In the context of fiscal deficits in India, several distinct sets of issues have been examined from time to time. Some of the important issues that have been noted in the literature are listed below:

1. Whether fiscal deficits of the central and state governments, considered together, and separately are sustainable.
2. Whether these governments are solvent, given their debt and deficit levels.
3. Whether the presence of high levels of structural fiscal deficits has constrained the usability of fiscal policy as a tool of stabilization in respect of output as well as prices.
4. Whether there is a meaningful asymmetry between the accumulation of fiscal liabilities by the central and state governments.
5. Whether there is potential for additional seigniorage in the system for financing fiscal deficits.
6. Whether there is a need to formulate rules and targets to stabilize debt and deficits, and how should these targets be derived.
7. Whether, apart from the size, the quality of fiscal deficit has progressively become more of a problem and, in particular, whether the rising share of revenue deficit in fiscal deficit, that is, government dis-savings have resulted in a fall of the overall savings rate, thereby adversely affecting growth.
8. Whether fiscal deficits have crowded out private investment by putting pressure on interest rates, thereby adversely affecting growth.
9. Whether continued high levels of fiscal deficits, resulting in growing interest payments, have crowded out government capital expenditure.
10. Whether public investment financed by fiscal deficits has the potential of crowding-in private investment, thereby positively affecting growth.

These issues are interdependent as the impact of fiscal deficits on growth affects its sustainability. Although the major focus of this study is on the implications of fiscal deficits for growth and stabilization, some of the extant literature on the above issues is briefly reviewed here.

Fiscal Stance: Inflation and Output Stabilization

One set of issues concerns whether the fiscal policy as a policy instrument has been used to obtain the appropriate fiscal stance, expansionary or otherwise, given the prevailing economic conditions (e.g., Joshi and Little (1994) and Reserve Bank of India (2002)). In this context, reviewing the situation over the period 1974–5 to 1989–90, Joshi and Little (1994) observed that there was a clear tendency in India for fiscal contraction when inflation was above trend and fiscal expansion when inflation was below the trend. They found that in nineteen out of twenty-nine years from 1970–1 to 1989–90, this tendency was clearly visible. On the other hand, the fiscal stance was much less responsive to stabilizing output. They observed that prima facie fiscal policy was destabilizing in no less than twenty-two out of the twenty-nine years under review in their study. In some of these years, when output was below trend, the fiscal authorities were inhibited from adopting an expansionary fiscal policy either by inflation or by balance of payment difficulties. In the pre-1990 situation, in their view, inflation was the main consideration guiding India's fiscal policy. Joshi and Little (1994) observed,

> there would have been more room for fiscal policy to be devoted to (stabilizing output), if the economy had possessed greater stocks of foreign exchange reserves and commodities, specially food grains, the use of which would have reduced inflation by increasing supplies, and would have either ameliorated or financed a deterioration in the balance of payments (p. 231).

In recent years, these constraints have ceased to be binding, with a comfortable position in regard to the foreign exchange reserves, stocks of food grains, and balance of payments. There is therefore a case for better aligning the fiscal stance to make it more responsive to output stabilization. The Reserve Bank of India (2002) in its Report on Currency and Finance for 2001–2, provides estimates of structural and cyclical fiscal deficits. In their estimates, fiscal deficits in India are predominantly structural in nature and the cyclical component is very small in magnitude, ranging between a deficit of 0.12 per cent of GDP and a surplus of 0.21 per cent of GDP. Automatic stabilizers exist if revenues respond more to output changes than expenditures. The RBI estimates that the elasticity of receipts of the combined government sector is 1.07 whereas that for combined non-interest expenditure is 1.06. Since the difference between the two magnitudes is small, even if there is an automatic stabilizer, it is likely to be weak. Discretionary fiscal measures are therefore required for stabilization.

Impact on Savings, Investment, and Growth

The links between fiscal deficit and growth, savings and investment rates, inflation and current account deficits have also been examined in many studies. The relationship between fiscal deficit and interest rate and the existence of crowding out are important considerations in determining the advisability of deficit-financed expansionary fiscal policies. Authors like Sundararajan and Thakur (1980), Pradhan et al. (1990), and Parker (1995) had earlier examined the issue of crowding out in the Indian context. More recently, Chakraborty (2002) finds that fiscal deficit does not put upward pressure on the interest rate, while Goyal (2004), using monthly data, argues that there is a two-way causality between fiscal deficit and interest rates. In his view, interest rates did not rise in recent years in spite of high fiscal deficits because of the larger liquidity available to the system. Reserve Bank of India (2002) has noted that raising public sector investment to boost aggregate demand in the economy crowds-out both private consumption and investment with no long-lasting impact on output. On the other hand, infrastructure investment by the public sector crowds-in private investment while public investment in manufacturing crowds out private investment.

Solvency of the Public Sector

In the accounting approach to public sector solvency, Buiter (1985 and 1988) suggests that sustainable deficit levels can be financed without raising debt levels relative to GDP under feasible rates of growth, real interest, and inflation. Following the neo-classical solvency approach, Buiter and Patel (1992) observe that the relevant criterion for the no-Ponzi game condition on public debt is to judge it by comparing the rate of growth of public debt relative to GDP with the real interest rate. If the debt ratio systematically grows faster than the real interest rate, the public sector is insolvent.

Buiter and Patel (1992) examined the issue of solvency of the Indian public sector by studying trends in debt, primary budget surplus, and seigniorage. Solvency requires that, with a finite time horizon, public debt in the last period becomes non-positive, that is, no debt is left for further servicing. If the time horizon is infinite, the existing debt should be serviceable by current and future primary surpluses and future seigniorage. This implies that, at any time, the present value of future public debt becomes zero in the limit. If it becomes less than zero, it indicates a situation of 'super-solvency'. The requirement of the present value of debt to be zero or less holds as long as the economy is not dynamically inefficient, that is, it is not the case that the interest rate is below the growth rate forever. For a dynamically inefficient system (where the growth rate is higher than the interest rate forever) Ponzi games can be viable. Buiter and Patel contend that while the interest rate can be below the growth rate for extended finite periods of time, the Indian economy is not dynamically inefficient in the long run, and that 'there are no social free lunches to be earned by increasing the public debt'. Calling the build-up of public debt in India, 'this remarkable fiscal high wire act', they contend that the continuation of existing patterns of behaviour will eventually threaten the solvency of the government. They also observe that solvency is a very weak criterion with which to evaluate the sustainability of fiscal and financial policy. They observe that a government can remain solvent even though its debt relative to GDP grows without bound if the long-term growth rate of the debt-GDP ratio, while positive, is less than the long-term value of the excess of the interest rate over the growth rate. Thus, unbounded debt-GDP ratios can still be consistent with solvency.

Implications for Sustainability

The issue of sustainability of debt should be considered as distinct from that of solvency. Sustainability can be seen as the capacity to keep a balance between costs of additional borrowing with returns from such borrowing, which could be in the form of higher growth that results in higher government revenues that can be used for servicing the additional borrowing. Sustainability issues should be viewed for combinations of debt and fiscal deficit, and not in isolation for either debt or fiscal deficit. Thus, a fiscal deficit of 10 per cent combined with say a debt-GDP ratio of 100 per cent will have sustainability implications that are quite different from those of a 10 per cent fiscal deficit when the debt- GDP ratio is 50 per cent. Thus, sustainability should not be treated as synonymous with the stability of the debt-GDP ratio at whatever level it might have reached.

The level of debt in combination with the interest rate determines the level of interest payments. Fiscal deficit minus interest payments determines the primary deficit. The primary deficit represents the extent of borrowing used by the government for current expenditures, revenue, and capital. The remaining part of the fiscal deficit is claimed by interest payments, which are transfer payments that go back into the income–expenditure stream.

In particular, government interest payments add to the disposable incomes in the private sector. This has implications for government revenues as well.

At the same time, interest payments add to the government's revenue expenditures leaving less of the current fiscal deficit for use for government capital expenditure. Increases in revenue expenditures, ceteris paribus, lead to a fall in the government's net savings, which has an adverse impact on the overall savings and consequently on the growth rate. However, private savings may be positively affected by a higher fiscal deficit because of the positive impact due to higher wealth in the private sector in the form of government bonds. As government capital expenditure on infrastructure and other vital public goods is increased, the growth impulse is positively affected. The impact of fiscal deficit and level of debt on savings and investment as a result of the configuration of these variables determines the impact on growth as well as the interest rate. Considering the various interrelationships involved, the appropriate framework is a macroeconomic model. Such a model can also bring together the monetary-side influences on interest, growth rate, and inflation rates. Even while recognizing that growth and interest rates are endogenously determined, a large literature is devoted to sustainability analytics treating growth and interest rates as exogenous. This approach can be considered useful only as a frame of reference. It is relevant to consider the impact of fiscal deficit and debt on growth and interest rates.

Debt would become unsustainable if fiscal deficits follow a course that leads to a self-perpetuating rise in the debt-GDP ratio, which affects negatively the growth rate and positively the interest rate, such that the existing levels of primary government expenditures cannot be sustained, given the configuration of growth and interest rates. A sustainable debt–deficit combination would be stable in terms of debt-GDP ratio and fiscal-deficit GDP ratio consistent with the permissible levels of primary expenditures.

An alternative method by which the sustainability issues have been examined in the literature is to look at the growth and interest rates as stochastic processes. Although such an analytical framework does not help directly in designing fiscal policy, it helps ascertain whether debt and deficits show signs of unsustainability. Papadopoulos and Sidiropoulos (1999) showed that a test for sustainability should check for the cointegration of government expenditures and revenues. If these are cointegrated with the cointegrating vector of (1, −1), the necessary condition for sustainability of debt is satisfied.

Jha and Sharma (2004) carried out empirical tests to ascertain whether government expenditures and revenues are cointegrated in India using long time series data. They found, based on a sample period starting in the early 1950s, that if structural breaks are taken into account, government expenditures and revenues were cointegrated, and therefore growth in government debt in India has been consistent with the requirements of sustainability. The presence of cointegration implies that adjustments in revenues and expenditures take place such that these move together. Thus, for example, if interest payments to GDP ratios increase, adjustments in other components of expenditure—notably, government capital expenditure which, by itself, may not be desirable—would take place so that the co-movement of expenditure with revenues is maintained.

Financing Deficits by Alternative Channels

The fourth issue that has received attention relates to the relative merits of financing fiscal deficits by domestic borrowing, external borrowing, or borrowing from the central bank. In theory, financing by external debt would lead to pressure on the exchange rate. Financing domestic debt by monetization would put pressure on inflation and that by domestic borrowing, on interest rates. For example, Moorthy et al. (2000), while examining the issue of bond-financing versus monetization in the context of debt stabilization, conclude that the emphasis on market borrowing rather than borrowing from the RBI as part of economic reforms in India in the 1990s proved to be beneficial. In Rangarajan et al. (1989), the intertemporal budget constraint was used to study the dynamic interlinkages between government deficits and alternative modes of financing these. In particular, given the set of revenue and expenditure parameters, relevant for the late 1980s, it was shown that the debt-financing scenario led to an explosive growth in the debt-GDP ratio, and the monetary-financing scenario led to an unacceptably high inflation rate within a short span of time.

Asymmetry in Central and Sub-national Debt

Another dimension that has received attention relates to the desirability of asymmetric treatment of central and sub-national debt and deficits on grounds of different degrees of endogeneity of interest, growth, and other relevant variables. For example, Chelliah (2001) has argued that 'we must recognize that the state is borrowing largely from outsiders and paying interest to them' and that 'state governments do not have access to created credit'. In his view, the constraints on sub-national deficits must be stronger than those of the central government. The interest rates applicable to the borrowing by the states, both average rates and marginal rates, are higher as compared to those for the centre, implying the need for more stringent norms for the same rates of growth of GDP.

Controlling Debt and Deficit: Rules and Targets

Borrowing by the government often appears to be a softer option than increasing taxes or reducing expenditures. That is why, as established by international experience also, it is important to provide exogenous limits on borrowing by governments, whether central or sub-national.

Such limits can be exercised through fiscal responsibility legislation, or other institutional arrangements like the Australian Loan Council and the Maastricht Treaty for member countries of the European Economic Community. The Maastricht Treaty on Economic and Monetary Union, for example, has two convergence conditions for the members of the European Monetary Union: (i) Country's overall budget deficit for each fiscal year must be equal to or below 3 per cent of the GDP, and (ii) a country's stock of public debt must be equal to or less than 60 per cent of the GDP. The 3 per cent limit is not meant to be exceeded in 'normal' economic downturns.

There has been a discussion in the literature as to whether deficit targeting works in practice. The main institutional reforms for controlling the growth of debt and deficit relate to (i) formal deficit and debt rules, (ii) expenditure limits, and (iii) requirements of transparency. In regard to the first, apart from the Maastricht Treaty norms, the UK has operated a Golden Rule since 1997 whereby borrowing is done only to finance capital spending. Several countries have deficit and debt rules at the sub-national level. In the US, all states except two have laws requiring balanced budgets and limiting the states to raise debt. The provinces and territories of Canada generally have fiscal rules with balanced budgets requiring them to take on debt only to finance investment projects. Canada has also focused on instituting a rigorous expenditure review process. Debt ceilings can serve as a useful complement to deficit rules. The main criticism of the deficit rules in general and balanced budget rules in particular is that they are invariant and therefore tend to be pro-cyclical. This is particularly important for national governments. For this reason, the deficit rules for the national government have increasingly been defined in terms of a cyclically adjusted deficit measure or as an average over the economic cycle so that the operation of domestic stabilizers and some room for discretionary policy within the cycle may be permitted.

Transparency in fiscal management has been emphasized by countries like New Zealand, Australia, and the UK. Transparency is best served when there is an explicit legal provision for it, requiring elaboration of the guiding principles of fiscal policy, a clear statement of objectives of changes in fiscal policies, the need for a long-term focus on fiscal policy, and requirements for providing fiscal information to the public. The UK, US, and New Zealand have enacted legislations for transparency, which require statements indicating the objectives for deficits and debt. International experience also suggests that expenditure rules have often proved to be effective. These rules typically emphasize ceilings on specific areas of expenditure, like discretionary expenditure as opposed to non-discretionary expenditure, and in some cases concerning particular programmes.

In the Indian context, as far as the central finances are concerned, a Fiscal Responsibility and Budget Management Act (FRBMA) was enacted in 2003. Some states have also enacted fiscal responsibility legislation. Subsequently, after the Twelfth Finance Commission recommendations, 26 out of 28 states have enacted fiscal responsibility legislation, with two exceptions being West Bengal and Sikkim. The central government has also framed Rules under the FRBMA. The Act and the Rules, as these presently stand, have provided for the elimination of the revenue deficit by 2008–9, with 0.5 percentage point of GDP as the minimum annual reduction target, and fiscal deficit to be brought to a level of 3 per cent of GDP, with 0.3 percentage point of GDP as the minimum annual reduction target. The FRBMA has some built-in flexibility in achieving revenue and fiscal deficit reduction targets as there is a provision that the specified limits may be exceeded 'due to exemplary reasons such as considerations of national security and national calamity'. The Act has also provided that the 'Reserve Bank of India may subscribe to the primary issues to the Central Government Securities' for specified reasons.

Analysing Sustainability of Debt and Fiscal Deficit

In Domar's analysis of the dynamics of debt accumulation, both interest rate and growth rate are taken as exogenous. Based on this assumption, results can be derived that can serve as useful benchmarks.

Sustainability Analytics under the Canonical (Domar) Model

In considering the dynamics of debt accumulation, the following notations will be used: b_t: debt-GDP ratio in period t; g_t: nominal growth rate in period t; i_t: nominal interest rate in period t; and p_t: primary deficit relative to GDP in period t. The standard equation for debt accumulation is written as[1]

$$b_t = p_t + b_{t-1}[(1+i_t)/(1+g_t)] \tag{7.1}$$

Equation 7.1 can be written as

$$b_t = p_t + x_t b_{t-1} \quad [\text{where } x_t = (1+i_t)/(1+g_t)] \tag{7.2}$$

If

$$b_0 = p_0,$$

we have,

$$b_1 = p_1 + x_1 p_0$$

$$b_2 = p_2 + x_2 p_1 + x_2 x_1 p_0$$

Generalizing, we can write

$$b_t = p_t + (x_t)p_{t-1} + (x_t x_{t-1})p_{t-2} + \cdots + (x_t x_{t-1} \ldots x_1)p_0 \tag{7.3}$$

If it is assumed that x_t is constant, imping g and i are constant for all t, We can write

$$b_t = p_t + xp_{t-1} + x^2 p_{t-2} + \cdots + x^{t-1}p_{t-1} + x^t p_0 \tag{7.4}$$

The canonical model (Domar 1944) requires the additional assumption that p's are also constant for all t. Since $x_t = (1+i_t)/(1+g_t) = x$ for all t, three cases arise (7.1) when $g = i$, (7.2) when $g > i$, and (7.3) when $g < i$.

In the first case, we can write

$$b_t = p + \sum_{i=0}^{t-1} p = (t+1)p \tag{7.5}$$

This implies that if $g = i$, the debt-GDP ratio is the cumulated sum of the primary deficits in all the previous periods. In the second case, when $g > i$,

$$b_t = p\{1 + x + x^2 + \cdots + x^{t-1} + x^t\} \tag{7.6}$$

The term within parenthesis is a geometric series with a common ratio $x < 1$. As t tends to infinity, this sum tends to $x/(1-x)$. Then the long run value of the debt-GDP ratio can be written as

$$b_t = p + px/(1-x) = p/(1-x)$$
$$b_t = p(1+g)/(g-i) \text{ as } t \to \infty \tag{7.7}$$

In the third case, when $g < i$, $x > 1$, and b_t will grow indefinitely.

Thus, a value of $p > 0$, will eventually become unsustainable for both cases when $g = i$ and when $g < i$. In the case when $g = i$, the debt-GDP ratio grows linearly by the size of the primary deficit, and when $g < i$, the debt-GDP ratio grows explosively if the primary deficit-GDP ratio is positive.

We will now focus on the case where $g > i$. From (7.7), the long-term equilibrium value of $b_t = b^*$ is given by

$$b^* = p(1+g)/(g-i) \qquad (7.8)$$

The fiscal deficit to GDP ratio (f^*) corresponding to a stable debt-GDP ratio (b^*) will be:

$$f^* = p.g/(g-i) \qquad (7.9)$$

Equations (7.8) and (7.9) provide a system of two equations in three unknowns, viz., b, f, and p, assuming values of g and i are given $(g > i)$, and consistent with a stable debt-GDP ratio.[2] It is indicated that high values of p will be associated with high levels of b and f. However, these equations do not provide a unique solution as the unknowns are more than the number of the equations.

Using equations (7.8) and (7.9) together, the relationship between b^* and f^* can be written as:

$$b^* = f^*.(1+g)/g \qquad (7.10)$$

The pair (b^*, f^*) gives that level of fiscal deficit-GDP ratio at which the debt-GDP ratio remains unchanged at b^*. As shown by Figure 7.1, equation (7.10) gives a family of straight lines rising to the right, showing combinations of fiscal deficit-GDP ratio and corresponding stable debt-GDP ratio, for a given growth rate. This line shifts upwards as growth rates are lowered.

Alternatively, the stabilization conditions can be expressed in an equivalent way in terms of the ratio of interest payments to GDP. Defining interest payments to GDP ratio as (ip_y), we have

$$IP_t = i.B_{t-1} \quad \text{or} \quad (ip_y)_t = i.b_{t-1}/(1+g) \qquad (7.11)$$

As debt is stabilized $b_t = b_{t-1} = b^*$ and $(ip_y)_t = (ip_y)_t^*$

$$b^* = (ip_y)^*.(1+g)/i \qquad (7.12)$$

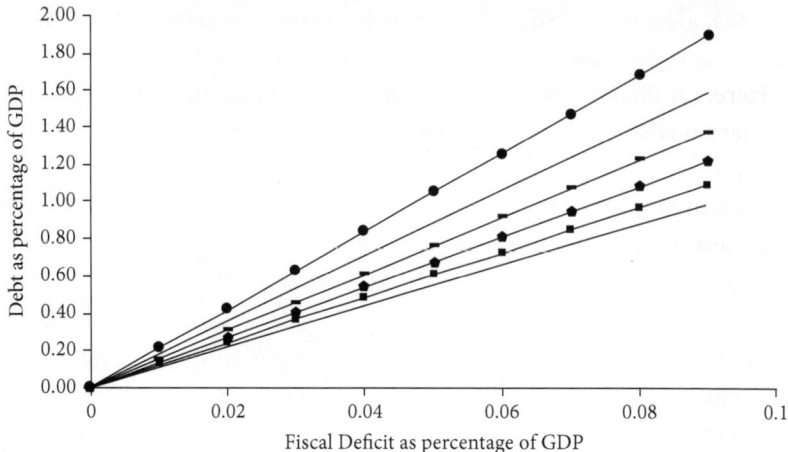

Figure 7.1 Stable Combinations of Debt and Fiscal Deficit to GDP Ratios for Different Growth Rates

Different Growth Rates Vertical axis: debt-GDP ratio; Horizontal axis: fiscal deficit GDP Ratio. For lower growth rates, the line is closer to the vertical axis; as growth rates are higher, for the same fiscal deficit ratio, debt-GDP ratios are lower.

The corresponding level of fiscal deficit to GDP ratio is given by

$$f^* = (ip_y)^* g/i \tag{7.13}$$

Equations (7.12) and (7.13) provide a set of two equations in terms of three unknowns, $(b, f, \text{and } ip_y)$. Again, the system can determine unique values of any two of the three unknowns, provided one of the unknowns is pre-specified. Clearly, additional information is needed to solve the system described by either (7.8) and (7.9), or (7.12) and (7.13).

The critical question is whether, when $g > i$, sustainability is implied for any value $p > 0$. To address this question, it is useful to recognize that g_t and i_t are neither constant nor independent of the level of p. In particular, both g_t and i_t should be taken as stochastic processes and dependent on the levels of debt and fiscal deficit relative to GDP. At any time t, the debt-GDP ratio b_t will be higher than its previous year's level b_{t-1}, as long as the primary deficit to GDP ratio in the current period p_t satisfies the following condition:

$$p_t = b_{t-1}(g_t - i_t)/(1 + g_t) = p_t^s \qquad (7.14)$$

Here, i_t is the average interest rate and p_t^s called the debt-stabilizing primary deficit to GDP ratio. As long as p_t in any given year is equal to or less than p_t^s for that year, the debt-GDP ratio will not rise in that year compared to its level in the previous year. Since p_t^s depends on the difference between $g_t - i_t$, it is important to consider how p should be determined in any year since it may affect g and i in that year.

The pre-specification of either the primary deficit to GDP ratio or the ratio of interest payments to GDP requires consideration of the appropriate fiscal stance in the medium to long term. The medium-term fiscal stance should aim at achieving the maximum possible trend growth rate. Such a fiscal stance should be consistent with the growth-maximizing combination of a stable debt-GDP ratio and a stable fiscal deficit to GDP ratio. The short-term fiscal stance should be designed to keep the economy close to the long-term growth and debt-GDP ratios using temporary variations in fiscal deficit. These issues are discussed in the next section.

The main lessons from the canonical model can be summarized as follows:

1. The debt-GDP ratio will rise continuously for positive values of the primary deficit relative to GDP if the growth rate is equal to or less than the interest rate.
2. If the growth rate is higher than the interest rate, and both of these are unaffected by the levels of fiscal deficit and debt relative to GDP, the debt-GDP ratio and the fiscal deficit-to-GDP ratio will eventually stabilize. Higher levels of primary deficit-to-GDP ratios will be associated with higher levels of stabilized debt-GDP and fiscal deficit-to-GDP ratios.
3. The level of fiscal deficit relative to GDP that keeps the debt-GDP ratio stable can be specified as dependent on the growth rate only.
4. The system of equations implicit in the canonical model can define combinations of stable debt-GDP ratio and fiscal deficit-to-GDP ratio but does not determine their best or most desirable values.
5. In deciding a suitable fiscal stance for the medium to long term, it is best to consider the debt-GDP ratio and fiscal deficit-to-GDP ratio together rather than only one of them.

6. The long-term fiscal stance requires additional information on the impact of debt and deficit levels on growth, and the assumption of constancy of growth and interest rates should be given up. In this case, the ratio of debt to GDP will rise progressively, even if the growth rate is higher than the interest rate, if the primary deficit to GDP ratio is above a threshold level given by p^s, which can be specified as dependent on the previous year's debt-GDP ratio, growth rate, and interest rate.

The following section provides an analytical framework within which the trend or structural values of a debt-stabilizing and growth-maximizing fiscal stance may be determined. The short-term fiscal stance can subsequently be decided around the long-term levels.

Sustainability, Optimality, and Stability

The canonical framework indicates permissible levels of primary deficits for given combinations of growth and interest rates, for different levels of debt-GDSP ratio. It does not indicate whether a higher or lower debt-GDP ratio may also be sustainable. It also does not indicate as to what may be the optimal ratio at which the debt-GDP ratio should be stabilized. These questions require a consideration of the impact of debt and deficit on interest rates and growth rates. Since various interrelationships are involved, in effect, a macro model with the specification of the relevant structural equations is required. However, to explain the conceptual framework for distinguishing between stability, optimality, and sustainability, we consider first a diagrammatic framework. It is assumed that both growth rate and interest rate may be functions of fiscal deficit, among other factors, and that this relationship is non-linear in both cases. As fiscal deficit levels relative to GDP rise initially, the growth rate rises up to a point. This is so because, initially, as fiscal deficit rises, government investment also increases, which crowds-in private investment and also positively affects private savings as the bond holdings of the private sector increase. As shown in Figure 7.1, higher levels of fiscal deficit would be associated with higher levels of debt-GDP ratio at which it can be stabilized. With the higher debt-GDP ratio, the interest payments to

GDP ratio also increase. Beyond a point, interest payments become so large as to result in a revenue deficit given other parameters, particularly the ratio of revenue receipts to GDP. As revenue deficit rises, government savings and capital expenditures fall. The overall savings rate also falls, and the growth rate begins to fall.

Also, as fiscal deficit relative to GDP rises, interest rates rise initially at low rates. However, at very large levels of fiscal deficit relative to GDP with the associated high levels of debt-GDP ratios, interest rates rise steeply. Figure 7.2 has four quadrants. In the north-east quadrant, the growth rate curve $[g = G(f,...)]$ shows growth rates at different levels of fiscal deficit relative to GDP under ceteris paribus assumptions, and the interest rate curve $[i = I(f,...)]$ shows interest rates at different fiscal deficit to GDP ratios under similar assumptions. Both growth and interest rates are in nominal terms. The growth curve lies above the interest rate curve for the range shown by OC on the x-axis. Throughout this range a country can afford to have a primary deficit.

In the south-east quadrant, the debt-GDP ratio is shown on the vertical axis. For any given growth rate, a curve showing the debt-GDP ratio for the level of fiscal deficit ratio can be shown, capturing the relationship $[b^* = f^*(1+g)/g]$. This relationship is the same as depicted in Figure 7.1,

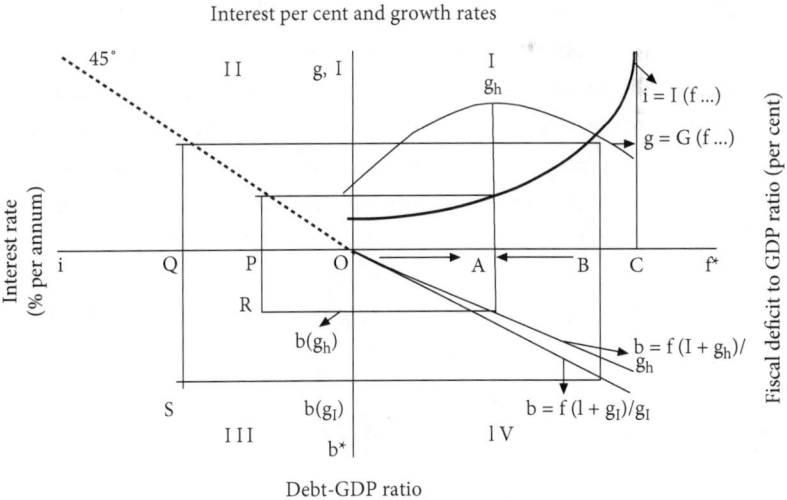

Figure 7.2 Aspects of Fiscal and Debt Sustainability

except that it is now shown upside down. For higher levels of growth rate the curve will shift inwards towards the x-axis, showing that with higher growth, the debt-GDP ratio can be maintained at a lower level for a given fiscal deficit-to-GDP ratio.

The interest rate associated with any fiscal deficit-to-GDP ratio in the first quadrant is taken to the horizontal axis of the second quadrant, that is, the north-west quadrant, through a 45° line. Using this and the debt-GDP ratio shown in the south-east quadrant, the ratio of interest payments to GDP can be shown as their product in the south-west quadrant. As an example, two growth rates are considered: a low growth rate (g_l) and a high growth rate (g_h). The line showing the relationship between fiscal deficit to GDP and the associated stable debt-GDP ratio is closer to the fiscal deficit axis (x-axis in north-east quadrant) for the high growth rate and closer to the debt-GDP ratio axis (y-axis in the south-west quadrant).

With the high growth rate, the interest payments to GDP ratio shown by ODCb (g_h) is much lower than that associated with the lower growth rate as shown by OKJb (g_l). Considering the first quadrant again, the levels of fiscal deficit in the range CD require primary surpluses to keep the debt-GDP ratio constant. But in this range interest payments relative to GDP would have become so high as to make obtaining primary surplus very difficult. To the left of point C on the x-axis, while primary deficit may be permissible, interest payments are too large, leading to government dis-savings resulting in growth rates that are less than the potentially achievable levels. In effect, the optimal level of fiscal deficit is given by OB, where growth is highest obtainable, primary deficit is consistent with sustainability, and interest payments are relatively low such that the government can make enough savings that can contribute to attaining the higher growth. Combinations of high fiscal deficit and debt relative to GDP are detrimental to growth. While it may appear that primary deficit can be maintained for a large range of fiscal deficit to GDP ratios, it is appropriate to search, in the context of a medium to long-term fiscal stance, for the growth-maximizing combination of fiscal deficit and debt relative to GDP, and attempt to hold the economy around this combination.

In order to ascertain the existence of such an optimum and identify its location, a fully articulated model of the economy is needed. In more practical terms, often it is useful to identify desirable changes in fiscal deficit relative to GDP from the existing level. Under certain circumstances, a reduction in the fiscal deficit is warranted and under others, an increase in it may be accommodated with beneficial effects. Policy considerations require distinguishing between long- and short-term components of fiscal deficit. The long-term levels of the combination of debt and deficit relative to GDP should be determined with a view to maximizing growth, given other parameters of the economy. The short-term component should be used as a counter-cyclical instrument. Thus, in a cycle, the short-term component of fiscal deficit can be positive in a recessionary phase and negative in the expansionary phase to keep the long-term configuration of debt and fiscal deficit levels relative to GDP stable. Desirable changes in fiscal deficit become difficult when the economy has gone through phases of large increases in the debt-GDP ratio due to the accumulation of primary deficit that may have remained uncompensated by the requisite excess of growth over interest rate. We review below the impact of high interest payments relative to GDP on savings and investment in India.

Fiscal deficits, savings, and investment in India

An understanding of the behaviour of savings and investment by the private and public sectors is important for considering their impact on fiscal deficit and vice versa. As long as the household sector is providing enough financeable savings, these may be absorbed by the public sector without putting pressure on interest rates. Also, it has been argued that any reduction in public savings is a loss to the overall savings rate on a one-to-one basis.

Trends in Savings and Investment in India

In this section, we look at the profile of the savings-GDP ratio (henceforth, savings rate) since 1950–1, and the relative contribution of the household, private corporate, and public sectors. The following symbols are used:

I = Gross domestic capital formation at current prices

I_a = Gross domestic capital formation at current prices adjusted for errors for errors and omissions (investment)

S = Gross domestic savings at current prices (savings)

I_h = Gross domestic capital formation by the household sector

I_c = Gross domestic capital formation by the private corporate sector

I_p = Gross domestic capital formation by the public sector

S_h = Gross domestic savings by the household sector

S_{hf} = Gross domestic financial savings by the household sector

S_c = Gross domestic savings by the private corporate sector

S_p = Gross domestic savings by the public sector

D_c = Shortfall of the savings of the private corporate sector relative to its investment

D_p = Shortfall of the savings of the public sector relative to its investment

E_h = Excess of the savings of the household sector relative to its investment

Z = Excess of adjusted gross domestic capital formation over gross domestic savings

E = Errors and omissions in gross domestic capital formation

From these, the following identities can then be written:

Gross investment is the sum of investments in household, private corporate, and public sectors:

$$I_h + I_c + I_p = I \tag{7.15}$$

Gross capital formation minus errors and omissions gives 'adjusted' investment:

$$I = I_a + E \tag{7.16}$$

Savings are the sum of household, private corporate, and public sector savings:

$$S_h + S_c + S_p = S \tag{7.17}$$

$$S + Z = I_a \tag{7.18}$$

The excess of public sector investment over its own savings is financed by the excess of domestic sector savings over domestic investment net of the private sector investment over their savings plus the adjustment terms.

$$(I_p - S_p) = (S_h - I_h) - (I_c - S_c) + Z \tag{7.19}$$

or

$$(I_p - S_p) - (S_h - I_h) = (I_c - S_c) + Z$$

or

$$D_p + D_c = E_h + Z \tag{7.20}$$

It is the excess of household savings over its domestic investment that is being used to finance the excess of investment over savings for both the public and the private corporate sectors. It may also be seen that the financial savings of the household sector are identically equal to the excess of total savings of the household sector over its investment ($S_{hf} = S_h - I_h$).

Figure 7.3 shows the profile of the savings-GDP ratio of the household, private corporate, and public sectors over the period 1951–2 to 2001–2. Starting from a level of just 6 per cent of GDP, the household sector savings ratio has shown a steady rise reaching levels of 22 per cent of GDP. The public sector relative to GDP had peaked in 1976–7 at 4.9 per cent. They fell marginally but had a local peak in 1981–2 at 4.5 per cent. Since then there has been a steady decline. The public sector savings to GDP

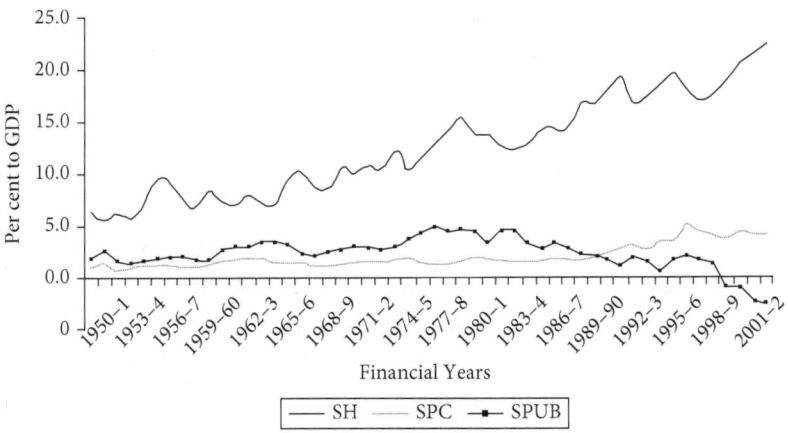

Figure 7.3 Savings Relative to GDP: Household, Private Corporate, and Public Sector

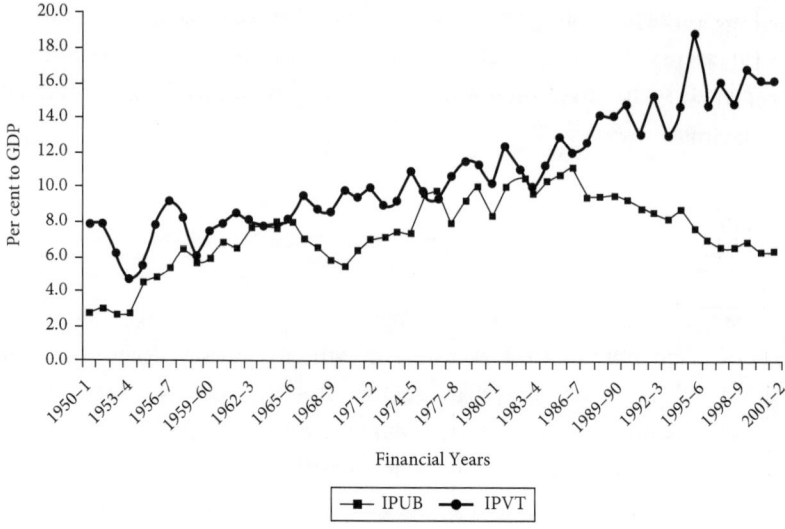

Figure 7.4 Investment Relative to GDP: Private and Public Sector

ratio turned negative in 1998–9 and the dis-saving relative to GDP continued to increase in magnitude, reaching a level of negative 2.5 per cent in 2001–2. This amounts to a fall of 7 percentage points from the level of 4.5 per cent achieved in 1981–2.

The savings ratio of the private corporate sector has been somewhat stagnant at below 2 per cent of GDP until 1987–8, after which it rose steadily to cross 4 per cent of GDP in 1995–6. Since then it has generally been above 4 per cent but is not rising any further. The public sector savings, which reached a peak in 1976–7 have now become negative.Figure 7.4 shows the time profile of public and private investment relative to GDP since 1950–1. Until 1988–9, both of these were rising along a trend path. Since then, while private investment has continued to rise along a trend path, public investment has fallen steeply. In the latter part of the 1990s, it may be noted that the private investment demand fell. In particular, the private corporate sector investment demand fell from a peak of 9.6 per cent of GDP in 1995–6 to 4.8 per cent in 2001–2. Among other factors, the fall in the nominal interest rates in the latter part of the 1990s is attributable to the decline in corporate investment.

Within the public sector, savings and investment of administrative departments and departmental enterprises is referred to as 'government' savings and investment. These are more directly related to fiscal deficit, and its impact on growth. The remaining public sector comprises non-departmental enterprises and quasi-government bodies. Table 7.2 gives the savings–investment profile of the different components of the public

Table 7.2 Gross Domestic Savings and Capital Formation of the Public Sector Relative to GDP

	Admini- strative depart- ments	Depart- mental enter- prises	Non- depart- mental enter- prises	Quasi- govern- ment bodies	Admini- strative departments and departments enterprises	(Per cent) Non- department enterprises and quasi-govt bodies
Gross Domestic Savings						
1993–4	−3.16	0.86	2.79	0.14	−2.30	2.93
1994–5	−2.68	0.99	3.23	0.12	−1.69	3.36
1995–6	−2.14	0.83	3.19	0.14	−1.30	3.33
1996–7	−2.41	0.75	3.25	0.09	−1.66	3.34
1997–8	−2.92	0.68	3.45	0.13	−2.25	3.58
1998–9	−5.23	0.57	3.53	0.14	−4.66	3.67
1999–2000	−5.10	0.57	3.36	0.14	−4.53	3.49
2000–1	−5.55	0.23	2.86	0.14	−5.32	3.00
2001–2	−6.22	0.04	3.29	0.14	−6.18	3.43
2002–3	−5.81	0.09	3.72	0.14	−5.72	3.87
Gross Domestic Investment						
1993–4	1.68	1.94	4.47	0.15	3.62	4.62
1994–5	1.93	1.80	4.85	0.16	3.73	5.01
1995–6	1.77	1.72	3.96	0.14	3.49	4.11
1996–7	1.66	1.54	3.71	0.12	3.20	3.83
1997–8	1.44	1.60	3.44	0.14	3.04	3.57
1998–9	1.61	1.40	3.37	0.19	3.02	3.56
1999–2000	1.70	1.48	3.58	0.18	3.18	3.76
2000–1	1.70	0.11	4.30	0.18	1.81	4.48
2001–2	1.61	0.81	3.23	0.19	2.41	3.41

(*continued*)

Table 7.2 Continued

					(Per cent)
Admini- strative depart- ments	Depart- mental enter- prises	Non- depart- mental enter- prises	Quasi- govern- ment bodies	Admini- strative departments and departments enterprises	Non- department enterprises and quasi-govt bodies

Excess of Investment over Saving

	Admini- strative depart- ments	Depart- mental enter- prises	Non- depart- mental enter- prises	Quasi- govern- ment bodies	Admini- strative departments and departments enterprises	Non- department enterprises and quasi-govt bodies
1993–4	4.84	1.08	1.68	0.01	5.92	1.69
1994–5	4.61	0.81	1.62	0.03	5.42	1.65
1995–6	3.91	0.89	0.78	0.00	4.80	0.78
1996–7	4.07	0.79	0.46	0.03	4.86	0.49
1997–8	4.36	0.92	−0.01	0.00	5.28	0.00
1998–9	6.84	0.83	−0.16	0.05	7.67	−0.11
1999–2000	6.81	0.90	0.22	0.05	7.71	0.27
2000–1	7.25	−0.13	1.44	0.04	7.13	1.48
2001–2	7.83	0.76	−0.06	0.05	8.59	−0.01

Source: National Income Accounts, Government of India.

sector. Comparing 1996–7 with 2001–2 figures, it is apparent that the draft of the government sector (administrative departments and departmental enterprises) as measured by the excess of investment over savings increased from 4.7 per cent of GDP to 8.6 per cent in 2001–2. This was clearly the result of the increase in the ratio of revenue deficit to fiscal deficit during this period. It did not lead to a rise in the interest rate because of the fall in private investment as well as government investment during this period. The key to improving the medium-term fiscal stance to sustain a higher growth rate is to reduce government dis-savings and increase government capital expenditure relative to GDP. These changes can happen when the pre-emptive claim of interest payments relative to GDP falls and/or government revenues relative to GDP rise.

Some Empirical Relations

In the argument that high levels of debt-GDP lead to high interest payments relative to GDP, which crowd out government capital expenditure and reduce the overall savings rate, two relationships are of critical importance:

1. The responsiveness of changes in the saving ratio with respect to changes in the fiscal deficit levels; and
2. The responsiveness of government capital expenditure to changes in the level of interest payments.

We provide some empirical estimates of the short-term and long-term relationships, using a sample period from 1950–1 to 2001–2. With the concept of cointegration proposed by Engle and Granger (1987), it is possible to distinguish between long-term equilibrium relations and short-term dynamics among variables. Identification conditions between cointegrated time series models or error correction models (also known as equilibrium correction models) have been explored in Johansen (1991) and Johansen and Juselius (1995). Their formulations have led to the conclusion that there is one set of conditions identifying long-term relations and another set of conditions identifying the short-term dynamics. In Hsiao (1997), it was shown that under certain conditions, virtually all the results for the stationary case also apply to structural models involving integrated variables. It is also demonstrated that the identification of long-term equilibrium relations is not independent of the short-term dynamics.

In the present analysis, the short-term dynamics of certain key relations are studied as a first step before an error correction model is estimated. The estimated structural relationships should be considered as embedded in a full structural model. However, here only a selected set of relationships are studied, which may be considered as inputs to a fuller model and as preliminary findings. The variables used in this exercise are defined below. Variables in real terms are derived by deflating by the implicit price deflator of GDP at factor cost (IPDFC). In the case of the interest rate, the inflation rate pertaining to the IPDFC is deducted to obtain the real interest rate. The first differences are shown by prefixing a variable by D, and the second difference, by prefixing a variable by DD.

The following variables are used for estimating the equations:

IPDFC: Implicit Price Deflator of GDP at Factor Cost

SPVR: private sector savings in real terms

PVYR: private disposable income in real terms

SPUBR: public sector savings in real terms

I3R: interest rate on deposits of 3 to 5 years

I3SR: ex-ante interest rate on deposits of 3 to 5 years obtained by deducting from I3R, the expected rate of inflation

IPVTR: private investment in real terms

ISBI: State Bank of India advance rate

RISBI: State Bank of India advance rate in real terms obtained by deducting the inflation rate

RCMRR: combined revenue receipts of the central and state governments in real terms

RCMIP: interest payments on the combined account of central and state governments in real terms

RCMCE: combined capital expenditure of the central and state governments in real terms

CMDFD: Combined Derived Fiscal Deficit

Private Savings Function: Impact of Public Savings

A critical hypothesis that requires to be tested is whether any fall in the public sector savings, implying an increase in revenue deficit, is compensated by a rise in private sector savings, and if that is so, whether the compensation is full or partial and whether the effect takes place with a lag. Real private savings appear to have a unit root not only in levels but also in first differences. It becomes stationary in the second difference with intercept and trend. The explanatory variables are PVYR and SPUBR. Both these are obtained by deflating the corresponding nominal series

Table 7.3 Dependent Variable: SPVR

Sample(adjusted): 1953–2002
Included observations: 50 after adjusting endpoints

Variable	Coefficient	Std Error	t-Statistic	Prob.
C	−18068.6	4,053.9	−4.457	0.000
PVYR	0.154422	0.030	5.085	0.000
SPUBR	−0.294430	0.111	−2.661	0.011
DSPUBR(−1)	−0.514448	0.210	−2.448	0.018
DPVYR(−1)	0.094398	0.076	1.245	0.220
SPVR(−1)	0.496261	0.111	4.459	0.000
R-squared	0.996579	Mean dependent var		94,558.22
Adjusted R-squared	0.99619	S.D. dependent var		94,033.24
S.E. of regression	5,804.129	Akaike info criterion		20.28269
Sum squared resid	1.48E + 09	Schwarz criterion		20.51214
Log likelihood	−501.0673	F-statistic		2,563.459
Durbin–Watson stat	1.73141	Prob(F-statistic)		0

Source: Authors' estimates.

by the IPDFC. Both these variables are stationary in the first difference with intercept and trend. A third explanatory variable is the expected real interest rate. The interest rate is represented here by the interest rates on deposits of three to five years. The corresponding interest rate is obtained by deducting from the nominal interest rate, the expected inflation rate. The inflation rate pertains to the IPDFC from which the trend inflation rate is estimated by using the H-P filter. Accordingly, a series for expected real interest rate (I3SR) is generated.

Table 7.3 gives results of the estimation of the error correction model (ECM), which estimates together the long-term relation and the short-term dynamics. While private savings respond positively to private disposable income, the effect of public saving is negative, implying that a fall in public savings is associated with a rise in private savings, but the compensation is partial. The effect is negative both in the level and the first difference. The positive sign and the magnitude of the lagged dependent term show that the long-term effect is higher than the short-term effect.

Table 7.4 Dependent Variable: RCMCE

Method: Least Squares
Sample(adjusted): 1953–2002
Included observations: 50 after adjusting endpoints

Variable	Coefficient	Std Error	t-Statistic	Prob.
C	824.1816	1,008.755	0.817028	0.4182
RCMIP	−0.452654	0.110548	−4.094651	0.0002
RCMRR	0.237316	0.053105	4.468815	0.0001
DRCMRR(−1)	−0.103212	0.09703	−1.063706	0.2931
RCMCE(−1)	0.545986	0.096808	5.639866	0
R-squared	0.951796	Mean dependent var		25,509.16
Adjusted R-squared	0.947511	S.D. dependent var		13,173.31
S.E. of regression	3,018.071	Akaike info criterion		18.95726
Sum squared resid	4.10E + 08	Schwarz criterion		19.14847
Log likelihood	−468.9316	F-statistic		222.1319
Durbin–Watson stat	1.941086	Prob(F-statistic)		0

Source: Authors' estimates.

Fiscal Deficit and Government Capital Expenditure

It has been argued in an earlier section that as interest rates increase relative to current revenues of the government, a process of adjustment starts in government expenditure. This may lead to a reduction in public investment, and particularly government investment relative to GDP. We look at the relationship between government capital expenditure, interest payments, and revenue receipts on the combined account of central and state governments. These are converted into real terms by deflating with the GDP deflator. All the three series are stationary in the first difference. Table 7.4 gives the estimated relationship within the ECM framework. It shows the impact of interest payments and revenue receipts in real terms on real government capital expenditure, the former negatively and the latter positively.

Growth in Combined Debt of Centre and States: A Historical Perspective

The decision as to the appropriate level of fiscal deficit in the current period has to take into account the levels of the accumulated debt relative to GDP, particularly in view of the impact it has on interest liabilities. In an earlier contribution, we looked at the experience of debt accumulation in respect of central debt relative to GDP (Rangarajan and Srivastava 2003). In this chapter, we look at the growth of the combined debt-GDP ratio and examine the relative contribution of cumulated primary deficits and the cumulated effect of the excess of growth rate over interest rate from 1951–2 to 2001–2. The interest rate in this discussion refers to the effective interest rate of the central and state governments, calculated as the ratio of interest payments in a year to the outstanding liabilities at the beginning of the year. Throughout the stretch of forty-five years from 1955–6 to 1999–2000, the real growth rate was in excess of the real interest rate. Since 2000–1, for three consecutive years, the real growth rate has been less than the real interest rate. During the 1990s, even when the GDP growth rate remained in excess of the interest rate, the gap between the two has been narrowing.

The standard specification of the equation describing debt dynamics with discrete time periods is given by equation (7.1) $[b_t = p_t + b_{t-1}\{(1+i_t)/(1+g_t)\}.]$ As discussed in Rangarajan and Srivastava (2003), writing $z_t = b_t - b_{t-1}$, equation (7.1) can also be written as

$$z_t = p_t - b_{t-1}[(g_t - i_t)(1+g_t)^{-1}]$$

or
$$p_t = z_t + b_{t-1}[(g_t - i_t)(1+g_t)^{-1}] \qquad (7.21)$$

Summing up over any two benchmark years 1 and T, we have

$$\Sum p_t = \Sum z_t + \Sum b_{t-1}[(g_t - i_t)(1+g_t)^{-1}] \quad (t=1,...,T) \qquad (7.22)$$

The term

$$A1 = \Sum z_t / \Sum p_t \qquad (t=1, ..., T) \qquad (7.23)$$

shows the extent to which the cumulated primary deficits translate into an accumulation of debt. On the other hand, the term

$$A2 = \Sum b_{t-1}[(g_t - i_t)(1+g_t)^{-1}] / \Sum p_t \qquad (t=1, ..., T) \qquad (7.24)$$

shows the extent to which the impact of cumulated primary deficits is absorbed by the excess of growth over interest rate. In Rangarajan and Srivastava (2003), this decomposition was used to analyse the profile of central debt in India. Here, we look at the accumulation of the combined debt of central and state governments in India. For the purpose of the historical review, debt includes external debt evaluated at historical exchange rates and state debt does not include reserve funds and deposits.

According to available information, the combined debt-GDP ratio of the central and state governments at the end of 1950–1 was 29.6 per cent. During 1951–2 to 1959–60 a little less than 13 percentage points was added to the debt-GDP ratio. An additional accretion of about 4 percentage pointstook place in the 1960s. In the 1970s, there was hardly any change in the debt-GDP ratio. It was in the 1980s and 1990s (up to 2002–3) that there was an increase respectively of 14.7 percentage pointsfor each period in the debt-GDP ratio. Table 7.5 and Figure 7.5 show the relative effects of the cumulated primary deficits and the factor reflecting the effect of growth–interest rate differential in the process of accumulation of combined debt of the central and state governments since 1951–2. The Indian experience shows that a significant part of the pressure of primary deficit could be absorbed by the excess of growth over interest rates. It

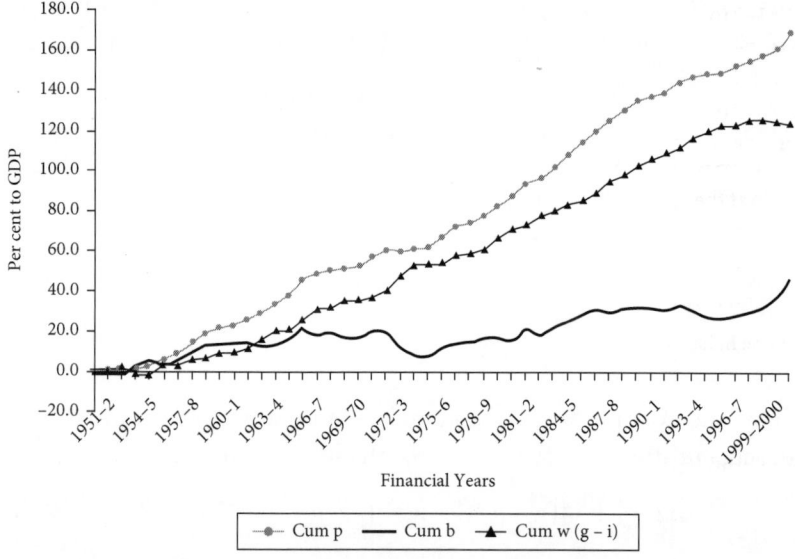

Figure 7.5 Growth of State Debt Relative to GDP: Relative Roles of Cumulated Primary Deficits and Excess of Growth over Interest Rates

Cum p: Cumulated primary deficit to GDP ratio

Cum b: Cumulated debt to GDP ratio

Cum w(g-i): Cumulated effect of weighted excess of growth over interest rate

Table 7.5 Decade-Wise Decomposition of Debt Accumulation
Relative to GDP

	Cumulated Changes in			Relative impact of cumulated primary deficit	
	Debt-GDP ratio	Primary Def-GDP ratio	Growth & interest rate differential	Increase in Debt-GDP ratio D/p	Absorption by growth–interest differential $w(g\text{-}i)/p$
1951–2 to 1959–60	12.89	19.39	6.50	66.47	33.53
1960–1 to 1969–70	3.87	32.18	28.31	12.03	87.97
1970–1 to 1979–80	0.07	26.18	26.12	0.25	99.75
1980–1 to 1989–90	14.71	52.09	37.38	28.24	71.76
1990–1 to 2002–3	14.67	39.09	24.42	37.53	62.47
1951–2 to 2002–3	46.21	168.94	122.73	27.82	72.18
Memo:					
1996–7 to 2002–3	19.55	19.77	0.22	101.14	1.13
Debt-GDP Ratio at the end of–					
1950–1	29.6				
2002–3	75.8				

Source: Indian Public Finance Statistics and National Income Accounts.

was able to absorb nearly 72 per cent of the cumulated primary deficits. Had this cushion not been available, cumulated primary deficits through 1951–2 to 2002–3 would have added about 169 percentage points to the combined debt-to-GDP ratio.

The decade-wise picture indicates that in the 1950s, 33.5 per cent of the impact of cumulative primary deficit was absorbed by the growth–interest rate differential. The remaining 66.4 per cent of the cumulated primary deficit of 19.4 percentage increased the debt-GDP ratio by

12.9 percentage points. In the 1960s, the pressure exerted by the cumulated primary deficit was relatively larger (32.2 percentage points). However, 88 per cent of this was absorbed by the differential of growth over interest rate, resulting in only a small increase of 3.9 percentage points in the debt-GDP ratio. During the 1970s, nearly a hundred per cent of the impact of the cumulated primary deficit was absorbed by the growth/interest rate differential, leading to a negligible increase in the debt-GDP ratio. In the 1980s and the 1990s (up to 2002–3), about 72 and 62 per cent, respectively, of the pressure of cumulated primary deficit could be absorbed by the $(g - i)$ differential. Figure 7.5 also shows how the accumulated primary deficit was the most persistent factors in causing the debt-GDP ratio to rise, and how the growth–interest differential was able to absorb a significant portion of it in several stretches of time.

However, for three consecutive years, 2000–1, 2001–2, and 2002–3, the nominal growth rate fell below the effective interest rate. In these years, instead of absorbing the impact of primary deficits, the growth–interest differential, being negative, worked in reverse by adding to the debt-GDP ratio. Further, since this effect depends on the previous year's debt-GDP ratio, its impact became progressively greater for the same shortfall in the growth rate relative to the interest rate. At the end of 2002–3 the combined debt-GDP ratio stood at 76 per cent when external debt is evaluated at historical change rates and for the states reserve funds are not included Rajaraman, Bhide and Pattnaik (2004). If these adjustments are made, the combined debt-GDP ratio at the end of 2002–3 is estimated to be about 85 per cent of GDP.

Analysing The Short- and Medium-Term Fiscal Policy Stance

The management of fiscal deficit needs to distinguish between the long-term or trend growth (after adjusting for the cyclical component of growth) and the structural or cyclically neutral deficit and the transitory deficit. The structural deficit must be determined within a sustainability framework aiming at maximizing the trend growth rate. The short-term component of fiscal deficit should be used to minimize the impact of cyclical changes while keeping the economy on its long-term growth path. The use of discretionary expenditure to stimulate the economy, when it is below potential output and contains inflationary pressure when prices are above trend levels, is meant to serve the objective of macroeconomic stabilization. Neo-classical analysis argues about the deleterious effect of high permanent deficits on savings and suggests stabilizing fluctuations around the equilibrium path with a high rather than low level of national savings.

In the Maastricht Treaty (MT) norms read with the Pact on Growth and Stability (PSG), it is provided for the member countries that under normal circumstances the structural balance should be zero and, when facing a slowdown, the net budget deficit could be up to a maximum of 3 per cent of GDP.[3] On a long-term basis, the debt-GDP ratio should not be allowed to exceed 60 per cent of GDP. It is only under an exceptional downturn or recession that the budget deficit may be allowed to exceed the 3 per cent reference value.[4]

Measuring Structural and Cyclical Components of Deficit

Several methods have been used in the literature for estimating structural deficits. Considering actual fiscal deficits as the sum of structural and cyclical components, if one of the two components is estimated, the other can be derived as a residual. Three principal methods have been used in the literature: (i) constant elasticities method, where the cyclical component is estimated first based on estimated of revenue and expenditure elasticities with respect to income, (ii) smoothed-ratio approach where the structural fiscal deficit is estimated first by smoothening the revenue and expenditure ratios to GDP, and (iii) structural time series approach where time-varying elasticities are used and the cyclical component is estimated first. There are some difficulties with each of these approaches. The more traditional approach of constant elasticities used by the Organisation for Economic Co-operation and Development (OECD), among others, involves a three-step procedure. First, the output gap is calculated by taking the difference between potential output and actual output; second, the response of revenue and expenditure categories to changes in the output gap is calculated by estimating the relevant elasticities, providing an estimate of the cyclical component of deficit; and finally, the structural deficit is calculated as a residual. As shown by Barrel et al. (1994) and Bradner et al. (1998), estimates of structural balances are highly sensitive to the method of estimating trend output and uncertainty surrounding the output-elasticities of expenditure and revenue categories. The structural time series approach, as suggested by Jaeger (1990), also has some prob-lems. In particular, the variances of the parameters are not well defined. It has been shown by Harvey (1989) that in such models, the exogenous variables must be bounded from above and should be non-stochastic. Url (1997) has pointed out that nominal potential output cannot be regarded as bounded from above. The smoothed-ratio approach, suggested by Cano and Kanutin (1996) provides a direct and simpler method of calcu-lating the structural deficit. In this approach, revenues and expenditures, expressed as ratios to GDP, are decomposed into a structural and residual component by using a Hodrick–Prescott (HP) filter.[5]

Let r_s and e_s be the trend ratios of revenues and expenditures relative to GDP (these can be disaggregated categories also), and r_c and e_c be corres-ponding cyclical components. Then the structural deficit to GDP ratio is derived directly as

$$f_s = e_s - r_s \qquad (7.25)$$

The cyclical deficit is obtained as a residual. Bradner et al. (1998) argue that this method has several advantages. The HP filter is relatively judgment-free since only one parameter, namely the length of the business cycle, has to be fixed. As a direct method, it is able to exclude transitory non-cyclical events. The linearity of the HP filter also facilitates using a disaggregated approach since the disaggregated structural components add to 1. This method is also not very demanding in terms of data require-ments. One disadvantage, however, is that it cannot capture the impact of fiscal policy changes if these are located at the end points of the sample.

Trends in Structural and Cyclical Deficits

In this analysis, a distinction is made between structural fiscal deficit and structural primary deficit by calculating the trend ratios of primary ex-penditure and interest payments relative to GDP separately. Thus,

$$f_s = (pe)_s - r_s + (ip)_s \text{ and } f_c = f - f_s \qquad (7.26)$$

The fiscal deficit to GDP ratio thus has three components: primary structural deficit, structural interest payments relative to GDP, and cyclical fiscal deficit. Table 7.6 shows the structural and actual fiscal deficits. Clearly, structural fiscal deficits account for a large part of the actual fiscal deficit in the 1990s. Structural interest payments to GDP ratio has increased continuously from 4.3 per cent in 1990–1 to 5.9 per cent in 2001–2, amounting to an increase of 2.6 percentage points . Structural primary deficit can be seen to have fallen from the peak of 4.14 per cent in 1990–1 to 2.75 per cent in 1997–8, before it started rising again. Although both factors have contributed to structural fiscal deficit, the impact of structural interest payments was larger in the 1990s and also more persistent.

Table 7.6 Combined Central and State Finances: Structural and Cyclical Deficits Relative to GDP

						(Per cent to GDP)	
	Actual Fiscal Deficit	Structural Fiscal Deficit	Cyclical Fiscal Deficit	Structural Primary Deficit	Debt-stabilizing primary deficit	Actual Interest Payments	Structural Interest Payments
1990–1	9.383	8.433	0.950	4.144	4.4757	4.397	4.288
1991–2	7.162	8.302	−1.140	3.822	3.2284	4.746	4.480
1992–3	7.240	8.171	−0.931	3.516	2.9542	4.792	4.656
1993–4	9.824	8.059	1.765	3.243	2.8343	4.953	4.816
1994–5	6.945	7.975	−1.030	3.012	4.3319	5.128	4.963
1995–6	6.778	7.947	−1.169	2.846	3.8711	4.962	5.101
1996–7	6.081	7.993	−1.912	2.757	2.5044	5.111	5.236
1997–8	7.660	8.118	−0.459	2.748	0.5467	5.159	5.370
1998–9	8.227	8.309	−0.083	2.801	1.9892	5.318	5.508
1999–2000	9.002	8.548	0.453	2.899	0.3002	5.682	5.650
2000–1	8.792	8.816	−0.024	3.022	−1.1835	5.727	5.794
2001–2	10.557	9.099	1.458	3.159	−0.4902	6.098	5.939

Source: Indian Public Finance Statistics and National Income Accounts, Government of India.

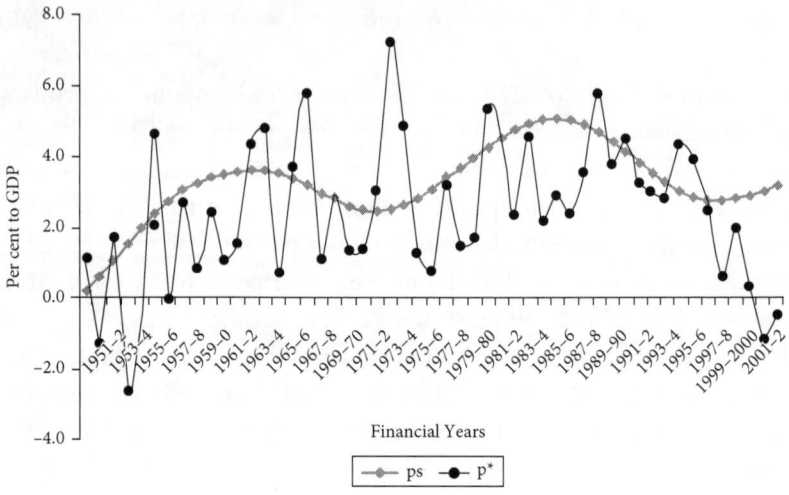

Figure 7.6 Comparison of Structural and Debt-Stabilizing Primary Deficit

Structural Primary Gap

The structural 'primary gap' is defined as the difference between the actual structural primary deficit and the debt-stabilizing primary deficit (p^s).

Table 7.6 also shows that the primary deficit has been higher than the 'debt-stabilizing' primary deficit defined as $\{b_{t-1}^{*}(1+g_t)/(g_t-i_t)\}$, in most of the years in the 1990s except 1990–1, 1994–5, and 1995–6. The structural primary balance has been used in the literature to assess the medium-term fiscal stance. The large values of the structural primary balance since the late nineties clearly indicate that the current medium-term fiscal stance is not sustainable.

The profile of structural and debt-stabilizing primary deficit since 1951–2 is compared in Figure 7.6. The structural primary deficit is shown by the bolder line. There were long stretches towards the end of the 1980s and the latter part of the 1990s when the structural primary deficit was much higher than the debt-stabilizing primary deficit. These were the episodes in time where large accretion of debt relative to GDP took place. This led to larger structural interest payments relative to GDP. Together, structural primary deficit and structural interest payments have caused structural fiscal deficits to be large.

Given the large structural deficit, the role that cyclical deficit can play has become extremely limited in periods of recession. It is expected that a suitable short-term fiscal stance would show opposite signs between cyclical deficit and departures of actual growth from trend growth—that is, when actual growth is below trend, the cyclical deficit should be positive and vice versa. It would be seen that throughout the period from 1965–6 to 1987–8, the short-term stance was in the correct direction. It is in the period since 1988–9 that the short-term stance has not been robust, except in the mid-1990s.

The FRBMA enacted by the central government in 2003, read with its Rules, defines the target of achieving a fiscal deficit level of 3 per cent of GDP by 2008–9. This can be evaluated in relation to the MT norms, taking into account the potential of a higher growth rate than what is implicit in the MT norms, where countries with nominal growth of about 5 per cent are supposed to maintain balance (zero fiscal deficit) under normal circumstances and up to 3 per cent of fiscal deficit when faced with a downturn. The higher growth rate in India implies that while a higher fiscal deficit may be permitted, it should maintain the debt-GDP ratio at lower levels so that the burden of interest payments is lower, enabling larger capital expenditures to promote medium-term growth. The FRBMA does not spell out strategies that can cope with economic downturns. It has, however, defined a path of adjustment to reach a level of fiscal deficit that may be consistent with a medium-term stance Chelliah (2004). The FRBMA is incomplete in two respects: (i) it does not define a debt-GDP ratio that would be consistent with the need for keeping the economy on its potential growth path, and (ii) it does not define suitable limits of departure from the medium-term stance to cope with cyclical fluctuations. It is also important that the centre's FRBMA is supplemented by state-level fiscal responsibility legislation.

*　*　*

This chapter has looked at the impact of fiscal deficits on savings, investment, and growth in light of the theoretical literature on the subject in the context of the fiscal deficit and debt on the combined accounts of the central and state governments. Fiscal deficits amount to a reduction in government savings, which may not be fully offset by a corresponding rise in private savings, leading to a fall in the overall savings rate. The impact of fiscal deficit on investment arises from its impact on both private investment and government investment. The adverse effects on private investment occur if fiscal deficits put pressure on interest rates and if private investment is sensitive to the interest rate. The effect on government capital expenditure is through committed interest payments, which rise if the debt-GDP ratio rises and/or the interest rate rises. In the context of debt accumulation in India, the main findings are summarized below:

1. Fiscal deficit and government debt in India have received growing attention from analysts and policymakers, particularly since the 1990s, when in most years the combined fiscal deficit was higher than 9 per cent of GDP. The concerns have become more serious in recent years when there has been an explosive rise in the debt-GDP ratio, even though the nominal interest rates have fallen. This is because during 2000–3, nominal growth rates fell even more. With the growth rate being less than the effective interest rate, the debt-GDP ratio increased both because of cumulated primary deficits and excess of interest rate over growth rate from 2000–1 to 2002–3.

2. Even if fiscal deficits may appear to be sustainable according to some studies, the critical issue relates to determining appropriate levels of debt and deficit relative to GDP at which these should be stabilized. This can be achieved by developing rules with given growth and interest rates and initial debt levels. However, since fiscal deficits and debt affect growth and interest rates, answers need to be derived using information on their impact on savings and investment, which ultimately determine the growth rate. The interest rates are also affected by the fiscal deficit, but there may also be exogenous influences, particularly international interest rates and the inflow of foreign capital.

3. When fiscal deficits are high in magnitude relative to GDP and largely structural in nature, the government's ability to mount counter-cyclical interventions is compromised, particularly when growth is below trend levels. This was clearly experienced in the late 1990s and the early part of the new decade.

4. In India, the household sector saves more than it invests, and the excess becomes available in the form of the financial savings of this sector to the private corporate sector and the government sector for their investment requirements that are not financed by their own savings. Although government dis-savings increased since the late 1990s, the pressure on interest rates was not witnessed because of a fall in investment demand by the private sector. This may prove to be temporary.

5. The overall growth rate depends on the overall savings rate and investment rate. There is reason to believe that when government savings fall, the private savings rate increases as wealth held in the private sector in the form of government bonds increases. This compensatory rise in the private sector savings rate has been partial. On the investment side, the government's own investment demand also fell as its debt-GDP ratio and the ratio of interest payments to revenue receipts rose. Empirical tests indicate that government capital expenditures do respond negatively to interest payments and positively to revenue receipts. If interest payments rise faster than revenue receipts, government capital expenditure falls. Private investment responds negatively to a rise in expected interest rates. In the 1990s and beyond, government capital expenditures relative to GDP fell not only because interest payments relative to GDP increased but also because the revenue receipts to GDP fell.

6. The FRBMA has certain positive features. It is incomplete in two respects. First, it does not indicate a suitable level of debt-GDP ratio along with the specified fiscal deficit target, and second, it does not provide a suitable strategy for coping with short-term fluctuations.

7. It is important that the centre's FRBMA is supplemented by state-level fiscal responsibility legislation because, taken together, states' borrowing and debt contribute significantly to the overall fiscal deficit and debt relative to GDP and have significant macro implications.

To achieve and sustain growth at high levels, it is required that the overall savings ratio is increased leading to a rise in the investment ratio, and fiscal deficit should be managed so as to serve this purpose.

Notes

1. Sometimes this equation is defined with an explicit term for the ratio of seigniorage to GDP. Seigniorage can be obtained in many forms. It may be explicit in the form of printed money. It may be implicit if the government is able to borrow with the help of the central bank at administered rates, which are less than what the market would determine otherwise. Seigniorage also arises if the government borrows from the central bank at non-zero interest rates, but gets dividends from the central bank on such earnings.

2. It can be shown that

$$\delta f^*/\delta g = -p.i/(g-i)^2$$

Similarly,
$$\delta d^*/\delta g = -p.(1+i)/(g-i)^2$$

The effect of an increase in the growth rate, given the interest rate and holding other variables unchanged, is to lower the equilibrium levels of fiscal deficit and debt.

Thus,

$$\delta f^*/\delta g = \delta[pg/(g-i)]/\delta g$$
$$= p[(1/(g-i) - g/(g-i)^2] = p[-i/(g-i)^2]$$

Similarly,
$$\delta d^*/\delta g = \delta[p(1+g)/(g-i)]/\delta g$$
$$= p[(1/(g-i)-(1+g)/(g-i)^2] = -p[(1+i)/(g-i)^2]$$

3. According to the PSG, in the medium term, the net deficit or the net borrowing to GDP ratio should be 'close to balance or in net surplus'. However, the net deficit may exceed 3 per cent of GDP under exceptional or temporary circumstances. The PSG acknowledges the need to distinguish between cyclical and structural components of budget balance. In any case, the 3 per cent reference value should not be exceeded during normal economic downturns.

4. An economic downturn is considered exceptional if there is an annual fall of real GDP of at least 2 per cent. A severe recession is defined as a downturn with a negative annual real GDP growth of 0.75 per cent or more.

5. The Hodrick–Prescott filter is a two-sided linear filter. It is widely used to obtain estimates of the trend component of a long series. This filter computes the smoothed series s of y by minimizing the variance of y around s, subject to the penalty that constrains the second difference of s. s is chosen so as to minimize the following expression:

$$\sum(y_t - s_t)^2 \qquad \text{(t varies from $1, 2, ..., T$)}$$
$$+ \lambda \sum\{(s_{t+1} - s_t) - (s_t - s_{t-1})\}^2 \qquad \text{(t varies from 2 to $T-1$)}$$

The penalty parameter λ is set so as to control the smoothness of the derived series s. For annual series, the recommended value of λ is 100. As λ approaches infinity, s will approach a straight line.

8

Thirteenth, Fourteenth, and Fifteenth Finance Commissions

In the previous chapters, we have reviewed the evolution of fiscal federalism in India up to the Twelfth Finance Commission. The period covered under the recommendations of the Thirteenth, Fourteenth, and Fifteenth Finance Commissions extends over sixteen years spanning from 2010–11 to 2025–6. In this long period, many major developments have taken place, affecting the finances of central and state governments, their deficit and debt profiles, and the distribution of fiscal transfers. These developments include the abolition of the plan/non-plan distinction in 2015–16, the implementation of a Goods and Services Tax in India with effect from 1 July 2017, the amendment of the Fiscal Responsibility and Budget Management (FRBM) Act of the central governments in 2018, and corporate income tax reforms in September 2019. The 2018 FRBM amendment brought about changes in the debt and fiscal deficit benchmarks for the central and the combined government and introduced a framework for macro-stabilization. There were also developments relating to the reorganization of two states. First, the erstwhile state of Andhra Pradesh was divided between Andhra Pradesh and Telangana in 2014, increasing the number of states from 28 to 29. Subsequently, the state of Jammu and Kashmir was reorganized in August 2019, which reduced the total number of states in India from 29 to 28 and increased the number of union territories with legislatures from 2 to 3. There were also global developments having significant consequences on the domestic economy and government finances. These include major upheavals in global crude prices and the economic shock due to COVID-19, which affected 2020–1 with aftershocks extending beyond this. With the backdrop of these developments, this chapter provides a critical overview of the context and recommendations of the Thirteenth, Fourteenth, and Fifteenth Finance

Federalism and Fiscal Transfers in India, Second Edition. C. Rangarajan and D.K. Srivastava, Oxford University Press.
© Rangarajan and Srivastava 2024. DOI: 10.1093/9780198930426.003.0008

Commissions. The changing context was often captured in the Terms of Reference (ToR) of these respective Commissions. Some of the notable changes in the ToR of these Commissions are discussed below.

Changing contours of Commissions' Terms of Reference

Apart from the regular clauses drawn from the constitutional provisions regarding tax devolution and grants, a number of other clauses were included in the ToR of different Commissions reflecting the evolving empirical realities of the concerned times. We first review these.

Thirteenth Finance Commission

Some of the notable items in the ToR of the Thirteenth Finance Commission are listed below.

1. The Commission was asked to 'review the state of the finances of the Union and the States, keeping in view, in particular, the operation of the States' Debt Consolidation and Relief Facility 2005–2010 introduced by the Central Government on the basis of the recommendations of the Twelfth Finance Commission, and suggest measures for maintaining a stable and sustainable fiscal environment consistent with equitable growth'.
2. The Commission was asked to assess the impact of the implementation of GST, including its impact on the country's foreign trade.
3. The Commission, in making its recommendations, was asked to take into consideration: (i) the need to improve the quality of public expenditure to obtain better outputs and outcomes; (ii) the need to manage ecology, environment, and climate change, consistent with sustainable development; (iii) the need for ensuring the commercial viability of irrigation projects, power projects, departmental undertakings, and public sector enterprises through various means, including levy of user charges and adoption of measures to promote efficiency.

4. Just as in the case of previous Commissions, the Commission was asked to utilize the 1971 population figures for determination of devolution of taxes and duties and grants-in-aid.

An additional item in the ToR asked the Thirteenth Finance Commission to review the roadmap for fiscal adjustment and suggest a suitably revised roadmap with a view to maintaining the gains of fiscal consolidation from 2010 to 2015. In doing so, the Commission was expected to take into account the need to bring the liabilities of the central government for oil, food and fertilizer bonds into the fiscal accounting, and the impact of various other obligations of the central government on the deficit targets.

Fourteenth Finance Commission

Some of the noteworthy ToR of the Fourteenth Finance Commission are given below.

1. The Commission was expected to suggest changes to the Fiscal Responsibility and Budget Management (FRBM) Act, keeping in view the fiscal consolidation roadmap recommended by the Thirteenth Finance Commission.
2. It was asked to assess the impact of the proposed goods and services tax (GST) on government finances and also suggest a mechanism to compensate states for revenue losses, if any.
3. The Commission was asked to look at the need to insulate the pricing of public utility services—drinking water, irrigation, power, and public transport—from policy fluctuations through statutory provisions.
4. Further, it was expected to determine the level of subsidies required for sustainable and inclusive growth, and equitable sharing of subsidies between the central and state governments.
5. The Commission, in making its recommendations, was also asked to take into consideration the need for making the public sector enterprises competitive and market oriented; listing and disinvestment; and relinquishing of non-priority enterprises.

6. Further, it was expected to take into account, the need to balance management of ecology, environment, and climate change consistent with sustainable economic development.

7. Just as in the case of previous Commissions, the Commission was asked to utilize the 1971 population figures for determination of devolution of taxes and duties and grants-in-aid. However, it was stated that the Commission could also take into account the demographic changes that had taken place after 1971.

An additional ToR of the Commission required it to take into account the bifurcation of Andhra Pradesh and re-examine various comparable estimates for financial projections.

Fifteenth Finance Commission

The Fifteenth Finance Commission was given two ToR and an extended overall period of six years. Their first report covered the original ToR and the year 2020–1. The second report covered the next five years from 2021–2 to 2025–6. The original ToR had provided that in the determination of devolution, wherever relevant, instead of 1971, the 2011 population data was to be used. This was a major change permitting a departure from the use of the 1971 population data in the tax devolution formula. The Commission was also asked to examine the rationale for continuing with revenue deficit grants and to introduce performance grants particularly relating to central objectives. Further, the Commission was asked to recommend a fiscal roadmap for controlling government debt and deficit and linking it to higher inclusive growth, principles of equity, efficiency, and transparency.

In the additional ToR, references to the following issues were quite important:

1. Revenue uncertainty, and by implication the need for making reliable forecasts by the Commission.

2. The need for creating an earmarked fund for defence and internal security.

Revenue Sharing: Vertical Dimension

States have been continuously demanding, in their Memoranda to different Commissions, that the share of states in the divisible pool of central taxes be raised to 50 per cent. The Thirteenth Finance Commission raised it only marginally to 32 per cent from 30.5 per cent, as recommended by the Twelfth Finance Commission. A major event in the form of the abolition of the distinction between plan and non-plan expenditures happened in 2015–6. This led to the Fourteenth Finance Commission raising the share of states in the divisible pool from 32 per cent to 42 per cent. In their analysis, recommending this change, they gave four reasons:

> However, a compositional shift in transfers from grants to tax devolution is desirable for two reasons. First, it does not impose an additional fiscal burden on the Union Government. Second, an increase in tax devolution would enhance the share of unconditional transfers to the States. We have factored in four important considerations: (i) States not being entitled to the growing share of cess and surcharges in the revenues of the Union Government; (ii) the importance of increasing the share of tax devolution in total transfers; (iii) an aggregate view of the revenue expenditure needs of States without Plan and non-Plan distinction; and (iv) the space available with the Union Government. Considering all factors, in our view, increasing the share of tax devolution to 42 per cent of the divisible pool would serve the twin objectives of increasing the flow of unconditional transfers to the States and yet leave appropriate fiscal space for the Union to carry out specific-purpose transfers to the States. (Clause 8.13 (p. 90) of the Report of the Fourteenth Finance Commission)

Of these reasons, the third consideration makes reference to the distinction between plan and non-plan revenue expenditures of the states. However, the Commission does not specify what the share of this factor is in the overall increase of 10 percentage points in the share of states in the divisible pool. It is observed that eventually the central government raised the share of cesses and surcharges, thereby reducing the size of the divisible pool as a percentage of the centre's gross tax revenues. This led to an effective neutralization, by the central government, of this ad-hoc increase of 10 percentage points in the share of states in the divisible pool by the Fourteenth Finance Commission (Table 8.1).

Revenue Sharing: Horizontal Dimension

Table 8.2 gives the relative weights assigned to different tax devolution criteria by the three recent Finance Commissions. The weight attached to the population criterion was brought down from 25 per cent given by the Twelfth and Thirteenth Finance Commissions, to 17.5 per cent by the Fourteenth Finance Commission, and then further to 15 per cent by the Fifteenth Finance Commission. Population criterion may be considered as a neutral criterion in the sense that it ensures the same per capita transfers to all states independent of per capita incomes or any cost considerations. By the mandate given in the ToRs, the Commissions had been compelled to use only the 1971 population data. As the gap between the year of recommendation and the year 1971 continued to increase, the use of the 1971 population data had become increasingly unrepresentative of the size of a state measured in terms of population. The Fourteenth Finance Commission was asked to take into account the demographic changes to partially correct the effect of using dated population data. As a result, demographic change was added as a separate criterion with a weight of 10 per cent. The Fourteenth Finance Commission defined the demographic change criterion simply as the share of a state in the 2011 census-based population. In the case of the Fifteenth Finance Commission, the ToR asked the Commission to use 2011 population data, which was the latest available census-based population data. Alongside, the Commission also used the demographic change criterion although with a different definition. This criterion was defined as the inverse of the total fertility rate. This was done to compensate states which had shown a lower growth rate of population during the period from 1971 to 2011. This criterion was given a higher weight of 12.5 per cent in the tax devolution scheme.

The weight attached to the distance criterion, which was 50 per cent in the case of the Twelfth Finance Commission, was reduced to 47.5 per

Table 8.1 Recommended and Effective Share of States in Sharable Central Revenues (%): FC12 to FC15 (2)

Commission	Recommendation period	Recommended share in divisible pool (%)	Effective share in gross central taxes (%)	Shortfall in effective share relative to recommended (% points)	Share of cesses and surcharges# in centre's gross tax revenues (%)
(1)	(2)	(3)	(4)	(5)	(6)
FC 13	2010–1 to 2014–5	32.0	27.9	–4.1	9.8
FC 14	2015–6 to 2019–20	42.0	34.9	–7.1	12.9
FC 15 (1)	2020–1	41.0	29.4	–11.6	20.2
FC 15 (2)	2021–2 to 2025–6	41.0	31.2*	–9.8*	18.0*

Source (basic data): Union Budget Documents, https://www.indiabudget.gov.in/ (Accessed on 5 October 2023); Reports of Twelfth to Fifteenth Finance Commissions, https://fincomindia.nic.in/commission-reports (Accessed on 5 October 2023); and Authors' calculations

*pertains to data for three years, 2021–2 (Actual), 2022–3 (RE) and 2023–4 (BE); #excludes GST compensation cess.

Table 8.2 Relative Weights for Different Tax Devolution Criteria: Thirteenth Finance Commission to Fifteenth Finance Commission

#	Criteria	FC 13	FC 14	FC 15 (1)	FC 15 (2)
1	Population	25	17.5	15.0	15.0
2	Demographic change	–	10	12.5	12.5
3	Income/fiscal capacity distance	47.5	50	45.0	45.0
4	Area	10	15	15.0	15.0
5	Forest cover	–	7.5	10.0	10.0
6	Tax effort	–	–	2.5	2.5
7	Fiscal discipline	17.5	–	–	–

Source (basic data): Finance Commission Reports (Twelfth to Fifteenth Finance Commissions), https://fincomindia.nic.in/commission-reports (Accessed on 5 October 2023) and Author's compilation.

cent by the Thirteenth Finance Commission. This was raised again to 50 per cent by the Fourteenth Finance Commission and then brought down to 45 per cent by the Fifteenth Finance Commission. It may be noted that the distance criterion is the main vehicle by which the Commission ensures higher per capita transfers for lower per capita income states. It is thus the main vehicle for the redistribution of resources through the scheme of fiscal transfers. With a substantial weight to this criterion, it is this criterion which has been responsible for a higher share in the divisible pool going to the poorer states.

There are two other sets of criteria. The first group captures cost disabilities, with factors such as area and forest cover. In the case of the area criterion, with many states having a very low share of area in the total area of states, the concept of a floor (share of 2 per cent) was introduced by the Tenth Finance Commission. This floor consideration has continued to be used by subsequent Commissions, including the three recent Commissions. This consideration reflects the minimum costs of establishment, even if the area covered by a state is small. In general, a larger area indicates a lower density of population and higher per unit costs of providing public and merit services.

The second group includes considerations pertaining to incentives such as tax effort and fiscal discipline. The fiscal discipline criterion was discontinued after the Thirteenth Finance Commission. The

Fourteenth Finance Commission did not use any incentive-related criteria.

Components of Grants

Table 8.3 gives the relative importance of tax devolution and grants in the recommended transfers for the Thirteenth, Fourteenth, and Fifteenth Finance Commissions. The share of devolution in total transfers through the Finance Commission was the highest at 89.2 per cent for the Fourteenth Finance Commission. It was reduced to 80.6 per cent in the final report of the Fifteenth Finance Commission. In the case of the Thirteenth Finance Commission, it was 85.7 per cent. A conscious view must be taken of the respective roles of devolution and grants in transfers. Grants assume greater importance if the equalization principle is given greater importance. Within the overall grants, the share of revenue deficit grants was the highest in the

Table 8.3 Relative Importance of Tax Devolution and Grants

Finance Commission	Share in Taxes	Revenue deficit grants	Disaster relief	Local body grants	Other grants	Total Grants	Total transfers
Recommended amounts (INR crore)							
FC 13	1427913	35863	25495	86468	90498	238324	1666237
FC 14	3889408	135155	53829	282667	0	471650	4361058
FC 15 (1)	855176	74340	22184	90000	14499#	201023	1056199
FC 15 (2)	4224760	294514	122601	427911	171636#	1016662	5241422
Shares (%)							
FC 13	85.7	2.2	1.5	5.2	5.4	14.3	100.0
FC 14	89.2	3.1	1.2	6.5	0.0	10.8	100.0
FC 15 (1)	81.0	7.0	2.1	8.5	1.4	19.0	100.0
FC 15 (2)	80.6	5.6	2.3	8.2	3.3	19.4	100.0

Source (basic data): Reports of FC 10 to FC 15, https://fincomindia.nic.in/commission-reports (Accessed on 5 October 2023) and Authors' calculations.

Note: For the period from Thirteenth Finance Commission to Fourteenth Finance Commission, transfers to states exclude the transfers made to Jammu and Kashmir.

For the first and the second reports of the Fifteenth Finance Commission, some of the grants listed here under other grants are still under the consideration of the central government. These have not been accepted so far.

first report of the Fifteenth Finance Commission at 7 per cent. The share of local body grants increased from 5.2 per cent during the Thirteenth Finance Commission period, to 8.5 per cent in the first report of the Fifteenth Finance Commission, and 8.2 per cent in the final report of the Fifteenth Finance Commission. Disaster relief grants have also increased in terms of their relative importance over time. Their share was the highest in the final report of the Fifteenth Finance Commission.

With respect to share in central taxes, actual amounts received by the states were quite close to the recommended or projected amounts by the Thirteenth Finance Commission. However, these were much lower in the case of the Fourteenth and the first report of the Fifteenth Finance Commission Table 8.4. This indicates that the projected magnitude of the divisible pool of central taxes was much higher than the actual realization. In the case of grants also, states actually received lower amounts compared with what was recommended by the Commissions. Since the magnitude of grants is fixed in nominal terms, the reason for receiving lower amounts of grants could be because of non-fulfilment of associated conditionalities by the states.

The Fourteenth Finance Commission had recommended a 10 percentage points increase in the share of states in the divisible pool of central taxes. One reason for this was the abolition of Plan grants, which was

Table 8.4 Actual Transfers Received by States (magnitude and shares)

Finance Commission	Share in Taxes	FC grants	Total transfers	Share in Taxes	FC grants	Total transfers
Actual amounts (INR crore)				As % of recommended amounts		
FC 13	1422720	180607	1603327	99.6	75.8	96.2
FC 14	3116820	428627	3545447	80.1	90.9	81.3
FC 15 (1)	595227	182531	777758	69.6	90.8	73.6
Shares (%)						
FC 13	88.7	11.3	100.0			
FC 14	87.9	12.1	100.0			
FC 15 (1)	76.5	23.5	100.0			

Source (basic data): RBI State Finances (2023), https://rbi.org.in/Scripts/AnnualPublications. aspx?head = State%20Finances%20:%20A%20Study%20of%20Budgets (Accessed on 5 October 2023) and Authors' calculations.

linked to normal central assistance based on the Gadgil formula. Also, the distinction between plan and non-plan expenditures was discontinued in central and state budgets. The Fourteenth Finance Commission, for this reason, did not recommend any state-specific or sector-specific grants. In their case, grants were limited to revenue deficit grants, local body grants, and disaster relief grants.

The Fifteenth Finance Commission did not examine the substantive issue of the rationale for continuing with the revenue deficit grants, although this subject was covered in their ToR. The Commission only observed that it was continuing with these grants. It may be recalled that the extant literature[1] on fiscal federalism in India has, in the past, heavily criticized the mechanism of revenue deficit grants because of the implicit incentive in this principle for fiscal indiscipline. This adverse incentive arises because if a state creates a history of high expenditures based on excessive borrowings, it will create a history of interest payments which will be considered as valid expenditure for purposes of determining revenue deficits. As long as states know that revenue deficit is a principle for determination of transfers, it is in their interest to incur large per capita expenditures financed by any means, including additional and unsustainable borrowings, and then ask the Finance Commission to underwrite the shortfall. This criticism was particularly valid in the presence of the mechanism of plan financing, where states attempted to maximize their plan size, which would entitle them to higher central assistance in the form of loans and plan grants. Although the mechanism of five-year plans has now been discontinued, the adverse incentive of revenue deficit grants has not fully gone away because of the continued financing of revenue expenditures through borrowing and continuation of centrally sponsored schemes (CSS) where, in many cases, states have to contribute their shares, which may also be financed by borrowing.

To some extent, the adverse incentive of revenue deficit grants can be mitigated by the application of normative principles in the assessment of state-wise expenditure needs and own revenues.

In the case of earlier Commissions, particularly some of the recent ones, revenue deficit grants were usually given for the erstwhile special category states which were small in size and had relatively larger cost disabilities. Costs of providing services are high in these states because of the hilly terrain and their special fiscal needs. In the Fifteenth Finance Commission, many of the larger states have also become recipients of the revenue deficit grants. It is clear from Table 8.5 that revenue deficit grants were recommended for seventeen states in the Fifteenth Finance Commission (second report) and for only seven states in the Thirteenth Finance Commission. In the case of the medium and large (ML) states, only one state was a recipient of the revenue deficit grants under the

Table 8.5 State-Wise Recommended Revenue Gap Grants Per Year (INR crore)

State	FC 13 2011–15	FC 14 2016–20	FC 15 (1st report) 2020–1	FC 15 (2nd report) 2021–2
Medium and large states				
Andhra Pradesh	503.2	4422.6	5897	6099
Haryana				26
Karnataka				326
Kerala		1903.8	15323	7563
Punjab			7659	5194
Rajasthan				2948
Tamil Nadu			4025	441
West Bengal		2352.0	5013	8023
Small and Hilly States				
Assam		675.8	7579	2837
Himachal Pradesh	1577.8	8125.0	11431	7440
Manipur	1211.4	2045.4	2824	1959
Meghalaya	562.2	354.0	491	627
Mizoram	798.2	2436.6	1422	1309
Nagaland	1629.2	3695.0	3917	4250
Sikkim			448	253
Tripura	890.6	1020.6	3236	3978
Uttarakhand			5076	5629

Source (basic data): Reports of Thirteenth to Fifteenth Finance Commissions, https://fincomindia.nic.in/commission-reports (Accessed on 5 October 2023) and Authors' compilation.

Thirteenth Finance Commission and only three states received this grant under the Fourteenth Finance Commission. However, in the first report of the Fifteenth Finance Commission, five ML states were recipients of revenue deficit grants. In the final report of the Fifteenth Finance Commission, this increased to eight states.

Article 275(1) of the Constitution enjoins the Finance Commission first to determine the 'principles' which should govern the grants-in-aid of the revenues of the state and then determine the 'sums' that are to be paid. Revenue deficit grants often did ensue in the gap-filling approach, even when moderated by the application of some partial norms. In determining the appropriate principle, a suitable approach would be to determine grants on the basis of the equalization principle, especially capturing cost and need disabilities. In fact, tax devolution can cover part of the fiscal capacity disability while grants should be used to focus on cost and need disabilities determined on the basis of suitable benchmarks. Such an approach to the determination of grants would be consistent with the provisions of Article 275(1).

Other Key Recommendations of the Three Recent Commissions

In the discussion below, we look at the salient recommendations of the three recent Commissions with respect to local governments, disaster risk management, debt and fiscal deficit management, and any other important issues.

Local governments

Thirteenth Finance Commission
As shown by Table 8.3 earlier, local body grants earmarked by the Thirteenth Finance Commission amounted to INR86,468 crore (excluding Jammu and Kashmir). The Thirteenth Finance Commission introduced an element of buoyancy in the volume of grants earmarked for local bodies by linking it to a recommended share in the divisible

Table 8.6 Weights Allotted to Criteria for Grants to Local Bodies by the Thirteenth Finance Commission

Criterion	Weights allotted (%)	
	PRIs	ULBs
Population	50	50
Area	10	10
Distance from highest per capita sectoral income	10	20
Index of devolution	15	15
SC/STs proportion in the population	10	
FC local body grants utilization index	5	5
Total	100	100

Source (basic data): Thirteenth Finance Commission Report, https://fincomindia.nic.in/com mission-reports (Accessed 5 October 2023) and Authors' compilation.

pool of Centre's taxes. However, in order to ensure that this was to be given as a grant and not a share in taxes, the Commission suggested that the recommended share be applied to the previous year's divisible pool and the relevant amount be converted into a grant. This grant was divided into two parts, namely basic grants and performance-linked grants. The performance-linked grants were subjected to a number of conditionalities. Both the general basic grants and general performance grants were allocated between rural and urban areas in accordance with their respective populations as per the 2001 Census. These population shares were 26.82 per cent for urban areas and 73.18 per cent for rural areas. The inter-se distribution of these grants across states was formula-based, as detailed in Table 8.6.

With respect to the general performance grants, quite elaborate conditions were specified by the Commission. The Commission recommended that states that did not comply with these conditions would forfeit these grants. These conditions are summarized below:

1. State governments must put in place a supplement to the budget documents for local bodies (separately for PRIs and ULBs) furnishing the details (other than those relating to Finance Accounts).

2. State governments must put in place an audit system for all rural and urban local bodies.

3. State governments must put in place a system of independent local body ombudsmen that would look into complaints of corruption and maladministration against the functionaries of local bodies, and recommend suitable action.

4. State governments must put in place a system to electronically transfer local body grants provided by the Commission to the respective local bodies within five days of their receipt from the central government.

5. State governments must prescribe through an Act the qualifications of persons eligible for appointment as members of the SFC consistent with Article 243I(2) of the Constitution.

6. All local bodies should be fully enabled to levy property tax (including tax for all types of residential and commercial properties) and any hindrances in this regard must be removed.

7. State governments must put in place a state level Property Tax Board, assisting all municipalities and municipal corporations in the state to put in place an independent and transparent procedure for assessing property tax.

8. State governments must gradually put in place standards for delivery of all essential services provided by local bodies. For a start, state governments must notify all municipal corporations and municipalities by the end of a fiscal year of the service standards for four service sectors, namely water supply, sewerage, stormwater drainage, and solid waste management.

9. All municipal corporations with a population of more than 1 million (2001 census) must put in place a fire hazard response and mitigation plan for their respective jurisdictions.

In practice, states found it difficult to comply with these conditions and thus, the actual amount of performance grants disbursed to the states was much less than the amount estimated and recommended by the Commission. In addition, the Thirteenth Finance Commission recommended that state governments may share with the local bodies some of the income that they receive from royalties.

Fourteenth Finance Commission

The Fourteenth Finance Commission increased substantially the re-commended size of the local body grants to INR 2,82,667 (excluding Jammu and Kashmir). They discontinued its linking with the divisible pool of central taxes. The local body grants were divided between PRIs and ULBs in the ratios of 69.7 per cent and 30.3 per cent, reflecting the relative size of rural and urban populations as per the 2011 Census. Just like the Thirteenth Finance Commission, the Fourteenth Finance Commission also recommended grants in two parts, namely a basic grant and a performance grant. The division of total grants into basic and performance was 90:10 for rural local bodies and 80:20 for ULBs. The basic grants were to be distributed among the panchayats based on the formula recommended by the respective State Finance Commissions. For ULBs, the Commission recommended an inter-se allocation of these grants based on a formula using population and area with relative weights of 90 per cent and 10 per cent. The distribution of performance grants was to be based on a number of performance criteria recom-mended by the Commission. The Commission also suggested that municipal bonds may be used as a source of finance for the ULBs.

Fifteenth Finance Commission

This section summarizes the recommendations of the Fifteenth Finance Commission with regard to the local governments, focusing on their final report. The Commission substantially enhanced the share of ULBs in the total local body grants to 34 per cent in view of the growing urbanization of India's population. They also earmarked certain performance-based grants for million-plus cities in India. They introduced separate grants for primary health facilities, incubation of new cities, and shared services such as maintenance of national data centres. The allocated amounts are given in Table 8.7.

A number of conditions were specified for the ULBs for the release of grants. These included showing consistent improvement in the collection of property taxes in tandem with the growth rate of the state's GSDP. In the case of rural local bodies, all three tiers—village, block, and district—were given grants. The inter-se distribution among all the tiers of panchayat is to be implemented by the state governments on the basis of the accepted recommendations of the latest State Finance Commission and

Table 8.7 Grants to Local Bodies as Recommended by the Fifteenth
Finance Commission

#	Grants	Magnitude (INR cr.)	Share (%)
1	Total grants for rural and urban local bodies	4,27,911	
	Grants for primary health sector	70,051	
	Other grants to be disbursed among the local bodies	3,57,860	
	of which Grants for RLBs	2,36,805	66
	Untied	94,721	40
	Tied	1,42,084	60
	Drinking water, rainwater harvesting, and water recycling	42,625	30
	Sanitation and maintenance of open defecation-free status	12,788	30
	of which Grants for ULBs	1,21,055	34
	Million-Plus cities Challenge Fund (MCF) for Million-Plus/Cities	38,196	32
	Grants for Non-Million-Plus Cities/Category-II Cities/Towns	82,859	68
	Untied	33,143	40
	Tied	49,716	60
	Drinking water, rainwater harvesting and water recycling	24,858	
	Sanitation and maintenance of open defecation free status	24,858	
2	Grants for incubation of new cities	8,000	
3	Grants for shared municipal services	450	
	Total grants	4,36,361	

Source (basic data): Final report of the Fifteenth Finance Commission, https://fincomindia.nic.in/commission-reports (Accessed on 5 October 2023) and Authors' calculations.

in conformity with the following bands of (a) not less than 70 per cent and not more than 85 per cent for gram panchayats, (b) not less than 10 per cent and not more than 25 per cent for block panchayats and (c) not less than 5 per cent and not more than 15 per cent for zilla panchayats, subject to the shares adding up to 100 per cent. It was also provided that of the total grants recommended for rural local bodies, 40 per cent be untied and 60 per cent tied to supporting and strengthening the delivery of two categories of basic services: (i) sanitation and maintenance of open defecation-free status, and (ii) drinking water, rainwater harvesting, and water recycling.

The Commission recommended that after March 2024, no grants be released to a state that has not complied with the constitutional provisions in respect of the State Finance Commission formation and acting on its recommendations.

Disaster Risk Management

The subject of dealing with natural calamities was given statutory backing through the enactment of a Disaster Management Act (DM Act) in 2005. During the course of the period under the recommendations of the three recent Finance Commissions, disaster risk management was given a stronger institutional structure and more robust funding. The erstwhile National Calamity Contingency Fund (NCCF) was merged into a National Disaster Relief Fund (NDRF) and the central and state governments were asked to set up National and State Disaster Mitigation Funds.

Thirteenth Finance Commission

The Thirteenth Finance Commission recommended that the existing NCCF be merged into the NDRF with effect from 1 April 2010, and that the balances in the NCCF at the end of 2009–10 be transferred to the NDRF. With respect to the financing of the NDRF, the Act had provided for crediting this fund with the amounts provided for this purpose by the central government. The Eleventh Finance Commission, which had come up with the idea of NCCF, had recommended for this fund a corpus of INR 500 crore.

The Thirteenth Finance Commission also recommended that state-level Calamity Relief Funds (CRFs) be merged into the State Disaster Relief Funds (SDRFs) with the balances in the CRF getting transferred to the SDRFs. It also recommended that the central and state governments jointly contribute to this fund in the ratio of 75:25 for general category states and 90:10 for special category states. The Commission recommended that the list of disasters be expanded to cover man-made disasters of high-intensity.

Fourteenth Finance Commission

The Fourteenth Finance Commission recommended an aggregate corpus for all states to be increased to INR 61,219 crore. It also recommended that the state's contribution to the SDRF be uniform for all states at 10 per cent, thereby abolishing the distinction between general and special category states for this purpose. It also recommended that the states utilize up to 10 per cent of their SDRF in their respective states for meeting expenditure needs of local disasters that were beyond the scope of those at the national level.

Fifteenth Finance Commission

The Fifteenth Finance Commission developed a new and elaborate framework to consider disaster-related risks. In determining the state-wise allocation of funds for disaster management, they considered a three-part framework which included a combination of capacity (as reflected through past expenditure), risk exposure (area and population) and hazard and vulnerability (disaster risk index). A total corpus of INR 1,60,153 crore has been recommended of which the share of the central government is estimated at INR 1,22,601 crore and that of states is estimated at INR 37,552 crore.

In respect of financing the disaster management requirements, including funding of the Relief and Mitigation Funds, the Commission recommended earmarked grants. The earmarked allocation for this purpose has been estimated at INR 11,950 crore, which is to be allocated for certain priority areas, namely two under the NDRF (expansion and modernization of fire services and resettlement of displaced people affected by erosion) and four under the NDMF (catalytic assistance to twelve most drought-prone states, managing seismic and landslide risks in ten hill states, reducing the risk of urban flooding in seven most populous cities, and mitigation measures to prevent erosion).

With a view to discouraging excessive and unsubstantiated demands from states, the Commission recommended that all central assistance through the NDRF and NDMF be provided on a graded cost-sharing basis. States should contribute 10 per cent for assistance up to INR 250 crore, 20 per cent for assistance up to INR 500 crore and 25 per cent for all assistance exceeding INR 500 crore.

The Commission also recommended setting up of a Recovery and Reconstruction Facility within the NDRF and SDRF. Assistance for recovery and reconstruction is generally a multi-year programme, and the assistance, shared between the union and states, needs to be released annually against expenditures and only as a percentage of total cost.

Debt and Fiscal Deficit Management

During the period covered by the three recent Finance Commissions, major changes occurred in the profile of government debt and fiscal deficit. In 2018, a major amendment to the centre's FRBM was brought about based on recommendations of the FRBM Review Committee chaired by Shri. N.K. Singh. Individual Commissions also made significant recommendations affecting the roadmap of fiscal and primary deficit and related parameters. Global events such as episodes of high crude prices, COVID-19, and ongoing geopolitical supply disruptions have also had a significant effect on the debt and deficit levels of the central and state governments relative to GDP. We consider below, the salient features of the analysis and recommendations of individual Commissions under review.

Thirteenth Finance Commission
The Thirteenth Finance Commission provided a new roadmap for fiscal consolidation for the centre and the states, which included the following targets.

- Reduction in the debt stock of the centre and the states to a target of 45 per cent and 25 per cent of GDP respectively by 2014–15.
- Elimination of revenue deficit with revenue account balance as a long-term and permanent target.

The Thirteenth Finance Commission had recommended different glide paths for general and special category states for reducing revenue deficits and for reaching a fiscal deficit target of 3 per cent of GSDP. The Commission also suggested the setting up of an independent review mechanism by the Centre to evaluate its fiscal reform process. The independent review mechanism was envisioned to evolve into a Fiscal Council with legislative backing.

The Thirteenth Finance Commission made some significant recommendations regarding interest and debt relief. It recommended that the interest rate on loans to the states from the NSSF contracted until 2006–7 and outstanding at the end of 2009–10 be reset at 9 per cent, in order to correct the interest asymmetry between the centre and the states. These loans carried an interest rate of either 9.5 per cent or 10.5 per cent, depending on the year in which the loans were contracted. Relief was to be provided on loans contracted until 2006–7, since a portion of the funds collected under the NSSF from 2007–8 onwards was borrowed by the central government. The Thirteenth Finance Commission also recommended that the NSSF be reformed into a market-aligned scheme covering aspects including interest rate and tenure.

The Thirteenth Finance Commission recommended that the loans from central government to states administered by ministries/departments other than the Ministry of Finance and outstanding at the end of 2009–10 which were not covered by the Twelfth Finance Commission under the Debt Consolidation and Relief Facility (DCRF), be written off. Additionally, the Thirteenth Finance Commission suggested that the practice of the centre providing loans to the states under CSS be avoided in future. The Thirteenth Finance Commission reiterated the Twelfth Finance Commission's recommendation that the central government provides a borrowing window for fiscally weak states that are unable to raise funds from the market.

Sikkim and West Bengal did not enact an FRBM Act and were therefore not eligible for the benefits under the DCRF facility introduced by the Twelfth Finance Commission. The Thirteenth Finance Commission recommended that such states be made eligible for consolidation of central loans in accordance with the terms of the DCRF. However, the Thirteenth Finance Commission clarified that no further debt waiver would be extended on the central loans consolidated and rescheduled by the Twelfth Finance Commission.

Fourteenth Finance Commission

The Fourteenth Finance Commission made certain salient recommendations regarding benchmark debt and fiscal deficit targets for the central and state governments and regarding the glide paths to reach these targets. Some of their main recommendations are summarized below:

1. Fiscal deficit of all states was anchored to an annual limit of 3 per cent of GSDP with states being eligible for a flexibility of up to 0.25 per cent over and above this limit if their debt-GSDP ratio was less than or equal to 25 per cent in the preceding year.
2. States were allowed a further borrowing limit of 0.25 per cent of GSDP if the interest payments were less than or equal to 10 per cent of the revenue receipts in the preceding year.
3. The flexibility of 0.5 per cent of GSDP could be availed of by a state only if there was no revenue deficit in the concerned year. If a state was not able to fully utilize its sanctioned borrowing limit of 3 per cent of GSDP in any particular year during the first four years of the recommendation period (2015–6 to 2018–9), it would have the option of availing this non-utilized borrowing amount only in the following year but within the award period.
4. The Commission also recommended that the central government may amend its FRBM Act and eliminate the concept of effective revenue deficit.
5. The Commission recommended the setting up of an independent Fiscal Council.
6. Keeping in mind the importance of risks arising from guarantees, off-budget borrowings, and accumulated losses of financially weak public sector enterprises when assessing the debt position of states, the Fourteenth Finance Commission recommended that both central and state governments adopt a template for collating, analysing, and annually reporting the total extended public debt in their respective budgets as a supplement to the budget document.

The Centre's 2018 FRBM Amendment

Following a commitment made in the Union Budget for 2016–7, an FRBM Review Committee was constituted on 17 May 2016. In its four-volume Report, the Committee recommended the enactment of a new Debt Management and Fiscal Responsibility Framework supplemented by Debt Management and Fiscal Responsibility Rules to replace the FRBM Act, 2003 and FRBM Rules, 2004 including their subsequent amendments. As per the amendment, the fiscal deficit became an operational target, and the revenue deficit target was dropped. Targets were set in terms of debt relative to GDP for the combined and central government at 60 per cent and 40 per cent respectively.

The centre's 2018 amendment to the FRBMA also provides for certain countercyclical interventions linked to five conditions in which a departure from the operational fiscal deficit target of 3 per cent of GDP can be made. These conditions relate to: (i) national security, (ii) act of war, (iii) national calamity, (iv) collapse of agriculture severely affecting farm output and incomes, and (v) structural reforms in the economy with unanticipated fiscal implications. The Act provides that if, as a result of one or more of the above conditions, there is a 'decline in real output growth of a quarter by at least 3% points below its average of the previous four quarters', then the fiscal deficit limit may be increased, but this increase 'shall not exceed one half percent of the gross domestic product in a year'.

It is notable that the combined debt-GDP ratio sharply increased to 74.6 per cent in 2019–20, exceeding the FRBM 2018 target of 60 per cent by a wide margin. The impact of COVID-19 further widened this margin significantly.

Fifteenth Finance Commission

The Fifteenth Finance Commission considered three alternative scenarios in order to specify potential deficit and debt paths for the centre and states. They used their assessed revenue paths as the benchmark and considered two alternative performances indicating lower than and higher than the indicated benchmark. The Fifteenth Finance Commission considered three possibilities: (i) if economic recovery is slower than assessed, (ii) if the Commission's macroeconomic assessment holds, and (iii) if economic recovery is faster than assessed. We may refer to these as Pessimistic, Benchmark, and Optimistic scenarios respectively. As shown by the actual fiscal deficit to GDP ratio of the central government (row 4 of Table 8.8), the reality proved to be worse than even the pessimistic forecast of the Commission.

Table 8.8 Fiscal Deficit to GDP Ratio for the Central Government (%): Fifteenth Finance Commission Forecasts

Scenario	2020–1	2021–2	2022–3	2023–4	2024–5	2025–6
Pessimistic	NA	6.5	6.0	5.5	5.0	4.5
Benchmark	7.4	6.0	5.5	5.0	4.5	4.0
Optimistic	NA	6.0	5.5	5.0	4.0	3.5
Actual Fiscal deficit to GDP ratio	9.2	6.7	6.4	5.9 (BE)		4.5*

Source (basic data): 15th FC report, https://fincomindia.nic.in/commission-reports-fifteenth (Accessed on 5 October 2023) and Authors' compilation.
*As per the 2022–3 Union Budget Speech of the FM.

For the state governments, the Fifteenth Finance Commission did not give three alternative scenarios for fiscal deficit. Instead, it suggested an indicative borrowing programme for the state governments Table 8.9. They also provided a degree of flexibility by indicating a year-wise extra borrowing space linked to certain incentives.

The actual fiscal deficit to GDP ratio of the states indicates that they have not been able to utilize available fiscal deficit limits or participate in the centre's stimulus programmes in the COVID-19 period and in subsequent years, preferring to remain closer to their Fiscal Responsibility Legislation (FRL) targets.

The Fifteenth Finance Commission also recommended the setting up of a High-Powered Inter-governmental Group to re-examine the centre's FRBM.

Other Key Recommendations

There are certain other notable recommendations given by these three Finance Commissions that are briefly discussed below.

Thirteenth Finance Commission
The Thirteenth Finance Commission took note of the increasing outlays on the CSS, which required a larger contribution from the states as well.

Table 8.9 Fiscal Deficit to GDP Ratio for States: Fifteenth Finance Commission Forecasts

	2020–1	2021–2	2022–3	2023–4	2024–5	2025–6
Indicative deficit path for state governments						
Fiscal deficit	4.5	4.0	3.5	3.0	3.0	3.0
Incentive-based extra borrowing space: range of all-state fiscal deficit under the recommended space for borrowing						
Upper limit (If all states use the full borrowing space available)	NA	4.5	4.0	3.5	3.5	3.0
Lower limit (states, on an average, reach the current FRBM limit)	NA	3.0	3.0	3.0	3.0	3.0
Actual fiscal deficit to GDP ratio*	4.1	3.7 (RE)	3.4 (BE)	–	–	–

Source (basic data): Final Report of the Fifteenth Finance Commission, https://fincomindia. nic.in/commission-reports-fifteenth (Accessed on 5 October 2023); RBI; https://rbi.org.in/ Scripts/AnnualPublications.aspx?head = State%20Finances%20:%20A%20Study%20of%20 Budgets (Accessed on 5 October 2023) and Authors' compilation. *sourced from the RBI

This has implied an increased share of states in the funding of CSS. It is implicit in this that states' capacity to contribute up to the needed share may be constrained and this may lead to non-utilization or partial utilization of funds for some of the CSS. The Commission recommended undertaking initiatives to reduce the number of CSS and to restore the predominance of formula-based plan transfers.

The Thirteenth Finance Commission had also set up a task force on GST to work out the revenue-neutral rate. It emphasized the concept of the 'Grand Bargain' and recommended the setting up of a statutory GST Council in place of the Empowered Committee of State Finance Ministers to facilitate the transition to GST.

Fourteenth Finance Commission

The Fourteenth Finance Commission recommended the creation of an autonomous and independent GST Compensation Fund with a legislative basis to provide reasonable comfort to the states in agreeing to adopt GST.

The Commission also recommended an expanded role for the Inter-State Council that was constituted on 28 May 1990 by a Presidential Order, to include the following additional responsibilities:

i) Identifying the sectors in the states that should be eligible for grants from the Union.
ii) Indicating criteria for inter-state distribution.
iii) Helping design schemes with appropriate flexibility being given to the states regarding implementation.
iv) Identifying and providing area-specific grants.

Fifteenth Finance Commission

The Fifteenth Finance Commission reviewed the issue of GST compensation. Noting that the present arrangement was scheduled to come to an end by June 2022, and that the states could experience a sudden revenue shock (Rao (2014)), the Commission recommended the continuation of the compensation cess up to 2025–6 to raise funds for paying off to the states the accumulated arrears. The Commission, however, did not recommend the continuation of the GST compensation arrangement in light of the revenue shock that the states were expected to suffer.

Another matter that was referred to the Commission related to the need and desirability of a separate mechanism to fund capital outlay for defence and internal security requirements. The Commission recommended the setting up of a dedicated, non-lapsable Modernization Fund for Defence and Internal Security. This recommendation, however, has only been accepted in principle by the central government. The Action Taken Report (ATR) of the Fifteenth Finance Commission has stated the following: 'The Government has accepted in-principle the creation of non-lapsable fund for Defence in the Public Account of India. Sources of funding and modalities will be examined in due course.'

Concluding Observations

In this chapter, the main developments during the period under the recommendations of the Thirteenth, Fourteenth, and Fifteenth Finance

Commissions have been discussed. During this period, some salient changes happened in the organization of states. In particular, the erstwhile state of Andhra Pradesh was divided between Andhra Pradesh and Telangana in 2014, increasing the number of states from 28 to 29. Subsequently, the state of Jammu and Kashmir was reorganized in August 2019, which reduced the total number of states in India from 29 to 28 and increased the number of union territories with legislatures from 2 to 3. In the field of taxation, the Goods and Services Tax was implemented in 2017, replacing a number of central and state indirect taxes. Also, major reforms were undertaken with respect to the Corporate Income Tax in 2019. Further, the plan/ non-plan distinction in government expenditures was abolished in 2015–6 and subsequently, the mechanism of plan grants was also discontinued. In the context of managing fiscal deficit and government debt, the centre's FRBM was substantially amended in 2018. These changes affected the working of India's fiscal federal system in a number of ways which have been reviewed in this chapter.

In regard to the vertical dimension of fiscal federalism, the main notable change was an increase of 10 percentage points in the states' share in the divisible pool of central taxes. In fact, the central government was partly able to absorb this sharp increase because of the elimination of plan grants, which used to constitute an average of 3 per cent of the divisible pool during the period 2009–10 to 2013–14. The Planning Commission was abolished and substituted by Niti Aayog with no financial powers. Subsequently, the central government increased the non-sharable cesses and surcharges to reduce the effective share of states in central taxes. Also, the central government has not been forthcoming in accepting state-specific and sector-specific grants, although the revenue deficit grants are being accepted along with grants for local bodies and managing natural calamities. In the context of the horizontal distribution of resources, the ways and weights associated with the use of the population criterion in the tax devolution formula were changed by these recent Finance Commissions. In particular, the Fifteenth Finance Commission was asked explicitly to use 2011 Census-based population data, discontinuing the earlier mandate of using the 1971 data. The weight given to the distance criterion, which is the main vehicle for determining redistributive transfers, was also progressively reduced as compared with the Twelfth Finance Commission and especially the Eleventh

Finance Commission. We also note that environmental considerations were brought in the tax devolution scheme through the introduction of a separate criterion pertaining to areas under forest. Incentives for fiscal discipline and tax effort were almost eliminated, with the Fifteenth Finance Commission according a low weight of 2.5 per cent to tax effort. In the case of grants, the Fourteenth Finance Commission had discontinued all grants other than revenue deficit grants, and grants for local governments and natural calamities. The Fifteenth Finance Commission reintroduced sector-specific and state-specific grants. However, the central government has put their acceptance on hold. This raises the broader question as to whether some of the need and cost disabilities reflected in these grants can be incorporated by modifying the scheme of tax devolution and ensuring that revenue deficit grants are not gap-filling grants. These should be determined by a more comprehensive normative approach which also reflects cost and need disabilities.

We have reviewed at length the 2018 amendment to the centre's FRBM and the performance of the central and state governments regarding their fiscal and revenue deficit profiles. We have highlighted the need for reexamining the centre's amended FRBM, emphasizing the importance of maintaining revenue account balance and linking it to government dissavings. There is also a need to establish symmetry in the fiscal deficit and debt targets relative to GDP for the central and state governments.

Note

1. Bhatt and Scaramozzino (2015), Bagchi and Chakraborty (2004), and Rangarajan and Srivastava (2008).

9

Future of Fiscal Federalism in India

Over the course of the last seven decades, fiscal federalism in India has covered considerable ground. It has evolved in a dynamic way, responding to the changing contours of the central and state finances in the context of continuing inter-state development disparities. The Finance Commission continues to occupy a prime position in the context of determining fiscal transfers from the central to the sub-national governments. In the current situation relating to economic and fiscal disparities, substantive changes and reforms are called for in order to address a number of outstanding and continuing issues. The role of the Finance Commission has also become more critical in correcting development disparities and some of the continuing inequalities in the standards of publicly provided services across states after the abolition of the Planning Commission. Some of the outstanding problems in this context may be classified in the following broad categories: (i) Resolution of vertical imbalance, (ii) Resolution of horizontal imbalance across states, (iii) Challenges posed by the implementation of GST and its needed reforms, (iv) Considerations of resource, environmental, and ecological externalities, (v) Managing fiscal imbalances and stabilization, and (vi) Reforms of institutional framework governing centre-state financial relations. The Sixteenth Finance Commission, whose Terms of Reference (ToR) were announced in a press release on 29 November 2023,[1] based on the Union Cabinet's approval of the ToR, will have the opportunity to address some of these formidable tasks. Subsequently, another press release on 31 December 2023 announced the appointment of Dr Arvind Panagariya as Chairman of the Sixteenth Finance Commission. The ToR have remained the same as earlier. The Commission has to submit its report latest by 31 October 2025. Its period of reference is for five years from 1 April 2026, that is, 2026–7 to 2030–1.

Federalism and Fiscal Transfers in India, Second Edition. C. Rangarajan and D.K. Srivastava, Oxford University Press.
© Rangarajan and Srivastava 2024. DOI: 10.1093/9780198930426.003.0009

Sixteenth Finance Commission

Departing from the extant practice of specifying a detailed ToR for the Finance Commission, the ToR of the Sixteenth Finance Commission only specifies the substantive content of Articles 280 and 275 of the Constitution. These ToRs are given below.

Terms of Reference

The ToR of the Sixteenth Finance Commission as indicated by the press release is as follows:

(1) The distribution between the Union and the States of the net proceeds of taxes which are to be, or may be, divided between them under Chapter I, Part XII of the Constitution and the allocation between the States of the respective shares of such proceeds;

(2) The principles which should govern the grants-in-aid of the revenues of the States out of the Consolidated Fund of India and the sums to be paid to the States by way of grants-in-aid of their revenues under article 275 of the Constitution for the purposes other than those specified in the provisos to clause (1) of that article; and

(3) The measures needed to augment the Consolidated Fund of a State to supplement the resources of the Panchayats and Municipalities in the State on the basis of the recommendations made by the Finance Commission of the State.

The Commission may review the present arrangements on financing Disaster Management initiatives, with reference to the funds constituted under the Disaster Management Act, 2005 (53 of 2005), and make appropriate recommendations thereon.

ToR, Sixteenth Finance Commission

Paragraph (1) of the ToR is based on Article 280(3), subclause (a) of the Constitution. Paragraph (2) of the ToR is based on Article 280(3), subclause (b) read with Article 275(1) of the Constitution. Paragraph (3) of the ToR is based on Article 280(3), subclauses (bb) and (c) of the Constitution (Srivastava, Bharadwaj, Kapur and Trehan (December 2023).

In the case of the earlier Finance Commissions, an elaborate set of ToRs was provided mainly on account of clause (d) of Article 280 of the Constitution which makes reference to 'any other matter referred to the Commission by the President in the interests of sound finance'. No specific matter has been referred to the Sixteenth Finance Commission under this clause. However, since this phrase is part of the Constitution, it should be open to the Commission to consider any relevant matter in the interest of sound finance. Some of the other constitutional articles which may have relevance for centre-state fiscal relations relate to Articles 292, 293, 270, and 271. Articles 292 and 293 provide that Parliament may prescribe limits for borrowing by the central government and give approval to any borrowing by the state governments if the central government has extended any loan to the state government which is outstanding in part or full or with respect to which a guarantee has been given. Article 270 deals with the distribution of union taxes between the central and the state governments. Clause (1) of this article is relevant. Clauses (1), 1(a), and 1(b) of this Article cover all central taxes including GST which are to be distributed between the central and the state governments under the recommendations of the Finance Commission. Clause (2) of this Article however relates to taxes which may be a part of the Union List but which may be assigned to the states. Another important article, namely Article 271, provides for the levy of the surcharge by the central government. The levy of cess, which has been mentioned in Article 270 (1) itself, can be levied under any law made by Parliament for this purpose Kotha, Agarwal, Sengupta, Singh (2018).

The heavy reliance on cesses and surcharges by the central government has been a subject of discussion in recent times,[2] as discussed in Chapter 8. This may continue to remain an important issue in the context of vertical distribution of resources between central and state governments.

'Disaster Management' as a subject is not mentioned in any of the three lists of Schedule VII of the Constitution. It means provisions regarding disaster management come under the Residuary Powers of the Union under entry 97 of the Union List. This matter has been referred to under paragraph 4 of the ToR of the Sixteenth Finance Commission.

The constitutional provisions are enough for the Commission to consider the entire ambit of centre-state fiscal transfers. The Commission is free to determine its approach and methodology as provided under Article 280(4), which clearly states that 'the Commission shall determine their procedure and shall have such powers in the performance of their functions as Parliament may by law confer on them'.

Period of Reference

The periodicity of five years which had been maintained since the Tenth Finance Commission covering 1995–6 to 1999–2000, was disturbed by the coverage of six years in the two Reports by the Fifteenth Finance Commission pertaining to 2020–1 and for the period 2021–2 to 2025–6 respectively. The Commission had faced certain difficulties in selecting a suitable base year on account of the change of the status of Jammu and Kashmir from a state to a union territory (UT) with legislature. Subsequently, the onset of COVID-19, which affected 2020–1, also had to be taken into account in forecasting economic and fiscal outcomes during the recommendation period of the Commission. Before the Fifteenth Finance Commission, it was the Ninth Finance Commission which had a reference period of six years.

The press release dated 29 November 2023 indicates that the Sixteenth Finance Commission will have a reference period extending from 2026–7 to 2030–1. The two constitutional articles relevant to the constitution of the Finance Commission are Article 280 and Article 281. Clause (1) of Article 280 provides that 'The President shall, within two years from the commencement of this Constitution and thereafter at the expiration of every fifth year or at such earlier time as the President considers necessary, by order constitute a Finance Commission which shall consist of a Chairman and four other members to be appointed by the President.' Thus, the Commission will stand constituted only after a Presidential notification. The Fifteenth Finance Commission was constituted through a Presidential notification on 27 November 2017. A second notification extending the term of the Fifteenth Finance Commission was issued on 29 November 2019.[3]

Number of States

When the Fifteenth Finance Commission was constituted in November 2017, India had 29 states. However, with the Jammu and Kashmir Reorganization Act of 2019, the erstwhile state of Jammu and Kashmir was made a UT with legislature, while Ladakh was made a UT without legislature. Thus, in the first and the final reports of the Fifteenth Finance Commission pertaining to 2020–1 and 2021–2 to 2025–6 respectively, recommendations were made for the distribution of resources between the central government and 28 states. This situation may change again if and when Jammu and Kashmir is made a state again, in regard to which the latest Supreme Court judgement[4] pertaining to this matter has made certain observations.

Benefits of a Short ToR

There are certain benefits to having a short ToR referring only to the constitutional provisions. This provides the Commission with a greater degree of flexibility in determining the scope of its work, its approach, and its methodology. In fact, what has been missed out in relation to the ToRs of the preceding Finance Commissions, may remove some undue constraints on the Commission. Some of the typical missed-out clauses may be listed as below:

1. **Specification of a Census year:** The ToR of some of the earlier Commissions had mentioned a specific Census year. Since it was a part of the ToR, the Commissions considered it a mandate to utilize population data of that Census year implying use of dated information. This unduly constrained the Finance Commission in choosing the most appropriate year with respect to which it may have considered population data to be most relevant. The Sixteenth Finance Commission will now have the necessary freedom to choose the relevant population data.
2. **Examining the status of fiscal imbalances:** The earlier Finance Commissions were asked to review the state of government finances of the central and state governments especially with respect to fiscal

deficit and debt. This consideration will nevertheless have to inform the Sixteenth Finance Commission's deliberations in the context of determining tax devolution and grants. Even if they focus on the revenue accounts of central and state governments, it is the substantive importance of interest payments which are part of revenue expenditure which has a bearing on government borrowing both by central and state governments. In fact, the dynamics of movement of interest payments is linked to the dynamics of fiscal deficit and debt.

3. **Inclusion of incentives:** Finance Commissions were often asked to consider providing incentives in their scheme of tax devolution and grants to promote multiple objectives, including the centre's flagship schemes, progress towards sustainable development goals (SDGs), progress made in increasing tax/non-tax revenues, structural reform programmes, and so on. Similarly, efforts and progress made in moving towards replacement rate of population growth were to be considered in devising the scheme of fiscal transfers for the Fifteenth Finance Commission. In their ToR, reference was also made to provision of grants in aid to local bodies for basic services, including quality human resources, and implementation of a performance grant system in improving delivery of services. In the case of the Thirteenth and Fourteenth Finance Commissions, there was a reference made to the 'need to balance management of ecology, environment and climate change consistent with sustainable economic development'. The Sixteenth Finance Commission would be free to devise its own approach and consider the introduction of incentives or compensation as needed with reference to tax effort, fiscal discipline, environmental externalities, and so on.

Thus, as long as Article 280(4) remains a part of the Constitution, any matter may be considered by the Finance Commission in the interests of sound finance.

Status of Data Availability

The latest population data that would be available to the Sixteenth Finance Commission based on the Census is 2011. The 2021 Census has not been conducted. Instead, the plan is to conduct a Census in 2026. Thus, for the reference period of the Sixteenth Finance Commission, if the Commission decides to use population data based on the 2011 Census, it would be dated by fifteen to twenty years, considering the first and the terminal years of the recommendation period namely, 2026–7 and 2030–1. The latest GSDP data currently available from the NSO pertains to 2021–2 for all states and 2022–3 for a selected list of states. Assuming that the Sixteenth Finance Commission uses data for three years, it may imply utilizing GSDP data pertaining to 2020–1, 2021–2, and 2022–3. The 2020–1 GDP/GSDP data would contain the deleterious effects of COVID-19 and 2021–2 data would reflect its base effects. 2022–3 would be the first year where, by and large, the GDP/GSDP data would have normalized.

Like the earlier Finance Commissions, the Sixteenth Finance Commission will also have to deal with the resolution of vertical, horizontal, and fiscal imbalances. It is due to the interlinkages of interest payments arising on government debt that the issue of sustainable fiscal deficit and debt gets linked to the subject of fiscal transfers. It is the post-transfer availability of resources that determines the fiscal scope of the central and individual state governments measured in terms of their primary expenditures.

Resolving Vertical Imbalance

Vertical imbalance in the collection of revenues and the distribution of responsibilities has been deliberately built into the constitutional scheme of assignment as given in Schedule 7. The centre has been provided relatively larger resources while the states have been assigned relatively larger responsibilities necessitating fiscal transfers from the central to the state governments. This imbalance also continues in regard to state and local governments. So far, the Finance Commissions have not clearly stated the objective principles on the basis of which the respective shares of the states considered together and the central government in the divisible pool of central taxes as well as in the magnitude of total transfers inclusive of tax devolution and all Finance Commission grants have been determined. Their approach has been incremental adjustments in historically determined shares, except for the Fourteenth Finance Commission where a one-step sharp increase was involved. States have been complaining, all along, about the deficiency of resources in relation to their responsibilities. There are also issues in regard to unconditional and conditional transfers, with states favouring the former. Some changes have also occurred in respect of the collection of revenues and expenditures after the introduction of GST.

In correcting vertical imbalance, there is a need for a rethink on the roles of the centre and states on expenditures (Srivastava, Bharadwaj, Kapur and Trehan (March 2024). It is argued that centrally sponsored schemes have ballooned over time and have 'encroached' on the territory of states. But it is also a fact that the performance of the central government is judged not only on the basis of actions taken that fall strictly within its jurisdiction but also on the initiatives taken in the areas which fall in the concurrent list and the state list. Centralized planning, which held sway for several decades, has something to do with it. In recent periods, stabilization expenditures such as Food Subsidy and Employment Guarantee Schemes have increased substantially. At the time of the election, the central government is held responsible for the state of the economy. Thus, there is a big difference between what the Constitution says and what the perception of the people is. This is an aspect which Finance Commissions cannot ignore.

The Fourteenth Finance Commission attempted to raise the share of states in the divisible pool of central taxes. This effort was more than neutralized by the central government by increasing the share of cesses and surcharges, which had the effect of reducing the size of the divisible pool. In addition, the central government has also not fully accepted the recommendations of the Fifteenth Finance Commission regarding grants other than those relating to revenue deficit grants, local body grants, and grants for natural calamities. Three aspects relating to the vertical dimension may be summarized as follows:

1. Stagnation of the tax-GDP ratios of the central and state governments.
2. Continuing under the provision of critical public and merit services in many states.

3. Continuing tensions in the vertical sharing of resources.

India's combined tax-GDP ratio for the central and state governments has been stagnating in the range of 16–18 per cent over a period of more than three decades. This stagnant pool for which both central and state governments may be responsible is one reason why the state governments ask for higher transfers and the central government is reluctant to agree to any scheme of effectively increased transfers. The centre's gross tax to GDP ratio has remained in the range of 8.1 per cent to 12.1 per cent during the period 1984–5 to 2022–3 (Figure 9.1).

With a relatively stagnating tax-GDP ratio, supplemented by a stagnating non-tax to GDP ratio, any upward flexibility to government expenditure to GDP ratio could only be provided by increasing the fiscal deficit to GDP ratio. If we consider the FRBM limit of 6 per cent of GDP as the permitted fiscal deficit relative to GDP for the combined

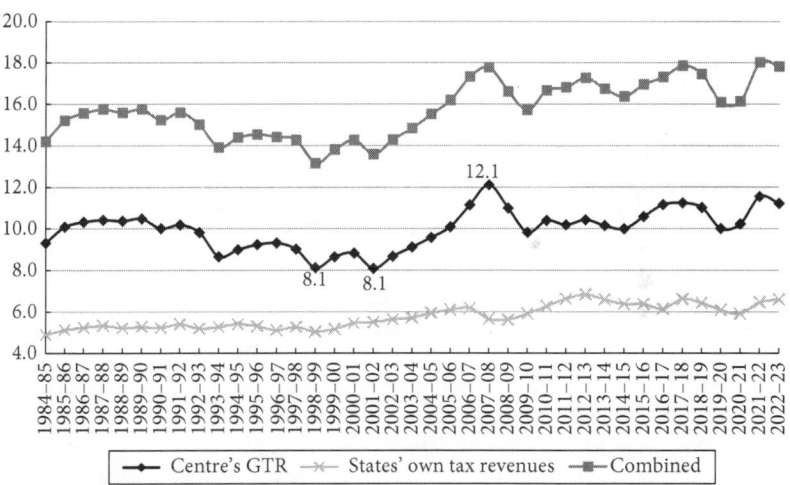

Figure 9.1 Tax-GDP Ratio: Centre, States, and Combined

Source (basic data): MoSPI; https://www.mospi.gov.in/ (Accessed on 7 October 2023), IPFS; https://dea.gov.in/indian-public-finance-statistics (Accessed on 7 October 2023), Union Budgets; https://www.indiabudget.gov.in/ (Accessed on 7 October 2023), CGA; https:// cga.nic.in/ (Accessed on 7 October 2023), RBI; https://rbi.org.in/Scripts/AnnualPublicati ons.aspx?head = State%20Finances%20:%20A%20Study%20of%20Budgets (Accessed on 7 October 2023), CAG; https://cag.gov.in/hi (Accessed on 7 October 2023), and Authors' calculation

government, the size of government in India as measured by total expenditure to GDP ratio appears to have stalled after reaching a level of 26 per cent to 27 per cent of GDP. This may not be an optimal size for the government for an economy like India's which needs to expand its expenditure for its underprovided public and merit services such as education, health, and infrastructure. If the size of the government is to be increased, it would be critical to increase the tax-GDP ratio on a sustained basis.

Empirically, a degree of stability was observed in the share of central and state governments in their combined revenue receipts for the Twelfth and Thirteenth Finance Commissions and some of the earlier Commissions. Here, in the estimation of relative shares of central and state governments, grants given by the centre to the states have been included on the side of the states. The pattern of this stability was changed in favour of states with the recommendations of the Fourteenth Finance Commission. From a share of 64.2 per cent in the combined revenue receipts during the Thirteenth Finance Commission period, the share of states jumped to 68.2 per cent in the period of the Fourteenth Finance Commission (Table 9.1). This is because of the higher level of transfers from the centre to states.

Table 9.1 Share[#] of Centre and States in Combined Revenue Receipts (per cent): Recent Commission Periods

Commission recommendation period	Centre	States
11th FC (2000–1 to 2004–5)	37.1	62.9
12th FC (2005–6 to 2009–10)	38.1	61.9
13th FC (2010–1 to 2014–5)	35.8	64.2
14th FC (2015–6 to 2019–20)	31.8	68.2

Source (basic data): IPFS; https://dea.gov.in/indian-public-finance-statistics (Accessed 7 October 2023), Union budget documents; https://www.indiabudget.gov.in/ (Accessed on 7 October 2023), RBI – State Finances: A Study of Budgets (Various issues); https://rbi.org.in/Scripts/AnnualPubli cations.aspx?head=State%20Finances%20:%20A%20Study%20of%20Budgets(Accessed on 7 October 2023), CAG; https://cag.gov.in/hi (Accessed on 7 October 2023)

[#] relates to the situation after fiscal transfers and adjustment for inter-governmental interest payments

Note: Data on grants from the centre to states after 2015–16 are taken from Statement 16, 'Budget Provision by Head of Account', contained in the Union Budget documents. It includes data on grants-in-aid to the UTs.

Clearly, the centre's access to revenue resources has fallen over time by a substantive margin. This fall is 6.3 per cent points if we compare the average for the Twelfth Finance Commission period (38.1 per cent) with that of the Fourteenth Finance Commission period (31.8 per cent). This has happened despite an increase in the non-sharable cesses and surcharges made by the centre, as already shown in Table 8.1. As a percentage of the divisible pool, the share of the centre's cesses and surcharges are estimated to average 15.5 per cent during the Fourteenth Finance Commission period (2015–16 to 2019–20) and 24.8 per cent during the first three years of the recommendation period of the Fifteenth Finance Commission (2020–1 to 2022–3 (RE)). The Sixteenth Finance Commission may need to examine the issue of the sharp fall in the share of the centre in the combined revenue receipts together with the centre's increasing reliance on cesses and surcharges.

Resolving Horizontal Imbalance

The horizontal dimension of fiscal transfers also has a number of outstanding issues which need to be resolved by the Sixteenth and subsequent Finance Commissions. Per capita GSDP in nominal terms has been used by the Finance Commissions as a proxy for measuring fiscal capacity, which in turn is used as a proxy for measuring state tax bases. There are a number of issues in this context. First, there is a need to augment the measurement of the state tax base by including variables other than the per capita GSDP. In fact, after the transition to the GST, per capita consumption expenditure on goods and services may be a more direct representation of the GST tax base. For other taxes that are still with the states such as VAT/GST on petroleum products, duties on alcohol, motor vehicle tax, and stamp duty and registration fees, more direct measures of the respective tax bases are needed. The second critical issue is that there are large disparities in the per capita GSDPs across states. In determining tax devolution through the distance criterion, it is the nominal per capita GSDP which is used to measure the distance from a benchmark per capita GSDP. This provides a redistributive mechanism in determining fiscal transfers and in this context, a differentiation between Medium and Large (ML) states and Small and Hilly

(SH) states is also not made. The states included in these two groups are given below.

- **ML group of states:** The ML group of states includes Andhra Pradesh, Assam, Bihar, Chhattisgarh, Gujarat, Haryana, Jharkhand, Karnataka, Kerala, Madhya Pradesh, Maharashtra, Odisha, Punjab, Rajasthan, Telangana, Tamil Nadu, Uttar Pradesh, and West Bengal.
- **SH group of states:** The SH group of states includes Arunachal Pradesh, Goa, Himachal Pradesh, Manipur, Meghalaya, Mizoram, Nagaland, Sikkim, Tripura, and Uttarakhand.

This classification is helpful to highlight the relatively higher per capita costs of small and hilly states due to the need for incurring a minimum amount of fixed costs for setting up the administrative and governance structure for a state, or because of higher per capita costs of provision of services due to the nature of the terrain.

Table 9.2 shows that the ratio of the highest per capita income state to the lowest per capita income state continues to be quite high. Considering all states together, this ratio was at 10.1 in 2020–1. This has marginally declined since 2011–2. Even within the group of ML states, this ratio was 5.4 in 2020–1. In fact, it is higher than the corresponding ratio in 2011–2. Within the SH group, this ratio has fallen to some extent but remains as high as 5.1 in 2020–1.

These trends imply that large redistributive transfers would still be called for in the future, as the process of convergence in per capita income levels across states has not been very strong. In fact, for the group of ML states, such convergence is not visible. The higher per capita income states continue to resist large redistributive transfers and relatively high weights to the distance criterion in the tax devolution formula. This problem would become progressively weaker if the process of convergence in growth across states becomes stronger. In fact, the Finance Commission transfers themselves serve as an instrument for accelerating the pace of this convergence.

Apart from fiscal capacity equalization through tax devolution, there is the question of the relative balance between tax devolution and grants as instruments of fiscal transfers. The role of grants in the context of Commissions other than the Fourteenth was to utilize them also as a

Table 9.2 Per Capita GSDP (INR)

State	2011–12	2015–16	2016–17	2017–18	2018–19	2019–20	2020–21
HR	1,16,408	1,83,249	2,04,727	2,29,705	2,47,532	2,66,393	2,61,455
TS	1,00,733	1,55,626	1,75,530	1,98,002	2,31,156	2,54,455	2,55,805
KA	98,567	1,62,796	1,86,072	2,04,934	2,25,144	2,44,381	2,59,803
GJ	1,01,075	1,60,284	1,79,427	2,01,650	2,23,430	2,38,978	2,38,716
KL	1,08,666	1,64,554	1,84,979	2,03,399	2,27,397	2,36,621	2,28,353
TN	1,03,743	1,58,072	1,74,054	1,94,834	2,15,785	2,29,657	2,37,131
MH	1,13,192	1,66,351	1,84,113	1,95,195	2,11,042	2,22,649	2,18,753
AP	76,997	1,19,777	1,34,879	1,54,020	1,70,180	1,87,076	1,95,275
PB	95,379	1,32,467	1,43,124	1,55,840	1,67,378	1,73,119	1,69,457
RJ	62,907	93,094	1,02,422	1,09,780	1,18,640	1,28,325	1,28,495
WB	56,693	83,456	90,426	1,00,014	1,14,045	1,24,182	1,32,932
OR	54,727	75,011	88,934	98,934	1,11,148	1,17,782	1,16,933
CH	61,305	81,907	94,083	99,452	1,10,291	1,17,700	1,17,615
MP	43,023	69,110	81,768	90,094	1,01,647	1,13,224	1,16,169
AS	45,538	68,868	75,869	83,871	90,616	1,00,501	97,508
JH	45,318	58,139	65,405	73,628	82,220	82,276	78,621
UP	35,917	53,113	59,249	65,203	70,565	74,688	71,325
BH	23,525	33,218	37,052	40,065	44,451	48,318	47,983
ML	68,012	1,01,990	1,13,929	1,25,046	1,37,743	1,47,473	1,48,109
Max to min (ML)	4.9	5.5	5.5	5.7	5.6	5.5	5.4
GA	2,89,192	3,65,806	4,15,411	4,54,172	4,67,795	4,85,645	4,86,851
SK	1,81,842	2,81,780	3,19,740	3,97,107	4,30,340	4,71,379	4,72,512
HP	1,05,376	1,59,842	1,74,249	1,91,554	2,03,823	2,17,226	2,12,470
UK	1,13,467	1,65,588	1,80,171	2,00,951	2,07,727	2,11,276	2,06,822
AR	79,530	1,27,474	1,35,665	1,51,754	1,69,351	1,98,769	2,04,935
MZ	65,347	1,27,004	1,41,614	1,64,982	1,84,756	1,76,365	1,49,050
NL	61,159	94,001	1,03,490	1,14,953	1,23,729	1,37,510	1,39,437
TR	51,999	93,248	1,01,385	1,11,151	1,25,405	1,34,973	1,34,325
ML	66,304	76,788	82,127	86,459	92,274	97,615	95,433
MN	44,649	61,906	66,050	78,284	81,364	90,996	97,064
SH	97,546	1,42,390	1,55,593	1,73,048	1,82,827	1,92,066	1,89,327
Max to min (SH)	6.5	5.9	6.3	5.8	5.7	5.3	5.1
All states	68,839	1,03,123	1,15,099	1,26,389	1,39,008	1,48,724	1,49,267
Max to min (ALL)	12.3	11.0	11.2	11.3	10.5	10.1	10.1

Source (basic data): MoSPI; https://www.mospi.gov.in/ (Accessed on 7 October 2023)

means for achieving equalization in the provision of public and merit services. When fiscal capacity equalization is only partially achieved, attempts to equalize at least the standards of services in selected public and merit services may prove to be desirable. However, after the sudden increase in the share of states in the divisible pool of taxes, the central government has become reluctant to accept the Commissions' recommendations with respect to state- and sector-specific grants, as has been the case with the Fifteenth Finance Commission. The only main vehicle of grants that is left is the revenue deficit grants under Article 275(1). The attempts to use a normative approach in determining these revenue deficit grants have been rather weak. The practice of determining 'gap-filling grants' largely continues, although some normative elements are introduced by the Finance Commissions from time to time. Given the relatively lower weight being accorded to grants as an instrument of transfers, it is imperative that in future, the Commissions move towards a full-fledged implementation of a normative approach in determining Article 275(1) grants. Further, focus on selected services such as education, health, and water supply and sanitation would improve the extent of overall equalization if full or near full equalization is attempted in these services. Some suggest that future Finance Commissions should examine the subject of non-merit subsidies in detail and exclude unjustified subsidies in the estimation of Article 275(1) grants. This can, however, run into a political problem. Certainly, a more careful look at non-merit subsidies may be called for if the states are simultaneously running a fiscal deficit well above the norm.

It is also possible to incorporate some elements of cost and need disabilities in the tax devolution formula itself (Srivastava, Bharadwaj, Trehan and Kapur (2019)).[5] Tables 9.3, 9.4, and 9.5 highlight differences in per capita expenditures for education, health, and water supply and sanitation across the three Commission periods. Table 9.3 shows differences in per capita average expenditures with respect to periods covered respectively by the Thirteenth, Fourteenth, and Fifteenth (first report) Finance Commissions. In the case of grants, it is feasible to distinguish between the ML group of states vis-à-vis the SH group of states rather than treating them together. This way, the overall resources required for equalization within each group of states would be lower, whereas inter-group differences in per capita costs would be better reflected. The

Table 9.3 State-Wise Per Capita Education Expenditures (INR)

State	FC13	FC14	FC15(1)
Kerala	3044	5049	4626
Haryana	2759	4298	5318
Chhattisgarh	2325	4265	5743
Maharashtra	2941	4142	5286
Assam	2405	4068	5848
Tamil Nadu	2538	4012	5278
Andhra Pradesh	1991	3879	3981
Rajasthan	1974	3701	4625
Karnataka	2317	3374	3979
Gujarat	2164	3233	3839
Odisha	1823	3225	4031
Punjab	2090	3148	3978
Madhya Pradesh	1573	2889	3642
West Bengal	1856	2672	3723
Uttar Pradesh	1379	2222	2230
Jharkhand	1321	2182	3016
Bihar	1184	1957	2991
ML States	**1972**	**3158**	**3861**
Max to min (ML)	**2.6**	**2.6**	**2.6**
Sikkim	9479	14366	20199
Goa	7012	11295	15463
Mizoram	7326	11007	16503
Arunachal Pradesh	5084	10868	10919
Himachal Pradesh	4849	7392	9719
Nagaland	4268	6970	8186
Uttarakhand	3723	5757	7654
Jammu and Kashmir	2703	5728	9382
Tripura	2877	5413	6737
Meghalaya	3341	5106	7972
Manipur	2695	3876	6847
SH States	**3753**	**6272**	**8990**
Max to min (SH)	**3.5**	**3.7**	**3.0**
All States	**2038**	**3273**	**4050**
Max to min (ALL)	**8.0**	**7.3**	**9.1**

Source (basic data): RBI; https://rbi.org.in/Scripts/AnnualPublications.aspx?head = State%
20Finances%20:% per cent20A per cent20Study per cent20of per cent20Budgets (Accessed 7
October 2023)

Table 9.4 State-Wise Per Capita Health Expenditures (INR)

State	FC13	FC14	FC15(1)
Kerala	914	1772	2218
Tamil Nadu	709	1303	2016
Rajasthan	564	1246	1603
Andhra Pradesh	643	1242	1729
Haryana	594	1183	1857
Chhattisgarh	482	1182	1961
Assam	499	1141	2158
Gujarat	531	1075	1530
Karnataka	580	1068	1477
Odisha	417	1019	1781
Punjab	614	975	1243
Maharashtra	535	938	1460
West Bengal	441	818	1205
Madhya Pradesh	411	792	1037
Jharkhand	287	666	1063
Uttar Pradesh	358	652	754
Bihar	198	457	765
ML States	**483**	**942**	**1338**
Max to min (ML)	**4.6**	**3.9**	**2.9**
Arunachal Pradesh	2217	5492	6521
Goa	2712	4948	7718
Sikkim	2404	4097	7594
Mizoram	2020	3774	5980
Nagaland	1382	2590	3291
Himachal Pradesh	1364	2349	3565
Jammu and Kashmir	1107	2190	3903
Meghalaya	1124	2112	3043
Tripura	802	1689	2443
Manipur	966	1600	2656
Uttarakhand	826	1489	1919
SH States	**1157**	**2136**	**3313**
Max to min (SH)	**3.4**	**3.7**	**4.0**
All States	**508**	**986**	**1411**
Max to min (ALL)	**13.7**	**12.0**	**10.2**

Source (basic data): RBI; https://rbi.org.in/Scripts/AnnualPublications.aspx?head = State%20
Finances%20:%20A%20Study%20of%20Budgets (Accessed 7 October 2023)

Table 9.5 State-Wise Per Capita Expenditures on Water Supply and Sanitation (INR)

State	FC13	FC14	FC15(1)
Haryana	453	628	792
Odisha	163	599	722
Karnataka	83	511	238
Rajasthan	249	392	450
Chhattisgarh	160	345	267
Jharkhand	124	343	250
Andhra Pradesh	102	303	125
Madhya Pradesh	100	252	99
Maharashtra	103	242	443
Bihar	46	197	289
Assam	127	195	258
Kerala	152	195	128
West Bengal	94	159	76
Gujarat	60	144	135
Tamil Nadu	57	137	137
Punjab	120	123	221
Uttar Pradesh	19	41	63
ML States	**101**	**235**	**242**
Max to min (ML)	**23.8**	**15.3**	**12.6**
Arunachal Pradesh	1514	4085	5448
Goa	1564	2187	3215
Mizoram	1117	1688	1880
Himachal Pradesh	983	1405	1305
Jammu and Kashmir	599	975	1383
Sikkim	371	737	1033
Meghalaya	456	653	816
Uttarakhand	450	427	379
Nagaland	230	423	458
Tripura	173	398	524
Manipur	198	177	356
SH States	**579**	**817**	**975**
Max to min (SH)	**9.0**	**23.1**	**15.3**
All States	**118**	**256**	**269**
Max to min (ALL)	**82.3**	**99.6**	**86.5**

Source (basic data): RBIhttps://rbi.org.in/Scripts/AnnualPublications.aspx?head = State%20 Finances%20:%20A%20Study%20of%20Budgets (Accessed 7 October 2023)

maximum to minimum ratio for the ML group in the case of per capita education expenditures is relatively lower than that for the SH group. In both cases, the differences are much lower than the corresponding differences in per capita GSDP levels. This means a full equalization in education can be achieved with relatively lower overall resources needed for redistribution.

This situation is also replicated in the case of health expenditures although the disparities are somewhat higher than those in the case of education expenditures. Table 9.4 gives the relevant state-wise and average figures. The argument for achieving better equalization with fewer resources is applicable in this case also.

The profile of per capita expenditures in the case of water supply and sanitation, however, shows much larger disparities (Table 9.5). Aiming for equalization across states within each group may call for larger redistributive transfers. However, the per capita expenditures involved for the ML group of states for water supply and sanitation are much lower. Thus, overall resource requirements may still be manageable in this case.

It is thus arguable that higher and more comprehensive equalization also covering cost and need disabilities can be achieved through grants rather than fiscal capacity equalization by allocating fewer resources for redistributive transfers.

Considering together tax devolution and grants, to evolve a comprehensive approach towards redistributive transfers, we may note that the distance criterion implies relatively larger shares for relatively lower-income states. At present, it is given the highest weight of 45 per cent. Any increase in this weight would imply a lowering of shares of the higher-income states. Many of the richer states argue for a lowering of the weight given to the distance criterion. At the same time, the needs of the lower-income states require to be given due attention. In fact, it is the lower-income states which will provide a relatively larger share of the so-called 'demographic dividend' to India in the future years, provided adequate attention is paid to the education and health needs of the population in these states. It may be useful to consider freezing the weight to the distance criterion at the current level, but some automatic upward adjustment in the resources transferred to the poorer states may be brought about through the route of grants. In fact, equalization of the provision of education and health services should be given priority in the overall scheme of resource transfers. Instead of using a large number of tax devolution criteria, the transfer of resources to individual states may be guided by the equalization principle using a limited number of criteria such as population, area, and distance, supplemented by a suitable scheme of grants. In the literature on fiscal federalism, it has been shown that the equalization principle is consistent with both equity and efficiency. This principle is used in well-established federations such as Canada and Australia. The basic consideration of reflecting needs, unit costs of providing publicly provided goods and services including merit services, and equity considerations can all be reflected through these three criteria provided these are more finely tuned by using additional and relevant information in the formulation of the devolution criteria.

The arguments about equalization in the context of horizontal transfers can and should be extended also in the context of local governments. In this volume, the subject of fiscal transfer to the third tier of government has not been discussed in detail. It is clear that local public goods have a significant role to play in improving the welfare of the citizens within their jurisdictions. Just as we have emphasized the importance of equalization in the inter-state distribution of resources, there needs to be an emphasis on carrying the principle forward to the level of local governments. This task has been constitutionally mandated to be overseen by State Finance Commissions. The performance of the State Finance Commissions has been rather heterogeneous across states. Much needs to be done to improve the position of resources of the local governments and the provision of local public goods. The primary role here is that of the states, even though the Finance Commission may also allocate a certain quantum of grants.

Challenges Posed by the Implementation of GST and Its Needed Reforms

The implementation of GST in India is still not complete. Many major goods could not be included in the present GST such as petroleum products, alcoholic liquor, real estate, electricity, and agriculture (see Mehta and Mukherjee (2021)). These items are of significant revenue importance both for the central and state governments. The continuation of taxation of these products outside GST provides a limited degree of residual revenue autonomy to both the central and state governments. Given the need to improve the revenue performance of GST, neither the central government nor the state governments are in favour of including these items excluded from GST.

Incomplete GST reforms appear to have entered a gridlock which none of the participating governments are willing to break out of, at least in the short to medium term. It is argued that there is only one way the GST reforms can be completed while ensuring revenue adequacy as well as revenue autonomy for the participating governments (see Srivastava (2022)). This way is to integrate environmental and demerit taxes in the GST by including a non-rebatable cess in the GST scheme of taxation, and giving a degree of autonomy for the participating governments to fix the rate of this cess. Such a cess or additional non-refundable levy may be levied by both the centre and the states and the rate of such a cess can be different for the centre and individual states. For instance, in the case of petroleum products and alcoholic liquor, these rates may be fixed with a view to raising revenues consistent with their current revenues from these items.

Another GST issue relates to its revenue performance. States were guaranteed a 14 per cent growth on their base year revenues at the point of transition. However, the assumptions on which such a growth rate was projected were not realized in practice. The actual growth of GST revenues as a whole from 2017–8 to 2021–2 was 5.7 per cent (excluding compensation cess) and 7.3 per cent (including compensation cess). Thus, the 14 per cent growth figure proved to be too optimistic. The low GST revenue growth numbers reflect relatively lower buoyancy which may be a function of GST's effective rate and the corresponding nominal GDP growth during the period. The compound annual growth rate (CAGR) of nominal GDP has also been lower from 2017–8 to 2021–2 at 8.3 per cent as compared to 11.1 per cent from 2013–4 to 2017–8.

Fortunately, the GST compensation mechanism is not to be extended beyond 2025–6. This will facilitate increasing the effective GST rate by incorporating increases in the rates in various GST rate groups. According to the RBI, the weighted average GST rate was estimated at 11.6 per cent for July and September 2019 as compared to the

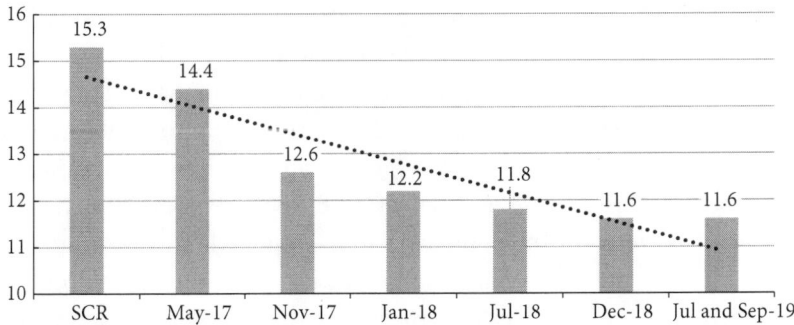

Figure 9.2 Weighted Average (Effective) GST Rate

Source (basic data): RBI Bulletin September 2019; https://rbidocs.rbi.org.in/rdocs/Bulle
tin/PDFs/RBIBULL092019_F9C3EF9F35AF34BC08C4736D2B6AC3E47.PDF (Accessed 7
October 2023) and Authors' creation

Note: SCR refers to Subramanian Committee recommendation

RNR of 14.4 per cent in May 2017, prior to the implementation of the
GST. In fact, the sequence of revisions in the GST rates through various
GST Council meetings led to the continuing reduction in the effective
GST rates as shown in Figure 9.2, sourced from the RBI (Bulletin
September 2019).

Thus, two major changes in the GST that are now needed relate to
raising GST's effective rate and increasing the scope of GST to cover
some of the major goods and services that have been left out in the initial
transition.

Considerations of Resource, Environmental, and Ecological Externalities

One dimension of fiscal federalism which has not found due consideration in the scheme of transfers determined by the Finance Commissions
so far relates to the endogenization of costs borne by some of the resource-
rich states that suffer from environmental hazards and pollution. These
costs pertain both to positive externalities such as those emanating from
forests, and negative externalities such as those emanating from the ex-
traction of minerals. In the case of forests, areas under forest provide

benefits to the country as a whole but large tracts of land are not available for cultivation or other alternative economic uses to the states where these forests are located. Similarly, not much attention has been paid to cost disadvantages associated with desert areas, proximity to oceans, proximity to international borders, and so on. In the case of mining of coal and various other minerals, considerable pollution leading to health hazards is suffered by the population in the states where these minerals are located. In the case of major minerals, except for the limited royalty received by the concerned states, there is not much compensation to the citizens of these states for the health hazards that they bear. For a discussion of these environmental costs, reference may be made to Srivastava and Kumar (2014) and Srivastava (2022).[6]

The sharing of water resources, particularly river water, is also a major aspect of inter-state relations which has a bearing on the fiscal and economic parameters of the states. The sharing of river water has been a source of tension among states and needs to be resolved.

Managing Fiscal Imbalances and Stabilization: The Relative Role of Centre and States

The centre's FRBM was amended in 2018, as discussed in Chapter 8. Provisions in this amendment have been rendered out of alignment because of the large departure of the general government debt-GDP ratio at the end of 2020–1, which is estimated to be more than 30 per cent higher than its target value of 60 per cent. Given the history of correction in the debt-GDP ratio, bringing it down to 60 per cent may prove to be extremely challenging. The average annual rate of change in the combined debt-GDP ratio over the period from 1990–1 to 2019–20 is 0.030 percentage points of GDP, with some patches where inter-year variations were relatively larger.[7] This historical experience shows that achieving a reduction of more than 30 percentage points would prove to be an uphill task. In recasting the fiscal consolidation framework, it will be useful to consider a feasible and realistic adjustment path to achieve the sustainable targets of debt and fiscal deficit.

While revising the existing FRBM framework, there is a need to correct the internal inconsistency between debt and deficit targets for the central and state governments. There is an inconsistency between the centre's debt-GDP target of 40 per cent with its fiscal deficit target of 3 per cent. Similarly, there is an inconsistency between the states' debt-GDP target of 20 per cent and their fiscal deficit target of 3 per cent.[8] There has to be symmetry between debt and deficit targets.

Also, the macro-stabilization conditions in the 2018 FRBM proved to be ineffective and impractical. In the new FRBM, it would be appropriate to consider a more practical and effective specification of the departures from the specified adjustment paths and target values for meeting the macro-stabilization objectives. It is also useful to recognize that in India, even the states may have a supplementary role in macro-stabilization for two main reasons. First, some of the states in India are quite large and their government expenditures may affect the overall aggregate demand. Second, there is a difference between the periodicity and amplitude of agricultural cycles vis-à-vis the non-agricultural cycles. States may have a more direct role in dealing with the agricultural cycles since agriculture is a state subject (for detailed discussion, see Srivastava et al. (2021)).

Reforms of Institutional Framework Governing Centre-State Financial Relations

In the context of institutional reforms relating to managing centre-state fiscal relations, the Finance Commissions have made various recommendations from time to time but with little response from the central government. Many of these problems need to be attended to in the future. Some of these are summarized below.

- **Absence of institutional memory of Finance Commission:** In the working of the Finance Commissions, the non-availability of a permanent secretariat and a continuing institutional memory can be identified as a major avenue whereby the working of the Commission can be made more efficient. Why this has not been done so far in spite of recommendations by almost all of the recent Finance Commissions remains an issue.
- **Sharing of GST data:** GST Council, through GSTN, has access to extensive economic data of critical importance. These include tax

revenue data, tax base data, input tax credit data, output tax data, import and export data, data on inter-state movement of goods and services, and so on. Several aspects of GST data are of critical importance. Preliminary analysis based on the GSTN, as summarized by the Economic Survey 2017–18, has already provided a number of valuable insights regarding the Indian economy.[9] Currently, such valuable data are not being shared. However, this data needs to be shared on a continuous basis among different tiers of the government and also with economists, analysts, and the public at large. There is a need to develop a clear format in which GST data should be made available to potential users through a centralized website.

- **Underperformance of State Finance Commissions:** State Finance Commissions have performed in a very heterogeneous way across states. Their appointments have been irregular and the status of implementation of their recommendations has also not met expectations. The availability of fiscal data regarding local governments has also been quite inadequate.

- **Role of National Development Council (NDC)[10] in the post Planning Commission era:** The role of the NDC after the abolition of the Planning Commission and the setting up of the NITI needs to be streamlined so that the NDC can effectively play the role of an apex body where state governments are represented, in the formulation of economic policy to guide India's overall development effort.

- **Energizing the Inter-State Council:** The Inter-State Council has been characterized by very few meetings and very little impact on the working of federal relations in the country. They have met only twelve times in twenty-eight years since 1990, showing an average of 0.4 meetings per year. Since the Inter-State Council is a constitutional body, more needs to be done if it is to play a proactive and meaningful role.

- **Loan Council:** The Twelfth Finance Commission had recommended (paragraph 15.7 of the Report) that the overall limit to the annual borrowing of states from all sources should be supervised by an independent body like a Loan Council, with representatives from the Ministry of Finance, Planning Commission (erstwhile), Reserve Bank of India, and the state governments.

This Council may, at the beginning of each year, announce borrowing limits for each state, taking into account the sustainability considerations. A Loan Council has worked effectively in the case of Australia, where capital expenditures by the sub-national governments are also incorporated while fixing borrowing limits. In due course, the Loan Council may be evolved into a full-fledged Fiscal Council.

Concluding Observations

Two core concerns of the Finance Commission relate to resolving vertical and horizontal imbalances in determining fiscal transfers to the sub-national governments. The vertical imbalance arises from the provisions of the Constitution which have provided relatively larger resources to the central government and relatively larger responsibilities to the state governments. The existence of a concurrent list provides for a number of joint responsibilities. Fiscal transfers from the central to the state governments have facilitated establishing a balance for the state governments such that post transfer, resources available to the state governments enable them to meet their larger responsibilities. Empirically, a degree of stability was observed in the share of central and state governments in their combined revenue receipts after transfers, especially for the period covered by the Eleventh, Twelfth, and Thirteenth Finance Commissions This share has ranged between 61.9 per cent and 64.2 per cent for the states and 35.8 per cent and 38.1 per cent for the centre (Table 9.1). With the Fourteenth Finance Commission, this stability was modified in favour of the states as they sharply increased the share of states in the divisible pool of taxes from 32 per cent to 42 per cent. This trend continued in the period of the Fifteenth Finance Commission. However, the central government has attempted to claw back some of the fiscal space ceded to the states by increasing the share of cesses and surcharges that do not form a part of the divisible pool, and by not accepting some of the state- and sector-specific grants in the case of the Fifteenth Finance Commission. In fact, the role of cesses and surcharges should be considered together with the sharp fall in the centre's share in the combined revenue receipts (Table 9.1).

In the case of horizontal imbalances, considerable differences in relative fiscal capacity and cost and need disabilities in providing public and merit services by the state governments continue to persist. There are various difficulties in recommending a scheme of fiscal transfers which is redistributive enough to ensure equalization of standards of services across states. Every Finance Commission has to make a call as to the extent of redistributive transfers that they are willing to recommend. As and when differences in per capita fiscal capacities reduce across states, the extent of redistributive transfers will also fall. It is still important to suitably measure the degree of equalization achieved by any scheme of fiscal transfers, so that the Commission is able to explicitly target the desired degree of equalization in their period of recommendation. There is also a need to consider the next generation of reforms in regard to the devolution formula. This would require the use of indicators such as population and area in modified ways, where additional weights are given to segments of population and area that account for higher unit costs in the public provision of services. Some illustrations have been provided in Srivastava (2022).

In this context, the subject of balancing resources and responsibilities at the level of local governments is also equally important. Here, the Constitution has provided for a critical role for the State Finance Commissions. It is important to extend the principle of equalization to the third tier of governance with a view to improving the welfare of citizens in the local jurisdictions both urban and rural.

Other important aspects in the context of horizontal transfers relate to endogenizing a number of environmental, ecological, and resource externalities. Mineral-rich states bear a significant amount of pollution costs and health hazards. Forest-rich states extend positive externalities by absorbing carbon emissions for the benefit of the other non-forest states. These externalities are not adequately reflected in the scheme of fiscal transfers, although some consideration has been given to the maintenance and development of forests by some of the recent Commissions. There has to be an attempt to replace the continuing gap-filling approach for determining Article 275(1) grants with a more genuine norm-based and equalization-consistent determination of these grants.

In the context of macro-stabilization, and the stabilization of debt and deficit of the central and the state governments, more reforms are needed in the centre's FRBMA and the Sixteenth Finance Commission may be required to play a significant role in recalibrating the path of fiscal balances of the central and state governments beyond suggesting modified benchmarks for sustainable debt and deficit targets.

GST reforms are also incomplete since a number of important taxes levied by the centre and the states are still outside of its ambit, including taxes on petroleum products, state excise duty, electricity duty, stamp duty and registration fees, and the motor vehicle tax. Many of these taxes are highly revenue productive. Some important ones such as taxes on petroleum products and state excise duties on alcoholic products relate to polluting and demerit goods. One method for including these within GST while maintaining their revenue productivity and their consumption constraining role is to levy on them a non-rebatable levy or cess within the GST framework. The Sixteenth Finance Commission may also consider ways in which it can facilitate the completion of the GST reforms.

The institutional backdrop of maintaining centre-state fiscal relations also requires further reforms. The setting up of a Loan Council and a permanent secretariat for the Finance Commission needs to be given adequate priority. In fact, the compilation of up-to-date economic and fiscal data can be considered a critical efficiency measure. Currently, every Finance Commission has to start virtually afresh in the compilation of data that they need. There are many agencies, such as the GST Council, which need to share GST collection data in far greater detail than they presently do. A suitable information base would also facilitate the work of State Finance Commissions. The data repository of a permanent secretariat of the centre's Finance Commission can also be accessed by the State Finance Commissions.

Notes

1. https://pib.gov.in/PressReleaseIframePage.aspx?PRID = 1980688
2. Final Report of the Fifteenth Finance Commission (2021). Paragraph numbers 3.63 to 3.65; Srivastava (2023b); Sharma and Swenden (2022); Srivastava (2022).
3. https://pib.gov.in/Pressreleaseshare.aspx?PRID = 1579123
4. https://frontline.thehindu.com/news/jammu-kashmir-supreme-court-upholds-abrogation-of-article-370-in-landmark-decision/article67627243.ece
5. This subject is discussed in greater detail in Srivastava (2023b).

6. Srivastava and Kumar (2014); Srivastava (2022).

7. Srivastava et al. (2021).

8. For a detailed discussion, see Srivastava (2023 a, c), Srivastava, Bharadwaj, Kapur and Trehan (2020, 2021).

9. Report of the Committee on Fiscal Statistics, National Statistical Commission, Government of India (September 2018); https://www.mospi.gov.in/sites/defa ult/files/committee_reports/Report%20of%20the%20Committee%20on%20 Fiscal%20Statistics.pdf

10. The National Development Council (NDC) or Rashtriya Vikas Parishad, is the apex body for deliberations on development matters in India. It was set up on 6 August 1952 to strengthen and mobilize the effort and resources of the nation in support of the Plan, to promote common economic policies in all vital spheres, and to ensure the balanced and rapid development of all parts of the country.

References

Abel, Andrew B.N., Gregory Mankiw, Lawrence H. Summers, and Richard J. Zeckhauser (1989), 'Assessing Dynamic Efficiency: Theory and Evidence', *Review of Economic Studies*, Vol. 56, pp. 1–20.

Alesina, Alberto, and Roberto Perotti (1995), 'Fiscal Expansions and Adjustments in OECD Countries', *Economic Policy*, Vol. 10, No. 21, pp. 207–48.

Alesina, Alberto, Reza Baqir, and Willian Easterley (1997), 'Public Goods and Ethnic Divisions', NBER, Working Paper No. 6009.

Annett, Anthony (2000), 'Socio Fractionalization, Political Instability, and the Size of Government', IMF, Working Paper 00/82.

Aubut, Julie, and F. Vaillancourt (2001), 'Using GDP in Equalization Calculations: Are There Meaningful Measurement Issues', IIGR, Working Paper, Queens University.

Australian Loan Council (1993), *Future Arrangements for Loan Council Monitoring and Reporting*, Department of Parliament Library, Parliament of Commonwealth of Australia, Canberra.

Bahl, Roy W., and Johannes F. Linn (1992), *Urban Public Finance in Developing Countries*, Oxford University Press, New York.

Barrel, R., J. Morgan, J. Sefton, and J. in't Veld (1994), 'The Cyclical Adjustment of Budget Balances', *National Institute Report*, No. 8, Report for the European Commission.

Barro, Robert J. (1974), 'Are Government Bonds Net Wealth?', *Journal of Political Economy*, November/December, Vol. 82, No. 6, pp. 1095–117.

Barro, Robert J. (1976), 'Reply to Feldstein and Buchanan', *Journal of Political Economy*, Vol. 84, No. 2, pp. 343–49.

Barro, Robert J. (1979), 'On the Determination of the Public Debt', *Journal of Political Economy*, October, Vol. 87, No. 5, pp. 940–71.

Barro, Robert J. (1987), 'Government Spending, Interest Rates, Prices, and Budget Deficits in the United Kingdom, 1701–1918', *Journal of Monetary Economics*, Vol. 20, No. 2, pp. 221–47.

Barro, Robert J. (1989), 'The Ricardian Approach to Budget Deficit', *Journal of Economic Perspectives*, Vol. 3, No. 2, pp. 37–54.

Barro, Stephen (2002), 'Macroeconomic Versus RTS Measures of Fiscal Capacity: Theoretical Foundations and Implications for Canada', IIGR, Working Paper, Queens University.

Barsky, Robert B., N. Gregory Mankiw, and Stephen P. Zeldes (1986), 'Ricardian Consumers with Keynesian Propensities', *American Economic Review*, Vol. 76, No. 4, pp. 676–91.

Bernheim, B. Douglas (1989), 'A Neoclassical Perspective on Budget Deficits', *Journal of Economic Perspectives*, Vol. 3, No. 2, pp. 55–72.

Bernheim, B. Douglas, and Kyle Bagwell (1988), 'Is Everything Neutral?', *Journal of Political Economy*, Vol. 96, No. 2, pp. 308–38.Bernnan, Geoffrey, and Jonathan

Pincus (1998), 'Is Vertical Fiscal Imbalance So Inefficient? Or the Flypaper Effect Is Not an Anomaly?', School of Economics, Working Papers 1998–2006, University of Adelaide, Adelaide.

Besley, Timothy, and Stephen Coate (2003), 'Centralized versus Decentralized Provision of Local Public Goods: A Political Economy Approach', *Journal of Public Economics*, Vol. 87, pp. 2611–37.

Bhatt, Antra, and Pasquale Scaramozzino (2015), 'Federal Transfers and Fiscal Discipline in India: An Empirical Evaluation', *Public Finance Review*, Vol. 43, No. 1, pp. 53–81.

Bird, Richard, and Andrey Tarasov (2002), 'Closing the Gap: Fiscal Imbalances and Intergovernmental Transfers in Developed Federations', International Studies Program, Working Paper Series, at Andrew Young School of Policy Studies, GSU paper 0202, Georgia State University.

Bird, Richard, and Pierre-Pascal Gendron (2000), 'CVAT, VIVAT, and Dual VAT: Vertical "Sharing" and Interstate Trade', *International Tax and Public Finance*, Vol. 7, No. 6, pp. 753–61.

Bird, Richard M. (1993), 'Threading the Fiscal Labyrinth: Some Issues in Fiscal Decentralization', *National Tax Journal*, Vol. 46, pp. 207–27.

Boadway, R. (1996), 'Review of the Uneasy Case for Equalization Payments by Dan Usher', *National Tax Journal*, Vol. 49, No. 4, pp. 677–86.

Boadway, R. (2001), 'Revisiting Equalization Again: RTS vs. Macro Approaches', IIGR, Working Paper, Queens University.

Boadway, R., K. Cuff, and M. Marchand (2002), 'Equalization and the Decentralization of Revenue-Raising in a Federation', *Journal of Public Economic Theory*, Vol. 5, pp. 201–28.

Boadway, R., and F. Flatters (1982), 'Efficiency and Equalization Payments in a Federal System of Government: A Synthesis and Extension of Recent Results', *Journal of Economics*, Vol. 15, No. 4, pp. 613–33.

Boadway, R., and P. Hobson (1993), 'Intergovernmental Finance in Canada', Canadian Tax Foundation, *Canadian Tax Papers*, No. 96, Toronto.

Boadway, R., and Jean-Francois Tremblay (2005), 'A Theory of Vertical Fiscal Imbalance', IFIR, Working Paper Series, April.

Boadway, R., M. Marchand, and M. Vigneault (1998), 'The Consequences of Overlapping Tax Bases for Redistribution and Public Spending in a Federation', *Journal of Public Economics*, Vol. 8, pp. 255–73.

Boadway, R. and Michael Keen (1996), 'Efficiency and the Optimal Direction of Federal-State Transfers', *International Tax and Public Finance*, Kluwer Academic Foundation, Vol. 3, No. 2, pp. 137–55.

Boothe, Paul (2001), 'The Stabilization Properties of Equalization: Evidence from Saskatchewan', IIGR, Working Paper, Queens University.Bradford, F. David, and Wallace E. Oates (1971a), 'Towards a Predictive Theory of Intergovernmental Grants', *American Economic Review*, Vol. 61, No. 2, pp. 440–8.

Bradford, F. David, and Wallace E. Oates (1971b), 'An Analysis of Revenue Sharing in a New Approach to Collective Fiscal Decisions', *Quarterly Journal of Economics*, Vol. 85, No. 3, pp. 416–39.

Bradner, P., L. Diebalek, and H. Schuberth (1998), 'Structural Budget Deficits and Sustainability of Fiscal Positions in the European Union', Working Paper, No. 26, Oesterreichische National Bank.

Brennan, Geoffrey, and James M. Buchanan (1977), 'Towards a Tax Constitution for Leviathan', *Journal of Public Economics*, Vol. 8, No. 3, pp. 255–73.

Brennan, Geoffrey, and James M. Buchanan (1980), *The Power to Tax: Analytical Foundations of a Fiscal Constitution*, Cambridge University Press, Cambridge.

Breton, Albert (1998) *Competitive Governments: An Economic Theory of Politics and Public Finance*, Cambridge University Press, Cambridge.

Buchanan, J.M. (1950), 'Federalism and Equity', *American Economic Review*, Vol. 40, No. 4, pp. 583–599.

Buchanan, J.M. (1952), 'Federal Grants and Resource Allocation', *Journal of Political Economy*, Vol. 60, No. 6, pp. 208–17.

Buchanan, J.M., and R.A. Musgrave (1999), 'Public Finance and Public Choice: Two Contrasting Visions of the State', *MIT Press*, Cambridge, Massachusetts, p. 272.

Buchanan, J.M., and R.E. Wagner (1971), 'An Efficiency Basis for Federal Fiscal Equalization', in J. Margolis (ed.), *Analysis of Public Output*, National Bureau of Economic Research, Princeton.

Buiter, W.H. (1985), 'Guide to Public Sector Deficit and Debt', *Economic Policy*, November, pp. 13–79.

Buiter, W.H. (1988), 'Some Thoughts on the Role of Fiscal Policy in Stabilization and Structural Adjustment in Developing Countries', NBER, Working Paper No. 2603, May.

Buiter, W.H., and Urjit R. Patel (1992), 'Debt, Deficits and Inflation: An Application to the Public Finances of India', *Journal of Public Economics*, Vol. 47, March, pp. 172–305.

Cano, L., and A. Kanutin (1996), 'Estimation of Structural Deficits in EU Countries', *mimeo*, LSE.

Careaga, Maite, and Barry R. Weingast (2000), 'The Fiscal Pact with the Devil: A Positive Approach to Fiscal Federalism, Revenue Sharing, and Good Governance', Working Paper, Stanford University.

Chakraborty, Lekha, S. (2002), 'Fiscal Deficit and Rate of Interest: An Econometric Analysis of the Deregulated Financial Regime', *Economic and Political Weekly*, Vol. 37, No. 19, 11 May.

Chanda, Asok (1965), *Federalism in India: A Study of Union-State Relations*, Hillary House, New York.

Chelliah, R.J. (1996), 'The Meaning and Significance of the Fiscal Deficit', in *Towards Sustainable Growth: Essays in Fiscal and Financial State Reforms in India*, Oxford University Press, New Delhi.

Chelliah, R.J. (2001), 'The Nature of the Fiscal Crisis in Indian Federation and Calibrating Fiscal Policy', *Money and Finance*, ICRA Bulletin, Vol. 2, Nos 4–5.

Chelliah, R.J. (2004), 'Implementing FRBM Act, 2003: Evaluating Kelkar Task Force Report', *Economic and Political Weekly*, September.

Chelliah, R.J. (2006), 'A Tract on Reform of Fiscal Federal Relations in India', Madras School of Economics, Monograph Series, No. 1.

Chernick, H. (1992), 'A Model of the Distributional Incidence of State and Local Taxes', *Public Finance Quarterly*, October, pp. 572–85.

Chrystal, Alec K., and D. Kevin (1987), 'Would a Higher Fiscal Deficit Stimulate the Economy?', *Fiscal Studies*, Vol. 8, No 1, February.

Collins, D.J. (2000), 'The Impact of the GST Package on Commonwealth State Financial Relations', *Australian Tax Research Foundation*, Research Study No.

34, Sydney.Commonwealth Grants Commission (1983), *Equality in Diversity Commonwealth Grants Commission* (Australia), Australian Government Publishing Service, Canberra.

Commonwealth Grants Commission (1994), 'The Distortionary Effect of Rising Taxes', in R. Robson and W. Scarth (eds), *Deficit Reduction: What Pain, What Gain?* The C.D. Howe Institute, 1994, pp. 44–72.

Commonwealth Grants Commission (1995), *Equality in Diversity: History of the Commonwealth Grants Commission*, 2nd edition, AGPS, Canberra.

Commonwealth Grants Commission (1999), *Report on General Revenue Grant Relativities, Volume II: Methods, Assessments and Analysis*, Commonwealth of Australia, Canberra, p. 184.

Commonwealth Grants Commission (2004), *Report on State Revenue Sharing Relativities*, Review, Canberra.

Commonwealth Grants Commission (2021), 'New Arrangements for Distributing GST', Occasional Paper No. 4. September 2021. doi: https://www.cgc.gov.au/publi cations/occasional-paper-4-new-arrangements-distributing-gst

Commonwealth Grants Commission (2023), 'GST Distribution to States and Territories in 2023–24', Occasional Paper No. 9.14 March. doi: https://www.cgc. gov.au/publications/occasional-paper-9-gst-distribution-states-and-territor ies-2023-24

Compson, M., and J. Navratil (1997) 'An Improved Method for Estimating the Total Taxable Resources of the States', Research Paper, US Department of the Treasury, Washington DC.

Comptroller and Auditor General of India (2003), *Report of the CAG on the Union Government*, Union Government (Civil), Accounts of the Union Government (1 of 2003), New Delhi.

Corden, W.M. (1997), *The Road to Reform: Essays on Australian Economic Policy*, Addison-Wesley, Melbourne.

Courchene, T.J. (1984), *Equalization Payments: Past, Present, and Future*, Ontario Economic Council, Toronto.

Courchene, T.J. (1992), 'Mon Pays, C'est L'hiver: Reflections of a Market Populist', *Canadian Journal of Economics*, Vol. 25, No. 4, pp. 759–91.

Dahlby, Bev (1996), 'Fiscal Externalities and the Design of Intergovernmental Grants', *International Tax and Public Finance*, Vol. 3, pp. 397–412.

Dahlby, Bev (2008), 'The Canadian Federal-Provincial Fiscal Equalization System', CESifo DICE Report, Vol. 6, No. 1, pp. 3–9.

Dahlby, Bev, and L.S. Wilson (1994), 'Fiscal Capacity, Tax Effort and Optimal Equalization Grants', *Canadian Journal of Economics*, Vol. 27, No. 3, pp. 657–72.

Dahlby, B., Feehan, J. P., Ferede, E., and Joanis, M. (2014), 'Four New Studies of the Canadian Equalization System', *The School of Public Policy Publications*, Vol. 6, No. 6, pp. 1–10.

Davoodi, Hamid, and Heng-fu Zou (1998), 'Fiscal Decentralization and Economic Growth', *Journal of Urban Economics*, Vol. 43, pp. 244–57.

Department of Finance, Government of Canada (2023, 29 September), 'Federal Transfers to Provinces and Territories'. Retrieved from Government of Canada: https://www.canada.ca/en/department-finance/programs/federal-transfers.html

Dixon, P.B., M.R. Picton, and M.T. Rimmer (2002), 'Efficiency Effects of Inter-Government Financial Transfers in Australia', *Australian Economic Review*, Vol. 5, No. 3, pp. 304–15.

Domar, E. (1944), 'The "Burden" of Public Debt and National Income', *American Economic Review*, Vol. 34, No. 4, pp. 798–827.

Eisner, Robert (1989), 'Budget Deficits: Rhetoric and Reality', *Journal of Economic Perspectives*, Vol. 3, No. 2, Spring, pp. 73–93.

Eisner, Robert, and Paul J. Pieper (1984), 'A New View of the Federal Debt and Budget Deficit', *American Economic Review*, Vol. 74, pp. 11–29, March.

Engle, R.F., and C.W.J. Granger (1987), 'Cointegration and Error Correction: Representation, Estimation and Testing', *Econometrica*, Vol. 55, pp. 251–76.

Feld, Lars P., and Gebhard Kirchgässner (1999), 'Public Debt and Budgetary Procedures: Top Down or Bottom Up? Some Evidence from Swiss Municipalities', in James Poterba and Jürgen von Hagen (eds), *Fiscal Institutions and Fiscal Performance*, National Bureau of Economic Research, Cambridge, pp. 151–80.

Feld, Lars P., and John G. Matsusaka (2003), 'Budget Referendums and Government Spending: Evidence from Swiss Cantons', *Journal of Public Economics*, Vol. 87, No. 12, pp. 2703–24.

Feldstein, Martin S. (1976), 'Perceived Wealth in Bonds and Social Security: A Comment', *Journal of Political Economy*, Vol. 84, No. 2, pp. 331–6.

FRBM Review Committee report (January 2017), 'Responsible Growth: A Debt and Fiscal Framework for 21st Century India', https://dea.gov.in/sites/default/files/Vol umepercent201percent20FRBMpercent20Reviewpercent20Committeepercent2 0Report.pdf

Gale, William G., and Peter R. Orszag (2002), 'The Economic Effects of Long Term Fiscal Discipline', *Urban-Brookings Tax Policy Center Discussion Paper*, 17 December.

Garnaut, R. (2002), 'Equity and Australian Development: Lessons from the First Century', *Australian Economic Review*, Vol. 35, No. 3, pp. 227–43.

Garnaut, R., and V. FitzGerald (2002a), 'Issues in Commonwealth-State Funding', *Australian Economic Review*, Vol. 35, No. 3, pp. 290–300.

Garnaut, R., and V. FitzGerald (2002b), 'Final Report of the Committee for the Review of Commonwealth-State Funding', Melbourne, Victoria.

Gordon, Roger (1983), 'An Optimal Tax Approach to Fiscal Federalism', *Quarterly Journal of Economics*, Vol. 97, pp. 567–86.

Government of India (1978), *Report of the Seventh Finance Commission*, Ministry of Finance, New Delhi.

Government of India (2000), *Report of the Eleventh Finance Commission*, Ministry of Finance, New Delhi.

Government of India (2002), *Indian Public Finance Statistics* (2001–2 and earlier issues), Ministry of Finance.

Government of India (2003), *Receipts Budget* (2003–4 and earlier years).

Government of India (2004), *Report of the Twelfth Finance Commission*, New Delhi.

Goyal, Rajan (2004), 'Does Higher Fiscal Deficit Lead to Rise in Interest Rates? An Empirical Investigation', *Economic and Political Weekly*, Vol. 39, No. 1, pp. 2128–33.

Graham, J.F. (1964), 'Fiscal Arrangements in a Federal Country', in *Intergovernmental Fiscal Arrangements*, Canadian Tax Foundation, Toronto.

Gramlich, Edward M. (1989), 'Budget Deficits and National Saving: Are Politicians Exogenous', *Journal of Economic Perspectives*, Vol. 3, No. 2, pp. 23–35.

Grewal, B.S. (1999), 'Federalism and Fiscal Equalization: Should India Follow the Australian Path?', in I. Copland and J. Rickard (eds), *Federalism: Comparative Perspectives from India and Australia*, Manohar, New Delhi.

Grewal, B.S., and R. Mathews (1983), 'Federalism, Locational Surplus and the Redistributive Role of Subnational Governments', paper presented at International Institute of Public Finance Conference at Budapest and published in part in Guy Turney and A.J. Culyer (eds) (1985), *Public Finance and Social Policy*, Wayne University Press, Detroit and in part in *Government and Policy*, 1986, Vol. 4, No. 3, pp. 317–324.

Grifiths, A.L., and K. Neren Berg (eds) (2002), *Handbook of Federal Countries*, Forum of Federations, McGill-Queen's University Press.

Harvey, A.C. (1989), *Forecasting Structural Time Series Models and the Kalman Filter*, Cambridge University Press, Cambridge, UK.

Hayek, F.A. (1945), 'The Use of Knowledge in Society', *American Economic Review*, Vol. 35, pp. 519–30.

Hobson, Paul A.R. (2001), 'What Do We Already Know about the Appropriate Design for a Fiscal Equalization Program in Canada and How Well Are We Doing?', IIGR, Working Paper, Queens University.

Hodrick, R., and E. Prescott (1981), 'Post-War U.S. Business Cycles: An Empirical Investigation', Discussion Paper No. 451, Carnegie-Mellon University, Pittsburgh.

Hsiao, C. (1997), 'Cointegration and Dynamic Simultaneous Equation Model', *Econometrica*, Vol. 65, No. 3, pp. 647–70.

Huther, Jeff, and Anwar Shah (1996), 'A Simple Measure of Good Governance and Its Application to the Debate on the Appropriate Level of Fiscal Decentralization', World Bank, Washington DC.

Inman, Robert P., and Daniel L. Rubinfeld (1996), 'Designing Tax Policy in Federalist Economies: An Overview', *Journal of Public Economics*, Vol. 60, No. 3, pp. 307–34.

Inman, Robert P., and Daniel L. Rubinfeld (1997a), 'Making Sense of the Antitrust State-Action Doctrine: Balancing Political Participation and Economic Efficiency in Regulatory Federalism', *Texas Law Review*, Vol. 75, pp. 1203–99.

Inman, Robert P., and Daniel L. Rubinfeld (1997b), 'The Political Economy of Federalism', in D. Muller (ed.), *Perspectives on Public Choice: A Handbook*, Cambridge University Press, Cambridge, pp. 43–64.

Inman, Robert P., and Daniel L. Rubinfeld (1997c), 'Rethinking Federalism', *Journal of Economic Perspectives*, Vol. 11, No. 4, pp. 73–105.

Jaeger, A. (1990), 'The Measurement and Interpretation of Structural Budget Balances', *Empirica*, Vol. 17, No. 2, pp. 155–169.Jha, R., and A. Sharma (2004), 'Structural Breaks, Unit Roots, and Cointegration: A Further Test of the Sustainability of the Indian Fiscal Deficit', *Public Finance Review*, Vol. 32, pp. 220–31.

Johansen, S. (1991), 'Estimation and Hypothesis Testing of Cointegrated Vectors in Gaussian Vector Autoregressive Models', *Econometrica*, Vol. 59, pp. 1555–80.

Johansen, S., and K. Juselius (1995), 'Identification of the Long-Run and Short-Run Structure: An Application to the ISLM Model', *Journal of Econometrics*, Vol. 63, pp. 7–36.

Joshi, Vijay, and I.M.D. Little (1994), 'Fiscal Policy', in *India-Macroeconomics and Political Economy: 1964–1991*, World Bank, Washington DC, pp. 225–243.

Keen, M. (1998), 'Vertical Tax Externalities in the Theory of Fiscal Federalism', IMF Staff Papers.

Keen, M., and S. Smith (1999), 'Viva VIVAT!', *International Tax and Public Finance*, Vol. 6, No. 2, pp. 741–52.

Kelkar, V. (2023), 'Towards Strengthening India's Cooperative Federalism: Initiatives for Multi-level Governance Reforms', 2nd B.P.R. Vithal Memorial Lecture, delivered at the Centre for Economic and Social Studies, Hyderabad on 1 December 2023.

Kim, Sang Loh (1995), 'Fiscal Decentralization, Fiscal Structure, and Economic Performance: Three Empirical Studies', Unpublished PhD Dissertation, University of Maryland.

Kirchgässner, Gebhard, Lars P. Feld, and Marcel R. Savioz (1999), *Die direkte Demokratie*, Helbing and Lichtenhahn, Basel.

Kontopoulos, Y., and Roberto Perotti (1999), 'Government Fragmentation and Fiscal Policy Outcomes: Evidence from OECD Countries', in James Poterba and Jürgen von Hagen (eds), *Fiscal Institutions and Fiscal Performance*, pp. 81–102, National Bureau of Economic Research, Cambridge.

Kotha, A.P., V. Agarwal, A. Sengupta, and R.P. Singh, (2018), 'Cesses and Surcharges: Concept, Practice and Reform. Practice And Reform' (August 2018), submitted to the Fifteenth Finance Commission.

Kotlikoff, Laurence J. (1988), 'Intergenerational Transfers and Savings', *Journal of Economic Perspectives*, No. 2, pp. 41–58.

Kotlikoff, Laurence J. (1995), 'Applying Generational Accounting to Developing Countries', *IED Discussion Paper Series*, No. 67, Institute for Economic Development, Boston University, December 1995.

Lahiri, A., and R. Kannan (2001), 'India's Fiscal Deficits and Their Sustainability in Perspective', Proceedings of NIPFP-World Bank Conference on India: Fiscal Policies to Accelerate Economic Growth, 21–22 May, New Delhi.

Lockwood, B. (2002), 'Distributive Politics and the Benefits of Decentralisation', *Review of Economic Studies*, Vol. 69, pp. 313–38.

Lockwood, B. (2005), 'Fiscal Decentralization: A Political Economy Perspective', *The Warwick Economics Research Paper Series*, (TWERPS), No. 721.

Madden, J.R. (1993), 'The Economics of Vertical Fiscal Imbalance', *Australian Tax Forum*, Vol. 10, No. 1, pp. 75–90.

Madden, J.R. (2002), 'Australian Fiscal Federalism, Global Integration and Economic Reform', paper presented at Workshop on Federalism in a Global Environment, Stanford University, 6–7 June 2002.

Mathews, Russell (1985) 'Fiscal Federalism in Australia', Conference Discussion Paper on Edward M. Gramlich's Paper, The Australian National University, Canberra.

Mathews, Russell (1993), 'The Theory and Practice of Fiscal Equalization', A Report for the Queensland Government, mimeo.

Matsusaka, John G. (1995), 'Fiscal Effects of the Voter Initiative: Evidence from the Last 30 Years', *Journal of Political Economy*, Vol. 103, pp. 587–623.

McGuire, Martin C., and Mancur Olson Jr. (1996), 'The Economics of Autocracy and Majority Rule: The Invisible Hand and the Use of Force', *Journal of Economic Literature*, Vol. 34, pp. 72–96.

McKinnon, Ronald I. (1997), 'Market-Preserving Fiscal Federalism in the American Monetary Union', in Mario Blejer and Teresa Ter-Minassian (eds), *Macroeconomic Dimensions of Public Finance: Essays in Honor of Vito Tanzi*, Routledge, London, pp. 73–93.

McKinnon, Ronald I., and Thomas Nechyba (1997), 'Competition in Federal Systems: The Role of Political and Financial Constraints', in John Ferejohn and Barry Weingast (eds), *The New Federalism: Can the States be Trusted?*, Hoover Institution Press, Stanford, pp. 3–61.

McLure, E. Jr (1983), *Tax Assignment in Federal Countries*, Australian National University, Canberra.

McLure, E. Jr (2000), 'Implementing Subnational Value Added Taxes on Internal Trade: The Compensating VAT', *International Tax and Public Finance*, Vol. 7, No. 6, pp. 723–40.

Mehta, D., and Sacchidananda Mukherjee (2021), Emerging Issues in GST Law and Procedures: An Assessment. NIPFP Working Paper, No. 21/347.

Moorthy, Vivek, B. Singh, and S.C. Dhal (2000), 'Bond Financing and Debt Stability: Theoretical Issues and Empirical Analysis for India', *Development Research Group Study*, Vol. 19, RBI, Mumbai, June.

Musgrave, Richard M. (1959), *The Theory of Public Finance*, McGraw-Hill, New York.

Musgrave, Richard M. (1961), *Public Finance: Needs, Sources and Utilization*, National Bureau of Economic Research, Princeton.

Myers, G.M. (1990), 'Optimality, Free Mobility, and Regional Authority in a Federation', *Journal of Public Economics*, Vol. 43.

Oates, Wallace E. (1972), *Fiscal Federalism*, Harcourt, Brace, Jovanovich, New York.

Oates, Wallace E. (1985), 'Searching for Leviathan: An Empirical Study', *American Economic Review*, Vol. 75, pp. 748–57.

Oates, Wallace E. and Schwab, Robert M (1996), 'The Theory of Regulatory Federalism: The Case of Environmental Management', in Oates, Wallace E (ed.), *The Economics of Environmental Regulation*, Edward Elgar Publishing Limited, UK, 1996, Chapter 18, pp. 319–31.

Oates, Wallace E. (1999), 'An Essay on Fiscal Federalism', *Journal of Economic Literature*, Vol. 37, pp. 1120–49.

Oates, Wallace E. (2001), 'A Reconsideration of Environmental Federalism', in *Resource for the Future*, November 2001, Discussion Paper No. 01–54.

Oates, Wallace E. (2002), 'A Reconsideration of Environmental Federalism', in J. List and A. de Zeeuw (eds), *Recent Advances in Environmental Economics*, Edward Elgar, Cheltenham, pp. 1–32.

Oates, Wallace E., and Robert M. Schwab (1988), 'Economic Competition among Jurisdictions: Efficiency-Enhancing or Distortion-Inducing?', *Journal of Public Economics*, Vol. 35, pp. 333–54.

Oates, Wallace E., and Robert M. Schwab (1991), 'The Allocative and Distributive Implications of Local Fiscal Competition', in D. Kenyon and J. Kincaid (eds), *Competition among States and Local Governments*, Urban Institute, Washington DC, pp. 127–45.

Papadopoulos, A., and M. Sidiropoulos (1999), 'The Sustainability of Fiscal Deficit in the European Union', *Advances in Economic Research*, Vol. 5, No. 3, pp. 289–307.

Parker, K. (1995), 'The Behaviour of Private Investment', IMF Occasional Papers, No. 134, International Monetary Fund, Washington DC.

Persson, Torsten, and Guido Tabellini (1999a), 'Political Economics and Public Finance', Alan Auerbach and Martin Feldstein (eds), *Handbook of Public Economics*. Vol. 3, Amsterdam, North Holland, pp. 1549–1659.

Persson, Torsten, and Guido Tabellini (1999b), 'The Size and Scope of Government: Comparative Politics and Rational Politicians', *European Economic Review*, Vol. 43, pp. 699–735.

Persson, Torsten, and Guido Tabellini (2000), 'Political Economics: Explaining Economic Policy', MIT Press, Cambridge, Mass.

Persson, Torsten, Gerard Roland, and Guido Tabellini (1996), 'Federal Fiscal Constitutions: Risk Sharing and Redistribution', *Journal of Political Economy*, Vol. 104, No. 5, pp. 979–1009.

Persson, Torsten, Gerard Roland, and Guido Tabellini (1997), 'Separation of Powers and Political Accountability', *Quarterly Journal of Economics*, Vol. 112, pp. 1163–202.

Phelps, Edmund S. (1961), 'Accumulation and the Golden Rule', *American Economic Review*, Vol. 51, 1961, pp, 638–43. Reprinted in Amartya Sen (ed.), *Growth Economics,* Penguin Books Ltd., England, 1970, Chapter 8, pp. 193–200.

Pommerehne, Werner W. (1977), 'Quantitative Aspects of Federalism: A Study of Six Countries', in Wallace E. Oates (ed.), *The Political Economy of Fiscal Federalism*, Heath-Lexington, Lexington, MA, pp. 275–355.

Pommerehne, Werner W. (1978), 'Institutional Approaches to Public Expenditure: Empirical Evidence from Swiss Municipalities', *Journal of Public Economy,* Vol. 9, pp. 255–80.

Pommerehne, Werner W. (1990), 'The Empirical Relevance of Comparative Institutional Analysis', *European Economic Review*, Vol. 34, pp. 458–69.

Pradhan, B.K., D.K. Ratha, and Atul Sarma (1990), 'Complementarity between Public and Private Investment in India', *Journal of Development Economics*, Vol. 33 No. 1, pp. 101–116.

Prud'homme, Remy (1995), 'The Dangers of Decentralization', *World Bank Research Observer*, Vol. 10, No. 2, pp. 201–10.

Qian, Yingyi, and Barry R. Weingast (1997), 'Federalism as a Commitment to Preserving Market Incentives', *Journal of Economic Perspective*, Vol. 11, No. 4, pp. 83–92.

Rajaraman, Indira Bhide, and R.K. Pattnaik (2004), 'A Study of Debt Sustainability at the State Level in India', mimeo, Reserve Bank of India.

Rajaraman, Indira, and Abhiroop Mukhopadhyay (2000), 'Sustainability of Public Domestic Debt in India', in D.K. Srivastava (ed.), *Fiscal Federalism in India: Contemporary Challenges, Issues before the Eleventh Finance Commission*, Har Anand Publications, New Delhi.

Rakshit, Mihir (2000), 'On Correcting Fiscal Imbalances in the Indian Economy: Some Perspectives', *Money and Finance*, ICRA Bulletin, Vol. 2, No. 2.

Rangarajan, C. (2022), 'Good and Bad Freebies', *Indian Express*, 16 June. doi: https://indianexpress.com/article/opinion/columns/punjab-govt-free-electricity-low-income-households-support-policy-7972197/

Rangarajan C., and D.K. Srivastava (2003), 'Dynamics of Debt Accumulation in India: Impact of Primary Deficit, Growth and Interest Rate', *Economic and Political Weekly*', Vol. 38, No. 46, November.

Rangarajan C., and D.K. Srivastava (2004a), 'Fiscal Federalism in Canada: Drawing Comparisons and Lessons', *Economic and Political Weekly*, Vol. 39, No. 19, 8–14 May, Working Paper No.18, NIPFP, New Delhi.

Rangarajan C., and D.K. Srivastava (2004b), 'Fiscal Transfers in Australia: Review and Relevance to India', *Economic and Political Weekly*, Vol. 40, No. 27, pp. 3709–22.

Rangarajan C., and D.K. Srivastava (2005), 'Fiscal Deficits and Government Debt in India: Implications for Growth and Stabilization', *Economic and Political Weekly*, Vol. 40, No. 27. Also Published as NIPFP Working Paper No. 35.

Rangarajan C., and D.K. Srivastava (2008), 'Reforming India's Fiscal Transfer System: Resolving Vertical and Horizontal Imbalances', *Economic and Political Weekly*, Vol. 43, No. 23. Also published as MSE Working Paper No. 31, 2008.

Rangarajan, C., and Srivastava, D.K. (2018), 'Balancing Conflicting Claims', *The Hindu*. 19 May 2018. doi: https://www.thehindu.com/opinion/lead/balancing-conflicting-claims/article62111589.ece

Rangarajan, C., and Srivastava, D.K. (2020), 'Growth Compulsions, Fiscal Arithmetic', *The Hindu*, 28 September. doi: https://www.thehindu.com/opinion/lead/growth-compulsions-fiscal-arithmetic/article32709726.ece

Rangarajan, C., and Srivastava, D.K. (2020), 'Slower Growth and a Tighter Fiscal', *The Hindu*, 9 May. doi: https://www.thehindu.com/opinion/lead/slower-growth-and-a-tighter-fiscal/article31538125.ece

Rangarajan, C., and Srivastava, D.K. (2021), How Far Can the Fiscal Deficit Be Stretched?, *The Hindu*, 23 February. doi: https://www.thehindubusinessline.com/opinion/how-far-can-the-fiscal-deficit-be-stretched/article33915755.ece

Rangarajan, C., and Srivastava, D.K. (2022), 'The Fiscal Rethink', *Indian Express*, 23 February. doi: https://www.magzter.com/stories/Newspaper/The-Indian-Express-Delhi/The-fiscal-rethink

Rangarajan, C., and Srivastava, D.K. (2023), 'Balance Fiscal Consolidation with Growth', *The Hindu*, 17 January 2023. doi: https://www.thehindu.com/opinion/op-ed/balance-fiscal-consolidation-with-growth/article66382844.ece

Rangarajan, C., and Srivastava, D.K. (2023), 'Charting the Path for the Sixteenth Finance Commission', *The Hindu*, 29 July 2023. doi: https://www.thehindu.com/opinion/lead/charting-the-path-for-the-sixteenth-finance-commission/article67132693.ece

Rangarajan, C., and Srivastava, D.K. (2023), 'Fiscal Consolidation in India: Charting a Credible Glide Path. EY Tax Insights', Issue 25, 25 March.

Rangarajan C., and Srivastava D.K. (2023), 'Growth, Fiscal Policy and Monetary Policy of India: Why and How to Overcome Economic Shocks', Consumer Unity & Trust Society (CUTS International).

Rangarajan, C., Anupam Basu, and Narendra Jadhav (1989), 'Dynamics of Interaction between Government Deficit and Domestic Debt in India', RBI Occasional Papers, September. Also included in Amaresh Bagchi and Nicholas Stern (1994) (eds), *Tax Policy and Planning in Developing Countries*, Oxford University Press, Delhi.

Rao, Kavita (2014), 'Revenue Implications of GST and Estimation of Revenue Neutral Rate: Estimates for 2011–12', National Institute of Public Finance and Policy, New Delhi.

Report of the Commission on Centre-State Relations (Volume III on Centre-State Financial Relations and Planning. http://interstatecouncil.nic.in/wp-content/uploads/2015/06/volume3.pdf

Report of the Committee on Fiscal Statistics, National Statistical Commission, Government of India (September 2018); http://mospi.nic.in/sites/default/files/committee_reports/Report%20of%20the%20Committee%20on%20Fiscal%20Statistics.pdf

Report on the Revenue Neutral Rate and Structure of Rates for the Goods and Services Tax (GST) (2015), Ministry of Finance (4 December 2015), http://www.gstcouncil.gov.in/sites/default/files/CEA-rpt-rnr.pdf

Report of the Task Force on Goods and Services Tax Submitted to the Thirteenth Finance Commission, https://fincomindia.nic.in/writereaddata/html_en_files/oldcommission_html/fincom13/discussion/report291209.pdf

Reserve Bank of India (2002), *Report on Currency and Finance*, Mumbai.

Revesz, Richard L. (1996), 'Federalism and Interstate Environmental Externalities', *University of Pennsylvania Law Review*, Vol. 144, pp. 2341–416.

Reynolds, Patricia (2001), 'Fiscal Adjustment and Growth Prospects', in T. Callen, P. Reynolds, and C. Towe (eds), *India at the Crossroads: Sustaining Growth and Reducing Poverty*, International Monetary Fund, Washington.

Rodden, Jonathan, Gunnar S. Eskelund, and Jennie Litvack (2003), *Fiscal Decentralization and the Challenges of the Hard Budget Constraint*, MIT Press, Cambridge.

Roubini, Nouriel, and Jeffrey D. Sachs (1989), 'Political and Economic Determinants of Budget Deficits in the Industrial Democracies', *European Economic Review*, Vol. 33, pp. 903–38.

Sato, Motobiro (2000), 'Fiscal Externalities and Efficient Transfers in a Federation', *International Tax and Public Finance*, Vol. 7, No. 2, pp. 119–139.

Saunders, C.A. (1990), 'Government Borrowing in Australia', *Journal of Federalism*, Vol. 20, pp. 35–52.

Scott, A.D. (1950), 'A Note on Grants in Federal Countries', *Economica*, Vol. 17, No. 68, pp. 416–422.

Scott, A.D. (1952), 'Federal Grants and Resource Allocation', *Journal of Political Economy*, Vol. 60, No. 6, pp. 534–536.

Seabright, Paul (1996), 'Accountability and Decentralization in Government: An Incomplete Contracts Model', *European Economic Review*, Vol. 40, pp. 61–89.

Searle, G.H. (2002), 'Changes in Producer Services Location, Sydney: Globalisation, Technology and Labour, *Asia Pacific Viewpoint*, Vol. 39, No. 2, pp. 237–55.Seshan, A. (1987), 'The Burden of Domestic Public Debt in India', *RBI Occasional Papers*, Vol. 8, No. 1.

Sharma, Chanchal Kumar, and Wilfried Swenden (2022), 'The Dynamics of Federal (In) Stability and Negotiated Cooperationu Single-Party Dominance: Insights from Modi's India', *Contemporary South Asia*, Vol. 30, No. 4, pp. 601–18.

Shigehara, Kumiharu (1995), 'Commentary: Long Term Tendencies in Budget Deficits and Debt', in *Budget Deficits and Debt: Issues and Options*, Proceedings of a Symposium (31 August–2 September), Federal Reserve Bank of Kansa City, US, pp. 57–87.

Srivastava, D.K. (2021), 'Fiscal Consolidation and FRBM in the COVID-19 Context: Fifteenth Finance Commission and Beyond', *Economic and Political Weekly*, Vol. 56, No. 33, pp. 48–55.

Srivastava, D.K. (2022), 'Intergovernmental Fiscal Relations in India: Time for the Next Generation of Reforms', MSE Working Paper 222.

Srivastava, D.K. (2023a), 'The Future of Fiscal Consolidation', *Economic and Political Weekly*, Vol. 57, No. 13, pp. 29–35.

Srivastava, D.K. (2023b), Evolving Contours of Centre-State Fiscal Relations: Inconsistencies, Ad-Hocism and Centralization', MSE Working paper 239. July 2023.

Srivastava, D.K. (2023c), 'Balancing Growth with Fiscal Consolidation', *Economic and Political Weekly*, Vol. 58, No. 12, https://www.epw.in/journal/2022/13/budget-2022/future-fiscal-consolidation-india.html.

Srivastava, D.K., and Kumar, K.K. (eds) (2014), *Environment and Fiscal Reforms in India*, Sage Publications, India.

Srivastava, D.K., and Pawan K. Aggarwal (1994), 'Revenue Sharing Criteria in Federal Fiscal Systems: Some Similarities and Differences', *Public Finance/ Finances Publiques*, Vol. 49, No. 3, pp. 440–459.

Srivastava, D.K., and Pawan K. Aggarwal (2000), 'Fragmentation of States and Criteria-Based Fiscal Transfer in India', in D.K. Srivastava (ed.), *Fiscal Federalism in India: Contemporary Challenges*, Har-Anand Publications, New Delhi, pp. 130–46.

Sundararajan, V., and Subhash Thakur (1980), 'Public Investment, Crowing Out, and Growth: A Dynamic Model Applied to India and Korea', *IMF Staff Papers*, Vol. 27, No. 4.

Srivastava, D.K., M. Bharadwaj, R. Trehan, and M. Kapur (2019), 'Designing and Implementing Equalization in India', presented at EY-MSE Roundtable on 'Fiscal Federalism in India: Contemporary Perspectives', organized at Madras School of Economics, Chennai in February 2019.

Srivastava, D. K., M. Bharadwaj, T. Kapur, and R. Trehan, EY Economy Watch (December 2023), EY, https://www.ey.com/en_in/tax/economy-watch

Srivastava, D. K., M. Bharadwaj, T. Kapur, and R. Trehan, EY Economy Watch (March 2024), EY, https://www.ey.com/en_in/tax/economy-watch

Srivastava, D. K., M. Bharadwaj, T. Kapur, and R. Trehan (2020), 'Impact of Covid-19 on Global Debt: A Study of Countries in the G-20 Group', *Modern Economy*, Vol. 11, 2101–21.

Srivastava, D. K., M. Bharadwaj, T. Kapur, and R. Trehan (2021), 'Covid's Economic Impact: Should India Recast Its Fiscal and Monetary Policy Frameworks?', *Journal of International Economics and Finance*, Vol. 1, No. 1, pp. 63–81.

Tabellini, Guido (2000), 'Constitutional Determinants of Government Spending', Working Paper, IGIER, Bocconi University.

Ter-Minassian, Teresa (ed.) (1997), 'Fiscal Federalism in Theory and Practice', *International Monetary Fund*, Washington DC.

Tiebout, C.M. (1956), 'A Pure Theory of Local Expenditures', *Journal of Political Economics*, Vol. 64, pp. 416–24.

Tiebout, C.M. (1961), *An Economic Theory of Fiscal Decentralization in Public Finance: Needs, Sources and Utilization*, Princeton University Press, Princeton, New Jersey.

Tocqueville, Alexis de (1945), *Democracy in America*, Vintage Books, A Division of Random House inc., New York, first published in 1838.

Url, Th. (1997), 'How Serious Is the Pact on Stability and Growth?', Working Paper No. 92, Austrian Institute of Economic Research.

Usher, Dan (2001), 'The Case for Switching to a Macro Formula', *IIGR*, Working Paper, Queens University.

Vedder, R., L. Gallaway, and C. Frenze (1987), 'Federal Tax Increases and the Budget Deficit, 1947–86: Some Empirical Evidence', Joint Economic Committee Minority Staff Paper.

Velasco, Andres (1999), 'A Model of Endogenous Fiscal Deficits and Delayed Fiscal Reforms', in James Poterba and Jürgen von Hagen (eds), *Fiscal Institutions and Fiscal Performance*, National Bureau of Economic Research, Cambridge, Massachusetts, US, pp. 37–58.

Vithal, B.P.R., and M.L. Sastry (2001), *Fiscal Federalism in India*, Oxford University Press, New Delhi.

von Hagen, Jürgen, and Ian Harden (1996), 'Budget Processes and Commitment to Fiscal Discipline', IMF Working paper.

Walsh, C. (1993), 'Vertical Fiscal Imbalance: The Issues', in D.J. Collins (ed.) *Vertical Fiscal Imbalance and the Allocation of Taxing Powers*, Australian Tax Research Foundation, Conference Series No. 13, pp. 31–53.

Weingast, Barry R. (1995), 'The Economic Role of Political Institutions: Market-Preserving Federalism and Economic Development', *Journal of Law Economics and Organization*, Vol. 11, pp. 1–31.

Wildasin, David E. (1998), 'Externalities and Bailouts: Hard and Soft Budget Constraints in Intergovernmental Fiscal Relations', *World Bank Policy Research*, WP 1843.

Wilson, John Douglas (1996), 'Capital Mobility and Environmental Standards: Is There a Theoretical Basis for a Race to the Bottom?', in Jagdish Bhagwati and Robert Hudec (eds), *Fair Trade and Harmonization: Prerequisities for Free Trade?*, Vol. I, MIT Press, Cambridge, MA, pp. 393–427.

World Bank (2003), *India: Sustaining Reform, Reducing Poverty*, Report No. 25797–1N.

Wrede, Mathias (2000), 'Shared Tax Sources and Public Expenditure', *International Tax and Public Finance*, Vol. 7, No. 2, pp. 163–175.

Yellen, Janet L. (1989), 'Symposium on the Budget Deficit', *Journal of Economic Perspectives*, Vol. 3, No. 2, pp. 17–21.

Zhang, Tao, and Heng-fu Zou (1998), 'Fiscal De-centralization, Public Spending, and Economic Growth in China', *Journal of Public Economics*, Vol. 67, pp. 221–40.

Index

For the benefit of digital users, indexed terms that span two pages (e.g., 52–53) may, on occasion, appear on only one of those pages.

Tables and figures are indicated by an italic *t* and *f* following the page number.

Action Taken Report (ATR) 310
actual expenditures 70
administrative scale 144, 169
aggregate transfers 74
Air [Prevention and Control of Pollution] Act, 1981 27
assignments of resources and responsibilities 3
augmented distance formula (ADF) 42
Australia
  council of governments 121
  donor states 115–16
  'donor' states 128–29
  equalization transfers, recent years in 159, 188–89
  expenditures, 2000–1, inter-jurisdictional shares in 120*t*
  fiscal federalism, working of 115
  fiscal transfers system, recent developments in 156
  general revenue assistance payments to states 163*t*
  gross state product, current prices at 128*t*
  GSP and richest states 128
  GST and FAG relativities, difference between 164, 165*t*
  hospital services assessment structure 168*t*
  inpatient services 167, 172*t*
  main state expenditure categories 166
  mean resident population 127*t*
  new equalization system 157

nominal GDP, state's share in 159*t*
per capita general revenue assistance 162*t*
per capita relativities 141*t*
relative to all-state average, per capita expenditure 148*t*
relativities, shares, and illustrative GST distribution 161*t*
states, population, income, and 2004 relativities 140*t*
states, population and state economies 127
state taxes in 164
state-wise per capita GDP 161*t*
state-wise population (2022) 160*f*
transition by year, summary 158*t*
vertical fiscal imbalance in 132–33, 132*t*
Australian Capital Territory (ACT) 115
Australian fiscal transfers system
  current status 115–16
  powers and functions, assignment of 117
Australian Loan Council 124
  role, change in 125
axiomatic framework
  comprehensiveness 212
  criteria-based tax revenue sharing 209
  horizontal equity 211
  neutrality 213
  normalization 1 and 2, 210, 211
  Tax revenue-sharing under, India 190

borrowing
  bailouts and controls on 176
Budget Balancing Assistance
  (BBA) 131–32

Calamity Relief Funds (CRFs) 302–3
Canada
  aggregate transfers 74
  allocation of tax powers 66
  centre's expenditure, in 71
  CHST 74
  constitution, Section 92(2) 66–68
  direct taxation 66–68
  economy features 65
  equalization grants 74, 77
  equalization payments 188
  equalization payments calculation,
    changes in 99
  federal and provincial debt 96
  federal country 64
  federal fiscal relations 64
  fiscal federalism, in practice 63
  levels of governments, major
    transfers to 75t
  open calculations 97
  per capita GDP, arranged in
    provinces 66f
  population and all- province GDP,
    share in 67t
  revenue sources 110
  Section 36(2) 77–78
  source-by-source approach,
    equalization entitlements 98
  TFF 74
  transfers calculation 65
  transfers composition 76, 77t
  vertical imbalance 69
Canada Assistance Plan (CAP) 86
Canada fiscal transfers system
  per capita health transfers,
    distribution of 107t, 109f
  provinces and territories,
    changes in 100
    horizontal dimension 103
    nominal GDP, share in 103f
    per capita equalization transfers
      distribution 105t

population, share in 104f
    support to provinces and
      territories 101t
    vertical dimension 100
  social transfers, distribution of per
    capita 108t, 109f
Canada Health and Social Transfers
  (CHST) 63, 74, 86
  cash transfers 87
  First Ministers/premiers of
    provinces 87–88
  forms 87
  general-purpose transfer 87
  relative importance of 76, 77t
Canada Health Transfers (CHT) 87–88
Canada Social Transfers (CST) 87–88
Canadian transfer system
  equalization, heart of 96
  no autonomous body 98
  outcome of 89–90
  recent developments 99
Canonical (Domar) model
  lessons from 259
  sustainability, analytics under 255
cash reserve ratio (CRR) 233
censored distance formula (CDF) 43
central debt
  accumulation of 228
  growth relative to GDP 230f
central government 3–4
centralization
  Australian system and
    expenditure 154
  expenditure after transfers in
    Australia 154
  extent in expenditures 120t
  growing, expenditure on state
    subjects 176
Central Statistical Organization
  (CSO) 65
central taxes, aggregate share of
  states 47
  alternative channel of fiscal
    transfer 48–49
  observations about 48
centralized tax system 3
centre's expenditure 71

CHST cash transfers 87
Commonwealth Government
  centralization in expenditures, extent
    of 118–19, 120*t*
  function assignment of 117
  own source revenues by 118, 119*t*
  power to levy all taxes 117
  SPPs 145
  vertical fiscal imbalance in 132–33
Commonwealth Grants Commission
    (CGC) 115–16, 122
  independent, impartial, and
    authoritative arbiter 123
  issues in context of assessment 147
Commonwealth Grants Commission
    Act 1973 122
Compensating VAT (CVAT) 185
Comptroller and Auditor General
    (CAG) 227–28
conditional grants 5
  purpose 5
congestible public goods
  efficiency and 9
Constitution
  Article 51A(g) 27
  Article 249, 26–27
  Articles 268/269 taxes 33–35
Constitutional (42nd Amendment) Act
    of 1976 27
core revenue-sharing criteria
  ADF 42
  CDF 43
  cost disadvantages, infrastructure
    reflect 44
  IIF 43
  income-based formulae 39
  MDF 41
  performance/incentives, criteria for 45
  population formula 43
  SDF 40
corporate income tax 68
cost disadvantages
  infrastructure reflect 44
criteria-based tax revenue sharing
  axiomatic basis 209
Culturally and Linguistically Diverse
    (CALD) 169–70

debt
  combined, centre and states
    growth in 272
  decade-wise decomposition,
    accumulation relative to GDP
    of 275*t*
  relative to GDP, growth of 274*f*
debt accumulation in India
  analysis of 224
  central 228
  data preliminaries 226
  debt-GDP ratio *see* debt-GDP ratio
  decade-wise decomposition, relative
    to GDP 229*t*, 230–31
  decomposing 225
  dynamics of 223–39
  interest payments on 223–24
  medium-term prospects 236
  primary deficit 235
  Receipts Budget 227–28
debt and fiscal deficits 239n.7
  alternative channels, financing
    deficits by 252
  analysing sustainability of 255
  central and sub-national debt,
    asymmetry in 253
  controlling 253
  corresponding level of 258
  fiscal and debt aspects, sustainability
    of 261*f*
  fiscal management, transparency
    in 254–55
  fiscal stance, inflation and output
    stabilization 248
  institutional reforms for
    controlling 254
  investment/savings/growth,
    impact on 249
  issues in Indian context 246
  public sector, solvency of 249
  rises, relative to GDP 261
  savings, and investment in India 263
  stable combinations, GDP ratios
    to 258*f*
  sustainability, implications for 250
Debt Consolidation and Relief Facility
    (DCRF) 305

debt-GDP ratio 236–37
  central debt relative to GDP,
      accumulation of 237
  interest rate associated with 262
  with liberalization and 237
  permissible levels of primary
      deficits 260–61
  potential build- up of 237
  south-east quadrant 261–62
  stabilize 237
  starting with 237
debt relief
  discontinuance of 202
debt-servicing crisis 20
debt sustainability
  Twelfth and Thirteenth Finance
      Commissions and 21
decade-wise decomposition
  debt accumulation relative to
      GDP 275t
decentralization
  constraining public sector growth,
      role in 16–17
  and economic development 22
  theorem 2
  welfare gains from 2
decentralized jurisdictions 4
democracies
  elected politicians (agents) 18
  principal-agent problems 18
  voters (principals) 18
Derived Fiscal Deficit 227–28
Diagnosis Related Groups
      (DRG) 169–70
disabilities 134
  classification 135
  factors see disability factors
  revenue and cost, factors
      affecting 136t
disability factors 143
  administrative scale 144
  socio-demographic composition 144
  specific purpose payments 145
  wages input costs 144
disaster risk management
  Disaster Management Act (DM Act)
      in 2005 302

distance 39–40

economic development
  fiscal decentralization and 22
Eighth Finance Commission 33
  horizontal equity, core criteria used
      by FC 35–36
  ToR of 52–53
  towards convergence 33
Eleventh Finance Commission 36–
      37, 182
  changes while computing distance-
      based shares of states 36
  concept of ceiling 37–38
  index of infrastructure 44–45
  index of tax effort, utilization 36–37
  MDF, modified by 41–42
  non-plan and plan revenue
      requirements 52–53
  per capita shares, modified
      formula 41–42
endogeneity, issues of 139
environmental federalism 24
  major and vital laws 27
Environmental [Protection] Act of
      1986 27
equalization 12 see also fiscal
      equalization; equalization grants
  alternative approaches to, Musgrave's
      views 12
  arrangements 8
  Australian and Canadian, difference
      between 188
  available data with TFC
      recommended, comparison of
      transfers based on 216t
  budget 135
  grants for health and education 200
  India, different from Australia and
      Canadia 189
  instruments of 15
  macro approaches to 84
  measuring extent, TFC
      recommendations 191
  payments 77–78
equalization grants 77
  ad Hoc adjustments 82

capacity, faulty indicators of 84
equalization payments share in total
    transfers 80–81, 81t
fiscal equity 77–78
lack of revenue effort,
    compensation for 83
measurement difficulties 83
needs and costs, non-consideration
    of 82
perverse incentives 82
problems 81
RST 78–80
Section 36(2) of *Constitution Act* 77–78
equity issues 152
error correction model (ECM) 271t
Established Programs Financing
    (EPF) 86
expenditure assessment
features 143
externalities 13
implications in federal system 13
types 13

federalism frontier 17
Fifteenth Finance Commission (FFC)
actual transfers received by
    states 294t
alternative scenarios 307
Article 275(1) of Constitution 297
ATR of 310
fiscal deficit to GDP ratio for Central
    Government *308t, 309t*
grants to local bodies as
    recommended by 301t
GST compensation 310
new and elaborate framework 303
recommendations 297, 300
recovery and reconstruction
    facility 304
relative importance of tax devolution
    and grants 293t
relative weights for different tax
    devolution criteria 292t
relief and mitigation funds 303
state-wise recommended revenue gap
    grants per year 296t
ToR of 288

Fifth Finance Commission
    ToR of 52–53
Finance Commission (FC)
    Article 270, 49
    Article 275, 49
    Article 280 of Constitution 315
    Article 280(3)(b) 49
    Clauses 315
    constitutional provisions 49
    core concerns, resolving vertical and
        horizontal imbalances 337
    criteria used for horizontal
        equity 35–36
    Eighth to Tenth, towards
        convergence 33
    First to Twelfth, aggregate share of
        states in central taxes 47
    fiscal performance indicators of 45
    normal periodicity of 30–31
    years covered under
        recommendations 30t
Financial Agreement Act 1928 124
Financial Assistance Grants
    (FAGs) 123
    general revenue assistance, form
        of 129–30
    reintroduction of 130
fiscal and revenue deficits
    centre and states of 178t
fiscal capacity
    measurement of 176
fiscal deficit
    attention received 282
    combined central and state
        finances 279t
    critical issue relates to
        determining 282
    government capital expenditure
        and 272
    magnitude relative to GDP,
        high in 282
    measuring structural and cyclical
        components of 277
    structural and cyclical, trends in 278
    structural and debt-stabilizing
        primary deficit, comparison
        of 280f

fiscal deficit and government debt in
    India 241–84
  and economy 246t
  Keynesian view 244
  neo-classical perspective 243
  Ricardian equivalence 245
  tax and spend' hypothesis 246
  theoretical perspectives 242
fiscal deficits 225
  and government debt in
      India 241–84
fiscal equalization *see also* equalization
  alternative 'equalization plans' 12–13
  conceptual issues 8
  defined by CGC as 134
  from disabilities to relativities 134
  horizontal transfers, system of 133
  mathematical presentation 135
  three approaches to distinguish by
      Musgrave 12
fiscal federalism 1
  common pool problem 18
  considerations of resource 333
  environmental, and ecological
      externalities 333
  evolution in India 29–61
  future in India 313–40
  intergovernmental transfers 5
  political economy aspects of 17
  in practice 63–113, 115–74
  soft budget constraints 20
  traditional theory 1–2
fiscal imbalances
  conditional grants and 5
  fiscal instruments, role in
      resolving 4, 7
  managing and stabilization 334
fiscal performance
  criterion related to
      improvement in 46
  indicators of 45
fiscal reform 20–21
fiscal residuum 8
Fiscal Responsibility and Budget
      Management Act (FRBMA) 255
  amendment 285–86, 306
  Review Committee 306–7

fiscal surpluses 9–10
fiscal transfer system 8
  predictability 6
  presence of externalities, in 13
  stability 6
Flypaper Effect 6
Forum of Federations (Canada) 1
Fourteenth Finance Commission
  actual transfers received by
      states 294t
  aggregate corpus for all states 303
  Article 275(1) of Constitution 297
  combined revenue receipts 322t
  debt and fiscal deficit
      management 306
  GST Compensation Fund 309
  local body grants 300
  Presidential Order 310
  recommendations 297
  relative importance of tax devolution
      and grants 293t
  relative weights for different tax
      devolution criteria 292t
  state-wise recommended revenue gap
      grants per year 296t
  ToR of 287–88
Fourth Finance Commission
      (FFC) 52–53

Gadgil formula 98
'Gap Filling Approach' (GFA) 55, 191
general revenue assistance 129
Gentlemen's Agreement 125
Goods and Services Tax (GST) 68
  challenges posed by
      implementation 331
  implementation in India 331–32
  introduced in Australia 115–16
  weighted average (effective) 333f
grants 15
Gross Expenditure Base (GEB) 89
growth and interest rate
  GDP ratio and excess, primary deficit
      to 236f
  profiles 231
  real 233f
  time profile of nominal 232f

Guaranteed Minimum Amount
(GMA) 131–32

Harmonized Sales Tax (HST) 68–69
Health Reform Fund (HRF) 74, 86
horizontal equity 211
horizontal fiscal equalization (HFE) 115
Australia's system of 116–17
Horizontal Fiscal Imbalance (HFI) 7,
89, 147
Australia, per capita expenditure
relative to all-state average 148*t*
Canada, in expenditure 94*t*
equalization approach to transfers 204
in expenditure 94*t*
expenditures 91
India 95*t*
per capita revenues 92*t*
resolving 323
revenue before and after transfers 90*t*
revenues 89
separating from VFI 181
horizontal transfers system
Australian system characteristics 154
disability factors 143
efficiency issues 152
equity issues 152
expenditure assessment features 143
fiscal equalization, system of 133
guiding principle, defined by
CGC 188–89
needs version 137
normative gap version 138
redistribution, extent of 148, 149*t*
revenue and expenditure side
equalizations 149, 150
revenue assessment features 142
standardized model version 137
total grants and relativities 139
total pool over years 149*t*

implicit price deflator of GDP at factor
cost (IPDFC) 269–70
income 39
India
central transfers, gross revenue
receipts and GDP 76*t*

debt accumulation, dynamics
of 223–39
fiscal deficits and government debt
in 241–84
GST, challenges posed by
implementation 331
horizontal imbalance, resolved
through 189
household sector and saving 283
institutional arrangements 65
no direct 'tax- base' sharing 69
relative share of centre and states
in 121*t*
savings and investment, trends in 263
tax revenue-sharing, axiomatic
framework under 190
vertical fiscal imbalance in 133*t*
vertical imbalance, long-term
stability in 181
institutional arrangements 119
Australian governments council 121
Australian Loan Council 124
CGC 122
commonwealth-state financial relations,
ministerial council for 122
special purpose ministerial
councils 122
institutional reforms
governing centre-state financial
relations 335
GST data sharing 335
institutional memory of FC,
absence of 335
Inter-State Council, energizing 336
Loan Council 336
NDC, role in post Planning
Commission era 336
state FC, underperformance of 336
Intergovernmental Reform Agreement
(IGA) 118, 131
aim 118
GST sharing and 131
intergovernmental grants
lump-sum grant 6
intergovernmental transfers 5
inter-jurisdictional competition 16
benefits of 18

inter-se sharing
   criteria and relative weights for
      determining 37t
   of income tax 34t
   union excise duties 34t
Inter-State Council
   characterized by 336
inverse income formula (II) 43

Kelkar Committee 186–87

Loan Council
   allocation 125
   Financial Agreement Act 1994 126
   institutional reforms and 336

Maastricht Treaty (MT) norms 277
Marginal Cost of Public Fund
      (MCPF) 13–14
market-preserving federalism 21
Modernization Fund 310
modified distance formula (MDF) 41
multi-tier governmental structure
   assignments of resources and
      responsibilities 3–4

National and State Disaster Mitigation
      Funds 302
National Calamity Contingency Fund
      (NCCF) 302
National Development Council (NDC)
   post Planning Commission era,
      role in 336
National Disaster Relief Fund
      (NDRF) 302
'national' public goods 3–4
National Small Saving Fund
      (NSSF) 202, 226–27
National State Domestic Product
      (NSDP) 39–40
needs version 137
Net Fiscal Benefits (NFBs) 77–78
neutrality 213
Ninth Finance Commission 33
   modified representative 58t
   non-plan revenue expenditure 60
   non-tax revenues 59

own tax revenues 57
   recommendations, making in 54
   ToR of 52–53
non-plan revenue expenditure
   Ninth Finance Commission 60
non-tax revenues
   Ninth Finance Commission 59
normative gap version 138
Northern Territory (NT) 115

optimality
   sustainability, stability and 260
Organisation for Economic
      Co-operation and Development
      (OECD) 19, 277–78
outstanding liabilities 238n.1
own tax revenues
   Ninth Finance Commission 57

pact on growth and stability (PSG) 277
per capita income 39
per capita transfers
   decomposition of
      recommended 218t
personal income tax (PIT) 68
population formula
   equal per capita transfers, criterion
      providing 43
predictability 6
primary deficit 239n.7
   accumulation 235
   GDP ratio and excess of growth over
      interest rates, to 236f
   primary expenditure, excess
      of 235–36
principal-agent problems
   adverse consequences 19
   democracies, in 18
private disposable income in real terms
      (PVYR) 270
   explanatory variables 270–71
private sector savings in real terms
      (SPVR) 270
   dependent variable 271t
property rights
   equity and efficiency,
      implications for 10

provincial expenditure 70
public sector savings in real terms
 (SPUBR) 270
 explanatory variables 270–71

RCMCE 270
 dependent variable 272*t*
real interest rate 232–33
 on government securities 233
Receipts Budget 227–28
 two modifications 228
Registrar General of India 65
Representative Tax System
 (RST) 78, 97
 characteristics 79
resolving horizontal imbalance 323
 education expenditures (INR),
  state-wise per capita 327*t*
 equalization', international
  practices 188
 health expenditures (INR), state-wise
  per capita 328*t*
 ML group of states 324
 per capita GSDP 325*t*
 SH group of states 324
 tax devolution and grants 330–31
 towards equalizing transfers 187
 water supply and sanitation (INR),
  state-wise per capita 329*t*
resolving vertical imbalance
 central and state GST rate
  components, determining 186
 and GST 184
 GST regime, nature of 184
  central 184–85
  concurrent or dual 185
  overall rate, determining 186
  state-level VAT 185–86
 India, long-term stability in 181
 justification for 180
Retail Sales Tax (RST) 68–69
revenue assessment
 features 142
revenue equalization 150
revenue gap grants
 methodology 56
 Ninth Finance Commission 57

revenue sharing 15
 arrangements 130
 criteria 38
 horizontal dimension 290–93
 horizontal equity principle 38–39
 vertical dimension 289–90

sale tax, GST 68
savings and investments
 different components profile 267*t*
 empirical relations 269
 household sector 283
 overall growth rate 283
 relative to GDP 265*f*, 266*f*, 266–68
 trends in India 263
Seventh Finance Commission
 Article 112, 51
 Article 275(1) 51
 capital purposes, grants
  recommended by 50, 51
 grants- in- aid, recommending 50–51
 resultant vertical distribution of
  resources, features of 181–82
 ToR of 52–53
sharable central revenues
 recommended and effective share of
  states in 291*t*
sharing criteria
 determination of relative
  weights of 176
short- and medium-term fiscal policy
 stance
 analysing 276
Sixteenth Finance Commission
  (SFC)
 2021 Census, based on 318–19
 data availability, status of 318
 number of states 317
 period of reference 316
 short ToR, benefits of 317
 tax-GDP ratio 321*f*
 ToR 313, 314
Sixth Finance Commission 52–53
socio-demographic composition 144
socio-economic status (SES)
  169–70
soft budget constraints 20

specific purpose payments (SPPs) 115, 129, 145
  Commonwealth Government, uses for 145
  introduced in 145
  questions on efficiency 146–47
  Statutory Commissions, administered by 146
spending power 69–70
stability 6
  sustainability, optimality, and 260
standard distance formula (SDF) 40
standardized model version 137
State Development Loans (SDLs) 202
State Disaster Relief Funds (SDRFs) 302–3
State Domestic Product (SDP) 39
state governments
  conditions specified by Commission 298–99
Statistics Canada 65
statutory liquidity requirements (SLR) 233
structural 'primary gap 280
sustainability 250–51
  analysing, debt and fiscal deficits 255
  Canonical (Domar) model, analytics under 255
  fiscal and debt aspects 261f
  optimality, stability and 260

tax-assignment problem 4
tax buoyancies
  vertical stability and 207
tax revenue-sharing
  under, axiomatic framework India 190
tax revenue-sharing criteria
  evolution 31
  income tax, inter-se sharing of 32t
  Phase I, separate criteria, income tax and union tax duties for 31
  Phase II, Eighth to Tenth Finance Commissions 33
  Phase III, full convergence 35
  union excise duties, inter-se sharing of 32t

taxes 4 *see also* Value Added Tax (VAT); Goods and Services Tax (GST),
  assignment problem 4
  devolution criteria, determining relative weights 196
  high excise 4
  and spend hypothesis 246
Tenth Finance Commission 36–37
  Alternative Scheme of Devolution, recommended 33–35
  'censored' distribution of area 37–38
  full convergence: from the alternative scheme of 35
Terms of Reference (ToR) 52–53
  census year, specification of 317
  considerations arising from 53
  examining, status of fiscal imbalances 317
  inclusion of incentives 318
  Paragraph 6(i) and (ii) of TFC 53–54
  SFC 313, 314
    Paragraph (1), (2), (3) 314–15
Territorial Formula Financing (TFF) 74, 86, 88
  gap-filling formula 89
theory of assignment 3–4
Third Finance Commission 51–52
  Asok Chanda's observation 51–52
Thirteenth Finance Commission
  actual transfers received by states 294t
  Article 275(1) of Constitution 297
  CRFs and SDRFs 302–3
  DCRF 305
  debt and fiscal deficit management 304
  different tax devolution criteria, relative weights for 292t
  FRBM Act 305
  glide paths for general and special category states 304–5
  loans 305
  local governments 297
    weights allotted to criteria for grants to 298t
  NCCF recommended 302
  recommendations 297

relative importance of tax devolution
and grants 293*t*
state-wise recommended revenue gap
grants per year 296*t*
task force on GST 309
ToR of 286–87
Total Taxable Resources (TTR) 85–86
transfers
composition of 176
gap-filling approach to
determining 176
Twelfth Finance Commission
(TFC) 175
concept of ceiling 37–38
constitution of loan council 203
fiscal developments 177
Paragraph 6 (iv) 52–53
recommended transfers
comparing equalizing benchmark
transfers with 195*f*
vertical and horizontal
components 195*t*
recommended transfers, equalization
transfers comparison 216*t*
states in central taxes, increase in
share 182

unconditional general revenue
assistance 129
Uniform Income Taxation Act of
1942 117–18

Value Added Tax (VAT) 66–68
central 185
compensating 185
dual 185
GST as 68
rate of compensating 185
state-level 185–86
veil hypothesis 6
Versano proposal 185
vertical externality 68
vertical fiscal gap 179–80
federal systems, in 179–80
vertical fiscal imbalance
(VFI) 7, 180–81
separating VFI from HFI 181
vertical imbalance 97
Canada in 69
in India 73*t*
Indian transfer system, resolving 203
measuring in Canada 70, 72*t*
resolving 179 *see* resolving vertical
imbalance319
vertical transfers
stability in 175
Viable Integrated VAT (VIVAT)
185–86

wages 11
wages input costs 144
The Water [Prevention and Control of
Pollution] Act of 1974 26–27